Labor and American Politics: A Book of Readings

Labor and

Edited by
Charles M. Rehmus
and Doris B. McLaughlin

American Politics

A Book of Readings

Ann Arbor
The University of Michigan Press

Acknowledgments

OUR PURPOSE in editing this work was to bring together in a single volume the leading materials from among the widely scattered literature on the subject of American labor's involvement in politics. Our hope is that this book will find a place as a text for courses on this subject, and that it will also be valuable as a supplementary reference work for those who are interested in labor history, pressure group theory, and American politics.

Part I, the historical background, is by no means intended to be a full record of the history of American labor. Instead, it is meant to highlight the often overlooked fact that organized labor in the United States has always been in politics. Part II, which shifts from the chronological to the topical approach, contains materials analyzing in detail the many facets of labor's contemporary political activities.

We are grateful to the Institute of Labor and Industrial Relations of The University of Michigan and Wayne State University for financial support and clerical assistance in connection with our work.

We should like particularly to thank Lawrence Rogin, whose original course in labor and politics at The University of Michigan provided a basic framework for our work. We also appreciate his suggestions on contemporary materials. We also received invaluable suggestions for historical materials from Sidney Fine. We are grateful to Joyce L. Kornbluh for editorial help and to Matthew Ash for research assistance. The staff of The University of Michigan Library helped us in many varied ways.

C. M. R.

D. B. M.

Contents

Part One

The Historical Background

Part One
Introduction:
The Historical Background

Chapter 1

Introduction

THE AMERICAN LABOR MOVEMENT has always been in politics, a fact which has often been obscured by its economic activities—its seeming preoccupation with on-the-job benefits—and by its frequent avowals of political nonpartisanship. Thus, our labor movement puzzles the foreign trade unionist. Since he usually is formally aligned with a political party himself, and may belong to a union which is beholden to the government for its very existence, he cannot understand why his American counterpart has not translated successes at the bargaining table into political gains. He would probably be surprised to learn that the first labor parties in the world were established in this country. The American citizen, too, accustomed to headlines emphasizing wage demands, strike threats, and the like, is likely to minimize labor's lobbying activities and to overlook the importance of the day-to-day activities of an organization such as the AFL–CIO's Committee on Political Education.

The widespread assumption that political activity has been relatively absent from the American labor scene stems primarily from the fact that the American labor movement has usually resorted to pressure politics, particularly at the national level, rather than to independent third-party action. There are many reasons why it has done so.

The majority of American wage earners had the right to vote by the early nineteenth century. Thus, when third parties emerged, their attempts to appeal to the labor vote ran up against long-standing allegiances to existing political parties. Such ties are hard to break, and no third party has ever been wholly successful at it.

Furthermore, organized labor has always represented a minority of the American electorate and "going it alone," particularly at the national level, would have been unrealistic. From time to time, local political parties, oriented exclusively to wage-earner demands, have existed in the more industrialized urban areas, but on a national basis labor has always sought alliances, most commonly with the farmer, when it has attempted third-party action. However, these third-party efforts have been largely unsuccessful and short-lived.

Labor's political course has also been governed by the characteristics, attributes, and attitudes of the American worker himself.

Some writers stress ethnic, geographic, and racial diversity as factors that have tended to limit unified worker action to immediate on-the-job demands. Others point to the relative scarcity of labor during much of our history, which has placed the worker, particularly the skilled artisan, in a favorable bargaining position and has made political pressure less important. The right to vote and the opportunity for a free education, granted here long before these privileges were available in other countries, has militated against class distinctions and has made political action on a class basis less feasible. Indeed, the American worker's lack of class consciousness is most often singled out as the characteristic that distinguishes him from his foreign counterparts. Along with his employer, the typical American worker has tended to believe in the efficacy of the capitalistic system and in the reality of the open society. His protests, over time, have not been directed against the system per se but rather against what he perceives as a malfunction within it which redounds to his disadvantage. This is not to say that there have not been workers genuinely disillusioned with the system but, rather, that ideas and desires of a fundamentally radical nature have not been representative of the mainstream of the American labor movement.

The first reading in this chapter, an article written before the merger of the AFL and CIO, emphasizes the American worker's lack of class consciousness, and his desire for "middle-class status and full citizenship." The article which follows, by Arnold Steinbach, stresses reasons for the lack of class distinctions, arising out of this country's unique heritage. "Labor as a Pressure Group" highlights structural elements in the American political system that have affected labor's role in politics. Bruce Millen's classification of political unionism ranks the union movements in various countries according to their emphasis upon political vis-a-vis economic functions and their relationship to government and political parties. In the concluding article, Adolf Sturmthal analyzes the major theories that have been developed concerning labor and political action, and offers one of his own.

Taken together, the readings in Chapter 1 indicate that while the American labor union movement cannot accurately be characterized as "political unionism," it is equally clear that it is not, as is sometimes assumed, concerned solely with wages, hours, and working conditions.

The remainder of Part One of this book is a general survey of the history of the American labor movement, with particular emphasis upon those periods in which it was most active politically. In one sense this history can be viewed as a record of conflict between those labor leaders who stressed the importance of political activity and those who argued the primacy of obtaining immediate economic gains for their followers. In the long run, the advocates of the latter course were the most influential in shaping labor policy; but even Samuel Gompers, the most dedicated adherent to the collective bargaining approach, was fully aware that economic activity alone was not enough if the American labor movement was to achieve its goals.

The U. S. Labor Movement: Its Ideological Orientation

THE STUBBORN REFUSAL of the American labor movement to behave according to the so-called "laws of history" utterly baffles the European intellectual.

Organized labor is the strongest of our organized political pressure groups. Political action has always been important to American unionism. It has never been a pure "business unionism" concerned only with dollars and cents. But political action has been a tool for the achievement of union ends. The opposite approach—the use of unionism as a tool for the advancement of a political "ideology," as in Europe—has been considered here a "betrayal of unionism." That is why there is not a national American labor party.

Inside the American labor movement, there is none of the ideological uniformity that characterizes European unions. A vast philosophical distance separates arch-Republican Bill Hutcheson of the carpenters from ex-Socialist Dave Dubinsky of the ladies' garment workers; yet they work together as vice presidents of the American Federation of Labor. And while the younger Congress of Industrial Organizations shows greater cohesion, the differences between Emil Rieve of the textile workers and Walter Reuther of the automobile workers might be enough to disrupt most European trade-union organizations. This diversity runs all the way to the individual local. Within the same union, within the same industry, within the same city, union practices, union policies, and even union oratory vary all over the lot.

American labor is not "working-class conscious"; it is not "proletarian" and does not believe in class war. Some parts of it are as uncompromisingly wedded to rugged individualism as the National Association of Manufacturers. Others want to "reform capitalism." If there were a standard or typical labor view on this subject, it would probably come close to that of George W. Brooks of the strong and

Excerpted, courtesy of *Fortune* magazine, from "The U. S. Labor Movement" which appeared in the February 1951 issue of that publication.

tough pulp, sulfite, and paper-mill workers (AF of L), who says "labor's objective of 'making today better than yesterday' is predicated on its acceptance of capitalism."

Yet the American union is a militant union—more militant, perhaps, than its European counterparts. Not only can it point to steadier gains for its members in the form of wages and benefits than any other labor movement; it has also been demanding for itself more and more managerial power within the business enterprise. And it is capable of fighting for both its economic and its power demands with a ferocity and bitterness (to say nothing of a vocabulary) that could hardly be matched by any class-war union.

For however much similarity there may be between the objective conditions that gave rise to unionism throughout the industrialized world, the American union is unique in the meaning it has for its member, in the purpose and function it serves for him: *it is his tool for gaining and keeping as an individual the status and security of a full citizen in capitalist society.* That it has made the worker to an amazing degree a middle-class member of a middle-class society—in the plant, in the local community, in the economy—is the real measure of its success. . . .

Twenty years ago it was easy to dismiss the peculiar characteristics of the American labor movement as signs of the "immaturity" of the American worker. The U. S. at that time, next to Japan, was the least unionized of the major industrial countries. Surely, so the argument ran, a bigger union movement in America would be as proletarian and as much dedicated to class war, as much anticapitalist and socialist, as the union movements of Europe. The most confident expression of this view came from Harold Laski, the lord high keeper of leftist illusions. But the same view had been held inside the American labor movement itself all during the twenties—for instance, by the young men around the Brookwood Labor College, many of whom later on showed up among the moving spirits of the CIO.

Today the U. S. may well be the most unionized of the free countries. Certainly, . . . practically all production employees in "big" and "middle" industry are organized. Union contracts determine wage rates everywhere in this country, in unorganized as well as in organized businesses, for clerical as well as for production employees. This switch from an open-shop to an organized economy took only twelve years—from 1933 to 1945. They were years of depression and war, of tension and upheaval. Yet today's successful, strong, and militant labor movement is as little "proletarian" or "socialist" as the small and unsuccessful labor movement of twenty years ago.

Since 1941 there have been three major developments within

American labor, all illustrating the same drift: the renascence of the AF of L; the strong anti-ideological shift within the CIO; and the eclipse of left-wing ideologies and philosophies within the labor movement itself.

All through the thirties and right up to World War II the AF of L was the "sick man" of American labor, if not given up for dead. It was obsolete if not senile, hidebound, unprincipled, inflexible, corrupt, and—worst swearword of all—"petty bourgeois." Yet today the AF of L has some eight-and-a-half million members—twice as many as it had in 1941. In addition the bulk of the "independent" unions are AF of L unions in their philosophy, their tactics, and their structure, though not in formal affiliation. Almost two out of every three American union members—10 million out of a total of 15 million—are thus organized on the AF of L basis and in unions that derive in unbroken descent from Samuel Gompers.

Neither economic developments nor the small changes in tactics that have occurred within the AF of L fully explain this renascence. Perhaps it is too much to claim, as some AF of L men do, that it is precisely its antiproletarian, procapitalist character that has been attracting the American worker. But one thing at least is sure: that the AF of L's middle-class character has proved no obstacle to its success, let alone, as was so confidently predicted only ten years ago, fatal to its very survival.

The CIO at its start was hailed as the fulfillment of the intellectual's dream of a "class-conscious" and "proletarian" labor movement. What has actually been happening to the CIO may be read in the career of the one bright young CIO radical of fifteen years ago who actually made good, the automobile workers' Walter Reuther, by all odds the most dynamic personality in American labor today.

Where Walter Reuther stood politically was never exactly clear. He was certainly not just an "ordinary socialist." There was always a strong resemblance to the Henry Ford of thirty years ago—the Henry Ford who sent the "Peace Ship" to Europe to stop World War I, who had an opinion on anything and everything, and whom the Chicago *Tribune* once called an "anarchist." There was also a bit of the technocrat in Walter Reuther, this being the element of continuity in his many "Reuther Plans." But there was no doubt whatever that he also believed in the class struggle, in some form of socialism, and in a labor party to bring about the "necessary change in the system." These beliefs (rather than his ability and competence as a union leader) gained him the admiration of all the sentimental "friends of labor" among the intellectuals, from the *New Republic* to the amateur politicians of Americans for Democratic Action.

Yet the biggest labor event of 1950—if not of the entire post-World War II period—was a contract negotiated by Walter Reuther that goes further in its affirmation both of the free-enterprise system and of the worker's stake in it than any other major labor contract ever signed in this country. The General Motors contract is the first contract that unmistakably accepts the existing distribution of income between wages and profits as "normal," if not as "fair." This at least was the interpretation that was given within the U.A.W. itself to the acceptance of the existing wage structure as the basis for the next five years. It is the first major union contract that explicitly accepts objective economic facts—cost of living and productivity—as determining wages, thus throwing overboard all theories of wages as determined by political power, and of profit as "surplus value." Finally, it is one of the very few union contracts that expressly recognize both the importance of the management function and the fact that management operates directly in the interest of labor.

The G. M. contract probably reflects what Reuther himself has come to believe over the last few years. . . .[1] But his own beliefs or words are really none too relevant. The important thing is that this contract—whose significance everyone in the labor movement grasped immediately—has become the program on which Reuther hopes to unify American labor under his own leadership. This is strong evidence of the CIO's shift toward the George Brooks concept of unionism, "predicated on its acceptance of capitalism." And the force behind the shift is precisely the CIO's success in gaining for the unskilled and semi-skilled worker in the mass-production industries what has been the goal of American labor in general: middle-class status and full citizenship.

Basic Roots of Differences Between United States and European Trade Unionism

Arnold L. Steinbach
U. S. Department of Labor

IN THE LIGHT of the closer contacts developing between American and European labor, it seems timely to look more carefully at the char-

---

[1] A statement by Reuther of his present view of the labor movement, and its role in politics, may be found in Chapter 12.—Eds.

Remarks made at a Conference on Human Resources and Labor Rela-

acter of European labor and the factors which operate to give it a character different from the trade union movement here. It is necessary to know whether these surface characteristics are truly basic or whether they grow out of even deeper forces which require understanding if our relationships vis-à-vis European labor are to be realistic as well as effective.

Different structural social and economic roots clearly have influenced the evaluation of different forms of society and labor movements around the world; they have given widely different meanings to terms used in expressing relations among the people or specific types of society such as "state," "democracy," "socialism," and "capitalism."

There are two basic elements, feudalism and classicism, which have had above all others a decisive influence upon the development and character of the European labor movement. Continental European society, except for the Scandinavian countries and Switzerland, evolved within a framework dominated by a combination of the remnants of a dying feudalistic system and the persistence of classic doctrines. It inherited from dying feudalism such problems as class distinctions, rigid obedience, and the desire to share in rank and privileges. Class distinction was subsequently given formal status by its development into the concept of class struggle. Rigid obedience manifested itself in such characteristics as party discipline within a "front" of democratic government, the "leadership principle," and a strict master-servant relationship. Predominance of rank and privilege has survived political and economic revolutions and, today, title or a white-collar classification is still more important socially than qualifications and efficiency.

In variation, Great Britain and the Scandinavian countries built upon feudalistic roots without the restrictions imposed by classic principles. However, in these countries, the lack of a combination of feudalism and classicism mitigated the aftereffects of feudalism. Class distinctions remained but not in their sharply accentuated forms as in continental Europe. Basic rights granted to the rank and file even during the feudalistic era changed the violence and direction of the pressure of a growing workers' class.

The United States' social and economic system, by contrast, was formed without the handicapping inheritance of either classicism or a feudalistic past. Their absence enabled the American worker to fight

tions in Underdeveloped Countries, held in Ithaca, N. Y., November 12–14, 1953.

Reprinted by permission of the New York State School of Industrial and Labor Relations.

for what he considered right and just in the economic arena without the circuitous route of a political class movement.

Classicism has influenced the present shape and character of continental Europe even more than feudalism. It infiltrated all sciences, economic theories, and even the day-to-day relationships of the people. Classicism grew out of the Roman law with its arbitrary and static rules. Even Canon law took its basic character from the classic philosophy of the Roman law.

In economics in particular, classicism led to the scholastic philosophy of the middle ages. Once the solution of a problem was found, such a solution came to be considered inviolable and permanent. Symbolically, it was entered in the "book," which in turn became the final basis for authority and order. Any opposition to its eternal truth came to be considered heresy or treason.

In Great Britain and the few European countries which were not engulfed in the statics of classicism, traditional nonclassic law with its adjustability and dynamics led in the economic sphere to the development of hypothetical or empirical philosophy during the middle ages. Under this empirical outlook, once a solution of a problem was found, such solution might thereafter be challenged and changed whenever events clearly pointed to other conclusions.

The United States fortunately gained its independence at a time when "liberté, egalité, and fraternité" had already become accepted slogans in large parts of what was then the articulate world. Thus, unlike the Europeans, we have never experienced the handicaps of feudalism. In addition, taking from our colonial past the Anglo-Saxon empirical philosophy, we have been free to govern by trial and error and by dynamics rather than by the static authority emanating from the "book." We did not hand our sovereign responsibilities to a "book" which would tell us how we should react to a specific situation. That is apparent in our concept of democracy.

These, then, seem to be fundamental factors whose varying applicability and operation have led to such wide variations in the evolution of modern labor movements in continental Europe, England, and the United States.

The industrial revolution was superimposed, therefore, upon different systems as they had developed from different roots. In continental Europe, it brought the excess labor from the farms into newly established factories—most illiterates who had for centuries lived in bondage geared to the lowest state of civilization. Wages were extremely low, working hours extremely long, and working conditions bad. They could not ask the employer to sit with them around the table to negotiate a collective agreement. He might have considered such a demand rebellion.

Before the workers could press for an improvement of their wages, hours, working conditions, and for collective agreements, they first had to gain recognition as equal partners. They had to acquire basic civil rights in the political arena before they could state their grievances in the economic arena. And to fight in the political arena they first had to develop political organizations before they could establish an independent and effective economic labor movement. The political labor movement thus became, initially, the mouthpiece of the economic demands of the workers. Intellectuals with liberal ideas, skilled workers of the guilds, and sometimes educated adventurers, rather than the rank and file, took the leadership in the political struggle.

Against whom did the workers direct their fight for recognition? The "book" was the stone wall barring recognition of worker needs and aspirations. For workers were not among the privileged groups who were strong enough to obtain "permanent" status when the "book" was compiled some hundred years ago. The traditional, privileged groups, when their power was challenged by increasingly articulate worker organizations, had only to hide behind the sacred rules of the "book" in order to preserve their status. The workers, however, could not understand the "ideology" of the "book," which was inadjustable to their needs. For them the "book," the final authority, became the symbol as well as the reality of their frustration, the wall which had to be destroyed before any desired change or adjustment could be achieved. The static authority of the "book" led, then, to the ideology of "toppling" or overthrowing an existing condition, an existing economic system. . . .

The differences in the organization, strategy, and tactics of trade unions in the various parts of the world are closely geared to the structural development of the society, the economic system and the labor movement. Certain characteristics of European labor are traceable to this fact. Labor's fight for recognition in Europe, under a system of feudal heritage and classicism, led to demands for having every gain written down in black and white, in the "book." Legislation, therefore, rather than collective bargaining, was the channel through which labor fought first its political battles for recognition and then its economic battles for an improvement of working conditions and living standards. Labor felt that the rights gained through bitter fighting could be less easily nullified if they were written into law. Collective bargaining processes, which increased with the spread of education and growth in maturity of the rank and file of the worker, became

mere stepping-stones for legislation and were restricted to the enumera-
tion of variable and fringe benefits. . . .

The political orientation of the European labor movement is
also rooted deep in history. Labor entered the economic arena only
by way of a political labor movement and the formation of class parties. Classicism and feudalism nurtured rigid rules and the formation
of ideologies. The ideology of the "book" was followed by counter
ideologies concentrated around the class distinctions and privileges
inherited from a feudalistic past. Works councils and codetermination
legislation, for example, are but the backwash of the earlier low status
of the workers in the society, community, and plant; of some kind of
inferiority complex in dealing with the economic partner; of a latent
distrust of the intentions of the "employer class"; and of the drive for
security in a period of recurring economic and political crisis. Such
security was always sought in legislation which, in line with scholastic
thinking, was the permanent "solution" of a given problem.

Labor as a Pressure Group

Charles M. Rehmus
University of Michigan

. . . [IT] IS TRUE that American unions today devote their major attention to control of the job, improved working conditions, and higher
standards of living for workers. They seek to achieve these objectives
primarily through collective bargaining rather than through class
propaganda warfare or through seeking political office directly. Nonetheless, American labor organizations have engaged in substantial political activities throughout their history—never more strongly than at
present. These activities, however, have assumed the pattern of pressure politics—attempts to influence public policy—rather than party
politics per se.

This choice, to be a pressure group rather than a party, makes
very good sense in terms of the nature of the American political system.
It would have been almost impossible for American labor to develop

Excerpted by permission of the publisher from "Labor in American Politics," in *Labor in a Changing America*, edited by William Haber, New York:
Basic Books, 1966.

a major political party with its base solely or primarily in the labor movement. There are a number of reasons for this.

1. The size of the United States and the diversity of interests in this Nation make it impossible for a party to come to power by appealing to a single interest or by relying on a single set of issues.

2. The composition of the major parties in the U. S. is extremely diverse, and the parties have always shared the labor vote. The American tradition of family influence on political party choice militates against a clearcut ideological division of the electorate based upon class differences.

3. The powerful position of the President of the United States in the American political system has meant that any truly national party must be a serious competitor for this office. A national organization must be developed if a party is to have an opportunity to elect a President. Labor's strength has always been concentrated geographically. Today, for example, organized labor has a substantial number of adherents in only ten or a dozen of the fifty states. This makes it practically impossible for labor to develop a national political party.

4. State laws favor existing political parties and encourage traditional voting habits. In many states new parties must meet extraordinary requirements in order to get on the ballot. Moreover, American candidates must be residents of the district in which they run for office. There are very few electoral districts that are composed primarily of labor voters. This complicates the problem of electing a substantial number of labor representatives to either state or federal legislatures.

5. American political parties have traditionally had low discipline and little centralized control over officials elected under their banner. American unions have likewise rejected specific direction from national bodies. Both of these traditions of autonomy would make a National labor party difficult to control.

6. Finally, and most importantly, the existing American political parties have shown a marked ability to come to terms with organized labor. The realism with which the large urban party machines in the U. S. have established political alliances with union leaders has ordinarily drawn off any substantial pressure for organized labor to set up a competing political organization.

In summary, for reasons of ideology and tradition, and because of the basic structure of the American political system, most leaders of organized labor have been uninterested in working toward an independent labor political party. This has been true particularly since the rise of the American Federation of Labor, and is still true today.

Types of Political Unionism

Bruce H. Millen

U. S. Department of State

"Political Unionism" Defined

THE TERM "POLITICAL UNIONISM" is subject to a variety of interpretations, since most labor organizations, including those in the United States, engage in political activity. It is necessary, therefore, to differentiate between the "economic union" that is to some degree involved in politics and the "political union" that carries on economic functions, but may subordinate them.

The political approach of American unions . . . is usually an extension of their economic function. Legislation related to the membership's interests as workers, consumers, or taxpayers will be supported, and candidates who favor the type of legislation wanted by the unions will be backed. Progressive legislation—such as aid to education—which has an impact beyond their own membership is also generally supported. With few exceptions, American labor leaders have employed the established political channels, and although a rally might be staged, for instance, in favor of a medical aid bill that is being debated by Congress, a strike would never be called for this purpose. In England, the trade unions are much more directly involved in politics through participation in the Labor Party, but, here too, much of the involvement is pointed toward goals more or less related to the traditional functions of economic unionism.

As I define it, the "political union" has certain specific characteristics:

1. The amount of time and thought invested in direct political work is a primary index. The political union's leaders are directly engaged in political operations and discussions day in and day out.

2. The goals of its leadership are very broad, in contrast to the usually circumscribed goals of union leaders in the United States, and may include revamping the major rules governing the society. The political union, through its support of "open-end" objectives, seeks improved living standards for its members, but may temporarily be willing to go slow in achieving them in the hope of winning political power.

Excerpted by permission of the publisher from *The Political Role of Labor in Developing Countries*, Washington, D. C.: The Brookings Institution, 1963.

3. The frequent use of direct mass action—a demonstration, a strike, or sometimes a staged riot—in support of nonindustrial objectives, and a propensity for tailoring the performance of economic functions to serve political ends are constant factors. Protest is almost never registered through as mild a method as a "write-letters-to-Congress" campaign that unions in the United States might mount.

4. Ideological conformity in the leadership is required, although the tolerable limits of dissent may vary. Communist labor movements are the most demanding, nationalist movements somewhat less so. Movements that are linked only loosely to a party or government are usually permissive, demanding only general support of the ideology.

5. There is a marked tendency toward "movementism"—i.e., the continual determination to form or participate in a broad-based political force aimed at capturing and maintaining political power. Trade unionism alone is considered an inadequate instrument with which to attain the political, economic, and social reforms sought by the union leaders.

There are, however, exceptions to the movement tendency, especially in certain Middle East countries where the political elites have, for the most part, attempted to control the labor groups instead of including them in a mass front. As a consequence, the union leadership is likely to engage in maneuvers that are still highly political but uninspired by an ideology.

6. In the early stages of a movement-building process, a political union often closely resembles a political party—and may indeed be a party. Eventually, however, the many problems encountered in the wider interest-spectrum of a party tend to press the union back to its specialized area of labor representation. But even here the interests it looks after are not only those of its own often small and unstable membership but also the broader ones of an idealized national labor force.

"Political unionism" and "economic unionism" are clearly not mutually exclusive means of action but two facets of the organized labor pattern, which often may alternate in the operations of a given union. In the operations of most Asian and African unions the political facet is durably and highly visible—much more so than in the unions of the developed countries—but blendings are found. A Ceylonese labor leader (who also headed a political party) described this to a group in Washington some years ago: "It is true that political leaders like myself originally got into the trade union field to strengthen the nationalist effort—but this did not mean that we were free to ignore the workers' job-related demands. We had to get something for them in order to hold their loyalty."

The characteristics of "political unionism" as stated above apply in general to the organizations that are the concern of this book. Yet it is necessary to remember that every organization mentioned here is fundamentally only representative of itself. It has always been impossible to encompass within any single term or phrase what it is that constitutes a "labor organization." Robert Franklin Hoxie spelled out the difficulty many years ago:

> The union program, taking it with all its mutations and contradictions, comprehends nothing less than all the various economic, political, ethical, and social viewpoints and modes of action of a vast and heterogeneous complex of working-class groups, molded by diverse environments and actuated by diverse motives.[1]

A labor organization is made up of human beings and is responsive to a wide array of problems sensed and felt. Thus each one, whether local union or national center, is unique. Moreover, there is a constant flux as the union acts and reacts to changing internal and external developments, so that the union of tomorrow is likely to be something different from the union of today.

In presenting a generalized picture, then, one runs the risk of oversimplifying or of overlooking important characteristics of labor organizations in an individual country. The wide range of union function and operation in any given country is difficult to span: describing an American union such as the United Auto Workers provides but little insight into the National Maritime Union or any of the unions of the construction trades; so, too, in Kenya, the characteristics of the Mombasa Port Workers Union are quite different from those of the General Agricultural Workers Union. But Kenya unions as a whole differ from United States unions more than they differ from each other —and that is the point this study is trying to make.

Types and Functions

Bearing in mind the caveat above—that each organization described in these pages is representative only of itself—it may nevertheless be useful to offer here a spectrum of categories into which the unions of various countries can be grouped. The categories necessarily over-

---

[1] Robert Franklin Hoxie, *Trade Unionism in the United States*, New York: Appleton, 1922, p. 35.

lap, and the situations in the developing countries are still so fluid
that the characteristics of any union may change rapidly. However,
the groupings will indicate wherein the present unionism of the new
countries differs from or corresponds to that of older countries. . . .

1. The unionism exemplified by the United States model is at
one extreme of the spectrum, that of the Soviet bloc at the other. As
pointed out earlier, the dominant note in the American labor movement
is the collective bargaining function, although political action in some
sense of the term has always been included in union programs. American unions are by tradition free and independent of government and
political parties. Historically, especially during the early stages of
labor organization, strong controls were at times exerted on union
activity, but in the main by private employers, who were, however,
often supported by judicial interpretation or administrative action of
public authorities.

2. Next on the spectrum are the unions of the North European
countries—typified by those of Scandinavia. Collective bargaining and
economic action rank high on their list of priorities, and functional
links with Social Democratic and Labor parties are usual. Many of
the organizations have engaged in direct political strikes, but as they
acquired political responsibility such activities became more rare.
Although the unions cooperate closely with political parties and formulate wage policy in keeping with party objectives, they have an independent source of power, and can, therefore, be considered "free and
independent." Obviously, however, to apply the phrase here supplements its American connotation.

3. Because Israel is in many respects unique, it belongs in a
class by itself. Although Histadrut, the labor federation, relates somewhat to the North European category in its basic socialist ideology,
the addition of Zionism and nationalism has imparted special characteristics and given it a "nation-building" philosophy. Histadrut is
as much an expression of political drive as it is of trade unionism;
links with political parties are close and for the most part mutually
beneficial. Collective bargaining has been a commonly used tool but
is not dominant. Because of its political ties, Histadrut is of course
not free and independent in the American sense of the term, but
because it is itself a power center within the complicated party structure, it is not a captive—and is certainly philosophically closer to the
American model than to the Russian.

4. The next point on the spectrum can be represented by Italy

or France—or India and Ceylon.[2] The dominance of ideological concepts here is the basis of highly politicized trade unionism carried on
within the framework of a competitive political system. There is a
history of left-wing radicalism, including revolutionary socialism and
communism, and the general or industry-wide strike for the attainment
of economic and political purposes is still retained as a weapon. Union
ties with political parties are the norm and permit, in varying degrees,
party influence on trade union matters. The extent of independent
power retained by the unions is a variable not only from country to
country of this category but also within each of the countries, depending upon which union-party relationship, among the several within the
open system, is being examined.

5. In the Middle East grouping (Israel aside) the labor organizations, with the exception of those in Lebanon, are or have been subject to stern control by the respective governments . . . they tend
therefore to be the "political-maneuver" type. The Turkish unions
have been gradually gaining additional rights recently, but still fall
far short of being free or independent. Collective bargaining is limited by both the nature of the economy and the restraints imposed by
government. The unions in Egypt have been striving for something
more substantive, but the government's ambivalence in seeking to
build a mass political organization and at the same time maintain close
watch over the component units has so far restricted them to this
grouping.

6. In Africa, many of the unions might properly be grouped
under the general heading of "political-maneuver" and controlled organizations, although the degree of restraint is probably somewhat less
than that exercised by Middle East governments. In countries that
are guided in part by conservative remnants of the old *patrone* par-

---

[2] Many of the Latin American and Caribbean countries would also seem to
fit into this general category, according to discussions I have had with trade union
and political leaders from this region. Too, Robert J. Alexander's description of
Latin American labor as one of the revolutionary forces and "an integral part of
the revolt against the traditional society" has a familiar ring. ("Organized Labor
and the Bolivian National Revolution," paper presented to the Research Seminar
on Comparative Labor Movements, Washington, D. C., 1962. This paper and
nine others by Seminar members were included in a book published by Northwestern University Press in 1963: *National Labor Movements in the Postwar
World,* edited by Everett M. Kassalow.) George I. Blanksten's comment that Latin
American labor articulates the views of large numbers who are otherwise unrepresented in the interest-group structure also matches the picture. (See "Latin
America," in Gabriel A. Almond and James S. Coleman, eds., *The Politics of the
Developing Areas,* New Jersey: Princeton University Press, 1960, p. 512.)

ties, the unions are generally expected to play a modest role, or none at all; the labor movements of Liberia, Dahomey, the Ivory Coast, and, possibly, Sierra Leone are illustrative of this. (In Sierra Leone there has been some evidence that changes are taking place.) The organizations do have a modicum of internal autonomy, but if they try to follow an independent course they have relatively little importance and are subject to controls.

In some of the African countries, however, a more dynamic type of union is dominant. These are the countries where the mass, structured party is in control or where there is evidence that a move in this direction is in process: Algeria, Tunisia, Guinea, Ghana, Tanganyika, Kenya, and, possibly, Senegal are representative. The labor movements here are highly political and, in the first four countries named, are also attempting to play a large political role. Although collective bargaining is not characteristically emphasized, it is not neglected. Most of the organizations are now coming under increasing government control, but because their operations are dynamic and because they give active support to government programs they have retained a voice in high councils and varying amounts of influence on over-all policy. The most extreme examples in this grouping—Ghana and Guinea—are much closer on the spectrum to the Russian model than to that of the United States.

7. Finally, of course, we reach the Soviet trade union system, in which I include the systems of all countries within the Sino-Soviet bloc. Collective bargaining is clearly subservient to the goals of the state, the trade unions are clearly subordinated to the Communist Party, and the question of union autonomy is irrelevant. The unions have been agents of the state since 1928, when Tomsky was replaced as head of the union federation by Kaganovitch as a consequence of the decision to force the unions to be production-minded rather than consumption-minded.

The rapidity of change in the developing countries makes it virtually certain that the above groupings will not remain static, but as of the summer of 1962 they appeared to be relevant to the situations observed.

Involved in the problem of rapid change, and making political unionism even more difficult to understand, is the shift in role when the labor arm of a political force moves from its pre-independence opposition to the colonial government to post-independence responsibility for cooperating with the new government. This shift has been especially common in much of Africa, where there are also assorted variations of it to add to our confusion. The case of the Union Marocaine du Travail in Morocco is one variation: the highly nationalistic

UMT moved into opposition after liberation; the oppositional course, however, has been more restrained than that taken prior to independence. There is also a distinction in role for unions operating under the one-party systems common to Africa, and those under multiple-party systems, as in India and Ceylon, where the observer encounters the many puzzling problems of competitive unionism. And all of this must be traced within the context of a fluid political situation.

Some Thoughts on Labor and Political Action

Adolf Sturmthal
University of Illinois

1—Systems of Thought

THREE SYSTEMS OF THOUGHT in the Anglo-Saxon world have dealt with the role of political action in the arsenal of the labor movement. In a chronological—only partly logical—order these are the theories of Marx, the Webbs, and Selig Perlman. For *Marx* political action was the fundamental and at the same time the supreme weapon of the working class. To the same degree to which the workers would develop class consciousness they would also accentuate their political organization, the leading organization among those which the working class creates for its emancipation. All other organizations are subordinate to the political party; they are not only under its leadership, they are also primarily recruiting grounds for the political organization. The ultimate battle in the class struggle is a political battle, in the sense that it is fought primarily by political organizations as well as that its object is the conquest of political power by the working class. For Marx political action forms, both quantitatively and qualitatively, an increasingly important part of labor action. With the progress of labor, we should, therefore, expect that political activity in the labor movement is increasingly emphasized.

With a very different kind of reasoning the *Webbs* arrived at a somewhat similar conclusion. In their view the objectives of the trade union required for their attainment the establishment and enforcement of what they called the "Common Rule." Collective bargaining

Reprinted by permission of the publisher from *Industrial Relations*, XVII, No. 3, Québec: Les Presses de l'Université Laval.

and mutual insurance may serve as instruments to this end; but, as the Webbs put it in the 1920 edition of their "Industrial Democracy," "the trade unionists, having obtained the vote, now wish to make use of it to enforce, by Legal Enactment, such of their Common Rules as they see a chance of getting public opinion to support." Political action for the purpose of legal enactment of common rules thus becomes a method of growing importance for the labor movement as its political power increases.

Selig Perlman's theory propounds an almost diametrically opposed view. The labor movement created and led in its early stages by intellectuals frees itself gradually from their spiritual leadership as labor evolves into self-confidence. Since it is the intellectual who has impressed upon the "manualists" the view that political action and social reform objectives are of paramount importance, labor gradually shifts its attention from politics and distant aims of social change to economic action and immediate objectives. The emancipation of the manualist from the tutelage of the intellectuals expresses itself in increasing emphasis on collective bargaining for short-run demands. A mature labor movement stresses collective bargaining to the neglect of political action (it is only a mirage, says Perlman).

2—Political Activity

This brief summary of the views of important thinkers indicates not only the disagreements which exist among them, but to some extent also the confusion between "scientific" and "normative" elements in their views. The "class-conscious" labor movement of Marx, the "mature" movement of Perlman are of course expressions of what the authors thought labor movements ought to do and not merely of what they would do. In addition, there seems to exist, perhaps more among the disciples than among the masters, a certain ambiguity of what the term "political activity" is to imply. It is perhaps useful first to clarify the term for our purposes.

Political action is sometimes—perhaps more in Britain than in the U.S.—identified with "independent political action" which in turn is interpreted to mean a Labor Party in the style of either the British Labour Party or the Scandinavian Social Democratic parties. In American discussions the term more commonly refers to either the nominating of candidates for public office or, in a somewhat looser fashion, to the attempt to achieve certain objectives by legislation or administrative action. In a vague way, emphasis on political action is sometimes identified with certain—usually radical—ideologies: political action is then regarded as equivalent with the effort to achieve certain changes

in the social system. Finally, we could suggest that the term be reserved for the work of organizations presenting solutions for a whole
range of problems, as distinguished from pressure groups which concentrate all their attention upon a small number of issues.

In what follows I intend to use the term in one of its most conventional meanings—namely, to denote a method for the achievement
of given objectives. Political action then implies the use of legislative
or administrative means by unions for the attainment of their objectives. More realistically, since no labor movement refuses to use legislation or administrative devices altogether and very few, if any, nowadays reject collective bargaining in toto, we shall be concerned with
the respective proportions in which these two methods—disregarding
all others—are used. Our assignment is thus to suggest hypotheses
that may assist in understanding the different mixtures of political
action and collective bargaining used by different labor movements.

3—Danger of Ethnocentrism

The main danger which such an attempt faces is that of ethnocentrism.
Let us consider what this danger may consist of in the case of the
United States. In making comparisons among different labor movements one or several of the following silent assumptions are commonly
or at least frequently at the base of the comparison:

1. The main or essential or at least short-run objectives of different labor movements are everywhere and at all times the same,
once labor movements have come into being. The achievements of
various labor movements can, therefore, be compared by the use of
one yardstick—e.g., the level or the rise of real hourly earnings.

2. The means of achieving these identical objectives would be
the same in all countries and at all times—if we disregard minor variations imposed by local peculiarities—if intellectuals did not intervene
and, from a certain moment on, misguide the movement.

3. The basic method *is* collective bargaining, with political
action at the most playing a subsidiary and supporting part to collective bargaining.

4. Left to themselves all labor movements will put increasing
emphasis on collective bargaining. We are heading for a universe
with an increasingly uniform labor movement in which the method-
mix accentuates collective bargaining at the expense of political action.

Merely stating these assumptions is sufficient to point out their
fragility and their fundamental ethnocentrism. To think of the labor
movements in the world in the image of present-day American business

unionism, i.e., as an organization whose horizon is bounded by wages and hours and working conditions is to misrepresent other movements, other phases of the history of the American labor movement and, perhaps, even some important aspects of American labor today. Statistically at least, in many of its behavior patterns, the American labor movement is the exception rather than the rule among the labor movements of the world. This applies particularly to its still rather distrustful attitude toward political action.

Equally significant, I believe, is the ethnocentric element in the role that many observers have assigned to collective bargaining. An almost mystic faith in collective bargaining has developed in this country. As long as the issue was that of collective bargaining versus unilateral determination of wages and working conditions—usually by the employer—the stress upon the virtues of collective negotiations was easily comprehensible. However, this faith in the unlimited virtues of collective bargaining seems less warranted when the choice is between collective bargaining and political action. Undoubtedly each of these methods has its virtues and its shortcomings and, what is more important, each operates best or most effectively under certain conditions. It will be the purpose of this paper to formulate some hypotheses about the conditions under which each of these methods seems likely to be most effectively employed. Let us proceed by way of a simplified theoretical model.

4—Theoretical Model

This model operates with four variables: economic development, changing objectives of the labor movement, changes in the fundamental situation on the labor market, and changes in the structure of the labor movement. In extreme shorthand the following propositions may be formulated:

1. With progressive economic development—which typically means industrialization—have come changes in the principal objectives of the different labor movements; so far the emphasis has ordinarily moved from the political, social, cultural, educational to the economic sphere.

2. Quite frequently industrialization has its takeoff in a situation which implies unlimited supplies of unskilled labor. The bargaining power of an all-inclusive labor movement is close to zero. Labor must then choose between political action or a limitation of its organization to high-skilled craftsmen. This choice will be greatly influenced by the existence or absence of strongly emphasized noneconomic objectives common to all or most workers.

3. With the progress of industrialization the excess supply of labor tends to be absorbed. However, this same process, by calling forth the rise of the semiskilled worker and other developments, weakens the bargaining position of the skilled workers. This tends to emphasize political action—but at this stage it often serves less as a substitute for bargaining, but rather as a necessary preparation for effective bargaining.

These propositions must be developed to be meaningful.

5—Economic Development

The problem we are considering must be visualized against the background of economic development—the progress of industrialization, rising per capita incomes, improving levels of education, ever higher social acceptance of manual labor, etc. This great change that has been going on in the Western world since the eighteenth century is now spreading around the globe. It has been accompanied by changes in the objectives of the labor movements.

During the last century and a half since organized labor movements have come into being, they have been instruments for the attainment of very different objectives at different times. Universal equal suffrage, greater educational opportunities for workers and their children (in particular universal compulsory free secular primary school education), greater social recognition for manual labor, recognition of social responsibility for some of the risks connected with manual work—all these and many more have been central objectives of various labor movements at different times. The struggle for universal equal suffrage filled an entire stage in the history of most Western labor movements—the heroic age of European socialism which lasted roughly until 1918 and was responsible to a large extent for the flavor of comradeship and dedication that was characteristic, until fairly recently, of so many of the Continental European labor movements. No one can fully understand the present crisis of European labor without reference to the void which the attainment of its democratic objectives left in the whole make-up of the movement. A history of the international labor movement could be written, simply in terms of those of its functions which it abandoned, partly because they were no longer necessary since some other organization had taken them over—e.g., education by the state, social security by a public system, etc.—or partly because the original objective had been attained. It seems possible that by further research certain interesting regularities could be ascertained in the sequence in which given objectives were emphasized, attained, or abandoned, the degrees of interconnection and overlap among them, etc. Intimate connections, in particular, could be established between certain types of objectives and emphasis or lack of emphasis on political action. The relative lack of interest in political action on the part of the American labor movement can be related to the fact that quite different from— say—its European counterparts, suffrage and public secular primary school education had been attained before the modern organization of American labor emerged.[1]

Let us now concentrate our attention exclusively upon that stage of the evolution in which the economic objectives of the labor movement have preeminence. For the sake of simplicity of the argument, I shall use the wage rate as the object of economic union demands. This means that I shall disregard for the moment all noneconomic demands—an important loss of realism, but fortunately only a temporary one in the development of our thought—as well as all economic demands not expressed in terms of changes of the wage rate. This, on the whole, is not a significant fact since these demands can be translated into rate changes and, in fact, are so treated on many occasions by the partners in the bargaining process.

The wage rate being a price, the proximate determinants of the price are supply and demand for the particular type of labor involved. The bargaining power of a union is then its ability to influence the wage rate either by changing the demand or supply schedules or by setting a rate different from the equilibrium rate. Generally speaking, bargaining power will be the higher, the easier it is to control the supply of labor that is available to fill the jobs, since the union has little direct influence upon the demand schedule.

In most countries, in the early phases of the industrialization process the supply of labor is very large in relation to the demand. This is expressed in what is called hidden unemployment or underemployment, i.e., a situation—existing particularly frequently in agriculture—in which the withdrawal of a significant portion of the labor force would be offset by minor adjustments in the work load of the remaining workers, without producing any substantial reduction in output. Arthur Lewis has discussed this situation in a study entitled *Economic Development with Unlimited Supplies of Labour*.[2]

---

[1] Quite possibly, in the twentieth century, anticolonialism, the struggle for national independence, may have taken the place of the conventional political objectives of labor in earlier history—universal suffrage, universal free secular grammar school education, etc.

[2] W. A. Lewis: *Economic Development with Unlimited Supplies of Labour*, The Manchester School of Economic and Social Studies, XXII, No. 2, May 1954; and the same: *Unlimited Labour: Further Notes*, XXVI, No. 1, January 1958.

This situation means that at the existing wage rate in industry an excess supply of labor is available. The industrial labor force can consequently be increased without any increase in the wage rate. In terms of economic theory, the supply of labor in the aggregate is perfectly elastic. No increase in wage rates is required to produce a higher supply of labor.

Where does this excess supply of labor come from? It originates essentially with four main sources:

1. *The excess labor force in agriculture.* In addition, the gradual transformation of subsistence agriculture into commercialized farming releases further parts of the agricultural labor force.

2. *Release of labor from the precapitalistic small-scale manufacturing and trading sector.*

3. *Population increase.* Industrialization goes sometimes—particularly nowadays—hand in hand with improved sanitation and the introduction of modern medical methods. This reduces the mortality rate and produces rapid increases in the rate of population growth.

4. *Immigration.*

Of these the first two—the release of labor from agriculture and the precapitalistic manufacturing and trading enterprises—are normally the most important sources of labor supply in the early stages of industrialization. They produce the excess supply that stands at the factory gates eager to take on factory jobs or that part of the agricultural labor force which recruiting agents in various guises can easily induce to leave the village, temporarily or permanently, to obtain industrial employment.

Industrial wage rates are, even under these conditions, higher than the average subsistence provided for in agriculture. But the differential between the wage rate for common labor in industry and the average subsistence in agriculture cannot be high. The pressure of the excess supply of labor prevents the differential from becoming larger than custom, morality, the need for a stable and reasonably healthy labor supply in the plant, higher living costs in urban communities, etc., require. Under these circumstances union action by way of collective bargaining is likely to have little effect upon the basic wage rate, that for unskilled labor in industry.

The situation is far better, from the union point of view, as far as the rates for skilled labor are concerned. Economic growth commonly produces a sharp increase in the demand for the higher skill grades of labor while the supply—as a result of low educational levels, mediocre training facilities, and rather high training costs in relation to current incomes—is fairly inelastic. The rise in the demand for higher skill qualifications is thus ordinarily sufficient to provide for an increased spread of the wage structure.

Unions operating in this kind of environment will be confronted with a choice whose implications are far-reaching. They may either limit their membership to highly skilled workers whose scarce supply provides the union with a powerful position at the bargaining table, or they may decide to represent all grades of industrial labor. In the latter case, they must find ways and means to relieve the pressure which unlimited supplies of labor exert upon the labor market. These ways and means may consist of restrictions on internal migration which effectively prevent the agricultural workers from accepting jobs in the urban areas and thus competing with the industrial workers for the scarce jobs in industry. Other devices are protective tariffs for agricultural goods. By increasing the average subsistence wage in agriculture the tariff reduces the significance of the industrial wage differential; at the same time, by improving the situation of the agricultural laborer, the tariff stems the tide of agricultural workers moving into industry. Restrictions on immigration are a relatively simple method to achieve the same objective. The unions, in a different solution of the problem, may achieve a universal "closed shop," i.e., they may hold complete control of the access to the various industrial occupations.

A labor movement limited to skilled craftsmen emphasizes collective bargaining. A movement conceived to include as many working class groups as possible, will have little market power. It will depend on political action either to give it control over the access to the labor market or to obtain direct enforcement of higher labor standards, circumventing, so to speak, the market.

On what does it depend which of these alternatives a labor movement chooses? As a working hypothesis I would suggest that one of the principal variables which determines the choice is the degree to which the labor movement serves as an instrument for the attainment of noneconomic objectives (in addition to economic goals) common to the workers in general. The demand for equal suffrage, for the removal of class distinctions directed against manual labor, for equal educational opportunities represents a common tie among all workers and turns the labor movement into a class movement. When the resentment over the class society outweighs the economic advantages that could be obtained by limiting membership to skilled workers, the movement aims at becoming an all-inclusive working class organization. Its main weapon, then, tends to be political activity. For its lack of power on the market place, it substitutes its political pressure—the power of its numbers. Given its desire to include unskilled working class groups, the emphasis on political action is rational, just as the use of market power is perfectly reasonable for an organization limited to higher skill groups.

All this applies to labor movements in the early stages of industrialization when there is an unlimited supply of labor. There are however, countries in which the takeoff into industrialization occurs while labor is in short supply. On the whole this means that there is no underemployment in agriculture and that the precapitalistic sectors in manufacturing and trade are relatively small. The labor supply for the growth of industry then must come from the natural population increase and from immigration. In countries of this type the bargaining power of unions is likely to be high at all times as long as industrial development proceeds at a sufficiently fast pace to absorb the increased labor supply originating in the growth of population and immigration. If the country happens to include a large underpopulated but fertile territory, labor shortage rather than an excess supply of labor is likely to be the main problem of economic development guaranteeing a maximum bargaining power for labor unions. In this situation collective bargaining is an effective device for unions. Immigration may, however, grow to the point where it endangers the bargaining power of—particularly unskilled—workers just as seriously as would internal pressure of underemployed agricultural laborers. Then the need will arise to make a choice between a politically inclined class movement and a market-oriented high skill group.

6—Supply of Labor

The excess supply of labor continues to exist until it is relieved by any of the following processes:

1. Capital formation progresses to the point where the excess labor supply is absorbed; this is most likely to happen by way of progressive industrialization since modernization alone would tend to reduce labor requirements in agriculture and in the precapitalistic sectors of manufacturing and trade.

2. Migration. This may be either internal migration from the areas of excess labor supply into those undergoing rapid economic growth capable of absorbing immigrant labor, or external migration from underdeveloped countries into rapidly advancing modern industrial nations.

As soon as the pressure of excess labor supply upon the labor market is relieved—which is long in advance of the total absorption of excess labor—wages for labor in the industrial sector begin to rise. There are two reasons for this: average subsistence in the precapitalistic sector rises by the removal of a number of participants in the distribution of the product without any appreciable drop in the product itself; this tends to increase the supply price of industrial labor. The bargaining power of unions in the modern sector is enhanced by the drop of the volume of excess labor. Collective bargaining now becomes an increasingly effective instrument in the hands of the labor movement, though it may appear to be the better part of wisdom to continue to use political devices for the purpose of raising incomes in the precapitalistic parts of the economy or in order to maintain a tariff that will increase real incomes in—say—agriculture. These devices will tend to reduce profits and, thereby the rate of economic growth in the long run, but at the same time will contribute to increases of wage rates in industry in the short run.

A special case of some significance is that of countries with "dual economies"—a substantial modern sector combined with a sector of either subsistence economy or at least a stagnant and relatively backward sector.[3] Our analysis leads us to expect that labor movements in these countries will tend to combine collective bargaining with political activity and that the role of bargaining increases with the growth of the modern sector.

7—Types of Labor

For a number of reasons, however, it would be misleading to assume that the logic of economic development would lead straight into the paradise of untrammelled collective bargaining and the corresponding decline of political action. Not only is it erroneous to regard social change simply as the function of one variable, but the independent variable itself—in this case the labor force represented by the unions—undergoes changes while economic growth proceeds. In practical terms this means:

1) That social mores once established persist beyond the life of the factors that gave rise to these mores. Thus the habit of regulating social relationships by law established in an era of unlimited supplies of labor continues into an era of increasing scarcity of labor;

2) The advance of modern industry has produced a new category of workers, in between the highly skilled and the common laborer, namely the semiskilled worker. With the development of mass production industries came the growth of this type of worker, for a period the most

---

[3] Cf., R. S. Eckaus: "Factor Proportions in Underdeveloped Areas," *American Economic Review*, XLV, No. 4, September 1955.

rapidly growing group of the labor force and one which so far has shown few signs of numerical decline. In many ways this group put its imprint upon the social life and particularly the labor movements of industrial nations since about the beginning of this century.

From the point of view of our analysis the emergence of the semiskilled worker in the later stages of industrial development means that the role of many types of skilled labor in the traditional meaning of the term—the craftsman and artisan—is greatly reduced. Entire operations which so far were in the hands of highly skilled workers are being taken over by semiskilled workers. At the same time it becomes easier for common workers to ascend into the ranks of the semiskilled. Rapid training processes are developed in the advanced industrial nations, training facilities are often provided for by the employees themselves, the growing wealth of the nation permits the development of many public training centers, and the rise of the general educational level of the population enables a growing proportion of the working class to benefit from advanced training.

Thus, the boundaries between the different types of labor become more fluid, one type can often be substituted for another, the monopolistic position of high-skill labor is weakened; semiskilled workers play an increasing part in the labor force and, consequently, the labor movements of advanced industrial nations. This is reflected in the strategy of the labor movement.

Strong unions arise in the modern mass-production industries shifting the center of gravity of the labor movement at least to some extent away from the old craft unions. While the latter would wish to put all emphasis on collective bargaining, the industrial unions in the mass-production industries combine collective bargaining with considerable stress upon political action. There is now no longer a large industrial reserve army concealed in underemployment in agriculture and in precapitalistic forms of manufacturing and trade. Even unskilled and semiskilled workers have, therefore, at least in principle considerable bargaining power. But the facility with which semiskilled workers can be trained combined with the rising levels of education of the population weakens the market position of the semiskilled workers. Substantial parts of the high-skill groups find that within limits and some adjustments in the work process semiskilled workers can be substituted for them. Group power is weakened. Unlike the relatively small groups of high-skill workers in early industrialization, large numbers of semiskilled workers or common laborers discover that changing levels of employment in industry in general and in their own industry in particular have vital influence upon their power on the labor market. A combination of bargaining and political action—with the latter preparing the ground and creating favorable conditions for the former—is the indicated strategy of the large industrial, and of many of the skilled craft, unions.

The weight of the industrial unions may be so large that the entire labor movement is swept along the way of mixed strategies or, there may be a prolonged split between the two groups with one putting the accent on bargaining—as for instance the building trades in the United States—and the other on political action as do the big industrial unions in this country.

8—Few Examples

What inferences can we draw from these models for an understanding of various labor movements? Let us consider a few examples.

1. Outstanding examples of labor movements which, in the early stages of industrialization, limited themselves to high-skill groups were the AFL and the French Syndicalists. Both operated in countries with limited supplies of labor: in the U. S. as a result of the development of a large continent, in France because of the low rate of population increase and the retardation in the decline of peasant enterprises as a result of the Meline tariff. If we remove the cover of ideological verbiage we find in both countries highly skilled craft groups relying on their market power: in the U. S. by collective bargaining, in France where collective bargaining was only in its infancy until World War I, simply by reliance on the effects of a scarce supply of skilled labor on its price. In both countries organized labor rejected political action, even developed disdain for the labor politician. Restrictions on immigration came in the United States toward the end of the century when mass immigration provided large supplies of common labor; the Meline tariff in France sufficed to slow down the decline of employment in agriculture and thus relieved the pressure of agricultural workers on the urban labor market. Even these measures were called in only in the nineties when the new type of semiskilled worker began to emerge, endangering the monopolistic position of the crafts.

2. In both countries it is possible to follow the impact of the rise of modern industry upon the arsenal of weapons used by labor. Up to 1914, the small shops around Paris with their many craftsmen and artisans were the stronghold of the antipolitical syndicalists while the large textile areas of the North and the coal mines of St. Etienne and the Pas de Calais with their masses of unskilled and semiskilled workers were bulwarks of the politically minded Marxians. Hothouse industrialization during World War I caused these small industries to

be replaced by some of the most advanced mass production establishments of France employing tens of thousands of semiskilled workers. This change was reflected in the ousting of the syndicalists and the victory of the Communists in the Parisian labor movement, and a consequent shift of emphasis to political methods.

In the U. S., the founding of the industrial unions was not only greatly facilitated by White House support and that of important State governors, but it led in turn to greatly enhanced union interest in participation in political campaigns. Over large parts of the U. S., the Democratic Party has for all intents and purposes become a labor party.

3. British development proceeded in three stages. Large supplies of labor prevailed for about the first five decades of the nineteenth century particularly as a result of the decline of agriculture. The British workers, deeply resentful of their class society, responded at first in a class movement of primarily political emphasis—the Chartists. In a second phase, with the gradual political reforms on one hand, the abolition of the corn laws on the other hand, came the withdrawal to skilled craft unions of high bargaining power—the development of business unionism. When in the last two decades of the nineteenth century the semiskilled workers appeared and organized, the unions began their shift to increased political activity—the founding of the Labour Party in 1900 or 1906 being the symbol of this new trend.

4. Particularly interesting, from the point of view of this analysis, are the cases of countries with a dual economy such as Mexico. In spite of very rapid economic growth, the problem of excess labor supply is still very grave and class feeling very intense—a result of the relatively recent emergence of Mexico from its feudal and colonial past. As a consequence, political action is the main weapon of the labor movement, but it seems increasingly also to set the stage for effective collective bargaining. By giving the unions full control over hiring—an almost universal closed shop—the government ensures bargaining power for the unions—in return for their political support. Political action, in this case, is the main weapon of the movement; in a subsidiary fashion it is also the key to effective collective bargaining.

5. Most of the underdeveloped countries that are now eager to enter the stage of industrialization, are areas of excess labor supplies. Since most of them are adopting modern forms of industry with its large requirements of semiskilled labor and the new labor movements have class objectives as well as strong feelings of class solidarity beyond the confines of a craft or occupation, the labor movements are of necessity political. The attempt to preach American style business

unionism in Ghana or Pakistan is doomed to failure; business unionism would be either inffective or run counter to the objectives of the movement and to the class consciousness of the workers or both; the circumstances do not permit the effective use of collective bargaining.

9—Conclusion

Many questions can undoubtedly be asked for which the suggested hypotheses provide no answer or no satisfactory answer. Nor do I claim that there is a single factor explanation for the behavior patterns of different labor movements at different times. What I do suggest is that the stage of economic development, the situation on the labor market, and the degree of class solidarity within labor, and the structure of the labor force are key factors which together explain a part, perhaps a good deal of the peculiar relationship that exists between labor and political action.

Chapter 2

Pressure Politics and
Workingmen's Parties

THE COLONIAL PERIOD IN AMERICA was marked by a scarcity of labor. While British authorities often enacted industrial codes to establish wage ceilings, in practice earnings often exceeded them by 50 percent and more. Although in theory strike action was forbidden, strikes did take place, were rarely punished, and often resulted in recognition of workers' demands. Property and income qualifications limiting the electorate generally precluded the wage earner's direct participation in colony-wide affairs. Nevertheless, the vote was often conceded to him in local elections.

The sharp class differentiation so characteristic of Europe was not present here. As one labor historian has indicated,

> . . . the settlers generally were inclined to hail the "virtuous" mechanic and to treat artisans with esteem. One almanac editor described the prevailing attitude neatly when he urged his countrymen "to prevent the execution of that detestable maxim of *European* policy amongst us, viz.: That the common people, who are three quarters of the world, must be kept in ignorance, that they may be slaves to the other quarter who live in magnificence. . . . He that will not work neither shall he eat," he declared, should be the American standard. To a great extent it was, and the workingman profited.[1]

As resentment against the British increased, wage earners actively participated in the agitation and attacks which culminated in the Revolutionary War. As this chapter's first reading indicates, colonial workers "combined *with* their employers in common political action rather than *against* their employers for economic advantage."

The only permanent form of worker organization prior to the Revolution had been mutual aid societies which pooled financial resources, often of both journeymen and masters, for sickness and death benefits. After the war, a new breed of business entrepreneur arose,

---

[1] Joseph G. Rayback, *A History of American Labor*, New York: The Macmillan Co., 1959, p. 21.

usually called the "merchant-capitalist," the wholesaler who contracted with individual shops for a specific volume of production and in turn distributed manufactured goods, at a profit, to retailers. The masters, caught between the demands of their journeymen for benefits that would result in increased labor costs, and the insistence of the merchant capitalists upon cheaper products, could no longer maintain the friendly informal relationship with their employees that had been possible in former years. The masters' attempts to keep wage rates down and to lengthen the work day made it clear to their journeymen that employer and employee interests were no longer identical. As a consequence, the old mutual aid societies became the basis for a different kind of organization, now composed solely of journeymen, and organized as a defense against both master and merchant capitalist.

Members of these organizations laid down rigid rules for entry and refused to work with nonmembers. Strikes, then called "turn-outs," were frequent during the first decades of the nineteenth century. Such activities were, however, largely limited to skilled artisans and semi-skilled operatives. Then, as for nearly a hundred years to come, the unskilled laborer had little bargaining power. Geographically, organized worker activities were largely confined to the larger industrial centers of the Northeast, such as Boston, New York City, and Philadelphia.

With the onset of a depression in 1819, the effectiveness of concerted worker action was severely undermined and the activities of the labor organizations came to a halt. A few were able to survive; many went under. But with the return of prosperity in 1822, new unions again sprang up. This pattern of disappearance and reemergence, following the ups and downs of the economic cycle, was characteristic of the trade union movement until the 1880's.

During the late eighteenth and early nineteenth centuries, labor's political activity was minimal. In general, workingmen supported Jefferson's Republican Party which, in turn, championed their interests. On occasions when employers turned to the courts, charging that labor organizations were a conspiracy in restraint of trade, Republican attorneys argued in labor's behalf and Republican newspapers came to its defense. Republican-controlled state legislatures granted wage-earners the vote. The alliance between the early Republican party and the labor movement broke down in the 1820's, however.

It was in these years that the world's first workingmen's parties were formed. The earliest was Philadelphia's, established in 1828. A severe depression in the winter of 1828–29 heightened interest in that city's labor party, and similar organizations sprang up throughout the country. As Edward Pessen's study of the workingmen's parties indicates, these organizations came into being only when appeals to the major parties, themselves engaged in factional strife, fell on deaf ears.

Once these third parties had met with some success, the major parties, particularly the Jacksonian Democrats (a new party resulting from a cleavage within the old Jeffersonian Republican Party), made efforts to woo workingman support. How successful these overtures were still remains a topic of heated debate among labor historians. The selection which follows Pessen's, by Joseph Rayback, analyzes the evidence marshaled on both sides of the question, "Did labor vote for Jackson?"

Following the Panic of 1837 and on into the 1850's, the air was filled with the appeals of idealistic and utopian reformers. Americans were bombarded with speeches advocating every conceivable "ism," from vegetarianism to utopian socialism, each a sure cure for all real or imagined ills. As Henry Pelling points out, each of these movements had its labor advocates. The panacea which attracted the most labor attention was that of land reform. The leader of this movement, George Henry Evans, had earlier been active in the Workingmen's Party of New York City. Now, rather than urging independent union political action, he was engaged in pressure politics, passing out petitions and cornering political candidates of whatever party, urging them to sign pledges stating that if they were elected they would promote the cause of homesteads for all. With the Democrats fervently courting labor support and even their opponents now making overtures, the idea of third party action by organized labor was again abandoned.

The altered climate in which the labor movement operated during this period is reflected in the change in judicial attitudes toward trade union activity. In the 1806 Philadelphia cordwainer's case and in a number of subsequent trials, workers who had organized to advance their interests were charged and convicted of engaging in criminal conspiracies. Increasing protest over the harshness of this position led to a partial victory for labor in 1842. A decision of the Massachusetts Supreme Court in Commonwealth v. Hunt resolved the question of the per se illegality of unions; henceforth labor organizations were not to be regarded as illegal conspiracies. The test of legality or illegality would depend not upon the act of organization but, rather, upon the organization's ends and the means it employed to obtain them. This decision, which followed English law and largely established a similar precedent in the United States, still left considerable room for judicial control affecting the activities and fortunes of labor unions. Nevertheless, labor's right to organize was now recognized.

Pressure tactics were used in attempts to obtain the ten-hour day, the one movement of the period that was concerned with solutions to the workers' job-related grievances. As Pelling notes, artisans in New York and Philadelphia had already won the shorter workday by the 1830's. But artisans elsewhere and factory operatives everywhere still continued to work as many as twelve to fourteen hours a day. In 1840, the Democratic President, Martin Van Buren, issued an executive order granting the ten-hour day to federal employees. While this indicated Democratic Party sympathy and served as a welcome example, similar legislation governing the bulk of American workers would have to come from the individual states.

All during the 1840's efforts were made to obtain ten-hour laws from state legislatures. The resulting legislation left much to be desired. At employer insistence, it commonly included a clause excepting from coverage any worker who entered into a special contract with his employer in which he indicated his willingness to work longer hours than the law allowed. Employers easily got around the new state laws by refusing to hire anyone unwilling to sign such a contract.

These failures caused those behind the ten-hour movement to become more aggressive in the next decade. In the 1850's they insisted that political candidates, of whatever party, sign a pledge of support for labor's position. Soon, both parties made effective ten-hour laws a part of their platforms. Apparently as a means of forestalling the threatened legislative interference, employers then voluntarily reduced the hours of work, usually to eleven per day. Whether this satisfied the workers, or whether the movement lost energy for some other reason is uncertain; in any event, impetus for the ten-hour day movement died out.

By the mid-1850's, labor, North and South, was caught up with the rest of the nation in the sectional conflict over slavery. Initially, northern labor's position toward the slavery question was ambivalent. Self-interest, as much as anything else, governed the northern wage earners' attitude. Many felt that if southern slaves were freed and migrated north in any numbers they would flood the labor market and drastically lower wage rates. Others claimed that since cheap southern labor was already affecting northern wages indirectly, emancipation would eliminate the unfair competition.

Once war was declared, however, the northern labor movement generally supported Lincoln's administration and the Union cause. Lincoln himself won organized labor's loyalty by opposing government intervention to halt strike activities. More important, increased production to meet military needs and the consequent demand for labor produced a very favorable environment for trade union activity, and labor organizations mushroomed during the war years. While these were predominantly local in scope, the number of unions organized on a national basis increased substantially as well.

There was also a spectacular growth in the number of city federations, organizations composed of representatives of all trade unions in a particular area. Theirs was primarily a propaganda function—to issue labor newspapers publicizing strike issues, to solicit strike funds and, in general, to present the views of the organized labor movement in the area. If a particular union was having difficulty with an employer, it was the federation's function to urge members of all other unions not to buy the products of the offending employer. Such boycotts proved to be very effective weapons. The federations also occasionally combined on a statewide basis to lobby against proposed antiunion legislation. However, the political potential inherent in such form of organization awaited a later day.

Political Action by Working Class Groups in the Revolutionary Period

Richard B. Morris
Columbia University

THE EVE OF THE REVOLUTION is marked by the appearance of numerous combinations of mechanics and laborers, masters and journeymen, primarily for political purposes. Together they protested against British imperial policy as it evolved after 1763. . . . Leadership was gradually wrested from the conservative merchants by the more radical working class groups. Operating through committees of mechanics, these groups seized the initiative in the adoption and enforcement of the nonimportation agreements[1] and in provoking incidents and organizing demonstrations. In this way the more conservative organs of protest were virtually supplanted.

Excerpted by permission of the author from *Government and Labor in Early America,* New York: Columbia University Press, 1946. Footnotes in the original have been deleted.
[1] Agreements among colonists to boycott British goods and the merchants handling them.—Eds.

The mariners were among the more radical and obstreperous element. In New York City they were organized as the Sons of Neptune, apparently antedating the Sons of Liberty,[2] for whom they may well have suggested the pattern of organization. [General Thomas] Gage reported that the "insurrection" of November 1765, in New York was supported by "great numbers of Sailors headed by Captains of Privateers, and other Ships." Shortly thereafter he referred to the sailors as "the only People who may be properly Stiled Mob," and charged that they were "entirely at the Command of the Merchants who employ them." The rank and file of the Sons of Liberty throughout the colonies were workmen, although the organizing and directing was in large measure in the hands of master craftsmen, rather substantial merchants, and professional men.

Certain outstanding examples may be considered to demonstrate the nature of working class cooperation for political ends and the solidarity of the urban artisan group. The hostility of the Boston workman to the Red Coat on the eve of the Revolution stemmed in part at least from resentment of the interloper, for the men of the regular army were allowed to accept private employment when they did not have military assignments. Quartered throughout Boston, the soldiers accepted work at very low rates of compensation. This sharp competition between soldiers and journeymen must be kept in mind in understanding the events leading to the Boston Massacre.

On the second of March 1770, three British privates in the 29th Regiment went to the ropewalk belonging to John Gray looking for work. A journeyman by the name of William Green insulted one of them, and the soldiers challenged him to a fight. After being worsted in fisticuffs, the soldiers ran back to the barracks in the immediate neighborhood and returned with several companions, who were driven off. The Red Coats then reappeared, reinforced to the number of some thirty or forty, armed with clubs and cutlasses, but the thirteen or fourteen hands of Gray's ropewalk were joined by fellow workers from neighboring ropewalks to the number of perhaps nine or ten, and the assault was again beaten off. Gray, the master, alarmed at the turn of events, made a personal complaint to Colonel Dalrymple, warning him that his soldiers were determined to even their score with the ropewalk workers. When Dalrymple placed the blame for instigating the riot upon Gray's journeyman, Gray discharged the accused on Monday morning, March 5th.

---

[2] Groups of colonists, formed to protest the Stamp Act.—Eds.

Testimony is virtually unanimous that the soldiers nursed their humiliation at the hands of the ropewalks journeymen and were making rash threats of avenging the insult promptly. On the evening of the fifth some British soldiers sallied out of Smith's barracks, beat up a number of persons, and were finally driven back to their barracks. Actually the incident followed the taunt of an apprentice boy hurled at a soldier, charging him with not paying a barber's bill to the lad's master. The soldier struck the apprentice, a general altercation ensued, and the exasperated soldiery fired, killing a number of persons, including Sam Gray, who had actively participated in the affray at the rope-walk on the preceding Friday. As to whether Gray was recognized and deliberately shot, or hit without special design, there was a conflict of testimony. Killroy, one of the soldiers positively identified as firing at the crowd, was known to have particapted in the fight at the rope-walks, as was Warren, another soldier.

The relationship of the ropewalk affair to the later massacre was admitted by the authorities, both British and colonial. Gage reported to Hillsborough:

> A particular Quarrel happened at a Rope-Walk with a few Soldiers of the 29th Regiment; the Provocation was given by the Rope-Makers, tho' it may be imagined in the Course of it, that there were Faults on both Sides. This Quarrell it is Supposed, excited the People to concert a general Rising on the Night of the 5th of March.

The Boston council also placed the blame for the affair of March 5, 1770, on the previous clash at the ropewalk, although on the details of the massacre civilians differed sharply from the military. According to the Boston authorities,

> the affair which more immediately was introductory to the said Massacre was a quarrell between some Soldiers of the 29th Regiment and certaine Rope-makers at the Rope-walk of one Mr. Gray. In the contest the Soldiers were worsted: and this reflecting, as they thought, on the honour of the Regiment there was a Combination among them to take vengeance on the Town indiscriminately. Of such a combination there is satisfactory proof.

On a number of occasions mariners and town artificers struck in protest against British military preparations. Gage reported to Hillsborough in 1768 that transports would not proceed from New York to St. Augustine, because "the Troops are designed for Boston," and the mariners had been "threatened by Some of the Chiefs of the discontented," and dared not "incurr their Displeasure." When, in 1774, Gage sought artificers to work on the fortifications of Boston, not only did the workers of that town refuse to work for him, but New Yorkers fully cooperated with the striking Bostonians. Gage finally induced some Boston carpenters and masons to start work on the barracks, whereupon a joint committee of the Boston selectmen and members of the committee of correspondence persuaded them to quit. Committees of correspondence of thirteen towns adjacent to Boston adopted joint resolutions deeming as "most inveterate enemies" any inhabitant of Massachusetts or the neighboring provinces who should supply the British troops at Boston with labor or materials. Gage was forced to send to Nova Scotia for fifty carpenters and bricklayers, and through Governor Wentworth's aid, obtained a few additional ones from New Hampshire; but the troops did not get into barracks until November. Early in the spring of 1775 mass meetings were held in New York City to protest the exportation of supplies for the use of the British garrison at Boston. The supply ship was seized by the Committee and the crew forbidden to proceed on the voyage.

At the very period when there was increasing concentration of workers in industrial establishments—a trend which was accelerated, first by the nonimportation agreements and subsequently by military needs—colonial journeymen put first things first, and combined *with* their employers in common political action rather than *against* their employers for economic advantages. In striking contrast was labor's role in Britain during those very same years. Franklin, writing in 1768, graphically described the lawless scenes in the British capital, where coalheavers and porters attacked the homes of coal merchants, while sawyers destroyed sawmills, watermen damaged private boats, and sailors would not permit ships to leave port unless their pay was raised. When the Revolution began it was reported that Britain was drained of ships for transport purposes by combinations of workmen and sailors for raising their wages, and strikers slowed down or disrupted production of English firms engaged in making clothing for the British army in America. Gage reported that "the News of the Tumults and Insurrections which have happened in London and Dublin . . . is received by the Factions in America, as Events favorable to their Designs of Independency."

The Working Men's Parties of the 1820's and '30's

Edward Pessen

Staten Island Community College,
City University of New York

THE UNIQUE FEATURE of the American labor movement during the Jacksonian era was the establishment of Working Men's parties. Beginning in Philadelphia in 1828, a Working Men's movement spread throughout the country, reaching its climax in the 1830's. . . . Since one of the classic features of the modern American labor movement is precisely the extent to which it has eschewed politics, the appearance of this movement is of obvious significance. This essay will examine aspects of the movement as well as some of the issues still in controversy concerning it.

If no attempt will be made here to give a blow-by-blow account of the rise and fall of the Working Men's parties, it is because it is by now a much-told tale. A substantial literature has appeared since George Henry Evans and his contemporaries in ante-bellum America first chronicled the activities of the New York Working Men.[1] . . . To date, though, the most comprehensive and probably still the most valuable study remains the pioneering effort of Helen Sumner in John R. Commons' *History* in 1918. In many respects it remains the basic structure on which all later works have built.[2]

The modern discussion, focusing as it has on a few major cities, has perhaps obscured what Miss Sumner's researches long ago uncovered: the ubiquitousness of the Working Men's party. Operating under a variety of names—"Working Men's Parties," "Working Men's Republican Associations," "People's Parties," "Working Men's Societies,"

Excerpted by permission of the author from "The Working Men's Party Revisited," *Labor History*, Vol. IV, Fall 1963. Substantial portions of the original article have been deleted; and footnotes renumbered.

[1] George Henry Evans, "History of the Origin and Progress of the Working Men's Party in New York," in *The Radical*, 1842–43; Hobart Berrien, *A Brief Sketch of the Origin and Rise of the Working Men's Party in the City of New York*, n.d.; Amos Gilbert, "A Sketch of the Life of Thomas Skidmore," in the New York *Free Enquirer*, March 30, April 6, 13, 1834; Jabez D. Hammond, *History of Political Parties in the State of New York*, Rev. ed. (New York, 1850), vol. II, 330–31.

[2] Miss Sumner wrote Part II, "Citizenship (1827–1833)," in Commons and Associates, *History of Labour in the United States* (New York, 1936), vol. I, 169–332.

"Farmer's and Mechanic's Societies," "Mechanics and Other Working Men," and just plain "Working Men"—they appeared in most of the states of the union. Pennsylvania was the home of the first known group, the Philadelphia party of 1828, which developed out of an earlier organization, the Mechanics' Union of Trade Associations. [The author goes on to list other towns in Pennsylvania and those in New York State, New Jersey, Washington, D.C., Ohio, Delaware, Massachusetts, Connecticut, New Hampshire, Maine and Vermont which also established such parties.] . . .

Most of our information concerning these parties comes from the pages of the dozens of journals which sprang up in this period in support of the Working Men. According to the *Delaware Free Press,* one of these journals, at least twenty newspapers in a number of states had appeared by August 1830, which might be classified as prolabor.[3] Miss Sumner found evidence of "some fifty newspapers in at least fifteen states" for the period of 1829-32. Naturally, these papers varied in the degree of support or attention they gave to the Working Men's cause but a substantial number of them can properly be described as organs of the political movement, so completely were they dedicated to the Working Men's issues both in their coverage and in their news slant. . . .

It would be understatement to describe the main questions raised by the recent literature as a challenge to the traditional thesis. For these questions concern nothing less than the fundamental nature of the Working Men's movement. They simply ask: Was the movement authentic? Was it composed of bona-fide wage earners battling in the interests of wage earners? Or was it spurious, consisting instead of wily politicians who wrapped themselves in the Working Men's mantle only to hide their real identity? . . .

The sharpest questions as to the authenticity of the Working Men's parties have been provoked by the accumulating evidence on the social and economic backgrounds of their members and leaders. The organ of the Philadelphia Working Men liked to think that in contrast to the two major parties of the time—the "Federalists," made up of lawyers and aristocrats, and the Jackson party, composed of bank speculators and office hunters—"on the Working Men's ticket . . . the candidates from first to last have been taken from the ranks of the people." But William Sullivan has shown that during its four years of existence the Philadelphia party nominated and supported very few

---

[3] Cited in *ibid.,* 286.

workers as candidates for office. According to his tabulation, of the party's one hundred candidates only ten were workingmen. Twenty-three were professional men, fifty-three were merchants and manufacturers, eleven were "gentlemen" and three had no occupations recorded. Among these were some of the wealthiest men in the city, including Charles Alexander, publisher of the conservative *Daily Chronicle*. These facts lead Sullivan to doubt that the Philadelphia organization was a true workingmen's party.[4] Louis Arky, on the other hand, found a high percentage of its early leaders—better than seventy-five percent, in fact—workers or artisans.[5]

The leading student of the New Jersey movement, Milton Nadworny, found little solid information about the occupations or incomes of the leaders and candidates there, although for Newark he ventures the understatement that "undoubtedly, not all of the men in the group were pure, unadulterated workingmen." Despite his findings that small businessmen and merchants often played leading parts in the movement, Nadworny nonetheless accepts it as essentially authentic.[6]

The New York City Working Men split into at least three factions shortly after their striking political success in the fall of 1829, and there is no doubt that the largest faction had little in common with true workmen. But prior to the infiltration of the party by opportunistic elements, culminating in their ascendancy by the time of the 1830 elections, the evidence indicates that bona-fide workers were active in its ranks. Of the eleven candidates put up for the State Assembly in 1829, ten were workers; the other, a physician, got significantly fewer votes than all the rest of his colleagues in the election.[7] In its early stages, according to George Henry Evans, the party sought not only to confine leadership to workingmen but to see that the leaders were journeymen rather than masters. That it was not successful, however, is shown by the fact that the following year even Evans' faction was supporting manufacturers as candidates for political office.

For that matter, Evans' definition of working man was a rather broad one. According to him, only one member of the seventy-man General Executive Committee of the New York party of 1830—a broker

---

[4] William A. Sullivan, "Did Labor Support Andrew Jackson?" *Political Science Quarterly*, LXII (December 1947), p. 575; and by the same author, *The Industrial Worker in Pennsylvania 1800–1840* (Harrisburg, 1955).

[5] Louis Arky, "The Mechanics' Union of Trade Associations and the Formation of the Philadelphia Working Men's Movement," *Pennsylvania Magazine of History and Biography*, LXXVI (April 1952), p. 173.

[6] Milton J. Nadworny, "Jersey Labor and Jackson" (Unpublished Master's thesis, Columbia University, 1948), pp. 58, 59–60, 75–76.

[7] *Working Man's Advocate*, November 7, December 25, 1829.

—was not a workingman. Evidently, he considered the five grocers, the two merchant tailors, the oil merchant, the teacher, and the farmer to be workers. The complete occupational breakdown for this committee unfortunately does not distinguish between masters and journeymen, but it does range over a broad category of occupations including carpenters, smiths, masons, painters, pianoforte makers, sash makers, and porter housekeepers. [Seymour] Savetsky, who is not inclined to take this organization's claims at face value, nonetheless concedes that on this committee "a majority . . . belong to the laboring element in the community." His close study of the property owned by this group established that just under fifty percent were propertyless, another ten percent had only personal property, while only three individuals owned property assessed at more than $10,000.[8] For the years after 1831 it has been rather conclusively shown, both by the contemporary, Jabez Hammond, and by Walter Hugins, writing in 1960, that the New York Working Men included a wide variety of social and economic types.

The Boston Working Men's party did not last long, though while it lasted it showed no animus towards men of wealth. Years ago I did a study of the social position of the candidates it supported in the municipal election of 1830 and in the state congressional contest of 1831. Their mayoralty candidate, Theodore Lyman, Jr., was a wealthy ship owner, while four of their seven aldermanic candidates were among the wealthiest men in Boston. Thirty-five of their sixty choices for the State Assembly belonged to that elite group whose property was valued in excess of $2,600.[9] Since less than two thousand persons in a population of seventy-eight thousand had this amount of property, it would appear that forty of the party's sixty-eight nominees belonged to the wealthiest segment of the community. I must admit, however, that I am now not so sure of what I wrote then, that these figures "do not imply anything fraudulent," and that they reflect "middle-class aspirations and a certain naiveté" more than they raise doubts "as to the true workingmen's character" of the Boston Working Men's party.[10] Doubts as to the actual nature of the party are indeed raised by such figures.

---

[8] According to Savetsky, the findings on the property holdings of the General Executive Committee members were based on a careful reading of fourteen volumes of tax rolls for the year 1830; Seymour Savetsky, "The New York Working Men's Party," (Unpublished Master's thesis, Columbia University, 1948), pp. 109–10.

[9] These figures are based on a study of the *List of persons taxed twenty-five dollars and upwards in Boston for 1834*, Boston, 1835.

[10] Edward Pessen, "Did Labor Support Jackson? The Boston Story," *Political Science Quarterly*, LXIV (June 1949), No. 2, p. 267.

Doubts have also been raised by the programs of the Working Men's parties. Joseph Dorfman has not been alone in noting that some of the measures they advocated bore no relation to the economic needs of workingmen. But it is true, of course, that workingmen had needs that ranged beyond the economic. That Working Men's parties raised aloft a standard which included a wide variety of political, social, intellectual, occasionally even religious, as well as economic issues, does not necessarily testify to anything but their breadth of interests and hopes.

The programs of the parties were amazingly similar. For, as Miss Sumner observed, "substantially the same measures were advocated by the workingmen in most of the western and southern cities, as well as in New Jersey, Delaware and New England, as were advocated by their comrades in Philadelphia and New York."[11] The program of the Philadelphia Working Men was to become the nucleus of all other programs. It included, above all, a call for a free, tax-supported school system to replace the stigmatized "pauper schools" which, according to Sullivan, provided a "highly partial and totally inadequate system of education for their children." The final copies of the *Mechanic's Free Press* contained on the masthead the following additional reforms: abolition of imprisonment for debt; abolition of all licensed monopolies; an entire revision or abolition of the prevailing militia system; a less expensive legal system; equal taxation on property; no legislation on religion; a district system of election.[12] In addition, the Philadelphians intermittently protested against the unsanitary and overcrowded housing conditions of workingmen; the high cost of living; the long hours, low wages, and poor conditions of labor, as well as the low esteem in which manual work was held; the hostility of the major parties towards labor; the mistreatment of labor unions; the lottery system—"the fruitful parent of misery and want to numberless heart-broken wives and helpless children, who have beheld the means of their subsistence lavished in the purchase of lottery tickets"; the "pernicious operating of paper money"; and such down-to-earth grievances as insufficient "hydrant water for the accommodation of the poor" and "the failure of the city to clean the streets in the remote sections of the city where the workingmen reside." And earlier they had pressed successfully for the passage of a mechanics' lien law to assure workingmen first claim on their employers' payrolls. Nor does this exhaust a list which from time to time carried criticisms of banks and banking,

---

[11] Sumner, "Citizenship . . . ," in *op. cit.*, 296.
[12] Cited in Sullivan, "Philadelphia Labor . . . ," 9–10.

charitable institutions, the sale of liquor, conspiracy laws—and, when invoked against unions—the use of prison labor, and the complexity of the laws and of the legal system. . . .

There is no question but that this was a broad program, substantial portions of which were supported by men and groups having nothing to do with labor. Imprisonment for debt, for example, was opposed by many people outside of the Working Men's movements— on broad humanitarian grounds in some cases, and on grounds of economic inefficiency in others. Its victims were not always the "laboring poor." The same is true for other of the reforms, including education. Yet it would be economic determinism of a very rigid sort, indeed, to insist that authentic labor organizations confine their programs to economic issues advantageous only to workers.

Much of the Working Men's program *was* in fact concerned with the economic interests of labor. Naturally, workers sought larger wages and better working conditions. But they also sought improved status in society, and some of them organized in order to support the perfectionist demands put forward by their idealistic leaders as the means of achieving this status. The program of the Working Men's parties reveals them to have been champions of social justice and a more perfect democracy, as well as critics of every kind of social abuse.

Still other questions as to the authenticity of the Working Men have been raised over the alleged closeness of their relationship with the Jacksonian party. While Arthur M. Schlesinger, Jr. sees a coalition between the two movements, critics of his thesis have interpreted the same evidence as indicating the essential fraudulence of the Working Men's parties, seeing them as being no more than front organizations for the Democrats. It is perhaps a source of comfort to these critics that their charges are similar to those made 130 years ago by some National Republican leaders and publishers.

With regard to this issue, as with others, the evidence is either inconclusive or too complex to permit black and white generalizations. Assuredly, from time to time on certain issues the two movements behaved as one. The organ of the Newark Working Men, the Newark *Village Chronicle and Farmers, Mechanics, and Workingmen's Advocate,* admitted in April of 1830 to its sympathy with the Jacksonians. And there seemed to be more than coincidence in the decision by the two parties in New Jersey that year to hold their nominating conventions for the State legislature in the same small town on the same date. Nor is it surprising that after the fall elections the Whig press denounced what it felt to be the collusion between the two parties. Five years later, the Newark Democrats still evidently depended to a large extent on the political support of the Working Men, while in 1836 the two groups jointly supported a number of legislative candidates. The leading student of the New Jersey Working Men concludes that they consistently supported the Democrats and their candidates.[13]

In New York City the striking political success achieved by the Working Men in 1829 seems to have been the result largely of a shift in the voting habits of people who ordinarily voted for the "Republican" or Jackson party.[14] The New York party broke into several splinter groups shortly after the 1829 election. The so-called *Sentinel* or *Advocate* wing, named after the journals published by the younger [Robert Dale] Owen and Evans, supported much of the Democratic program, especially its antimonopoly features. In fact, according to Savetsky, this faction was simply absorbed or assimilated into the New York Jacksonian organization after its defeat in the elections of 1830.[15]

In New England the decision in 1833 of the New England Association to support as their gubernatorial candidate, Samual Clesson Allen, the erstwhile champion of Andrew Jackson and opponent of the Bank of the United States, led more than one Whig journal to denounce the unholy alliance of Working Men and Jackson men. This same fact serves as the basis for Schlesinger's conclusion that at this time the Massachusetts Working Men increasingly threw themselves behind Jackson's monetary program.[16] Yet this same New England Association Convention urged the formation of a prolabor national political organization. When the Association again nominated Allen for Governor at its last convention in September 1834, at Northampton, it simultaneously urged rejection of the candidates of the major parties for State office. A close study of its programs, conventions, resolutions, and actions indicates that from its birth in Providence in December 1831, until its demise not three years later, this organization was little concerned with, let alone sympathetic to, the Democratic Party. As for the Boston Working Men's Party, not only did it show no support whatever for the Jacksonian party, but its slate of candidates for the Board of Aldermen and the State House of Representatives included a good number of National Republicans. . . .[17]

---

[13] Nadworny, *loc. cit.*, 55, 68–69, 75.

[14] This is the conclusion of Savetsky, according to whom the Working Men were essentially Democrats grown disenchanted with Tammany; *loc. cit.*, 110, 115.

[15] *Ibid.*, 60.

[16] Arthur M. Schlesinger, Jr., *The Age of Jackson* (Boston, 1945), 158.

[17] Two of its seven candidates for alderman were National Republicans, according to the Boston *Courier*, December 9, 1830, and the Boston *Daily Adver-*

In New York City not only [Thomas] Skidmore, but Evans and Owen and their supporters as well, regularly voiced their opposition to both major parties. Despite their occasional agreement with the Democrats on a particular issue, their press warned that Jackson had no interest in important reform. If the mid-century commentator, Jabez Hammond, can be believed, the men who "flocked to the standard of the Workingmen" in New York State were "opposed to the Albany Regency and the Jackson party."[18]

The Philadelphia Working Men had no objections to supporting candidates of whatever social background or political persuasion. Yet their journal saw no contradiction in denying any connection with either of the major parties; in fact, it stressed the danger represented by the Democrats, "for as most of us are deserters from their ranks they view us with the same sensation as the mighty lord would the revolt of his vassals: there cannot be so much danger from the Federalists as, generally speaking, we were never inclined to trust them."[19] In the elections of 1829, the one year in which the Philadelphia Working Men achieved an outstanding success, they combined with the anti-Jacksonians in support of eight local candidates, while endorsing only one Jackson supporter. Sullivan has concluded that "an analysis of the [Philadelphia] Working Men's Party reveals that both in its composition and its predilections, it was amazingly regular in its support of the anti-Jackson forces."[20]

Even for New Jersey the situation was more complex than the allegations of some National Republicans would make it appear. The original platform of the New Jersey Working Men refused to align the group in support of Jackson. As the Working Men of Morris showed in 1834, they had no compunctions about nominating a Whig to office. His success goaded the Democrats into charging that the Whigs used the Working Men as tools! The following year an election rally of Newark's Working Men's party expressly stated that it preferred neither of the major parties. And although in 1836 there was a degree of cooperation between the two groups, there was evidently a falling

---

tiser and Patriot, December 11, 1830. Fifteen of the sixty state candidates were also nominated by the National Republicans, while a number of the rest were prominent members of the party, according to the *Columbian Centinel*, May 7, 1831.

[18] Hammond, *op. cit.*, 331.

[19] *Mechanic's Free Press*, April 12, 1828, cited in Sullivan, "Did Labor Support Andrew Jackson?," 571.

[20] Sullivan, "Philadelphia Labor . . . ," 13.

out (before the end of the year) that may have been due to the Working Men's resentment at being used by the Jackson party.[21]

Two points should be stressed. The program of the Working Men's Parties called for reforms that in most cases went unmentioned by the Democrats, whether on a local, state, or national level. This would indicate that the movement's organizers were motivated precisely by the failure of the Democrats—not to mention the National Republicans—to work towards goals these organizers deemed of the highest importance. In addition, despite the attempt by some historians to treat the political issues and the major parties of the era in striking ideological terms, as though they represented diametrically opposed social and class viewpoints, the facts are otherwise. As Charles Sellers, Glynden Van Deusen, Bray Hammond, Richard Hofstadter, and others have shown, the major parties had similar views on many important issues, differing more in tactics than in fundamental objectives, with neither party dedicated to a drastic alteration of the fabric of society. Of course there were Democrats and Democrats. But Jackson himself, and the leaders of the Democratic party in most of the states, were practical men. All of which is to say that it is to misinterpret the nature of the Democratic state machines or the national Democratic party of Andrew Jackson's day to believe that so loose, opportunistic, all-inclusive, and eclectic a coalition would devote itself to the kinds of reform urged by the Working Men.

What conclusions can be drawn about the relationship between the Working Men, led by radicals who often sharply criticized the Democratic party, and Jacksonian democracy? To the extent that it, too, opposed aristocratic privilege and monopoly, the Working Men's movement may perhaps be interpreted as part of a broadly defined "Jacksonian Revolution." But neither organized nor unorganized workingmen became a fixed part of a Democratic political coalition. And if the Jacksonian movement was in fact a movement primarily devoted to achieving a freer competitive capitalism,[22] the Working Men clearly had demands which went far beyond that objective. Yet in the large view which seeks to impose a pattern on the era, reforms of varied character, championed by diverse groups—each seeking the achieve-

---

[21] Nadworny, loc. cit., 67, 69–73.

[22] See Richard Hofstadter, The American Political Tradition (New York, 1948), 56; Bray Hammond, Banks and Politics in America (New York, 1943), passim; Joseph Dorfman, The Economic Mind in American Civilization (New York, 1946), II, ch. 23; Richard B. Morris, "Andrew Jackson, Strikebreaker," American Historical Review, LV (October 1949), 68.

ment of its own objectives—somehow merge together in a broad, all-embracing reform movement. It is only in this general sense that the Working Men of the Jacksonian era can be said to have been a part of the large, sweeping movement towards whose political expression —the Democratic party—they often displayed indifference if not actual hostility.

If it does nothing else, the discussion of the various controversies concerning the authenticity of the Working Men's parties should clearly establish one thing: it is impossible to generalize about the movement as a whole, as though all of its constituent parts were alike in all important particulars. There were Working Men and Working Men. The origin of some was obscure; of others, dubious. Some arose out of economic struggles, others out of concern for status. Some came to be dominated by opportunists, others by zealots. Thus, the only safe generalization perhaps would be that no two parties experienced precisely similar careers.

Yet it is also clear that despite inevitable differences in their circumstances and behavior these organizations, arising more or less simultaneously and calling for like reforms, had much in common. Common to the Working Men's parties in the major cities, in my opinion, was their authenticity—at least for part of their history. By authenticity I mean that they were formed by workers or men devoted to the interests of workers, sought to attract workers to membership in or at least to support of the new organizations, worked for programs designed to promote the cause and welfare of workers, and entered politics because of the failure of the major parties to concern themselves with important reforms and in the hope that these parties could be goaded or influenced into showing such concern. The authenticity of a party that conforms to this standard is not lessened by the fact that in supporting candidates to office, it asked only that they support the program, or important elements of it, while it evinced no interest in the size of their bank accounts or their social status. Nor is there anything suspect in the fact that parts of the program might also be supported by nonworkers.

The origins of the Working Men in Philadelphia, New York City, Newark, and the cities of New England, stressing as they did either the working class backgrounds or the aims of their founders, strengthen the belief that the parties were not misnomers. It is true that the parties contained many men who by present definitions would not qualify as workers. But the definition of that earlier day was much more flexible. The prevailing concept was that all who performed "honest toil" were working men. Even to such a radical as George

Henry Evans in 1830, only lawyers, bankers, and brokers could be designated as persons not engaged in the kind of useful occupation qualifying them for membership either in the Working Men's party or the working class. (It is interesting testimony to the growing conservatism of the New York City Working Men that a resolution incorporating Evans' sentiments was defeated as too restrictive. In the fall of 1829, on the other hand, there was strong support for the principle of confining leadership in the party to journeymen and, in Evans' words, denying a vote to any "boss who employed a large number of hands.") Additional light on this issue is thrown by the similar discussion that arose among the Philadelphia Working Men. According to the *Mechanic's Free Press,* early in the party's history (in the summer of 1828) it was decided that while employers might be present at meetings, they could not hold office. Yet one year later its Ricardian Socialist editor, William Heighton, could write: "If an employer superintends his own business (still more if he works with his own hands) he is a working man. . . . If this view of things be correct, shall we look with a jealous eye on those employers who prefer being considered working men? Who are willing to join us in obtaining our objects?" Not only for political candidates but also for mere membership in the party, the important issue evidently had become simply whether the man would join in "obtaining our objects."

It is also true that at a certain point in its career the New York party, for example, seemed to be in the hands of men who had little sympathy with its expressed program. But contemporary participants and later scholars alike are unanimous in agreeing that these elements infiltrated the party only after the dramatic success it achieved in the 1829 elections and succeeded in taking it over only by the use of money, inner party intrigue, extralegal tactics, and newspaper excoriation, all the while continuing to pay lip service to reform. The New York Working Men underwent a *transition* that powerfully testifies to the fact that in its heyday it was not only an authentic but also an impressive organization, even frightening to some politicians. Perhaps nothing more dramatically suggests that the New York and other Working Men's parties were bona fide than the opposition, to put it mildly, they inspired in Democratic and National Republican politicians alike, and above all in most of the press. The Boston *Courier* was not alone in arguing that "the very pretension to the necessity of such a party is a libel on the community." The underlying thought of its editors, the Buckinghams, was that rich and poor, publishers and typesetters, skilled and unskilled—all are workingmen and therefore there was no need for a separate Working Men's party.

In the nation's cities, however, not only did a Working Men's party appear; it would be more accurate to say that it burst forth on the political community like a meteor, either electing its candidates, or obtaining the balance of power on its second attempt, as in the City of Brotherly Love or, in other cities, immediately after putting forward its original slate. Less than two weeks before the election, in New York City, for example, a ticket nominated for the State Assembly elected one and came near to electing several other of its candidates, amassing better than 6,000 out of 21,000 votes cast. And yet in this as in other cases the political success was decidedly ephemeral. Decline set in almost immediately, culminating a brief few years later in the party's demise and disappearance.

What accounted for the almost immediate downfall of the Working Men's party? From that time to this, attempted explanations have not been lacking. Some Philadelphia leaders bitterly blamed the workers themselves, both for their blindness to their own true interests and for their lack of courage. Other sympathizers attributed the failure to the party's mistaken policy of supporting wealthy candidates, themselves personally sympathetic to monopolies.[23] Thomas Skidmore, himself cashiered out of the New York party for his radical views and his uncompromising fight for them, charged that the party's doom was sealed by its permitting rich men to take over, men who had no business in the party in the first place. Evans, his one-time opponent, later came to agree with him.[24] Hammond also noted that the New York State party had within its ranks men who made their living at jobs they professed to criticize, not excluding banking. By his view, "this party, if it deserves the name of a political party, was too disjointed and composed of materials too heterogeneous to continue long in existence."[25] New York friends of the Boston Working Men, on the other hand, explained the pathetic political showing of the New England party by its preoccupation with issues, such as religious infidelity, that were not properly the concern of a workingmen's political organization.[26]

In her summary of the causes of the failure of the Working Men's parties, Miss Sumner listed, in addition to some of the factors

---

[23] The columns of the *Mechanic's Free Press* for 1830 and 1831 carry many of these post mortems.

[24] The *Working Man's Advocate*, March 6, April 17, 1830; the *Free Enquirer*, March 20, 1830; *The Radical*, January 1842; the *Friend of Equal Rights*, April 14, 1830, cited in *Working Man's Advocate* of April 17, 1830.

[25] Hammond, *op. cit.*

[26] See the *Working Man's Advocate* for May 1831, especially the issue of May 11.

mentioned by contemporaries of the movement, the onset of a general prosperity which turned the attention of workers from "politics to trade unionism"; dissension—"legitimate" when resulting from hetero- geneity, "illegitimate" when started and nurtured by "professional poli- ticians of the old parties, who worm themselves into the new party"; the inexperience of leadership with regard to the practical problems in managing a political party; the hostile activities of the parties' open enemies; and, "last but not least, the taking up of some of its most popular demands by one of the old parties."[27] Most recent literature on the subject tends to confirm many of her judgments. . . .

Their own political ineptitude and inexperience, internal bicker- ing, heterogeneous membership, lack of funds, and the infiltration of their ranks by men interested only in using them, all played an im- portant part in bringing about the downfall of the Working Men; so did the opposition of the press, and the shrewdness and adaptability of the Democrats. Several related points also might be mentioned. Better than the major parties then or now, the Working Men's party represented the Burkean definition of a political party as a group of men united in behalf of certain political, social, and economic princi- ples. Its membership may have been broad but the party's program was not all things to all men; it was certainly not a grab bag aimed primarily at winning office for those who professed to support it. In the American society of Tocqueville's day a distinctly class-oriented program could not expect success at the polls.

On the other hand, for a party that presumes to speak out in behalf of labor to open its lists to individuals who embody the opposite of everything it stands for is perhaps fatally to blur its image—at least in the minds of workingmen—while failing to shake the loyalties of other citizens for the traditional parties who were so much better at practical politics. Speak out the Working Men did, in a message that was idealistic and radical; and as the message became clearer, an American public seeking the main chance and increasingly optimistic about its possibilities, lost interest in the nay-saying of the radical dis- senters who formulated the Working Men's program. It may well be, then, that a reform party was doomed to failure in the American society- in-flux (bemoaned by a James Fenimore Cooper), whose characteristic members quivered in anticipation of the material fortunes to be made. Such optimism, when shared by workers, is the stuff that kills off ideological politics.

Notwithstanding their failings and their ephemeral vogue, a

---

[27] Commons, et al., *op. cit.*, I, 326.

final assessment of the Working Men's parties cannot fail to note their significance. Immediately after the results of the striking Working Men's showing in New York became known, the Democrats promised to pass the lien law for which the new party had been agitating. Nor was it a matter of a lien law alone. Even in the short run, the Democrats in New York and elsewhere hastily showed greater concern than ever before for the various reform provisions of the Working Men's program.[28] Thus one of the factors that helped bring about their disappearance as a separate political entity was also an indication of their strength. If it is the function of radical parties in America to act as gadflies, to goad and influence rather than win elections, then the Working Men succeeded admirably.

Of course the degree of success they enjoyed is hard to measure. The Working Men were not alone in championing public education, abolition of imprisonment for debt, banking reform, reform of the militia system, factory laws, general incorporation laws, recognition of labor's right to organize unions, shorter hours of work for labor—to name some of the leading issues. It is impossible to fix with precision their contribution in comparison with that of other individuals and groups who supported one or another of these measures. But there would seem to be no question that the role of the Working Men's parties was an important one, in some cases even greater than is usually believed. In the struggle for the creation of a public school system free from the stigma of charity or pauperism, for example, it has long been the fashion (certainly since Frank Carlton pointed it out) to accord considerable credit to the Working Men. Yet, as Sidney Jackson has shown, not only did the Working Men agitate for the establishment of such a system; they also advocated sophisticated qualitative measures that seem remarkably prescient. Among the changes they sought were an improved curriculum, less concerned with pure memory and "superannuated histories," less emphasis on strict discipline, better physical conditions for children, better trained and better paid teachers, and better equipped schools, free of clerical influences.[29] In

---

[28] Walter Hugins sees a smashing victory accomplished by the New York State Working Men in 1834, several years after they had formally disbanded as a separate party. In his words, "though forced by circumstances to disband as a political party, the Workingmen had reached the climax of their power and prestige. The party of Jefferson and Jackson had seemingly embraced the principles [antimonopoly] of the party of 'Mechanics and Working Men.'" *Jacksonian Democracy and the Working Class* (Stanford, 1960), p. 35.

[29] Sidney Jackson, "Labor, Education, and Politics in the 1830's," *Pennsylvania Magazine of History and Biography*, LXVI (July 1942), 282–84.

sum, Helen Sumner's generous estimate does not seem overdrawn: "The Working Men's party, in short, was a distinct factor in pushing forward measures which even conservative people now recognize to have been in the line of progress toward real democracy." [30]

Did Labor Vote for Jackson?

Joseph Rayback

University of Alberta

OLDER HISTORIANS INTERESTED in the role of labor and some contemporary historians have concluded, primarily on the basis of opinions of editors and labor leaders who lived in the 1830's, that workingmen's parties were organized and operated by workingmen who had deserted the party of Jefferson. In their opinion these workingmen returned to their old party, now led by Jackson. Various factors were involved in this return: workingmen recognized the Jacksonian Democracy as the party of the common man; they were attracted by the promises of Jacksonian politicians and by the fact that the Jacksonians began to fulfill their promises—in New York, for example, the Democrats enacted a part of the workingmen's platform by passing a mechanics' lien law in 1830, by abolishing imprisonment for debt, and by reforming the militia system in 1832. Finally, they were attracted by the fact that Jackson was an enemy of the Bank of the United States, which workingmen hated. The old-school historians conclude that labor voted for Jackson in 1832 and became an integral part of the Democratic party.

In recent years other historians have cast doubt on these conclusions. Their research into the period, while recognizing contemporary opinion, is based primarily upon an analysis of the occupations of members of Worky committees and conventions and Worky candidates, and upon an analysis of election returns. Concerning the composition of the workingmen's parties they have come to the following conclusions: in Boston the party, from its origin, was largely led by manufacturers and shopkeepers. In New York, the skilled artisans created and ran the party during its first campaign, but skilled artisans

---

[30] Commons, et al., *op. cit.*, I, 332.

Excerpted by permission of the publisher from *A History of American Labor*, New York: The Macmillan Company, 1959.

held only forty-two seats on the seventy-man Executive Committee established to run the party after the split with Skidmore in 1830; most of the remaining members were "manufacturers." In the city of Philadelphia the party was also organized by skilled artisans, but beginning in 1829 its leadership was strongly infiltrated by anti-Jacksonians. In other Pennsylvania cities—Harrisburg, Lewiston, and Pittsburgh—the workingmen's parties were only remotely connected with labor; they were developed by anti-Jacksonians to split the labor vote. The implication in these conclusions is that the manufacturers and anti-Jacksonians were able to lure workingmen into the camp of the Jacksonian opposition, at this period known generally as the National Republicans or Anti-Masons.

Analysis of the election returns, with the most careful and thorough work on the cities of Boston and Philadelphia, appears to substantiate the implication. Although the Democratic vote increased in Boston, the city was overwhelmingly anti-Jackson in 1828 and 1832, and against Van Buren in 1836. The Philadelphia situation was more complex. The city voted for Jackson in 1828; most of the wards where workingmen lived were strongly Jacksonian that year. Thereafter, however, the Jackson and Democratic vote dropped from a high of 56 percent in 1828 to 37 percent in 1832 and 34 percent in 1836. There was a slight rise in 1840. Further analysis of election returns from the rest of the state leads to the conclusion that, except for the county of Philadelphia, "the wage earners were the first to drop from the Jackson bandwagon." In short, the workingmen went over to the Jackson opposition. In general it appears that the new-school historians would agree with this conclusion.

The historian who tries to weigh these contradictory conclusions is faced with many problems. Admittedly, the conclusion of the old-school historians is based on less "scientific" evidence than that of the new school. But does that mean their conclusions should be lightly cast aside? The old-school historians have strong supporting evidence for their conclusion that workingmen became Democrats: in the period after 1833 agitation regarding workingmen's demands was very strong in the Democratic party; no comparable agitation developed within the Whig party. This could mean that the Democratic party was indeed the party of the workingmen, or at least the more articulate and politically conscious workingmen, and that the Whig party was not.

In addition the historian must examine carefully the scientific evidence of the new-school historians. One statistical study of the Boston returns which uses correlative coefficients reveals that, in spite of the election results, the majority of workingmen were pro-Jackson. In short, the scientific evidence concerning Boston has been contradicted by a scientific technique using the same evidence.

There are other weaknesses. It cannot be assumed that all "manufacturers" or wealthy men were anti-Jacksonians; such an assumption would be carrying the doctrine of economic determinism too far. It cannot be assumed, moreover, that anti-Jacksonians in the workingmen's parties successfully lured workingmen into the anti-Jackson camp; they might have repelled workingmen. It cannot be assumed that the obvious decline of the Democratic vote in Philadelphia was caused only by the desertion of workingmen; it might as readily be assumed that the decline was due in whole or in part to the desertion of Jackson and his party by other elements living in the city, elements which had been attracted to Jackson when they did not know his philosophy and deserted him when they came to know him better. Finally, even if the conclusions concerning Pennsylvania labor are correct, it cannot be assumed that these conclusions apply elsewhere. Among the industrial states of the union, Pennsylvania has seldom followed the prevailing or typical political trend.

The historian can safely conclude only the following: the workingmen's parties of the early Jackson period disappeared because the parties were not "respectable," which made workingmen who were members feel inferior; because workingmen turned once more to trade unionism in order to achieve economic ends; and because they in one way or another were persuaded to join the Democratic or Whig parties or both to gain political ends.

The Panic of 1837 and Its Aftermath

Henry Pelling
Queen's College, Oxford

THE PANIC OF 1837 marks a breaking-point in the history of American labor. The fresh start of the 1840's was made in a new atmosphere. One important feature of the new period was the great increase in immigration, especially from Ireland, which rose to a peak after the

Excerpted by permission of the publisher from Henry Pelling, *American Labor,* The Chicago History of American Civilization Series, University of Chicago Press, © 1960.

potato famine toward the end of the decade. These Irishmen, mostly unskilled and ill-educated, crowded into the larger cities, especially Boston and New York, and rapidly squeezed the native American worker—including the free Negro—out of the humbler occupations such as domestic service and general labor. As time went on, they began to take a high proportion of the less skilled jobs in the factories of New England. The distinct tendency of wages in the factories to decline in the 1830's and 1840's, the westward movement of New England farmers, and the expansion of other occupations for women such as schoolteaching, led to the disappearance of that unique phenomenon, the cultured operative of the Lowell system.[1] Her place was usually taken by the Irish immigrant, who was at first quite content with a low wage and poor conditions of work. With so many occupations falling to the foreign newcomer, whose habits of life seemed to the native American not merely strange but crude, it is not surprising that a general hostility to the immigrant grew up in those parts of the Union where they settled in large numbers.

This hostility took various forms, and varied considerably in intensity, depending in part upon the degree of "foreignness" of the immigrants concerned. The English and Scots, being both Protestant and English-speaking, merged readily into the native population—a process rendered easier by the variety of skills which they brought with them. The Germans automatically encountered some prejudice owing to the language barrier and because some of them were Catholics; and, in New York at least, there were at first frequent complaints about their competition in the skilled trades. In the end, they came to be recruited into the trade societies of the city, either in separate German-speaking locals or mixed in with their English-speaking colleagues.

The unskilled Irishmen, almost invariably Catholics, and for the most part congregating in city slums, in spite of their knowledge of the English language proved the least assimilable at a time when anti-Catholic prejudice was strong in the United States. They were quite capable of maintaining prejudice and creating disturbances among themselves, as was shown as early as 1834 in the astonishing gang warfare among Irish laborers on the Chesapeake and Ohio Canal, which caused Andrew Jackson to send in the federal troops. But as time went on, religious rioting between Irish Catholics and native Americans became not uncommon in the larger cities; and in 1844 thirteen people

---

[1] The "Lowell system" refers to the practice, in Lowell, Massachusetts textile mills, of hiring young unmarried women of the surrounding farm area and providing pleasant working conditions and lodgings for them.—Eds.

were killed in disturbances of this character at Philadelphia. Later, the Mexican War and the rise of the slavery issue to a predominant position in national politics caused a diminution of anti-Catholic feeling; but the continued growth of immigration, combined with the disintegration of the Whig party, led to the emergence of the strongly nativist Know-Nothing movement in the early 1850's. In areas of heavy urban settlement by foreigners, such as New England and the middle Atlantic states, Know-Nothing candidates secured striking electoral successes in the years 1852–56, although hardly anything of their policies of immigration restriction and limitation of voting rights was enacted.

It seems paradoxical at first sight that this period of labor history has been described as the era of "humanitarianism." Yet the title is not too difficult to explain. At a time when the workers themselves were divided by ethnic conflicts, when traditional crafts were being replaced or at least considerably disturbed by mechanical processes, and when the factory workers themselves largely consisted of women and children, it was difficult for a genuine labor movement to develop. Consequently, the way was open for middle-class reformers to air their views as to the best remedies for existing ills, and often to pass themselves off as the genuine representatives of labor. Fourier's utopian principles of social reorganization, for instance, were constantly propagated at workingmen's conferences by the assiduous Albert Brisbane, and owing to the support of Horace Greeley, the popular journalist, they secured considerable attention in the press. Self-supporting Fourierist or Owenite colonies were set up in suitably isolated places, but with little permanent success. These experiments did, however, encourage workingmen to take an interest in consumers' cooperation in the later 1840's. A number of "protective associations," as the cooperatives were called, came into existence for a brief period, only to disappear in most cases before many months had passed.

The most practical by far of the proposed solutions of labor's ills put forward at this time by middle-class reformers was the land-reform policy of George Henry Evans. Evans sought to rally the workers behind his National Reform Association with the object of securing a division of the national domain into homesteads for all. This program had a certain appeal to the urban workers, in view of the increasing difficulties which faced the poor man who wished to set himself up on a western homestead. But, of course, many families of comparatively limited resources were still managing to go west and acquire land; and so it proved difficult for Evans to persuade very many people that this issue ought to be the predominant one in national politics.

All the same, . . . his ideas were more successful in the end than were those of his fellow reformers.

All these reformers had the characteristic in common that they approached the problems of labor as it were from the outside. They were not themselves artisans, still less factory operatives, at the time that they were agitating for change. Rather they were zealous philanthropists, anxious to assist in solving the world's problems. Such generous enthusiasm was increasingly to be met in other spheres of activity; in fact, it was an indication of the increasing leisure available to those sections of the community which stood above the level of the manual worker. Abolitionism, the cause of women's rights, and the temperance movement were other directions in which the energies of the great American middle class came to be spent at this time.

The genuine labor movement of the 1840's was, as we have implied, feeble and ineffective. In the more prosperous years in the middle of the decade, a number of mechanics' and laborers' associations came into existence in New England. At Lowell there was even a Female Labor Reform Association, run by one of the factory girls, Sarah G. Bagley. These bodies were organized without distinctions of craft, and their principal object was to reduce the hours of labor to something like the ten-hour standard that many of the artisans of New York and Philadelphia had secured in the 1820's or 1830's. In 1845 they held an Industrial Congress for the ventilation of their grievances, and other industrial congresses were held in subsequent years, some of them of national scope, some of them for individual states. The trouble was that these congresses all too often turned into factional disputes between the various middle-class reformers of the time.

Slowly, however, the skilled artisans began to organize their individual crafts on a local basis, to disentangle themselves from the reformers, and to overcome the ethnic rivalries which had weakened them for a decade. The Crimean War provided a breathing space in which immigration temporarily declined, and generally prosperous conditions strengthened their position. Even the factory workers were able to win a reduction of their hours to eleven or ten; and the state legislatures were at long last willing to pass laws to the same end. Some of the craft societies once again began to contemplate the possibility of associating with societies of their own craft in other towns— an object that became all the more desirable as transportation facilities improved and the size of the market both for labor and for goods steadily enlarged. It had already been customary for local societies of the same craft to offer each other's members certain reciprocal privileges;

now this could be systematized and the different locals could cooperate in fixing conditions of work and wages. In this way national unions came into existence, though naturally they were at first no more than weak federations of substantially autonomous local societies. The first to be formed was the National Typographical Union (1852), and this lead was followed by several other trades, of which the apparently successful ones were the Stone Cutters (1853), the Hat Finishers (1854), the Molders (1859) and the Machinists (1859). The building trades, having less need to establish uniformity of prices, were slower to establish links of this character. But in any case, the whole movement had made very little real progress before the outbreak of the Civil War.

Chapter 3

Politics and Lobbies—
The Post-Civil War Era

BETWEEN 1860 AND 1900, the United States became an industrial giant. Its people, who had been largely self-employed on farms or in small rural villages, poured into the burgeoning cities, seeking employment for wages.

In 1860, only about five million Americans were urban dwellers. By 1900, the number had increased fivefold. Employment in manufacturing establishments increased from 1,300,000 in 1860 to 4,250,000 in 1890. The character of industrial employment changed as well. The sprawling factory, mill, and foundry replaced the small shop; the corporation began to supplant the individual entrepreneur. Widespread introduction of machines constantly threatened the skilled artisan with loss of his job. The unskilled and semiskilled faced continuing competition from the ex-farmer as well as from an ever-growing number of immigrants.

The effects of financial panics and economic depressions upon wage earners were, of course, devastating. Unemployment was widespread during cyclical downturns, and those who had jobs worked irregularly and at reduced wages. Moreover, this was the period when employers regarded "labor" as a commodity, and the individual worker himself came to feel that he was a mere cog in a machine society. One inventor, reflecting on the callousness of the period, remarked that "he could sell a time-saving device in twenty places and a lifesaving device scarcely at all."[1]

These changes would have been enough to give the average American worker a sense of insecurity and a feeling of anonymity. Moreover, his efforts to assert his rights through concerted action met the combined hostility of the courts, employers, and the government.

The courts became increasingly hostile toward union activity. Judges issued sweeping injunctions with increasing regularity. The

---

[1] Quoted in Eric Goldman, *Rendezvous With Destiny*, rev. ed., New York: Vintage Books, 1956, p. 29.

most famous of these, issued in connection with the Pullman Strike in 1894, forbad not only the leaders of the union but "all other persons whomsoever" from attempting to persuade railroad employees "in any manner whatever" to participate in the strike action.

Employers threatened to discharge and blackball any employee who joined a trade union. Employer propaganda equated trade union activity with radicalism, anarchism and general "un-Americanism." When strikes occurred, employers fired the strikers, threw additional armed guards around the plants, and brought in nonunion employees as replacements. They called upon the local police for help and appealed to the governor to send in the state militia. In disputes involving the railroads, intervention of federal troops became increasingly frequent.

In the main, business and "respectable" elements in the country approved of the measures taken against trade unions. Many of them considered concerted action to tamper with the workings of the marketplace a kind of heresy. When, in an effort to draw the sting of the Labor Reform party, the Republican party included in its 1872 platform the statement that "the servant of civilization [should have] his just share of mutual profits," the *Nation* was incensed. Its editors sternly warned that those who were capable of understanding the purity of labor market economics ought not to hold out vain hopes to workers for their own selfish political ends.

Given the climate of hostility and repression, it is not surprising that worker protest at times culminated in violent and explosive situations. The Railroad Strike of 1877, the Haymarket Riot, the Homestead Strike, the Pullman Strike, and the march of Coxey's Army were dramatic events of the era. Strikes were so characteristic of the mid-1880's that the period from 1882 to 1884 is often called "the Great Upheaval." Labor's activity, however, was not confined solely to these dramatic episodes.

During the late nineteenth century, workers used more mundane forms of united action in attempts to confront and solve the problems they faced. The groups they joined were sometimes economically oriented trade unions; sometimes political organizations; sometimes a bit of both.

As the country's transportation network expanded, trade unions sought increasingly to organize nationally, in an attempt to control the price of labor in increasingly national product markets. It is estimated that by the early 1870's over thirty national trade unions existed. Much like the earlier workingmen's organizations, however, these organizations were gravely affected by business recessions. Soon after the

Panic of 1873, less than a third of these early national unions continued to function. With the return of prosperity, the number increased again, and 39 national unions were listed in the 1880 census.

Workingmen's political organizations ranged from small local clubs to national parties. Direction of political activity at the local level often fell to the city labor federations, or "trade assemblies." These organizations did not always function in the same way. Some pressed only for a single issue, like enactment of eight-hour day legislation. Others allied themselves with one or the other major political party and sought to gain their ends through pressure tactics. Still others formed the nucleus of third party movements.

Of those organizations created to espouse a single issue, the eight-hour leagues probably had the widest appeal. The foremost champion of the movement was a Boston machinist, Ira Steward, whose ceaseless devotion to the cause earned him the title "the eight-hour monomaniac." Steward argued on behalf of shorter hours both as a device to spread available work, thus reducing if not eliminating unemployment, and as a means of increasing the workingman's leisure time.

Reminiscent of the earlier ten-hour movement, the eight-hour advocates used political pressure tactics. They sought to pledge political candidates and sent petitions and delegates to state legislatures and to Washington. As a result of their efforts an eight-hour day was established for federal employees in 1868, and six states enacted similar legislation. Enforcement at the federal level was spotty at best, however, and the state laws contained the same escape clause as had the earlier ten-hour legislation. Political efforts on behalf of a shorter work day had thus proved fruitless once again.

The eight-hour issue remained very much alive, however, and for many years to come it would crop up intermittently as a political issue. Primarily, however, it became an economic weapon, utilized by trade unions both as an organizing device and a collective bargaining demand.

The third parties—the National Labor Reform Party of the early seventies, the Greenback-Labor Party of the late seventies, and the Union Labor and United Labor parties of the eighties—did not seek to draw their membership solely from among urban workmen but sought wider support. These national political parties attempted to appeal to the farmer by highlighting rural complaints that railroad and banking "monopolies" and "middlemen" were causing high shipping and interest rates, and farmer complaints regarding low prices for their produce. By denouncing trusts and advocating currency and banking reform, the new parties also tried to win the vote of business elements.

These third party efforts succeeded in attracting the attention of the major political parties which, in some areas, presented "fusion" candidates. In off-year elections—particularly in 1878 and 1886—third party efforts met with considerable success. Results were disappointing, however, in presidential years.

Even at their best these parties were never wholly successful in attracting workingmen away from traditional party allegiances. In part, the failure of these organizations was due to the political naiveté of their leaders. More than once, these organizations were unwittingly the launching pads for opportunistic politicians. Third parties also suffered from perennial lack of funds. Much of the credit for their poor showing, however, must go to the efforts made by the two major political parties to combat their potential rivals.

Marc Karson's reading, the first in this chapter, briefly describes the earliest of these labor-oriented third party efforts, the Labor Reform Party. As Karson indicates, this organization grew out of the National Labor Union, which he describes as "the first national labor federation in America." From the beginning, the NLU was politically oriented. Initially, the NLU attempted nonpartisanship, endorsing candidates without regard to their party if they would pledge themselves to the NLU program. Once elected, however, NLU-supported candidates generally proved disappointing. Given this, the NLU decided to enter the political arena directly, with consequences contributing to its eventual demise.

Interestingly enough, the most significant labor organization of the late seventies and eighties, the Noble and Holy Order of the Knights of Labor, combined economic and political activities and, for a time, was highly successful in both.

The Order, founded in 1869, was originally the brainchild of nine Philadelphia garment cutters. For the first few months of its existence, the Knights of Labor differed little from other budding craft unions, except in its insistence upon secrecy. Within a year, however, the garment cutters were initiating "sojourners" into their ranks, i.e., workers in other crafts, in the hope that these would eventually "swarm" from the parent organization—now called Assembly No. 1—to form new assemblies among co-workers in their own crafts.

At first local assemblies were made up of workers of a single craft, but as the Knights grew, many of the local organizations, particularly in the less industrialized areas, were "mixed." When this was true, the local unit was of course less effective as a collective bargaining vehicle.

Membership in the Knights of Labor was not limited to skilled artisans. The organizations welcomed "all branches of honorable toil." However, the "drones" in society—doctors, bankers, stockbrokers—were not acceptable; nor were professional gamblers or persons engaged in the sale of alcoholic beverages. Always excepting these, the Knights' creed, "an injury to one is an injury to all," reflected the organization's governing principle of labor solidarity; the belief in "the great brotherhood of toil." Much of the Karson reading is devoted to the history of this unique organization. The selection which follows, by Edward T. James, describes what the Knights of Labor accomplished in politics.

The Karson reading notes that the Knights were extremely active in state and local political campaigns in 1886. Perhaps the most interesting race that year was that for Mayor of New York City. Labor's candidate for the post was Henry George, author of the widely read *Progress and Poverty,* and foremost advocate of the Single Tax. The last reading in this chapter, by Allan Nevins, describes the New York campaign.

In taking political action in New York City, the Knights followed the course they often took, combining with other elements in the labor movement in an attempt to gain their ends. Thus Terence Powderly, head of the Knights, joined Daniel DeLeon, who in later years became the leader of the Socialist Labor Party, in stumping for Henry George. Samuel Gompers, whose American Federation of Labor was already rising to challenge the Knights, also campaigned actively for Henry George. By that time Gompers had already begun to come to the conclusion that a labor organization ought to avoid active participation in politics. After George's defeat, he described his own part in the campaign as "this curious determination to disregard experience." [2]

Despite the emergence of the AFL and the Socialist Labor Party during this period, the Knights of Labor was the foremost labor organization in the United States during much of the last half of the nineteenth century. The all-inclusiveness of the organization proved to be its greatest weakness, however. Some have said that as a throwback to reform unionism the Order was looking backward, seeking simple answers in a complex industrialized society. Others have argued, however, that in some respects the Knights was the precursor of the twentieth century CIO, and simply was ahead of its time. In any event, the Noble and Holy Order of the Knights of Labor did not find fertile ground in the last decades of the nineteenth century.

---

[2] *Seventy Years of Life and Labor,* New York: Dutton, I, p. 312.

The National Labor Union and the Knights of Labor

Marc Karson

Kingsborough Community College,
City University of New York

IN [THE] POST-CIVIL WAR PERIOD, the National Labor Union, the first national labor federation in America, was created. William Sylvis, president of the Iron Molders' Union, was the guiding spirit of the new organization. Beginning with the first convention of the National Labor Union in 1866, the emphasis was on political activity. The convention declared itself in favor of the eight-hour day by legislative enactment, producers' cooperatives, public land reforms, the organization of un-skilled workers and the early establishment of a national labor party. Conventions in the succeeding two years repeated the earlier position in these matters and went on to argue the questions of the acceptance of Negro workers in the union, of national currency reforms, and of cooperation with the international labor movement.

The debate on organizing Negro workers within the National Labor Union was unable to reach a permanent conclusion. Even those like Sylvis who argued for the admission of Negro workers into the unions did not believe in the moral right of Negroes to social and po-litical equality.[1] Sylvis' view was that if they remained unorganized, they would be a potential threat to the economic standards of organ-ized white workers. Of a total of 142 delegates who attended the 1869 convention, none were Negroes, and the convention urged that col-ored representatives from all states be sent to the next convention. A committee was also appointed to organize the Negroes in Pennsylvania.

The question of currency reform, however, became the domi-nating issue within the National Labor Union. The union emphatically announced its opposition to high interest rates, the national banking system, bank notes, and tax-exempt government bonds, and advocated the government issuance of cheap paper "greenbacks" as legal tender. As for international relations, the National Labor Union was the first

---

Reprinted from "The Political History of the American Labor Movement in the Nineteenth Century" from *American Labor Unions and Politics, 1900–1918*, by Marc Karson. Copyright © 1958 by Southern Illinois University Press. Reprinted by permission of the Southern Illinois University Press. For convenience of the reader, footnotes which appear in the original have been renumbered.

[1] Grossman, Jonathan, *William Sylvis, Pioneer of American Labor,* New York: Columbia University Press, 1945, pp. 229–32.

sizable national American labor organization to show a strong interest in the European labor movement. Correspondence of fraternal goodwill was conducted with the International Workingmen's Association, and, in 1869, A. C. Cameron represented the organization at a Congress of the International in Basle, Switzerland.

The national labor party contemplated by the first congress of the National Labor Union in 1866 did not immediately come into being, although a platform for the party was adopted at the second convention in 1867, and local nominations of workers for political office were recommended. The platform favored the eight-hour workday law, producers' cooperatives, workers' housing, a Department of Labor, government management of railroads, express, water transportation, and the telegraph system. Opposition was voiced to strikes, the national banking system, and monopoly in money and land. Initial organizational preparation for the new party started in 1870, when the convention appointed an executive committee for the national convention to nominate candidates for the party. However, by the time this convention got under way in 1872, most of the trade-unions had deserted the National Labor Union because they objected to its predominantly political nature and its preoccupation with currency reforms. The convention nominated Judge David Davis, who later refused the nomination when he learned that Horace Greeley had been nominated by the insurgent Liberal Republican party. Thus the political fate of the National Labor and Reform party without its original candidate and without trade-union support, was doomed. Its final candidate, Charles O'Conner, a New York Democrat and slavery defender, polled a meager 29,489 votes. The position of the National Union itself was equally dismal. In the next few years after 1872, it tried vainly to arouse the workers' interest and then completely collapsed, its more militant political figures turned to the Socialist movements and others to the Greenback party.

In Massachusetts a union move into independent party politics almost paralleled the rise and fall of the National Labor Union. A Labor Reform party was organized in Massachusetts in 1869 with particular trade-union support of the shoemakers' union, the Knights of St. Crispin. In 1869, the party elected 21 members out of 80 to the lower house of the Massachusetts legislature, but within a few years its strength was negligible. Its end was hastened by the general decline of the Knights of St. Crispin and by dissension between the renowned abolitionist, Wendell Phillips, who favored currency reforms, and Ira Steward, self-educated mechanic and national crusader for the eight-hour day.

The serious depression from 1873 to 1878 was a time of acute distress for workers and unions, and the worst period of labor violence ever witnessed in America. There were demonstrations of the unemployed in New York and Chicago and strikes among the textile workers in New England and the coal miners in Pennsylvania. Terrorism instigated by the secret Irish ring of "Molly Maguires" prevailed in the anthracite regions. During the nationwide railroad strike, in July 1877, federal troops at Pittsburgh wantonly shot into a crowd of workers, killing twenty-six persons. The workers retaliated by destroying $5,000,000 worth of railroad property. For the most part the trade-unions were unable to withstand the effects of the depression. Only eight of about forty national unions, weakened in membership and finances, managed to survive this period.

A unique trade and labor organization that withstood the depression of the 1870's was the Noble Order of the Knights of Labor. Its first local assembly was organized in late December 1869, by Uriah Stephens from the remnants of the Garment Cutters' Association of Philadelphia. In recognition of the employers' practices of lockouts and blacklists, and as a result of Stephens' early training for the Baptist ministry and his membership in the Masons, Odd Fellows, and Knights of Pythias, the Knights of Labor was constituted as a secret association with a mystic ritual. Its general purpose was a broad one dedicated to uplifting and improving the status of all laboring people—farmers and intellectuals, whites and blacks, skilled and unskilled, male and female. In fact, everyone was eligible for membership except bankers, stockbrokers, lawyers, gamblers, and liquor dealers, though it was stipulated that three-fourths of the membership of each assembly was to be composed of wage earners. During its three-decade existence the objectives of the Knights of Labor were modified by its leaders and by the composition of its membership but its advocacy of labor solidarity and its idealistic attitude toward reform remained as permanent characteristics. In contrast to the exclusiveness of the existing craft unions, its appeal was built around the motto "An injury to one is the concern of all."

The Knights of Labor, however, was not a proletarian, revolutionary organization in the Marxian image. Its national leaders neither preached the Marxian doctrines of the class struggle, nor did they believe in the use of the strike as a weapon to gain their objectives. Rather, they intended to rely on education and propaganda against the banking power, not against the employers. Believing that the economic system was not operating for the welfare of the people, they wanted to make the necessary corrections by law so that profitable self-employ-

ment in business or on the land would be available to all those who
sought it. Like many humanitarian reformers that had preceded them
in the century, their ultimate ideal lay in a cooperative society. Their
contribution to advancing this ideal was in developing the solidarity
of working people by organizing them into one big union and educating them to the need for economic and political reforms.

The Knights of Labor first achieved national stature in 1878
when they created a general assembly which had supreme central
authority over the 100 local and district assemblies already function-
ing. The next year Terence Powderly was elected head of the Knights
to succeed Stephens who had resigned. . . . [One paragraph omitted.]

The convention of 1878, which had established the general assembly, also adopted a platform emphasizing that legislation would
correct the abuses of wealth and enable the Order to achieve its objective of elevating the people. The Knights' leaders also showed a personal active interest in politics. In the Congressional campaign of
1878, Stephens was an unsuccessful Greenback-Labor candidate, while
Powderly, as a candidate of the same party, fared better and was elected
mayor of Scranton and reelected in 1880. Other leaders of the Knights,
James L. Wright, Robert Schilling, Charles H. Litchman, John M.
Davis, Ralph Beaumont, and George Blair also were Greenback-Labor
candidates in 1878. Nevertheless, the Knights in principle did not at
this time support any one party or urge the creation of a new party.
The 1878 general assembly adopted no plan for political action to help
it secure the laws its platform demanded. The next general assembly
in 1879 agreed that the local assemblies could participate in political
campaigns in whatever manner they felt was in consonance with the
Order's interests. A resolution at the same convention to bar the general officers from engaging in politics was rejected. At the 1880 general
assembly, Phillip Van Patten, secretary of the Socialist Labor Party,
succeeded in having the policy of nonpartisan politics on a local basis
recommended to the local assemblies. The recommendation carried
the reservation, however, that no political action could be undertaken
unless three-fourths of the local members were in favor of such political
action; furthermore, no member was required to vote in political elections according to the preference of the local's majority. A motion at
the same convention to submit a recommendation to the locals and
district assemblies that they support the National Greenback-Labor
Party was tabled after a lengthy discussion.

Although Powderly repeatedly warned the Order that politics
should not be discussed within the organization, he agreed to the
addition to the Preamble in 1884 which stated that most of the demands

of the platform "could only be obtained through legislation, and that it is the duty of all to assist in nominating and supporting with their votes only such candidates as will pledge their support to these measures, regardless of party."[2] Legislative demands included in the platform at this time called for compulsory arbitration, a graduated income tax, the prohibition of the importation of foreign labor under contract, a postal savings bank, and government purchase and operation of the telegraph, telephone, and railroad systems. Succeeding general assemblies within the next decade adopted planks favorable to the restriction of immigration, the initiative and referendum, compulsory school attendance for children up to the age of fifteen, free school textbooks, the abolition of the militia, and the secret ballot.

In 1884 the Knights began the political technique of lobbying in state capitols and in Washington, D.C., as a means of securing their legislative demands. At that time they were a growing organization of over seventy thousand members frequently engaging in strikes which, although contrary to the principles of the Order and the wishes of its general officers, were nevertheless acknowledged by Powderly as aiding the movement's growth. The votes of the legislators on measures relative to labor also began to be recorded by the Order as a basis for precisely determining those politicians who were friendly and those who were harmful to the interests of labor. The Knights also had some success in having state conventions of the political parties incorporate demands of the Knights in their platform.

Around 1885 the Knights appeared to be the most successful labor organization ever yet developed in America. They had 100,000 members, their strike and boycott activities were meeting with considerable success, and when the powerful Southwestern Railroad magnate, Jay Gould, capitulated to their strike demands in 1885, their membership spurted in the next year to over seven hundred thousand.

The Knights' political activities in the campaign of 1886 were also very encouraging. In New York, Henry George, the Single-Taxer candidate of the United Labor party supported for mayor by the Knights, Socialists, and local trade-unionists, officially was credited with 68,000 votes to the winning Democratic candidate's 90,000. In Chicago, Milwaukee, St. Louis, Newark, and several smaller cities, labor candidates with the backing of the local Knights' organization made creditable showings. In a few of the smaller cities labor administrations actually were elected and a number of Knights were elected to state

---

[2] "Knights of Labor Preamble," quoted in Richard T. Ely, *The Labor Movement in America*, London: Heinemann, 1890, p. 86.

offices and to the national Congress, as candidates of the Democratic or Republican parties. The spring municipal elections of 1887 revealed that independent labor tickets with Knights' support were continuing to show sizable strength.

By the autumn of 1887, however, it was apparent that the strength of the Knights was waning. Independent labor candidates in spite of support by the Knights met with crushing defeat in their bids for political office. The Knights' membership itself showed a decrease in 1887 of 200,000 from the previous year but, worst of all, almost all of this loss occurred in the large industrial cities. In the next three years this decline steadily continued with some 300,000 additional members departing from the Order. Very likely many of the workers who had joined in 1885 and 1886 in anticipation of such benefits as the eight-hour day quickly grew disillusioned when they found that the Order neither fulfilled this expectation nor brought them any other remarkable material improvements. Other immediate factors responsible for the decline were increased opposition from the employers and their associations who had become alarmed at the Knights' sudden growth, unsuccessful strikes, the failure of cooperative enterprises, incompetent leadership, internal dissension over policies and politics, and the departure of skilled workers from the mixed assemblies into national craft unions. . . . [Two paragraphs omitted.]

A more fundamental explanation for the decline of the Knights is that it advanced idealistic postulates illogical in view of the conditions created by the industrial revolution. First, it considered that no conflict existed between employers and employees and that the inequalities in the social system were mainly caused by the "money power." Second, it considered that the interests of all workers were sufficiently identical to prompt all groups of workers to act unselfishly for the common good. Third, it gave its attention to ultimate and remote reforms before it had strong roots in the environment and before it was able to demonstrate that it could regularly secure immediate material returns for its supporters.

The membership of the Knights diminished so seriously that by the end of the 1880's control of the Order rested with a coalition composed of farmers and Socialists. Both of these groups were politically minded and, as a result, in 1889 the national leaders of the Knights took the first step toward political cooperation with the Farmers' Alliance. An agreement was reached whereby both organizations would lobby jointly before Congress for legislative demands that had mutually been decided upon. The following year the general assembly finally declared the need for national independent political party action.

Powderly was instructed to call a conference for the purpose of establishing an independent party in time for the 1892 national campaign. Thus the People's Party made its appearance. Its candidate for President was General James B. Weaver, the Greenback candidate of 1880 who still represented agrarian discontent with monetary, land, and transportation conditions. In the election the People's Party polled more than a million votes, predominantly from the agricultural south and west. The year after the election, Powderly was replaced by James R. Sovereign, a farmer-editor from the midwest. The Knights' steadily narrowing concept of its purpose as an organization mainly preoccupied with land reform had now become almost complete except for its retention of certain assemblies dominated by Socialist Labor party adherents. The latter clung to hopes of reviving the Knights into an organization that would once again gain a mass following among the industrial workers and then promote the ideals of labor solidarity and class emancipation.

The Knights in Politics

Edward T. James
Radcliffe College

THERE WAS NO QUESTION in [Uriah] Stephens' mind about the importance of politics to labor. "All the evils that labor rests under," he wrote in 1878, "are matters of law and [are] to be removed by legislation. . . ." To a member who had evidently argued that the Knights should have nothing to do with politics, Stephens replied with fervor: "Is the 8 *hour law*, or *Prison labor*, or *universal education*, or *child & female labor* or the *machinery question* or *land and the landless* . . . political questions. Can you discuss the *interests of labor* in any manner without running into *political economy*. . . . Our order *is not a political one* [and] never can be, but we must in a fraternal manner discuss the Economics of our condition." "Shall monopolists have polit[i]cs all to themselves?"

The policy Uriah Stephens had thus worked out was presented to the General Assembly of January 1879, where it was formally ap-

---

Excerpted by permission of the author from "American Labor and Political Action, 1865–1896: The Knights of Labor and Its Predecessors," Ph.D. thesis, Harvard University, 1954. Footnotes in the original have been deleted.

proved. Before the end of the year, however, it was given quite a different meaning from what Stephens had intended, though without sacrificing his essential principle of keeping political action on an unofficial basis.

In Stephens' conception the Knights were to discuss the political issues of the day in their assemblies but act on them only through outside channels, joining as individuals in a political club or party. Other members, however, wished to make more direct use of the organized strength of the Order. At the same General Assembly which approved the Stephens' policy Grand Secretary Charles Litchman, after echoing its main points, went on to suggest a somewhat different procedure: that a local assembly at the close of its meeting might formally adjourn but remain on as a group to consider political action. . . .

A set of rules to this effect was adopted by the next session of the General Assembly, in September 1879, and incorporated in the Order's constitution. A district or local assembly, it was provided, might "take such political action as will tend to advance the interests of the Order, or the Cause of Labor," leaving it "to the discretion of each Local Assembly to act with that Party in its vicinity through which it can gain the most." The subject could be discussed however, only after the regular business had been concluded and the assembly formally closed. Even under this arrangement political action could be authorized only by a three-quarters vote of the members present, each member (or each local assembly, in the case of the districts) having been expressly notified that such a proposal was to be considered. A final safeguard declared with emphasis: *"No member shall, however, be compelled to vote with the majority."*

These remained for many years the Order's official rules governing political action. . . .

[In 1884], though no change was made in the actual rules governing political action, as drawn up in 1879, a sentence in the instructions for local assemblies now made it plain that this was one of the Order's fundamental purposes. After pointing the familiar moral that "strikes, at best, only afford temporary relief," the passage added: "members should be educated to depend upon thorough organization, co-operation and political action, and, through these, the abolishment of the wage system. (Here was the reformist philosophy of the Knights in a nutshell.)

"Political action" had nowhere been expressly defined, though the 1879 rules implied that it meant the support of a particular party ticket. The 1884 constitution, however, gave quite a different impression. "It should be borne in mind," declared the new preamble to the platform, ". . . that most of the objects herein set forth can only be obtained through legislation. . . ." Hence "it is the duty of all to assist in nominating and supporting with their votes only such candidates as will pledge their support to those measures, regardless of party." . . .

[The first attempt of the Knights to influence national legislation came in 1884, on the initiative of the Window Glass Workers.] These craftsmen had organized what was in fact a nationwide trade-union, strong in bargaining power and business-like in principles, though bearing the misleading designation of Local Assembly 300. In 1882, when the assembly went on strike in the East for higher wages, employers retaliated by bringing in Belgian glass blowers bound under long-term contracts to a lower rate of pay. L. A. 300 succeeded at first in persuading many of the Belgians to join the walkout, but several firms promptly isolated the foreigners in company boarding houses and secured court injunctions to restrain the Knights from entering into any communication with them. Faced with this legal obstacle, the glass workers consulted a lawyer. He suggested that they seek a Congressional ban on the importation of foreign contract labor.

In a tariff-minded industry the idea was logical enough. L. A. 300 had a "constitutional lawyer" draw up such a bill and succeeded in getting it introduced into Congress. Here was a situation where the Knights as a whole could help. Hence the glass workers brought their measure before the next session of the General Assembly, which voted approval and directed the Executive Board to get up a petition to Congress for circulation among the members. Some 35,000 signatures were thus obtained, but the Board did not rest with this step. When the bill came up for a hearing early in 1884, it summoned all the chief officers of the Order to Washington to lend support.

Thus on February 1, 1884, [Grand Master Workman Terence V.] Powderly, Frederick Turner (the new General Secretary) and the five members of the Executive Board testified before the House Labor Committee, along with six representatives of L. A. 300. Though a few other workingmen appeared, it was overwhelmingly a Knights of Labor panel. Their statements were duly embodied in a favorable committee report. The bill . . . passed the House in June, though Senate delay postponed its final enactment until early 1885. . . .

The 1885 General Assembly [of the Knights] . . . balked at a full-scale program of lobbying, but some locals were already doing work of this sort at their own state capitals, and others were showing a strong interest in the election of legislators.

Here and there, in addition, Knights were taking a hand in city and county elections, as they had in the Greenback period and would continue to do into the Populist era. The urge often came after a successful organizing drive, and the results usually followed the cyclical pattern of initial success and subsequent disillusion. In many cases the technique was to run an independent Labor or Workingmen's slate. . . . In other instances the Knights seem to have heeded the advice of their national officers and sought to work within the regular parties. Two Michigan lumbering towns serve as examples. In Ludington they "went in to the . . . Caucuses and Conventions and nominated their Men" in the spring of 1884. "We run a K of L on the Democrat & Republican ticket for City Marshall and the Saloon men Run a Man on the Stump [.] we scooped them [.] the K of L Elected city Marshall City treasure[r] Two out of Four Aldermen Two out of Four Supervisors and Two Constables." The Bay City Knights the following spring likewise "dictated to two conventions who should be nominated. . . ."

But more characteristic of this period was the concern over state legislation. Here the chief reliance for a time was to send workingmen themselves to the legislative halls. Even in the Greenback era the Knights had won isolated successes of this sort. Between 1883 and 1885 they did better, electing members in at least six states, from Massachusetts in the East to Ohio in the West and Tennessee in the South.[1] Michigan, where the order had grown unusually fast, made perhaps the best record. In 1882 the Knights had sent three members to the legislature; in 1884 they came through with no less than 18 (Republicans and Democrats alike) and even elected one Knight to Congress.

Considerable hope as to what these men could accomplish was entertained at first, not least by the victorious Knights themselves. To some extent the hope was fulfilled, as several of them successfully pushed through laws like the Kansas mine-regulation act . . . or the Michigan ten-hour law for women and children sponsored by the Detroit printer and Knight Lyman Brant. But whatever their success it was obviously not due to weight of numbers nor, it can be safely assumed, to sheer persuasive logic. If a bill favoring labor was passed, it was because the garden-variety legislators respected the potential voting strength of the workingman. That strength could just as well be brought to bear from outside the legislative halls as from within.

Appeals of this sort might simply involve a trip to the capital to get a particular measure introduced, perhaps by the lawmaker from the home district. Some such tactic may well have been used by the Utica, New York, assembly which sponsored a factory-regulation bill in 1884, or the Maine one next year with its labor-bureau bill. Or again,

---

[1] The other states are New York, Connecticut, and Michigan.

if there were a local assembly in the capital city, it might now and then put in a word at the state house, as happened in Hartford, Connecticut.

The term "lobbying," however, properly applies to a more systematic and sustained campaign than any of these. Even so, by 1885 a few assemblies were meeting the standard. The work of the Washington Knights with Congress would certainly qualify. So would an instance in Texas, where two Galveston Knights appeared before a legislative committee in behalf of a pair of labor proposals, then skillfully rounded up support from other groups in the state including an assembly in the home town of a recalcitrant senator. Both their bills were enacted.

Most thoroughgoing in their tactics during this period were the Knights in Massachusetts. As early as February 1884 they were regularly sending representatives to "all committee hearings where labor is concerned," relying on the Knights in the legislature to keep them posted. At such events, reported their leader, A. A. Carlton, "the railroad and manufacturing corporations have each their attorney to manage their affairs . . . but on a perfect equality with them, and so recognized by the committee, appears the District Master Workman of District Assembly No. 30. . . ."

Even the most systematic lobbying, however, might be resisted or evaded. Little by little the Knights, like other pressure groups before and since, were driven toward the conclusion that effective lobbying also required effective electioneering. If a candidate, or a party, could be pinned down at campaign time to the support of a particular labor demand, the lobbyist's task would be correspondingly easier. Most important, if always most difficult, was the follow-up: the attempt at the next election to swing votes to those legislators who had proven their loyalty and to defeat those unfaithful to their pledge or otherwise unfriendly.

Only rarely did the Knights of Labor ever attempt this last technique either on the state or national level; and never, of course, did they think the problem through to its full implications. But in a few scattered instances by 1885 they were beginning to employ the simpler device of exacting promises from candidates and party conventions. Thus in New Brunswick, New Jersey, that fall they "placed the [state] Senatorial candidates under an obligation" to support several bills they desired. So also with the political parties themselves. In both Massachusetts and Ohio in 1885 local Knights delegations visited the Republican and Democratic conventions, seeking to get certain specific demands written into the platforms. In Massachusetts both parties gave way; in Ohio only the Democrats.

Such was the scope of the legislative efforts of the Knights in their years of growing strength and prestige. Viewed in perspective, how successful had they been? Something of a pattern again emerges. The laws most readily passed, both on the state and national levels, were those which were relatively innocuous, like the establishment of bureaus of labor statistics. Legislators, in striking a balance between conflicting pressure groups, always welcome a step which will please one interest without really hurting the others. Even the federal law against alien contract labor worked no great hardship on any sizable business group, and in addition the bill as passed was weak in its enforcement provisions. This again was another defense-in-depth employed by the politicians when under fire from labor: to accede to the demand but denature it in the process. A Michigan law establishing a general ten-hour day, like the state eight-hour laws of the 1860's, contained the classic loophole of this sort: the provision that longer hours could be established by contract.

The Henry George Campaign

Allan Nevins

Huntington Library

TAMMANY WAS SUFFERING from a severe fright. That year [1886], a great wave of labor unrest had rolled across the land. An angry strike had occurred on Jay Gould's railroads in the Southwest, a wage dispute at the McCormick Reaper Works in Chicago had culminated early in May in the bloody Haymarket Riot, and altogether nearly 1,500 strikes had occurred, crippling or closing about 10,000 establishments. In New York City, labor troubles on the street-car lines and a boycott of the Thiess Brewery had both resulted in violence and arrests. The Knights of Labor were at the height of their power, and many discontented workingmen were eager to resort to political action. Particularly in New York did they have good reason for doing so. The street railway strikes were embittered by the fact that the venal Board of Aldermen had granted franchises which gave the rapid transit interests enormous profits, while their employees worked twelve, fourteen, and even sixteen hours a day for a pittance. In April, almost the entire Board of Aldermen had been indicted for taking bribes, and labor leaders per-

Excerpted by permission of the publisher from *Abram S. Hewitt*, New York: Harper & Brothers, 1935.

ceived an opportunity to capitalize the public indignation. They prepared to run a labor candidate for mayor.

In midsummer a labor committee called upon Henry George to
offer him their nomination. His *Progress and Poverty,* published seven
years before, had brought him international fame and made him the
idol of the poor and oppressed. To workers he seemed the shining
apostle of a better social order. George at first demurred. Fearing that
he would humiliate himself and his cause by an ignominiously small
poll, he said, when the committee made a second call, that he would
not run unless pledged at least thirty thousand votes. The response to
this demand surprised even the labor leaders. Pledges rolled in like
a flood till 34,000 had been received. Tammany saw with alarm that
fully half of its vote would probably be swept away by the Henry
George movement. Indeed, the New York *Tribune* estimated that
three-fourths of the labor vote would come from Tammany's ranks. In
consternation, Boss [Richard] Croker and the County Democracy dis-
patched an emissary, William M. Ivins, to tell George that if he would
keep out, the County Democracy and Tammany would join in sending
him to Congress. Ivins also said: "You cannot be elected mayor, but
your running will raise hell, and we don't want that." George leaped
to his feet. "You end my uncertainty," he said. "I do not want the labor
and responsibility of the mayor's office, but I do want to raise hell.
I will run!" . . .

[A few days later, the Republicans nominated Theodore Roosevelt as their candidate, and soon thereafter Abram Hewitt agreed to
be the Tammany standard bearer.]

It was inevitable that the battle should swiftly develop into a
fierce attack upon Henry George as an incendiary theorist and agitator.
"We believe," said the *Nation,* "that nothing has occurred in the history
of New York threatening its welfare so seriously as the George movement." In other words, [Editor E. L.] Godkin asserted that Henry
George was more dangerous than Fernando Wood or the Tweed Ring.
This was nonsense; yet Curtis and *Harper's Weekly,* Pulitzer and the
World, Whitelaw Reid and the *Tribune,* all denounced George as a
wild revolutionary, while Carl Schurz assailed him as an apostle of
class warfare. It was not merely his essential doctrine, that land monopoly and unearned increment are the chief sources of social injustice,
which deeply alarmed property-holders in a city distinguished by high
land values and immense fortunes built upon unearned increment.
There was also the fact that in his writings Henry George had denounced monopoly and plutocracy with flaming eloquence, and had
pictured the wretchedness of the East Side, the misery of our submerged
tenth, in a way which conservatives might well call violent. . . .

Though George had not a single newspaper, his party organized a brilliantly effective canvass. In almost every precinct, Henry George Clubs were established. A small army of speakers, led by Samuel Gompers and Daniel De Leon, took the field. While it included so many of the lunatic fringe that Godkin remarked that nothing like it had been seen since [Horace] Greeley's campaign in 1872, it won votes. George himself, from cart-tails at noon and platforms at night, spoke indefatigably. Undersized, bald save for a fringe of reddish hair, his strong jaw emphasized by a sandy beard, when speaking he was the very picture of a fighter. Reporters called him "the little red rooster" or "the little game cock," phrases he did not like, for he was vain and lacking in humor, but which did him no harm. Crowds followed him everywhere, and at huge rallies hats were passed to pay the hall-rent.

On the Saturday night before election there was a great parade of George's followers. No fewer than 30,000 men and women, and some believed 70,000, in a cold drenching rain, without music and with few torches, passed the reviewing stand in Union Square, cheering as they went. "That night," Gompers wrote, "we felt confident of the election of George." No such parade had ever been seen before in a city campaign. Yet the canvass closed, as it had begun, with the betting 10 to 3 on Hewitt. An extraordinary registration had been announced: approximately 230,000 voters had enrolled, or 10,300 more than had voted for mayor in 1884, when the Presidential campaign had swelled the total. It was certain that many Republicans had swung to Hewitt. "If the panic grows," Roosevelt had written [Henry Cabot] Lodge, "thousands of my supporters will go to Hewitt for fear George may be elected—a perfectly groundless emotion." The newspapers exhorted them to do so, while Carl Schurz appealed especially to the German Republicans. In the last hours of the contest it was whispered that [Republican Boss Thomas C.] Platt had promised Croker to swing his followers to the Democratic candidate, but this was mere rumor. Hewitt himself made numerous appeals to Republicans. "As for Mr. Roosevelt," he told a meeting of merchants, "I trust that at some future time he will receive the reward due to his energy, his ability, and his character, but he has made a mistake. He has allowed himself to be made the tool of designing men."

Early on election day reports came in to headquarters that the Republican machine was making district deals at the expense of Roosevelt. There is evidence that about 2 P.M. Platt's lieutenants actually sent out word that since Roosevelt could not succeed, Republicans should all vote to assure Hewitt's triumph over Henry George. These votes were needed, for Hewitt himself predicted that the labor ticket would poll between 70,000 and 80,000 votes. "The race between Mr. George and myself," he added, "will be closer than my friends think."

By ten o'clock that night it was evident that Hewitt had been elected, and by midnight that his plurality over Henry George exceeded 20,000, while Roosevelt had run a bad third. . . . The official totals later gave Hewitt 90,552 votes; George 68,110; and Roosevelt 60,435. . . .

Hewitt was willing to admit the striking import of the vote which Henry George, without real political organization, without newspapers, and without money, had polled. "The significant fact standing out as the result of the election," he generously said, "is that 68,000 people have deliberately declared that they have grievances which ought to be redressed, and that they have no expectation that the existing parties will give them the relief they desire."

Chapter 4

The American Federation of Labor and Voluntarism

As MUCH AS THE KNIGHTS OF LABOR were out of step with late nine-teenth-century America, so another labor organization which emerged in the last decades, the American Federation of Labor, was suited to it. Where the Knights were all-inclusive, the AFL was exclusive. Where the Knights were concerned for the semiskilled and even unskilled workers, the AFL left these groups to fend for themselves. In the main, it concentrated only on the skilled element, the "aristocracy of labor."

Even as the Knights were growing in strength, some of labor's "aristocrats" were not attracted to the Order. Others who joined the Knights initially later abandoned it for membership in the more tra-ditional craft unions, which emphasized rigid apprenticeship rules and other restrictive devices, and focused their activities on the attain-ment of economic ends. Initially the leaders of the Knights were not threatened by these separatists. Indeed, through their political arms, the city and emerging state labor federations, the craft unions often cooperated with the Knights in the political arena.

Beginning in the late 1880's, however, as the nation recovered from an economic slump, the picture began to change and the interests of the growing national craft unions collided with those of the expand-ing Knights. Hostility was most pronounced where a Knights' local assembly was composed solely of one craft and for collective bargain-ing purposes was much like a local craft union. In a town where such a local assembly already existed, a national trade union organizer either had to cede the field or prepare for a fight. Malcontents often left union locals to join a Knights' local assembly, and just as easily would desert local assemblies to form a branch of a national union. Wherever such rival organizations existed jurisdictional disputes were inevitable. It was this conflict which caused the trade unions to form the American Federation of Labor in 1886.

An earlier attempt at federating craft unions, begun in 1881, had failed. The leaders of the earlier organization, known as the Fed-eration of Organized Trades and Labor Unions, had never actually re-solved the question of whether their prime purpose was to rival the

Knights or to function as a forum on questions of concern to the entire American labor movement.

One of the leaders who had argued loudly that the old federation should rival the Knights and restrict itself to trade union affairs was Samuel Gompers, and it was he who was elected the AFL's first president. He continued to hold this post, except for one year, until his death in 1924.

In 1886, Samuel Gompers headed an organization with at most 140,000 members. The Knights, in contrast, numbered over 700,000 at that time. By 1924, the Federation had almost three million members, while the Knights had long since passed from the scene. The ultimate success of the AFL was due in no small measure to one man, Samuel Gompers. Labor historian Foster Rhea Dulles wrote that as soon as Gompers was elected, he set up

> . . . headquarters in an eight-by-ten-foot office made available by the Cigar Makers [Union], with little furniture other than a kitchen table, some crates for chairs, and a filing case made out of tomato boxes, [and] . . . set about breathing vitality into the new organization with a zeal, devotion, and tireless energy that largely accounted for its survival. He wrote innumerable letters, always in his own hand, to labor leaders throughout the country, for a time edited the *Trade Union Advocate* as a means of publicizing his campaign; issued union charters, collected dues, handled all routine business; managed conventions and went on speaking and organization tours, and slowly but persistently transformed the American Federation of Labor from a purely paper organization into a militant and powerful champion of labor's rights. He felt himself to be engaged in a holy cause and from the day the AFL came into being until his death thirty-eight years later, it was his entire life.[1]

In actuality, the Federation was more the servant than master of its constituent unions. Gompers' chief function was to advise and persuade. The AFL president had very little power over the individual national unions that belonged to the Federation. He was expected to organize skilled workers into local units, which he was to nurse to maturity, and then turn over to the appropriate craft union. He could not call strikes but was expected to come to the aid of member unions when they took such action. He could not collect money from individual trade unionists but depended upon a set portion—and a small one at that—of the dues collected by the constituent trade unions. In

---

[1] *Labor in America,* New York: Thomas Y. Crowell Company, 1949, p. 162.

theory, the Federation had authority to settle jurisdictional disputes between unions competing within the same trade. In practice it seldom exercised it.

From the start, Gompers emphasized immediate economic gains to be won at the bargaining table. Nevertheless, from the Federation's beginning, its constituent international and local unions engaged in some political activities.

The prime vehicles for such activities were the state and local central bodies which, much like the older local and state labor federations, were composed of all unions in a given area. Initially, these units often included labor organizations not affiliated with the AFL. As the Federation grew in power and membership, however, the state and local central bodies tended to exclude non-AFL affiliates.

The state federations' prime function was lobbying. In line with Federation policy, however, the legislation they sponsored or endorsed focused on health and safety measures or was designed to protect women and children. Day-to-day shop rules, wages, and hours of work for the adult male were considered the province of the individual unions, to be obtained through negotiations with employers.

While the earlier local labor federations frequently engaged in third party action, the AFL-dominated local central bodies came, more and more, to work with whatever major party controlled a city's political machine. Their main objectives were to ensure a friendly police force, favorable building codes, and other local ordinances.

Gompers' approach to political activity, so far as the Federation was concerned, was essentially negative. His main objective was to ensure minimum governmental interference in trade union activity—a kind of labor laissez-faire. He advocated a policy which has come to be known as "voluntarism." Voluntarism involved two main ideas: first, government interference in union-management relations should be kept to a minimum; and the worker should look to his union, not to the state, for help. Second, the labor movement should avoid either independent political action or identification with any one political party. This concept stemmed from experience with hostile governmental action and from the minority position of organized labor.

Selig Perlman, the chief theorist of the AFL, summarized the fundamental importance of voluntarism to the new Federation in the following passage:

> It was indeed a new species of trade unionism that thus evolved. It differed from the trade unionism that the native American labor movement had evolved earlier in that it grasped the idea, supremely

correct for American conditions, that the economic front was the only front on which the labor army could stay united.[2]

Gompers' insistence upon a nonpartisan political role for the Federation was severely tested in the early years of that organization's existence. After the onset of the 1893 depression, Gompers was forced to battle those who wanted to turn the Federation into a political vehicle. Hostility to his policy by the socialist members present at the 1894 convention caused his only defeat for the AFL presidential office. Following his reelection in 1896, when interest in the free silver cause and the Bryan campaign was at its height, he felt called upon to remind trade unionists:

> The industrial field is littered with more corpses of organizations destroyed by the damning influences of partisan political action than from all other causes combined. . . .[3]

While Bryan received Gompers' personal support, he did not win the AFL's official endorsement. According to the theory of voluntarism, individual trade union members were expected to participate and make their weight felt in politics but the AFL, as an organization, was not to become permanently committed in the political arena.

The first reading in this chapter is by the late John R. Commons, prominent labor economist of the University of Wisconsin. The article discusses the structure and policies of the American Federation of Labor in terms of the background and experiences of the leaders who formulated them. In the political context, it is significant, as Commons points out, that the method of assigning votes to convention delegates deliberately strengthened the economically-oriented elements of the Federation at the expense of the political.

The second reading is the 1906 "Bill of Grievances" submitted by the AFL Executive Council to Congress and the President. By that time, the strength of the Federation had reached nearly one and one-half million. Fortified by this showing, and inspired by the successes of the newly founded British Labour Party, the leaders of the AFL felt it was time to air their complaints against governmental hostility. The covering letter contains a paraphrase of the slogan that was so closely identified with Gompers and the Federation's nonpartisan political stance: "Reward your friends and punish your enemies."

---

[2] *The Theory of the Labor Movement,* New York: Macmillan Co., 1928, p. 197.

[3] *American Federationist,* III (1896), p. 130.

Gompers proposed publishing the voting record of legislators on bills of interest to labor. The selection by Harwood Childs, "Voluntarism in Action," contains a sample of the kind of record kept. Childs also describes the other activities typical of the Federation in connection with political matters.

Gompers' article, "Should a Labor Party Be Formed?" was written to thwart the post-World War I movement in which agitation for third party action culminated in the La Follette campaign of 1924. Gompers' arguments in this article are typical of those he used whenever the question of the formation of a labor party was raised.

Michael Rogin's critique of "voluntarism" is the last reading in the chapter. Rogin differs with the widely held view that the doctrine was a pragmatic and libertarian philosophy developed in the best interests of the average American worker. Instead, he says, it protected only a narrow segment of the American labor movement and, in time, functioned primarily to help the AFL perpetuate itself as an organization.

The American Federation of Labor

John R. Commons

[THE] AMERICAN FEDERATION OF LABOR is the experimental outcome of labor movements in America, Germany, Great Britain, and France. Here in North America the two nations of Canada and the United States, the continental variety of economic conditions, the mixed sovereignty of forty-eight states and one federal government, the domination of local politicians combined in two national parties, the successive waves of immigration from all lands and a remarkable mobility of labor, have afforded the scope and imposed the necessity of bringing together in one federation over an entire continent as many varieties of unionism as may be found in other lands more limited and uniform in their circumstances. The leading originators of the federation, in 1886, had previously, in 1881, taken over, almost verbatim, the constitution of the British Trades Union Congress, and that imported form of organization is perpetuated in forty-eight state federations of labor. Other originators of the federation had participated in or struggled

Reprinted from *Encyclopaedia of the Social Sciences*, with permission of The Macmillan Company. © 1930 by The Macmillan Co., renewed 1958 by The Macmillan Co.

against three preceding strictly American organizations—the National
Labor Union, the Greenback Labor party, and the Knights of Labor—
each of them a product of the deflation of prices after the Civil War.
The federation had to adapt itself to the individualistic psychology of
these American movements unknown to other countries. Still other
originators had participated in the American trade unions which began
or expanded in the Civil War under American, British, Scotch, and
latterly Irish leaders.

The anarchistic exiles from the Paris Commune of 1871 and the
communistic exiles from Germany's attempted suppression of socialism
furnished, during the miserable decade of the seventies, leaders of
desperate strikes, of street demonstrations, and finally the "Ten Philosophers" from whose eager deliberations the American Federation of
Labor derived its first organization in the cigar shops of New York, 1879.

From the National Labor Union (1866–72) and the Greenback
Labor party (1874–80) the men who later organized the American
Federation of Labor learned a painful lesson: the futility of a labor
party which had necessarily to be founded on alliances with frantic
farmers and small businessmen against their organized opponents, the
bankers and big businessmen under the guidance of expert managers
of American machine politics. Such alliances could last only while the
slump in business continued.

From the Knights of Labor (1869–86) they learned that miscellaneous organized labor was incompetent to manage productive cooperation with the purpose of displacing capitalism by a voluntary
cooperative commonwealth; and they learned that this same miscellaneous labor, while it might win sudden mass strikes, could not keep
the winnings.

From the French exiles they learned that street demonstrations
brought to the front the facile intellectual agitator against whom the
workers in the shops were helpless and by whom they were misled;
the American leaders could not even share the French anarchists'
glorification of street barricades.

From the German communists and the teachings of Marx they
learned that their immediate opponents were the employers who owned
the shops, and that their enduring alliances must therefore be not with
farmers and small businessmen, since these included their own employers, but with other wage earners in the shops of competing employers. But they had also learned from the National Labor Union and
the Greenback Labor party that a labor party in America must include
these same farmers and businessmen against whom, as employers,

they must proceed, as communists, by confiscating their shops and usurping their management.

From the British and American unionists and from the Knights of Labor they learned that labor could not be lifted as a mass, nor business and banking defeated as a mass, and that sporadic organizations in single shops could not accomplish improvement; that their immediate opponents were the competing employers in the same line of business, and their organizations of labor must be separated along competitive lines so as to extend to these competing employers and no further. They learned, too, from the British unionists, but not the American, that they must build for permanent organization which could withstand the cycles of business depression and unemployment.

This learning by experience was the outcome of the deliberations of the "Ten Philosophers," about whom Gompers writes in his autobiography. Gompers, the Jewish cigar maker from London, and [Adolf] Strasser, the German cigar maker, proceeded to organize on the British model first the New York and then the national cigar makers and later the whole labor movement. This last organization was known as the Federation of Organized Trades and Labor Unions of the United States and Canada.

It was found after five years' experiment with this British model (1881–86) that it really concealed two different functions—legislation and organization—which had to be separated, intensified, and subdivided in order to fit the variety of American conditions. Out of the reorganization based on these discoveries came the American Federation of Labor, in 1886. Legislation had to be split into federal, state, municipal, Canadian, and provincial. So the new organization, for legislative purposes, split the Trades Union Congress [its British model] eventually into forty-eight state congresses and the Canadian Trades and Labor Congress with federations for the provinces of Canada, in order to fit the political divisions of the whole North American continent, and changed "United States and Canada" in its name to "American." Several of the trade unions similarly prefixed the word "international" to their names, meaning thereby "North American." While the British organization had its one parliamentary committee and its annual congress of all the unions, which eventually became, by alliance with the socialists, the British Labor party, the American federation has its executive committee and congressional lobbyists at Washington, affiliated with an independent congress at Ottawa for the Dominion of Canada, but supreme over the federations of the states and Porto Rico.

Like the British organization, and also like the Knights of Labor,

the federation has its city central federations, which in Russia became
the Soviets. These local federations in America are also linked up with
municipal politics, and have even conducted independent municipal
campaigns, the most notable being the unsuccessful Henry George
campaign of 1886 in New York, conducted by the Central Labor Union
in alliance with socialists and single taxers, and the successful McCarthy
campaign of 1909 in San Francisco.

The second function, separated from the other functions and
immensely emphasized in America, is organization of the unorganized
into local unions, their allocation to membership in the several national
and international unions, and mutual support among all the unions in
offense and defense on the economic field. The American Federation
of Labor has as high as a thousand diminutive "federal labor unions"
directly under control of headquarters at Washington. These are always in process of formation and dissolution as recruiting stations for
existing or new national unions. The federation supports from its own
funds from twenty to fifty general organizers in various localities, who
give their assistance to incipient unions and older unions. It appoints
special organizers for concerted action or sympathetic strikes, as in the
case of the steel strike of 300,000 workers in 1919, or in the organization of the 35,000 Italian subway workers in 1902 in New York. The
strikes themselves are conducted by the affiliated unions; but the federation officials and organizers lend their aid, and at times are a means
of collecting large sums of money as their substitute of "moral and
economic force" for the sympathetic strike.

The union label, an American invention first adopted in California to exclude Chinese workers from the shops and then copied
wherever the consuming power of union labor could help, has been,
for unions like brewery workers, cigar makers, employees on workingmen's garments and others, an instrument of importance in the program
of mutual support. . . .

The economic problem of organization became the decisive point
in the reorganization of 1886. The experience of five years with the
British model showed that nothing could be done with the national
political parties. The letters of the federation were unanswered and
its agents unheard. Besides, at that time Congress had not undertaken
labor legislation, the federal courts had not begun to use the injunction
against labor unions or to declare unconstitutional the labor laws of
the states. There were very few such laws anyhow, and they were
state laws, since the states were then deemed to be sovereign in such
matters. Hence the reorganization of 1886 provided for state federations whose main purpose should be legislation, while the national

federation specialized on the expansion of economic organization in all the states. Its headquarters were established in Indianapolis, a thousand miles from Washington but a convenient railroad center for reaching all parts of the country. Not until 1896, after federal injunctions and judicial unconstitutionality had nationalized labor legislation, were headquarters moved to Washington, where the executive committee could reach the Congress, the President and the departments. Federal labor legislation eventually became equal and even superior in importance to widespread organization, for the federal injunction challenged the right of unions to exist except on paper, and unconstitutionality challenged the usefulness of state federations of labor.

But in 1886 the problem of organization was supreme. The contest with the Knights was approaching its climax. The legislative constitution of the preceding five years was not fitted to this task. It provided only for a legislative committee without executive power between sessions. Nor were the trade unions of the country interested in national legislation—they were interested in defending themselves against the Knights, who in that year had reached the height of their power. Hence at a national conference of the officials of twenty-five unions and the legislative committee of the Organized Trades and Labor Unions, the latter disbanded and the national unions formed the American Federation of Labor. Samuel Gompers, secretary of the former legislative committee, was made president, and was reelected to this postion every year, except one, until his death in 1924.

The federation proceeded, in 1887, to strengthen the voting power of the national unions. Delegates from national and international unions were given one vote for each one hundred members, leaving the delegates from city and state federations with only one vote. Thus in the convention of 1924 the eight carpenters' delegates cast 3152 votes and the one delegate from the central union of New York City cast one vote.

This method of voting, it will be seen, makes the American Federation of Labor not a popular representative assembly for legislative or political purposes, like the former British or German or French conferences, or like the former General Assembly of the Knights of Labor, or the former National Labor Union, but makes it a congress of ambassadors from sovereign unions, "weighted" according to the size of the union. The delegates from the unions are usually the national presidents and executive officers of the unions.

Thus no individual workingman is a "member" of the American Federation of Labor. He is a member only of his union, and it is his national union that is the member of the federation. There is even no

dual citizenship, as there has been since the Civil War under the political constitution of the United States, where every citizen owes allegiance both to the federal union and to the state of his residence. Each
workingman is a "citizen" only of his own union, and gets representation
in the federation only through the executive officers of his national
union. Consequently the federation has no jurisdiction over individuals (except in the small federal labor unions above mentioned). Furthermore, since the federation has no funds of its own except the
meager fund of one cent per member per month which the national
unions each contribute in a lump sum, the federation remains with only
"moral" jurisdiction over its constituent unions. It is a loose confederacy
—not a federal union.

The result is that no "left wing" or "anti-administration" movement within any national union can get representation, or even a vote,
in the federation convention, except as it comes from a city or state
federation where the voting is legislative, democratic, and equal for
each local union, no matter how weak or strong it may be. As a matter
of fact nearly all of the socialistic or communistic resolutions offered
in the conventions of the American Federation of Labor have come
from these local delegates, occasionally from a socialistic or politically
minded national union, and then, after speeches, they are voted down
ninety-nine to one. They have freedom of speech but no weight.

No wonder that the dissatisfied and sometimes revolutionary
elements in this country and in others criticize the federation bitterly
as "a machine," "boss ridden," "reactionary," even "a corrupt conspiracy
of tyrants." The federation was organized and has been maintained
expressly for organization purposes and to keep out disunion. Like the
American political parties it is a "machine"—indeed its principle of
organization has been named "business unionism" by [Robert F.] Hoxie,
a discriminating student of labor movements. In the American conflict of races and religions and of geographical sections, in a system of
machine politics and highly efficient mechanized capitalism, and in
the absence of any "class consciousness" or "solidarity" of labor, which
in other countries is the heritage of centuries of military suppression,
the American federation has just one "pure and simple" business—how
to create a united front which is able to deal as one man with any situation regarding higher wages, shorter hours, slower speed, stricter
shop control of jobs and permanence of unionism. The federation was
created not as a political movement to overthrow capitalism or get
control of government, but as a movement within the ranks of labor
to bring about permanent organization over a continent where everything conspired against both organization and permanence.

Hence when it came to dealing in 1895 with the Socialist Trade and Labor Alliance, or in 1905 with the syndicalistic Industrial Workers of the World, or in 1923 with the Communists, whose movements threatened to disrupt some of the unions, the federation was in a position to take drastic united action, expelling and suppressing them. The federation is truly a militant organization, but in a country where there is no class consciousness that unites labor regardless of organization, its militancy runs sidewise against disruptive labor movements even more uncompromisingly than frontwise against employing capitalists.

This lateral and frontal militancy within a disruptive environment affords an explanation of several peculiarities either wholly absent or unobtrusive in other countries and at former times in America. These are the small proportions of organized to unorganized labor, the wide spread of wages between high paid and low paid labor, dual unions, jurisdictional strikes, trade agreements and strict shop rules. . . .

The federation has been from the start antipolitical and antilegislative. The trade agreement is evidently economic legislation, not political legislation. In this respect the policy of the federation fits the political system. American political parties are not founded on "principles"—they are business organizations of local professional politicians offering such promises, often different in different parts of the country, as they think will capture the voters. This means that they always take over from an independent "third party" whatever platform promises they think will dissolve that party and win its votes, if it appears to hold the balance of power. In the hope of this result the federation has always opposed a labor party and has always presented its legislative demands to the two dominant parties and to individual candidates, with recommendations that union members should vote for friendly candidates regardless of parties. This method is patently the only thing to do for an organization of only 15 percent of the voters. Sometimes the method gets results where strikes fail. After the federated unions lost the eight-hour strike in the steel industry in 1919, the Republican party leaders were reported to have induced the Steel Corporation to grant the demand voluntarily, which the corporation did in order to relieve the party of the incubus created by its victory over 300,000 workers. Similar paradoxes have occurred in the federation's history. The fact that administrative officers of government are usually elected by popular vote, whereas in other countries they are appointed by a legislative committee in control of the government, makes it even more important for the federation's executives to use their influence with the administration rather than legislature. It is in the administration of laws —local, state, and federal—that the organizations both of labor and of capital accomplish their aims of nullifying objectionable laws, enforcing favorable laws, or interpreting colorless laws. This process does not require a political party.

But the method is precarious. Consistently, therefore, the federation's policy is antilegislative. The primary reasons advanced against such legislation as that dealing with social insurance, hours of labor, minimum wage, and the like are rooted in fear of government interference with the liberties of wage earners, thus reducing them to a "status." The "self-help" of laborers organized in unions, by which is meant the establishment of shop rules, enlarges the liberties of the individual workers. Yet the federation's policy calls for legislation in cases where laborers, like children, are too weak to organize and, in less degree, where women are involved.

Labor's Bill of Grievances

Headquarters, American Federation of Labor

Washington, D.C. *April 7, 1906.*

To All Trade Unionists of America.

Dear Sirs and Brothers: The Bill of Grievances, printed below, formulated and adopted by the Executive Council of the American Federation of Labor, is expressive of the decision which organized labor of America has made manifest in its various conventions and union meetings. The presidents of all affiliated international unions were invited to meet the Executive Council at the headquarters of the American Federation of Labor, March 21, 1906, and participate in a conference concerning matters affecting labor's interests congressionally and administratively. The presidents or their duly credentialed representatives participated, and unanimously and enthusiastically endorsed and signed the document and participated with the Executive Council in the presentation and reading thereof.

Some garbled accounts of this matter have appeared in the press. In order that our fellow trade unionists may be in possession of the document in its original form, and that their actions may conform thereto, this is presented to you in its entirety.

Reprinted by permission of the AFL–CIO, from Vol. XIII (1906), *The American Federationist.*

Let the inspiring watchword go forth that—

We will stand by our friends and administer a stinging rebuke to men or parties who are either indifferent, negligent, or hostile, and, wherever opportunity affords, to secure the election of intelligent, honest, earnest trade unionists, with clear, unblemished, paid-up union cards in their possession.

Fraternally yours,

FRANK MORRISON,   SAMUEL GOMPERS,
Secretary.   *President, American Federation of Labor.*

Bill of Grievances.

HONORABLE THEODORE ROOSEVELT, *President of the United States;*
HONORABLE WM. P. FRYE, *President pro tempore, United States Senate;*
HONORABLE JOSEPH G. CANNON, *Speaker, House of Representatives, United States.*

GENTLEMEN: The undersigned Executive Council of the American Federation of Labor, and those accompanying us in the presentation of this document, submit to you the subject-matter of the grievances which the workmen of our country feel by reason of the indifferent position which the Congress of the United States has manifested toward the just, reasonable, and necessary measures which have been before it these past several years, and which particularly affect the interests of the working people, as well as by reason of the administrative acts of the executive branches of the government and the legislation of the Congress relating to these interests. For convenience the matters of which we complain are briefly stated, and are as follows:

Eight Hour Law.

The law commonly known as the Eight Hour Law has been found ineffective and insufficient to accomplish the purpose of its designers and framers. Labor has, since 1894, urged the passage of a law so as to remedy the defects, and for its extension to all work done for or on behalf of the government. Our efforts have been in vain. . . .

[The document then goes on to list additional grievances under the headings "Convict Labor," "Immigration," "Chinese Exclusion," "Seamen's Rights," and "Ship Subsidy," and continues with . . .]

Trusts and Interstate Commerce.

The anti-trust and interstate commerce laws enacted to protect the people against monopoly in the products of labor, and against discrimination in the transportation thereof, have been perverted, so far as the laborers are concerned, so as to invade and violate their personal liberty as guaranteed by the constitution. Our repeated efforts to obtain redress from Congress have been in vain.

Anti-Injunction Bill.

The beneficent writ of injunction, intended to protect property rights has, as used in labor disputes, been perverted so as to attack and destroy personal freedom, and in a manner to hold that the employer has some property rights in the labor of the workmen. Instead of obtaining the relief which labor has sought, it is seriously threatened with statutory authority for existing judicial usurpation.

Committee on Labor.

The Committee on Labor of the House of Representatives was instituted at the demand of labor to voice its sentiments, to advocate its rights, and to protect its interests. In the past two Congresses this committee has been so organized as to make ineffectual any attempt labor has made for redress. This being the fact in the last Congress, labor requested the speaker to appoint on the Committee on Labor members who, from their experience, knowledge, and sympathy, would render in this Congress such service as the committee was originally designed to perform. Not only was labor's request ignored, but the hostile make-up of the committee was accentuated.

Right of Petition Denied Government Employees.

Recently the President issued an order forbidding any and all government employees, upon the pain of instant dismissal from the government service, to petition Congress for any redress of grievances or for any improvement in their condition. Thus the constitutional right of citizens to petition must be surrendered by the government employee in order that he may obtain or retain his employment.

Redress for Grievances.

We present these grievances to your attention because we have long, patiently, and in vain waited for redress. There is not any matter of which we have complained but for which we have, in an honorable and lawful manner, submitted remedies. The remedies for these grievances proposed by labor are in line with fundamental law, and with the progress and development made necessary by changed industrial conditions.

Labor brings these its grievances to your attention because you are the representatives responsible for legislation and for failure of legislation. The toilers come to you as your fellow citizens, who, by reason of their position in life, have not only with all other citizens an equal interest in our country, but the further interest of being the burden bearers, the wage-earners of America. As labor's representatives we ask you to redress these grievances, for it is in your power so to do.

Labor now appeals to you, and we trust that it may not be in vain. But if, perchance, you may not heed us, we shall appeal to the conscience and the support of our fellow citizens.

Very respectfully,

SAMUEL GOMPERS,	DANIEL J. KEEFE,
JAMES DUNCAN,	WM. D. HUBER,
JAMES O'CONNELL,	JOSEPH F. VALENTINE,
MAX MORRIS,	JOHN B. LENNON,
DENIS A. HAYES,	FRANK MORRISON,

Executive Council, American Federation of Labor.

Voluntarism in Action

Harwood Lawrence Childs

Princeton University

SINCE ABOUT 1908 the American Federation of Labor has played an active part in elections, national as well as local.[1] No attempt is made to support candidates financially, but candidates whose public records have shown their sympathy for the labor movement are afforded every kind of support that the publicity agencies of the Federation can give. The organization keeps detailed records of public officials and will submit upon request the stand which any legislator has taken upon measures of interest to labor. The following is a typical sample of a legislator's record[2] as kept by the Federation:

Excerpted by permission of the author from *Labor and Capital in National Politics,* © 1930 the Ohio University Press, Columbus.

[1] See "Abstract of President Gompers' Testimony Before the House Lobby Investigation Committee," *American Federationist,* December 1913, XX, p. 1002.

[2] Similar records are kept for all legislators and the officers of the Federation have complete summaries showing the legislative record of every Congressman throughout his terms of office.

MASSACHUSETTS
Senator Henry Cabot Lodge, Republican
Residence: Nahant, Mass.
Legislative Record on Measures of Interest to Labor

66th Congress   *Attitude Toward Labor*

Oct. 21, 1919—Amendment to strike out antitrust clause
　　　　　favoring Labor in the First Deficiency bill   Unfavorable

Nov. 5, 1919—Motion to strike Labor Charter from
　　　　　League of Nations   Unfavorable

Dec. 19, 1919—Motion to strike clause making strikes un-
　　　　　lawful from Cummins railroad bill   Not Voting

Jan. 26, 1920—Americanization bill—Education of illiterates   Favorable

Feb. 23, 1920—Cummins-Esch railroad bill—acceptance of
　　　　　conference report containing the obnoxious
　　　　　antilabor and other objectional provisions   Unfavorable

Apr. 1, 1920—Motion by Senator Phelan to increase the
　　　　　appropriation for the Bureau of Concilia-
　　　　　tion, Department of Labor   Not Voting

Apr. 3, 1920—Retirement bill—Myers amendment prohib-
　　　　　iting affiliation of Federal Employees with
　　　　　Organized Labor   Favorable

67th Congress

Nov. 3, 1921—Senator Smoot's amendment to H.R. 8245
　　　　　providing for a sales tax which would shift
　　　　　the burden of taxation from the well-to-do
　　　　　to those least able to bear it   Paired, Unfavorable

Nov. 4, 1921—Senator Smoot again offers amendment
　　　　　providing for the sales tax   Paired, Unfavorable

68th Congress

Apr. 18, 1924—Passage of immigration restriction bill   Favorable

May 27, 1924—Passage of Postal Employees' wage increase
　　　　　bill with Borah corrupt practices amendment Favorable

June 2, 1924—Passage of Child Labor amendment to the
　　　　　Constitution of United States   Favorable

·   ·   ·   ·   ·   ·   ·   ·   ·   ·   ·   ·   ·   ·   ·   ·   ·   ·   ·   ·

Favorable to Labor	14
Paired favorable to Labor	0
Unfavorable to Labor	8
Paired unfavorable to Labor	2
Not voting	8
Answered present	0
Total	32

The direction of the nonpartisan political campaigns of the American Federation of Labor is usually placed in the hands of a National Non-Partisan Political Campaign Committee composed of three members of the Executive Council acting as an executive committee. This committee sends circulars to national, international, state, and local organizations, which outline plans to reelect public officials favorable to labor and to defeat those not in sympathy with the organized labor movement. The following are excerpts from a circular of this character:

> Greeting: The insidious campaign now being carried on to discredit forward-looking members of Congress makes it imperative that the organized wage-earners and their sympathizers make every preparation to take an aggressive part in the primaries which will be held in the various states and the election in November 1926. . . . A careful record of the votes made in the present session of Congress and previous Congresses will be compiled and sent to all organized labor. . . . It will be helpful to the American Federation of Labor Non-Partisan Political Campaign Committee if the officials of the various state federations of labor and central bodies will send in a list of candidates for United States Senators and members of the House of Representatives. . . . Every state federation of labor, every city central body, and every local union should appoint non-partisan political campaign committees. . . . Mass meetings should be held. . . . The campaign should not be confined to the organized wage-earners. . . . Much depends upon the outcome of the primaries and the elections. . . . It is our wish that every campaign committee will write to the American Federation of Labor for information that will be of value as to candidates.
>
> Yours fraternally,
> WILLIAM GREEN [3]

---

[3] *Proceedings of the Forty-Sixth Annual Convention of the American Federation of Labor,* 1926, pp. 71–72. [Green succeeded to the presidency of the AFL upon Gompers' death, in 1924.—Eds.]

Every attempt is made to adapt Federation pressure to the situations in different states. The individual records of Congressmen are sent to their respective congressional districts, and member organizations are urged to appoint legislative committees to keep records of their state legislators. Printed reports on legislation before Congress and the state legislatures are sent to colleges, member organizations, and the labor press. For example, on July 29, 1922, a special circular was sent to nearly 40,000 nonpartisan political campaign committees outlining what should be done to make the campaign a success.[4] In this endeavor to elect candidates favorable to labor the Federation cooperates with groups such as farmer organizations and the American Legion, and conferences are frequently held with representatives of these groups in Washington.[5] Hundreds of letters from individuals are answered on all phases of the campaign. Just before the primaries are held in the different states, organizers are frequently directed to visit local bodies and urge the support of favored candidates. One of the first instances of an attempt on the part of the Federation to bring about the defeat of a candidate for Congress was in the case of Charles E. Littlefield of Maine in 1906.[6] Since that time the influence of the Federation has been felt in most Congressional districts at election time. The following description taken from a report of the Non-Partisan Political Campaign Committee illustrates fairly well the procedure and the types of pressure brought to bear. After reciting a number of measures on which Representative Garrett of Tennessee had acted in a manner unfavorable to labor, the committee went on to state:

> On March 5, 1926, President Green wrote a letter to the Tennessee State Federation of Labor in which he referred to Representative Garrett's record in Congress. . . . President Green sent a representative to the Convention of the Tennessee State Federation of Labor who made still further representations of the necessity of defeating Representative Garrett. The secretary of the State Federation of Labor had previously sent President Green's letter to all papers in the state. . . . Finally Representative Garrett began to be alarmed at the reports coming from his district and in June, during the session of Congress, he hastened home to patch up his fences. Few wage-earners live in Representative Garrett's district, it is mostly a farming district, but the appeal made by the labor movement was so successful that he was barely elected by only about 1200 majority.[7]

---

[4] *Proceedings*, 1923, pp. 46–55.

[5] *Ibid.*, pp. 51, 52.

[6] "Abstract of President Gompers' Testimony Before the House Lobby Investigation Committee," *loc. cit.*

[7] *Proceedings*, 1926, pp. 72–74.

The American Federation of Labor not only takes an active part in Congressional and Senatorial elections but also brings its influence to bear upon the national party conventions. President Gompers and others associated with him took an active part in the informal proceedings connected with the party conventions of 1908 and 1912. Mr. Gompers set forth in his autobiography an account of Federation activities at that time.

> The Republican Convention was to meet in Chicago in June and the Democratic Convention in Denver in July. The Executive Council of the AF of L met in Chicago just prior to the Republican Convention, to prepare the planks and platform which we would urge be inserted in the convention's declarations. In that meeting we considered the report of our legislative committee. Additional workers had been detailed to the legislative committee in order that we might have the labor record of every member of Congress and that there should be no misunderstanding on the part of any members of Congress as to the gravity which labor attached to its grievances and its demands for remedial legislation. . . . James Duncan, Daniel J. Keefe, and I were selected to appear before the Committee on Platform. Mr. Keefe arranged for two interviews with Mr. Wade Ellis and we discussed labor planks. . . . So relentless was Mr. Cannon in his hostility to labor that, despite the fact that it was considered good form for candidates to stay away from conventions, he hastened to Chicago to add his personal activity against us. The committee refused to give us a hearing before the whole committee, but arranged for us to confer with a subcommittee. . . .
>
> As stated above, the platform contained an evasion on labor's paramount issue and the convention nominated as its standard bearer William Howard Taft known as the "injunction judge." James Van Cleave and the Republican reactionaries jeeringly told Labor to "Go to Denver." . . . That was in accord with our program and our Executive Council proceeded to Denver and we presented the identical propositions which we had presented to the Republican Platform Committee. There we were accorded a hearing before the full Platform Committee of which Judge Alton B. Parker was chairman. We were subjected to considerable questioning and exchange of views, with the result that the committee did include most of the requests that we presented.[8]

---

[8] Samuel Gompers, *Seventy Years of Life and Labor, An Autobiography,* E. P. Dutton and Co., 1925, II, Chapter XXXV, pp. 255 ff. "Labor expects to exercise just as great, if not a greater influence in the 1928 national political campaign as in any previous campaign, not excepting 1916" was a statement made by the President of the Federation in January 1928. In pursuance of this aim a nonpartisan committee was appointed to direct the political campaign. Beginning in the primaries an effort was made to elect friendly delegates to the National

It would be impossible to enumerate all of the various patterns of activity followed by the Federation as it seeks to establish its influence during elections. Every legal device which the ingenuity of the leaders and the finances of the organization will allow is used to bring about the desired results. These results are not capable of exact measurement because of the fact that the election of any public official is rarely due entirely to the support of any single group. The claims of the Federation, therefore, must be accepted with some reservations in spite of their suggestiveness. In its 1923 report the Executive Council of the Federation stated:

> Through the activities of the American Federation of Labor National Non-Partisan Political Campaign Committee, as directed by the Executive Council, twenty-three candidates for United States Senators who had been loyal to labor and the people were elected and eleven reactionary Senators defeated.
>
> Of the friendly Senators elected eighteen were Democrats and five Republicans. Of the candidates for representatives 170 were elected either because directly supported by the A F of L National Non-Partisan Political Campaign committees or by reason of the opposition to their opponents. Of these 105 were Democrats, 63 Republicans, 1 Farmer-Labor, and 1 Independent.[9]

These figures do not, of course, indicate the strength of the labor group as such in Congress, that is to say, the number of Congressmen elected directly from the ranks of labor. In the sixty-ninth Congress these numbered seventeen; two Democrats, thirteen Republicans, one Farmer-Labor, and one Socialist. The bulk of labor's support depends not upon labor men as such but upon Congressmen who show by their votes on test measures that they can be counted upon by organized labor.

Conventions, to get out friendly votes in the election, and ultimately to elect officers friendly to labor's program. For a general description of the program and methods to be employed see New York *Times*, January 25, 1928. For a list of the planks presented to the political party conventions in June 1928, see *Weekly News Service*, June 16, 1928.

[9] *Proceedings*, 1923, p. 50.

Should a Labor Party Be Formed?

Samuel Gompers

IN THE LAST FEW WEEKS there have been published certain situations which exist and certain movements which were about to be inaugurated. In a few of the cities that situation and that movement have become accentuated. In Chicago, New York City, and two or three other places the labor movement has expressed itself through the central bodies in favor of the formation of a political labor party.

No man has the right to look upon such a move lightly, or without deep consideration or deep concern. Either the proposed movement about to be inaugurated for the establishment of a political labor party is good, or it is bad. Either it is advantageous or it is injurious, and the purpose of my asking that we meet this afternoon is to present to you some facts upon that subject.

You who were in the movement of long ago will remember that to which I refer. We had in the United States a fairly growing labor movement of some trade unionists in some form of a federation called the National Labor Union. That organization went along, inspired good spirit and activity among the workers, and then called a national convention for the purpose of nominating a president of the United States. That convention met and nominated Justice David Davis, a judge of the Supreme Court of the United States, as its candidate for president, and after nominating Mr. Davis adjourned and never met again. The trade unions then in existence fell off in membership until the organizations became very weak and ineffective. Some organizations fell by the wayside. Labor was in a most deplorable condition, without opportunity for defense and robbed entirely of any power to press forward its rightful claims.

In 1885–86, after a few years of precarious early existence, the American Federation of Labor tried to build up and extend its influence and organize the workers into their unions.

In 1884 the American Federation of Labor declared for the introduction of the eight-hour workday, May 1, 1886. It proposed negotiations with the employers to the accomplishment of that high purpose. The movement gained great impetus and large advantages followed, but on May 2 or 3, 1886, a bomb was thrown at a meeting which was being held at Haymarket Square, Chicago, which killed and maimed

Reprinted by permission of the AFL–CIO, from Vol. XXVI (1919), *The American Federationist.*

more than twenty policemen. The meeting was supposed to have been held in the interests of the eight-hour movement. The wrath of the people which was aroused against those in charge of the Haymarket meeting gave the eight-hour day a severe blow and setback. However, the eight-hour day was secured for the workers in several industries and a reduction in the hours of labor from 16 to 12 or from 12 to 10 became almost universal in the United States. But the eight-hour movement as such was destroyed for the time being.

Due in part to that incident and to the resentment of the workers because they had lost so much that they could have obtained and due to certain local conditions, political rather than economic, in various cities the local movement undertook political campaigns and organized a political party in Chicago, Milwaukee, St. Louis, Boston, and New York. This resulted in the organized labor movement of New York City launching into a campaign which nominated Henry George as Mayor of the city. It was my privilege to enter into that campaign with the men (there are a few of them in this room now) who were active at the time. I aided to the very best of my ability. Henry George received 68,000 votes and came very near election. Some claim that he was really elected, but that in the last hours many of the supporters of Theodore Roosevelt who was the mayoralty candidate of the Republican party abandoned him and cast their votes for Abraham S. Hewitt who was the Democratic candidate for Mayor.

After the campaign closed and the election was held, the movement took on another phase. It was called the Progressive Labor Party. They admitted to membership not only the men of organized labor but what had popularly been called by a great many the "brain with brawn" or "brain with labor." The campaign was carried on with such scandalous results, that nearly all the men of labor who had some self-respect had to hold themselves in the background for fear that they might be besmirched with the incidents which occurred in the campaign. . . .

I mention these things of our own country, and now I want to mention a few things of other countries of which I have been a personal, intimate, and close observer.

In Germany, the trade union movement having been dissolved by Bismarck and the organizations of labor not having the right to exist, went to its death for the time. Then when there was a slight moderation of that order, the trade union movement of that country was organized from the top down. There were executive officers who imposed their will upon the rank and file. There was no democracy of administration, of construction, or of the right of the membership to determine policies. Benefits were paid by the officers of the general organization. These officers had the power to determine whether the workers were entitled to the insurance and other benefits. It was a matter of power vested in the executives. You can imagine how necessary it was for the rank and file to endeavor to curry favor with the executives in order that they might not be discriminated against unfairly.

In 1905 I was in Hamburg and Bremen, in consultation with the officers of the general labor movement of Germany, among whom were [Karl] Legien and [Adolf] Von Elm. They were not permitted to hold public meetings dealing with any subject affecting labor or the government. . . . The unions were struggling for the right to meet as unions and to have the guarantee of the law for their legal right to maintain their organizations and to hold such meetings; in other words, the right of free association. I had the assurance of Von Elm, Legien and others that the Socialist political party of Germany denied the demand made by the trade unions to work to secure from the government a law guaranteeing the workers the right to organize as a free association of workers. The Socialist political party of Germany, which is the only political party claiming to be the workmen's party, denied the union labor movement of Germany the right to take political action in order to secure the lawful right for its existence.

The French organized labor movement is not extensive. Some of the most completely organized unions are wholly out of touch with the Confederation Generale du Travail, that is the French Federation of Labor, because they want to exercise their individual right of trade unionism and trade union action. . . . The political party [Socialist Party] dominates the trade union movement of France. . . .

In England there is the British Trade Union Congress, the British Federation of Trade Unions, and the Labor Party. For the discussion of business when the conventions of either party are not in session, they meet jointly in conference through the Parliamentary Committee of the British Trade Union Congress and the Executive Committee of the Labor Party. Quite a number of the members of the Parliamentary Committee of the British Trade Union Congress are members of the Labor Party, and quite a number of them who hold their seats in Parliament are members of the Labor Party. As a matter of fact, the Executive Committee of the Labor Party dominates the entire movement of England.

At a conference held at Derby, England, in September 1918, the executive officers of the Labor Party presided and dominated the proceedings. And all the time that I was in England I never heard of a phrase like this: "The British Trade Union movement and the Labor

Party." I never heard it said: "The Parliamentary Committee of the British Trade Union Congress and the Executive Committee of the Labor Party." It was always the Labor Party and the Trade Union Congress. The Labor Party of England dominates the labor movement of England. . . .

The fact is that an independent political labor party becomes either radical, so-called, or else reactionary, but it is primarily devoted to one thing and that is vote-getting. Every sail is trimmed to the getting of votes. The question of the conditions of Labor, the question of the standards of Labor, the question of the struggles and the sacrifices of Labor, to bring light into the lives and the work of the toilers—all that is subordinated to the one consideration of votes for the party. . . .

In our movement we have done some things. We have brought together more than three million workers, organized into our trade unions and belonging to the American Federation of Labor. In addition there are between four and five hundred thousand workmen in the Railroad Brotherhoods not affiliated with us but yet in accord with our work and our policies. In other words, there are nearly four million of organized trade unionists in the United States. There is not always harmony; there is disagreement; there is opposition, all of it important, all of it tending to crystallize the sentiment of unity and devotion to the cause of Labor. The American labor movement occupies the field of activity without yielding one inch to any other body. . . .

Who are we going to have as the leaders of this new political labor party here? I understand that there is impatience among our fellows. It is creditable to them that they are impatient. There is not any man in all America, or in all the world, more impatient than I with the progress that has been made, with the position we occupy. I want more, more, more for Labor. I think I have tried and am trying to do my share. My associates of the Executive Council have tried to do their share, but there is such a thing as attempting to overrun, and by overrunning to defeat the object we would gain for the wage-earners and to throw them into the hands of those who do not know the honest aspirations of Labor or who would direct them for personal aggrandizement.

I have been the President of the American Federation of Labor for many, many years. I regard that position as the most exalted that I could occupy. I have no aspiration to hold this or that position. It is not that I ask you to follow me. I ask that the trade union movement be given its fullest opportunity for growth and development so that it may be the instrumentality to secure better and better and better and constantly better conditions for the workers of our country. . . .

It is not true, as some carping critics allege, that the American Federation of Labor is a nonpolitical organization. As a matter of fact, the workers of the United States and the organized labor movement act voluntarily in the exercise of their political right and power. We have changed the control of our government from the old-time interests of corporate power and judicial usurpation. We have secured from the government of the United States the labor provision of the Clayton Anti-trust Law, the declaration in the law that the labor of a human being is not a commodity or article of commerce. In that law we have secured the right of our men to exercise functions for which, under the old regime our men were brought before the bar of justice and fined or imprisoned. We have secured the eight-hour workday not only as a basic principle but as a fact. We have secured the Seamen's law giving to the seamen the freedom to leave their vessels when in safe harbor. The seamen of America are now free men and own themselves. We have secured a child labor law, and although it has been declared unconstitutional, we are again at work to secure a law for the protection of our children. Better than all, we have established the concept in law and in administration that the interest and welfare of the workers are paramount, and this not only in the laws of our republic but in the laws of our states and municipalities.

There are other laws in the interest of labor which we have secured, more than I can mention off-hand, but far above all these are the improvements brought into the lives and work of the toilers by their own actions as organized workers. We have established unity of spirit; we have brought about the extension of organization among the formerly unorganized, and our organized free existence to function and to express ourselves is now practically unquestioned.

Suppose in 1912 we had had a labor party in existence; do you think for a moment that we could have gone as the American labor movement to the other political parties and said: "We want you to inaugurate in your platform this and this declaration." If one of the parties had refused and the other party consented and took its chance, would the American Federation of Labor have been permitted to exercise that independent political and economic course if the labor party had been in existence? How long would we have had to wait for the passage of a law by Congress declaring law, in practice and in principle that the labor of a human being is not a commodity or an article of commerce—the most far-reaching declaration ever made by any government in the history of the world.

Voluntarism: The Political Functions of an Antipolitical Doctrine

Michael Rogin

University of California, Berkeley

PERHAPS THE MOST COMMON STATEMENT made about the American labor movement is that it is essentially pragmatic. This observation usually refers to its nonideological character in contrast with the 'doctrinaire Marxism' of European unions. When Sam Gompers spoke of the 'pragmatism' of the American Federation of Labor, however, he referred to American labor's rejection, not only of European socialism, but also of American Social Darwinism as well. Social Darwinism, which provided the operative ideals for many post-Civil War Americans, was optimistic about individual capacity for economic achievement and fatalistic about political or collective action to change economic conditions. In the name of individual freedom and immutable natural laws, Social Darwinists opposed union organization. Social Darwinist doctrines were generally accepted in the America of the period. They were particularly useful for businessmen anxious to block the growth of unions.

Gompers opposed the doctrines of Social Darwinism as meaningless abstractions, contradicted by the concrete experience of American workers. Laboring men had learned that the Horatio Alger dream was for most of them only a dream, and that they could only improve their situation collectively. In contrast to the Social Darwinist advice to workers, the AFL stressed the benefits of voluntary collective action and labor unity. Yet even as this AFL outlook became articulated, the Federation adopted many many Social Darwinist texts. Eventually voluntarism, as the Federation called its 'pragmatic' philosophy, conflicted with the needs of the workers and with the growth of the AFL. This happened because voluntarism became, not the practical expression of American working-class experience, but an organizational ideology protecting the craft union officials of the AFL.[1]

In its original conception, the unifying theme of voluntarism was that workers could best achieve their goals by relying on their

Reprinted by permission of the publisher from *Industrial and Labor Relations Review*, XV, No. 4 (July 1962), © Cornell University.

[1] The idea that ideologies which allegedly come from the grass roots in fact serve organizational purposes is developed by Philip Selznick in *T.V.A. and the Grass Roots* (Berkeley, Calif.: University of California Press, 1949).

own voluntary associations. Voluntarism defended the autonomy of the international craft union against the coercive interference of the state, the AFL itself and, implicitly, the union membership. Concretely this meant that Federation spokesmen favored trade union autonomy from the Federation and opposed internal union factions. Moreover, it meant opposition to alliance with any political party, as well as to positive state action such as wage-and-hour laws and unemployment insurance.

It would be a mistake to treat voluntarism, the doctrine of an organization, as a coherent and systematic political theory. Gompers and other AFL spokesmen defended voluntarism with practical arguments. They argued that the AFL could best achieve its goals within the organization by relying on the voluntary cooperation of the internationals. In their attack on politics, they pointed to the difficulty of getting workers to agree on political programs. They stressed the obstacles to the passage of favorable legislation. Perhaps the main emphasis was on the role of courts in emasculating labor legislation and in issuing labor injunctions.

Increasingly as the AFL matured, however, voluntarism was also defended with abstract and theoretical arguments. These arguments, reminiscent of the rhetoric of the Social Darwinist employers against whom the unions had organized, stressed the benefits of an abstract freedom at the expense of more immediate considerations. Opposing unemployment insurance at the 1930 convention, delegate Olander said,

> Every system of unemployment insurance here contemplates supervision and control by both federal and state governments and will require registration, not only of aliens among the workers, but of all of us. . . . Have we lost courage to the point where we regard freedom as no longer the greatest essential of life and the most necessary element in human progress?[2]

At the same time that the AFL used such theoretical arguments to justify craft-union autonomy and to attack state action, it asserted that voluntarism was a "pragmatic philosophy."[3] Voluntarism, it was claimed, was practical and functional, adapting policies to meet the

---

[2] AFL, *Proceedings*, 1930, p. 311.

[3] Samuel Gompers, "Robert Hunter's New Dilemma," *Federationist*, Vol. 23, May 1915, p. 355. In "Theories of the Labor Movement," in Brooks, Derber, McCabe, and Taft, eds., *Interpreting the Labor Movement* (Madison, Wis.: Industrial Relations Research Association, 1952), p. 38, Philip Taft agrees that the AFL had a "philosophy of simple pragmatism."

emergent needs of the labor movement. Traditionally, labor historians have not analyzed voluntarism as an organizational ideology, but have accepted its pragmatic claims at face value, ignoring the AFL's theoretical defence of voluntarism. The traditional view has been that voluntarism was the most effective response of American workers to their concrete needs, that it was modified in practice, and that Gompers was a realist who "would not have hesitated to abandon voluntarism had he been convinced that another philosophy would produce more lasting results."[4]

In his *Theory of the Labor Movement*, Selig Perlman provided the theoretical basis for this view of the AFL, where he explained its attitudes, particularly its concentration on job control and economic matters, on the basis of the "manualist consciousness" of the workers. To this consciousness of "organic labor," Perlman, like Gompers, contrasted the antipragmatic, abstract, and philosophical conceptions of intellectuals.[5]

The pragmatic element in voluntarism was real enough, but not the only element. Certainly the AFL was nonrevolutionary, and pragmatic in that sense. But pragmatic has other meanings. When Perlman and Gompers called voluntarism pragmatic, they meant that it was useful for the generality of American workers and arose from their actual experience. Once the organization enters the analysis, however, this general pragmatism can no longer be assumed. Voluntarism was indeed practical and protective for a particular small constituency, but it was merely formalist and doctrinaire for the larger constituency for which the American Federation of Labor claimed to speak. In fact, voluntarism was an abstract philosophy, which neither arose nor maintained itself simply out of organized labor's unfavorable experience with the state. In the service of the organization,

---

[4] George Higgins, *Voluntarism in Organized Labor in the United States: 1930–1940* (Washington, D.C.: Catholic University Press, 1944), p. 30. A typical statement of this general position is found in William English Walling, *American Labor and American Democracy*, Vol. 1 (New York: Harper and Brothers, 1926), p. 22: "In other countries labor organizations have been founded largely on general ideas and an effort has been made to base economic and political policies on these ideals. In America, on the other hand, general ideas have arisen exclusively out of labor's daily experience."

[5] Selig Perlman, *A Theory of the Labor Movement* (New York: Augustus M. Kelley, 1949), pp. 5–6, 40–41. The first edition was published in 1928. The continued dominance of the Perlman tradition is reflected in the recent publication of Philip Taft's two-volume history of the AFL. *The A. F. of L. in the Time of Gompers*, and *The A. F. of L. from the Death of Gompers until the Merger* (New York: Harper and Brothers, 1957, 1959).

voluntarism became as doctrinaire and abstract as the Social Darwinism which it opposed.

Organized Labor and the Pragmatist Revolt

If voluntarism is to be treated as an organizational ideology, the early AFL must first be understood in the context of the developing social thought of its time. Generally, throughout the nineteenth century the American labor movement had been part of the general reform movements in the nation. The Knights of Labor had been concerned with virtually the whole range of problem agitating American society. The American Federation of Labor, largely neglecting these broad concerns, was a new departure in American labor.[6]

The craft unions' decision to unite workers on the narrow basis of common craft interest has been rightly attributed by Perlman to the difficulty of maintaining an organized labor movement. But, unlike their predecessors, the AFL craft workers strove to create homogeneous unions so that the diverse interests of American workers would not tear the unions apart. As an organization built on this narrow class-constituency of craft workers,[7] the AFL's ideology was meant to protect only the interests of this constituency. But heir to a labor tradition which spoke not only for all workers but for all common men, it attempted to present itself as the spokesman for all American workers.[8] Much of its legitimacy came from its claim to represent this broad constituency, and the organizational ideology had to perpetuate that claim. To identify the voluntarism of the AFL with the pragmatism of its time, however, obscures the fact that what is functional for one

---

[6] For a similar departure in agricultural politics, see Grant McConnell, *The Decline of Agrarian Democracy* (Berkeley, Calif.: The University of California Press, 1953). I treat the AFL as attempting to create a homogeneous organization through building itself up on a narrow craft worker constituency, yet claiming to speak for the broad constituency of the working class. This approach was suggested by McConnell's treatment of the Farm Bureau.

[7] For confirmation of the fact that the AFL was overwhelmingly an organization of skilled workers, see James O. Morris, *Conflict Within the AFL* (Ithaca, N.Y.: New York State School of Industrial and Labor Relations at Cornell University, 1958), pp. 10–13. Craft worker predominance increased as the AFL matured, so that the organization became more homogeneous and less representative of American workers.

[8] Gompers often made this claim. For example, "The organized labor movement is the advance guard. It is the militant expression of the desires of all the workers" (Samuel Gompers, "The Issues that Face America," *Federationist*, Vol. 28, May 1920, p. 427). Similarly, by deriving the actions of the AFL from the manualist consciousness of labor as a whole, Perlman implied that the Federation represented all workers.

group may be dysfunctional for others, and ignores the differentiated groups within the American working class.

As the ideology of the American Federation of Labor, voluntarism was subject to currents which influenced other American thought. The founders of the AFL, discontented with the status quo, shared the outlook of American social thinkers at the turn of the century. Here was the same devotion to concrete reality, the same attack on abstract, formal, and metaphysical approaches found in Dewey, Robinson, Holmes, Beard, and others. Morton White, in his *Social Thought in America,* has called attention to the antiformalist character of American social thought in this period.[9] In challenging the conservatism of the late nineteenth century, the new trade unions thus joined the revolt against formalism. When questioned by the Socialist, Morris Hillquit, Gompers acknowledged that the various spheres of social life were interrelated and vigorously denied that the AFL restricted its activity to any one field. Asked whether it had a general social philosophy, Gompers replied,

> It is guided by the history of the past, drawing its lessons from history. It knows the conditions by which working people are surrounded. It works along the line of least resistance and endeavors to accomplish the best results in improving the conditions of the working people, men, women, and children, today and tomorrow. . . .[10]

A claim to realism, based on 'historicism' and 'cultural organicism,' was also the main positive element in the thinkers about whom White writes.[11] Moreover, the similarities between their antiformalism and that of the AFL were not confined to generalities. For example, the legal theory of the revolt against formalism stressed the historical development of the law and rejected the view that the law evolved in accordance with a formal-logical pattern. Legal formalism was used against the trade union, so that Gompers wrote:

> The change that labor aims to effect in the courts is to infuse into legalism ideals, interpretations, and a conscience that are social. Professor Roscoe Pound defines the social formula of justice as an attempt

---

[9] Morton White, *Social Thought in America: The Revolt Against Formalism* (Boston: Beacon Press, 1957), p. 6 et passim. By formalism is meant, here and throughout, abstract ideas which particular groups claim to be in the general interest but actually use to attack action against their own interests.

[10] *The Double Edge of Labor's Sword* (Chicago: Socialist Party, 1914), pp. 122–23.

[11] *Op. cit.,* p. 12.

to secure individual interests because, and to the extent that, they are social.[12]

The antiformalist theory of law recognized the social transformation that was taking place in America. All the writers stressed the primarily economic character of this transformation. Recognizing the limitations on freedom caused by the new economic power, Dewey distinguished between real and formal freedom. Formal freedom was a condition for effective freedom, but there were other conditions, such as the power to achieve one's goal.[13]

By its very existence, of course, the AFL attested to the importance of economic liberty. The antiformalist distinction between real and formal freedom was thus crucial to an organization whose purpose was to fight for real freedom against a dogmatism of formal freedom. In a speech in Chicago in 1908, Gompers said:

> Rights? Yes, there is no hesitancy on the part of our courts to grant us certain rights—for instance, the rights to be maimed or killed without any responsibility to the employer; the right to be discharged for belonging to a union of labor; the right to work as long hours for as low wages as the employer can impose upon working men or women. These rights—these academic rights which we do not want—are frequently conceded, but there is a denial to us of the rights that are essential to our welfare.[14]

This distinction between essential and academic rights, real and formal freedom, is related to the recognition that, as Gompers put it:

> We are not in an ideal world. . . . We are in the bitter struggles of an unjust society. . . . To shift applications of axioms that spring from the principles of abstract liberty to a totally different set of axioms that arise from manifest injustices of a present society—that is the mental juggle of dishonest liberty and property defense leaguers.[15]

John Dewey expressed this thought in a sentence. "No ends are accomplished without the use of force."[16] It would seem that Gompers could accept this formulation. Thus he wrote,

---

[12] Samuel Gompers, "Labor by Law, Not by Discretion," *Federationist*, Vol. 21, January 1913, p. 45. Cf. White, *op. cit.*, p. 17.

[13] White, *op. cit.*, pp. 101–2.

[14] Samuel Gompers, *Labor and the Common Welfare* (New York: E. P. Dutton and Co., 1919), p. 58.

[15] Samuel Gompers, "A Perverted Conception of Rights," *Federationist*, Vol. 20, June 1912, p. 466.

[16] White, *op. cit.*, p. 163.

In a hundred different directions the freedom of the citizen in modern society is restricted in the interests of the general welfare, or of public good, or health and morals. . . .

Professor Seligman's very acute analysis of economic liberty clearly exhibits the truth that we can never enjoy liberty in any absolute sense, that "all social progress is a result of certain repression of the liberty of some in the interests of all." [17]

If this were the only side of Gompers' attitude toward coercion, there would be no ambivalence in the pragmatism of the AFL or in its relation to the revolt against formalism. Voluntarism, however, rejected the antiformalist acceptance of force and opposed all restrictions on liberty. In his last speech to the AFL, Gompers said, "I want to urge devotion to the fundamentals of human liberty—the principles of voluntarism. No lasting gain has ever come from coercion." [18] It is this principled attack on force that differentiated voluntarism from the revolt against formalism. But if voluntarism is to be treated as a theory, its departure from the pragmatism of the period must be explained.

Individualism and the Problem of Coercion

The most obvious revolt of the trade union was against the formalism of individualism.

To say that a working man loses his individualism or his sovereignty in joining a union of labor is begging the question entirely. The fact of the matter is as soon as a man enters an industrial plant he loses his individuality and becomes a cog in a great revolving machine. [19]

It is by sacrificing his theoretical freedom of contract as an individual and by merging himself in an association with his fellows that the wage earner in many trades finally secures improved conditions of living. [20]

The attack on abstract individualism—expressed concretely in the organization of unions—was the essence of the AFL's revolt against formalism. But the creation of groups led to an abstract "group individualism" which destroyed that revolt. Laboring men, revolting against a conservative formalism which had protected the interests of the

---

[17] Samuel Gompers, "Trade Unions and Liberty," *Federationist*, Vol. 12, July 1905, p. 447.

[18] AFL, *Proceedings*, 1924, pp. 5–6.

[19] Gompers, *Labor and the Common Welfare*, p. 58.

[20] Gompers, "Trade Unions," p. 448.

business classes, had built new organizations. But these new organizations had to be legitimized to members, to the public, and had to be protected against attack from without and within. The main function of the ideology of voluntarism was to protect these organizations.

The American Federation of Labor had implicitly taken a formalist text from Rousseau. "The problem," Rousseau had written, "is to find a form of association . . . in which each, while uniting himself with all, may still remain as free as before."[21] According to Dewey, in joining unions workers sacrificed a largely meaningless freedom for a meaningful freedom. But the arguments the Federation presented to defend the closed shop, the boycott, and other union activities indicated that, where union activity and organization were concerned, it departed from Dewey's realistic position. Coercion, it was argued, ceased to be always present and always necessary, and disappeared both from within the union and from a totally organized economy.

In defending union activities, Gompers used the word "freedom" in the same formalist sense that he bitterly attacked when it was used against the trade union. Attempting to legitimize the union against the Spencerian attacks, he accepted the absolutist judicial notions current at the time, and used them to defend the trade union. Thus, in opposing the injunction, the Federation cited the constitutional guarantees of the first amendment. But it cited them as absolute prerogatives, which under no circumstances might be abridged. This "absolute-rights" theory was not supported by the legal realists. Holmes wrote, "No conduct has such absolute privilege as to justify all possible schemes of which it may be a part."[22] Defending the closed shop, Gompers wrote:

> Organized workmen have the right to refuse to work with unorganized workmen. Such a refusal is an exercise of their own right of contract and it cannot therefore be a violation of the right of anyone else. . . . The employers are free—free in a legal or moral sense of course—to choose between the organized and the unorganized. If he [sic] prefers the former for economic reasons, because they are more efficient or productive, the latter have no grievance either against him or against the workmen chosen.[23]

---

[21] Jean-Jacques Rousseau, *Social Contract*, Everyman's Edition (New York: E. P. Dutton Co., 1950), pp. 13–14.

[22] Edwin E. Witte, *The Government in Labor Disputes* (New York: McGraw-Hill, 1932), pp. 59–60.

[23] Samuel Gompers, "Labor and Equal Rights," *Federationist*, Vol. 2, June 1900, p. 165.

It had been the argument of Brandeis, and of the trade union, that the whole problem of coercion existed in the economy because the exercise of one party's 'right of contract' was likely to be a violation of someone else's rights in a world of unequal power. This insight had undermined the classical conception of a free and spontaneous (that is, unregulated) economy. But what Gompers sought to do was simply to raise spontaneous economic action to a higher level. An economy of organized groups would operate without coercion and could, therefore, be unregulated.[24] Politics (that is, the exercise of power) had become necessary because of the existence of and need for groups, but Gompers affirmed "that right is not made wrong, nor wrong right, by mere numbers. What a thousand men may do individually, they may do as a combination."[25] In so defending the boycott, Gompers failed to recognize that the difference between one worker acting and a thousand workers acting as one is that the thousand have more power. Gompers justified their acting by implying that unions were not exercising power; the proper justification is that other power already exists in the society. By defending the abstract, formal freedom to boycott, Gompers ignored the coercive power exercised by boycotting unions. He was thus able to preserve the fiction that coercion was absent in an economy of competing groups. If coercion were absent, state action in the economy would simply substitute force for freedom.

In the arguments it used to defend trade union activities, regardless of their effects, the AFL departed from the main revolt against formalism. Because its defenses of trade union action were philosophic and formalistic, however, it hardly follows that these defenses were impractical. The antithesis of pragmatism in that sense and formalism simply obscure the real issue. In fact, the formalism of the AFL was meant to be useful, but it was useful for the organization.[26]

---

[24] In his autobiography Gompers wrote, "I have often allowed myself to dream of the possibilities of production if all were free to work unretarded by the existing restraints. . . . Foremost in my mind is to tell the politicians to keep their hands off and thus preserve voluntary institutions and opportunities for individual and group initiative. . . . *Seventy Years of Life and Labor*, Vol. 2 (New York: E. P. Dutton and Co., 1925), p. 26. Except for the inclusion of groups, this reproduces the views of Social Darwinists and businessmen of the late nineteenth century.

[25] Samuel Gompers, "Invading Labor's Rights," *Federationist*, Vol. 12, February 1904, p. 129.

[26] At no point in the argument do I mean to imply that the advocacy of voluntarism by the leaders of the AFL was insincere. The argument that voluntarism served organizational functions does not go to the question of whether its

The Internal Uses of Voluntarism

If voluntarism departed from the revolt against formalism because it was an organizational ideology, then it becomes important to understand the organizational interests it served. Voluntarism served functions for the union leaders analogous to the functions served for radicals by Leninism. Both theories subordinated the organizations to the goals of a particular constituency. Thus, within the AFL, voluntarism legitimized the power of the large craft union internationals, and it legitimized the power of the leadership both within the Federation and within the internationals themselves.

Applying the principles of voluntary action to support the freedom of the international unions, the Federation denied to itself the right to intervene in the affairs of its affiliates. Thereby, voluntarism ignored the problems of coercion that existed within the internationals. Many commentators have arged that the Federation was too weak to interfere with its affiliates. Indeed, the policy of nonintervention was based on a recognition of power realities, but according to voluntarism, the policy was directed to the goal of freedom. By converting a power reality into a moral attitude, the Federation implicitly denied that power was a problem at all within the unions. By denying that an unequal distribution of power existed, voluntarism helped perpetuate the existing distribution. An ideology which attacked force was used to justify an existing distribution of force.

Voluntarism not only avoided the problem of internal government, it also contributed more directly to the support of craft union officialdom. In its attack on force, voluntarism expressed the ideal of an organization without internal conflict. Implicitly, force was unnecessary because the unions were homogeneous institutions making up a homogeneous federation in which agreement on ends could be achieved voluntarily. Gompers' farewell speech makes it clear that the ideal of unanimity is associated with an absolute denial of coercion.

"I want to urge devotion to the fundamentals of human liberty —the principles of voluntarism. No lasting gain has ever come from compulsion. If we seek to force we but tear apart that which, united, is invincible. There is no way whereby our labor movement may be assured sustained progress in determining its policies and plans other than sincere democratic deliberation until a unanimous decision is reached." [27]

---

proponents were 'really' motivated by self-interest, organizational interest, concern for the membership, or concern for the whole working class.

[27] AFL, *Proceedings*, 1924, pp. 5–6.

Of course, there was unanimity on few issues in the Federation and compromise, or the imposition of the view of the most powerful, was the actual practice. But by arguing that Federation decisions had unanimous approval (since they adhered to the principles of voluntarism), Gompers made it appear that there were no dissident points of view and no unequal distribution of power behind the expressed decisions of the Federation. He thereby attempted to legitimize the AFL externally as the spokesman for "labor," and internally against potential membership revolts.

Moreover, since unions were homogeneous, internal organization of differing points of view was unnecessary. Thus Gompers attacked a socialist faction in his own cigar-makers' union.

"We must ourselves permit of the free and untrammelled expression of opinion by the members of an organization, and not by a clique formed within the organization to control the business, the legislation, and the election of officers who are to control the affairs of the organization." [28]

The belief in homogeneity of interests, and the resulting attack on actions, served to make the group a concrete reality. By ignoring the problem of differential power in the economy, voluntarism had given the group an appearance of external reality and promoted a theory of group individualism. Similarly, voluntarism ignored the problem of union government. Oblivious to different points of view within the Federation, voluntarism legitimized the most powerful view, that of craft union officialdom. Ignoring the conflict between leaders and members, voluntarism legitimized the leaders as the spokesmen for the group. And if the leadership was the legitimate group spokesman, then those criticizing the leaders became attackers of the union. [29]

Voluntarism, in fact, is a theory of democracy which emerges from the homogeneity of a small group. It finds clear expression in Rousseau.

> But when factions arise, and partial associations are formed at the expense of the great association, the will of each of these associations becomes general in relation to its members, while it remains particular in relation to the state. . . . It is therefore essential, if the general will is to be able to express itself, that there should be no partial society within the state. . . . [30]

---

[28] AFL, *Proceedings*, 1915, p. 442.

[29] See Grant McConnell, "The Spirit of Private Government," *American Political Science Review*, Vol. 52.

[30] Rousseau, p. 27. For an excellent discussion of the relation between size and democratic institutions, see J. David Greenstone, "Local Union Government:

When this theory of democracy is applied within a large and diverse society, as it was in the nineteenth-century French liberals' attack on parties and in Gompers' attack on factions, it helps to perpetuate oligarchy. Operationally, the leaders represent the general will of the group. In the absence of organized centers for opposition to the current 'general will,' changing it, or changing those who represent it, becomes difficult.

Thus voluntarism, by ignoring the problem of power in the name of an abstract defense of freedom, legitimized the existing power distribution and attacked the legitimacy of attempts to change it. And if the power of craft union officialdom was behind the Federation's defense of trade autonomy, this same power led it to take positive action to support the large craft unions and their leaders.

Thus, despite the theory of voluntarism, the Federation interfered with the trade autonomy of the small internationals at the behest of the larger ones. The 1899 resolution on trade autonomy adopted by the AFL convention declared that the Federation was founded on the principle of the absolute self-government of all the crafts and guaranteed the weaker crafts the same protection as the stronger.[31] This was the theory, but it was not the organizational reality. In jurisdictional disputes between large and small crafts, not only did the Federation often use the theory of voluntarism to refuse to intervene to help the smaller crafts, but it also often intervened to help the larger craft unions. The Mule Spinners, for example, argued that to be forced by the Federation to amalgamate with the Textile Workers violated their trade autonomy. This argument, theoretically impeccable, did not stop their forced amalgamation.[32] Coercion was used against those elements whose antagonism was least likely to hurt the AFL.

In the area of internal union affairs, in spite of its professions of noninterference within the internationals, the Federation sided with the established leadership against rank-and-file revolts. Regardless of the conditions, no factions which had seceded or had been expelled from international unions were recognized. Nor did the Federation ever go so far as to appoint investigating committees. When President

---

Social and Political Determinants." Unpublished Master's thesis, University of Chicago, Department of Political Science, 1960, pp. 3–25.

[31] AFL, *Proceedings*, 1899, p. 136.

[32] AFL, *Proceedings*, 1919, p. 147. Compare Federation acceptance of the Building Trades' Council, under pressure from the strong building unions, in spite of early opposition to this partial association within the Federation (AFL, *Proceedings*, 1901, p. 184; 1903, pp. 212–13, 221; 1904, pp. 266–67). These are only two of many examples.

Berry of the Printing Pressmen entered the 1923 AFL convention after having suppressed an insurgent strike with some of the most unsavory techniques in labor movement history, he was greeted by Gompers as a savior of the labor movement.[33]

Selig Perlman has contrasted the "vanguard" attitudes resulting from the abstract approach of intellectuals to the working class with the pragmatic manualism of trade union consciousness.[34] It appears from the analysis here that voluntarism concealed a "vanguard" approach to the labor movement by trade union leaders.

The Opposition to Social Legislation

From the early years of the Federation, voluntarism was applied within the Federation in the ways suggested above. In the years before the first World War, however, a socialist opposition kept internal discussion alive and provided a challenge to the leadership. Therefore, during this time, the constraining effects of voluntarism on internal democracy were limited. In the 1920's, there was little or no opposition within the Federation and voluntarism became the unchallenged practice of the organization. And though voluntarism became more dominant within the Federation, its application to internal government did not change. Internally, voluntarism always defended the freedom of trade union leaders.

Externally, however, the meaning of voluntarism changed radically, as the position of the AFL changed in relation to the external world. In the beginning, voluntarism emphasized what the workers could obtain, unaided, through their own organizations. Abstractions which interfered with action and the practical solution of problems were attacked. Describing his early experience Gompers wrote, "My mind intuitively rejected the iron law of wages, the immutable law of supply and demand, and similar so-called natural laws. . . . My unfailing support of voluntary principles reflects my aversion to any theory of economic fatalism."[35]

The AFL's de-emphasis of politics was based on this activist view of what voluntarism meant. "Why wait for the slow process of law," asked Vice-President Duncan, "when we can exert a sure and certain economic power?"[36] Despite such views, the AFL neither emphasized politics nor withdrew completely from political activity. In

---

[33] Sylvia Kopald, *Rebellion in Labor Unions* (New York: Boni and Liveright, 1923), p. 234.

[34] Perlman, pp. 285–95, et passim.

[35] Gompers, *Seventy Years*, Vol. 2, p. 1.

[36] AFL, *Proceedings*, 1902, p. 182.

its very earliest years, the Federation engaged in lobbying and had an extensive political program. From approximately 1899 to 1904, while the AFL was growing rapidly, it became more and more opposed to political activity. Increasing employer and state opposition, however, forced it into a greater emphasis on political action until 1914, when the Clayton Act was passed. Despite this clouded victory, until the New Deal the Federation was to hold the most extreme antistate position in its history.

World War I experience hastened the development of this position. In 1914 the Federation had already opposed eight-hour laws, and antistate articles began to appear frequently in the *Federationist*. While World War I brought AFL leaders into participation in government, more significantly, Federation officials had the experience of participation with management. To Federation leaders, the war experience taught the value not of government action but of union cooperation with industry. Before the war, Gompers had denied that there was a harmony of interests between labor and capital. After the war he asserted that this harmony existed.[37] Their aggravated anxiety to win a place as the partners of industry made the Federation leaders even more opposed to state interference than they had been before the war.

At its inception, the AFL had asserted the power of workers to change their conditions through legislation as well as through union action. It therefore favored public works, nationalization of the telegraph, and other positive state action. But as the Federation grew, these positive proposals were either explicitly repudiated or ignored. Arguing that the economy must be let alone so that the free institutions within it could operate without restriction, the Federation opposed wage-and-hour laws and unemployment insurance. Its main political efforts were directed to getting the state out of labor affairs, through the removal of such restrictions as the injunction and the application of the anti-trust laws to labor.[38]

---

[37] In 1914 Gompers said, "I say they are not. . . . I know of no means by which the interests of the employers and the workingmen can be made harmonious in the full and broad sense of the term" (*Double Edge of Labor's Sword*, pp. 132, 138). In 1924 he wrote, "Labor, as such, may have interests that seem to clash with the interests of other factors in industry, but as a part of the great world of industry, labor, management, science, all share in the responsibility for the productivity and general well-being of industry. . . ." ("Politicians' Economic Ignorance," *Federationist*, Vol. 32, September 1924, p. 745). It is no accident that this sentiment appeared in an article attacking politicians.

[38] The Federation also favored certain positive legislation, but only to help those groups that were not perceived as able to help themselves. These groups were primarily women, children, and federal employees.

In the history of the Federation, then, the original meaning of voluntarism became completely altered. At first, voluntarism stressed the power of free labor unions to obtain their goals. Thirty years later, in the name of freedom, it denied to unions the right to act politically. Opposing action in support of social insurance, Gompers explained,

> Sore and sad as I am by the illness, the killing, the maiming of so many of my fellow workers, I would rather see that go on for years and years, minimized and mitigated by the organized labor movement, than give up one jot of the freedom of the workers to strive and struggle for their own emancipation through their own efforts.[39]

In the areas of collective bargaining and union organization, the AFL also became less activist. Federation spokesmen justified their new emphasis on labor-management cooperation with the argument that cooperation was superior to force. The result was dismal organizing campaigns which tried to convince management rather than the workers of the virtues of unionism. Voluntarism had come to mean cooperation instead of self-help. Not self-help but management-help was the alternative to self-help through politics.

Voluntarism thus changed its meaning as the Federation became an established organization. In the early period the young organization, heir to a reform-oriented labor tradition whose legitimacy the AFL hoped to claim for itself, found it inconvenient to oppose all state action. Moreover, while the Federation was fighting for an end to the labor injunction through legislation, it was oriented toward politics, and was more interested in an alliance with politically minded unionists and reformers than in an attack on positive state action. While the anti-state applications of voluntarism were already visible before 1914,[40] with the passage of the Clayton Act in that year, which established the AFL's social legitimacy, antistate voluntarism became dominant.

In the years following the passage of the Clayton Act the most striking application of antistate voluntarism was the Federation's opposition to social legislation favored by most other reformers.

Throughout its pre-New Deal history, the AFL opposed unemployment insurance and minimum-wage laws for men. Though before

---

[39] Samuel Gompers, "Voluntary Social Insurance vs. Compulsory," *Federationist*, Vol. 24, May 1916, p. 333.

[40] Thus the Federation at first opposed old-age pensions with voluntarist arguments, although in the wake of progressive and socialist agitation it eventually went on record in support of old-age pensions, AFL, *Proceedings*, 1902, pp. 134–40; 1903, p. 115; 1904, p. 201; 1905, p. 179; 1906, p. 233; 1907, p. 218; 1908, pp. 99–102; 1909, p. 198.

the turn of the century it had gone on record in favor of laws regulating hours, in 1914 it 'reaffirmed' its opposition to such laws.[41] Here again the difference between the AFL and the progressive movement of the period requires explanation.

The basis of AFL opposition to social legislation was the craft union leader's conception of his union's self-interest. James Duncan, president of the Stone Cutters and a vice-president of the Federation, made this clear in the debate on the hours' resolution at the 1914 convention.

> There are many trades working in this Federation whose men are working less than eight hours at the present time. In a number of localities our trade, looking for a new contract, has it state, "For a shorter workday." They have seven and one-half hours and they will get down to seven, and we hope through our trade union activities to get down to six-hour law by and by. If you have an eight-hour law you will see the handicap we will have in arguing with our employers for seven and seven and one-half hours a day.[42]

This was the antiformalism of an established craft, fearful of the harmful effects of a law for which, as an organization, it had no need. But it was precisely the pragmatic argument of Duncan that could not suffice in an organization which claimed to represent not only the powerful craft unions but also the unorganized workers. What was practical for Duncan was erected in his defense into a formalism that was not practical for the great majority of workers.

Many craft workers did not need to favor wage-and-hour legislation because they could obtain the benefits through their organizations. Here the interests of the class-based craft membership predominated. The unions, however, were powerless to provide other benefits such as unemployment insurance.[43] Here concern for organizational maintenance was crucial. The original attack on the antilabor character of the existing state was generalized to a fear of any positive state action. Large-scale political action might create institutions such as political parties or autonomous political action committees which would compete with the unions for the workers' loyalties. Large programs of state aid might turn workers' devotion away from the union and

---

[41] AFL, *Proceedings*, 1894, p. 46; 1899, p. 107; 1910, p. 421.

[42] AFL, *Proceedings*, 1914, p. 437.

[43] The evidence for this is provided in Abraham Epstein, *Insecurity: A Challenge to America* (New York: Harrison Smith and Robert Haas, 1937), pp. 248–49, et passim. It is true that some unions had benefit programs, but these were totally inadequate to meet the needs of the membership in a severe depression.

toward the state.[44] With these fears, the craft union officials were not willing to expend the resources involved in supporting large-scale political and state action.

Antiunion activities by an antilabor state also contributed to the AFL's opposition to social legislation. But these activities should not obscure the antistate posture deriving from the Federation's position as an established organization. In this respect, the Federation paralleled the laissez-faire capitalists against whom it had organized.

The Federation opposed social legislation for reasons which it perceived as pragmatic. But it was pure formalism, and not pragmatism, to insist that the voluntary association of the workers could be relied upon to provide such benefits as unemployment insurance. In fact, the AFL used ideological arguments to oppose practical reforms to ameliorate the condition of the workers. This is a far cry from the pragmatism claimed for it by Gompers and Perlman.

Gompers opposed a New York minimum-wage law for women on the ground that it was "a curb upon the natural rights and opportunity for development of the women of our country and of the industry."[45] In contrast, when the Federation was supporting hours' legislation for women in 1910, John Mitchell had ridiculed a similar argument:

> The very ground upon which this woman made her complaint— namely that she could not earn enough money in ten hours to maintain herself—renders ridiculous and absurd her plea that her liberty had been abridged.[46]

Gompers also attacked the Socialists for substituting ultimate goals for immediate demands:

> The workers have chosen as a policy or pragmatic philosophy . . . immediate and continuous improvement instead of waiting for that

---

[44] On this last point a statement by John Frey opposing unemployment insurance is revealing. "If you feed lions cooked meat, they are not going to roar. If you want the lions to roar you will have to hold raw meat under their noses, and then they will roar. The only way to get wage-earners interested in the trade union movement and make it a driving force is to convince them that . . . it is only through the strength, the fighting strength of that economic organization that you are going to get higher wages and shorter hours." AFL *Proceedings*, 1932, p. 342. Frey was one of the two or three most powerful men in the post-Gompers AFL.

[45] *Double Edge*, p. 100. This is a socialist pamphlet, but the words are Gompers'.

[46] John Mitchell, "The Workingman's Conception of Industrial Liberty," *Federationist*, Vol. 18, May 1910, p. 407.

far-off period when all the universe shall ring with the rare sweet harmony of perfect accord.[47]

But he also attacked compulsory health insurance:

It is a mere palliative, for economic justice, when established, will bring the relief sought for, and in greater measure, if obtained by the workers through organization, and this can only be done through freedom of action.[48]

Gompers often attacked the Socialists for being concerned with the prevention of evil to the exclusion of amelioration of evil. But in opposing unemployment insurance in 1931, the Executive Council of the Federation explained, "There are just two approaches to this problem: prevention and relief." [49]

This is not the place to recount the struggles in the Federation over social legislation. But this summary of its position and arguments suggests that voluntarism was not simply a pragmatic response of American workers to their situation. Rather it was a formalism which, in the name of abstract ideology, interfered with the workers' practical solutions to their immediate problems. The Federation's abstract notions of natural rights and freedom were pragmatic, not in content but in function, and not in general but for a particular constituency. While in some areas organizational needs corresponded to broad constituency needs, in the area of social legislation the two conflicted.

Moreover, in continuing to adhere to voluntarism after the 1930's depression began, the leadership interfered with organizational interests. True to voluntarism, Federation spokesmen continued their abstract and moral preaching against social legislation and by so doing probably aided the formation of the CIO. Official adherence to the philosophy of voluntarism even into the depression is explainable less by the realism of the Federation's leaders than by their commitment to a rigid philosophy which interfered with practical action in their own interest.

Voluntarism and Local Politics

I have argued that the AFL's opposition to social legislation was perpetuated more by organizational and craft worker concerns than by the antistate feeling of American workers as a whole. This is further supported by an analysis of the role of voluntarism in sustaining local labor political alliances.

---

[47] Gompers, "Robert Hunter's New Dilemma," p. 355.
[48] Quoted in Taft's history, Vol. 1, p. 365.
[49] AFL, *Proceedings*, 1931, p. 142.

Defending Perlman's *Theory*, Philip Taft has written of "its insistence that an understanding of labor and unionism must come from
a study of its institutions and practices rather than from theorizing
about historical missions."[50] The insistence of the *Theory* that the
AFL survived, "mainly because it knew how to resist the lure of politics,"[51] and the acceptance of the Federation's claim to nonpartisan
politics at face value, however, have led historians largely to ignore
the significant local political area of labor's "institutions and practices."

The dominance of the Perlman theory, even among political
scientists concerned with the labor movement, has meant that little
material is available on the actions of craft unions in city politics.
Nevertheless, an examination of the material that is available on New
York, Chicago, Philadelphia, and Detroit indicates that, far from resist-
ing politics, many locals were actively connected with city machines.[52]

In the name of voluntarism, the Federation opposed not only
city machines but all forms of party loyalty.

> The American Federation of Labor has often declared and often
> emphasized that as our efforts are centered against all forms of indus-
> trial slavery and economic wrong, we must also direct our utmost ener-
> gies to remove all forms of political servitude and party slavery. . . .[53]

Yet, when the Socialist J. Mahlon Barnes introduced a resolution "that an organizer's commission shall not be granted to an employer of labor or to any person who occupies a public office, either
elective or appointive, under a political party," the AFL convention
defeated it.[54]

While the craft unions were not generally interested in national
legislation, they were very much involved with politics on the local
level. Local unions were concerned with codes, licensing and appren-

---

[50] Taft, "Theories of the Labor Movement," p. 31.

[51] Perlman, p. 219.

[52] A partial list of such material follows: Henry John Gibbons, "The Labor
Vote in Philadelphia's Political Upheaval," *Charities and the Commons*, Vol. 15,
Feb. 5, 1906; Lawrence Rogin, "Central Labor Bodies and Independent Political
Action in New York City: 1918–1922," (Unpublished Master's thesis, Columbia
University, Department of Political Science, 1931); Stephen V. and Vera H.
Sarasohn, *Political Party Patterns in Michigan* (Detroit: Wayne State University
Press, 1957); Harold Seidman, *Labor Czars* (New York: Liveright Publishing Co.,
1938).

[53] AFL, *Proceedings*, 1906, p. 32.

[54] The committee which reported this resolution favored its passage, true
to the principles of voluntarism. AFL, *Proceedings*, 1902, p. 154.

ticeship laws, and other legislation; political appointments to inspectors' jobs and to other jobs less directly connected with union welfare; political pull for obtaining contracts, help in strikes, and the like; and often their share of political graft. The common theme was jobs for members; this required involvement in politics. Far from being anti-political, many locals were intimately concerned with politics; yet they gave lip-service to the antipolitical theory of voluntarism.

These local political unionists, connected with Republican machines in Republican cities like Detroit and Philadelphia and with Democratic machines in Democratic cities like New York, supported voluntarism because it did not challenge their power. First, voluntarism required no commitment on political issues that might upset a local alliance. Of equal or greater importance, both the doctrine of voluntarism and local union officials opposed independent political action, the former because it was political, the latter because it was independent. To local unionists a national policy of nonpartisanship meant they could be Democratic in Democratic cities and Republican in Republican cities.

Consequently, a large part of the constituency of the AFL was not opposed to politics as such, but only to national politics. At the same time the local political alliances contradicted voluntarism, voluntarism protected them. Research thus far suggests that voluntarism received its prime support, not from forces that were antistate out of some pragmatic manualism, or out of antistate experience, but from forces that were very willing to use the state for their purposes, and indeed used it often.

It is arguable that a coalition of forces that were not antipolitical united behind Gompers' antipolitical philosophy because it happened to serve their interests. The use of voluntarism as an internal weapon in the fight against the Socialists also lends support to this interpretation. Voluntarism legitimized the fight for power by giving it philosophic justification. The research of Marc Karson into the role of Catholics in fighting the Socialists in the AFL is also relevant.[55] These Catholics were not antistate at all. The more progressive like Father John Ryan, supported social legislation, and the bulk of active Catholic trade unionists were probably involved in local politics. But the Catholics supported Gompers, and voluntarism, as alternatives to the Socialists.

---

[55] Marc Karson, *American Labor Unions and Politics* (Carbondale, Ill.: Southern Illinois University Press, 1958), pp. 212–84.

Conclusion

Voluntarism, then, claimed to be a pragmatic philosophy which based itself on freedom and on the experience of all American workers. In fact it was an abstract philosophy, which received its prime support from a constituency whose experience and interests were significantly different from that of American workers as a whole.

Internally, voluntarism meant that the leaders were free to coerce the union membership. Externally, voluntarism protected the freedom of the craft union to bargain for a seven-hour day while the unorganized workers were forced to work far longer. Externally, voluntarism also kept the leaders free from having to press for unemployment insurance while the unemployed were forced to exist—where they could—on the dole. Finally, voluntarism kept city locals free—not free from politics, but free to form political alliances with city machines. If I have stressed the conflict of these organizational needs with broader constituency needs, this has been only to question the Perlman tradition. At times, organizational needs served constituency needs. Voluntarism, however, was above all an organizational ideology, serving organizational needs.

Chapter 5

Challenges to Voluntarism

BOTH WITHIN AND OUT OF THE AFL there were critics of Samuel Gompers' concept of voluntarism.

The first reading in this chapter, by Gerald Grob, deals with two of these challenges to Gompers' policy. The first consisted of agitation to have the AFL endorse the People's party—the so-called Populists— in the late nineteenth century. The second, and by far the more important challenge to AFL nonpartisanship, was the pressure to turn the Federation into a vehicle for the promulgation of socialism.

Formally launched in 1892, primarily as a vehicle for agrarian protest, the People's party made numerous overtures to the working-man. The party platform stressed the identical interests of the farmer and urban worker and, in an attempt to gain labor support, included planks endorsing a shorter work week and restriction of immigration. Although not unsympathetic to the Populists, Gompers nevertheless argued that an alliance between an organization composed of wage earners and a predominantly agrarian political organization was "unnatural," inasmuch as many of the Populist farmers were themselves employers. His view finally prevailed.

While the AFL at the national level avoided any endorsement of the Populists, at the state and local levels an effort was made by the socialists to forge a farmer-labor alliance. These attempts, centered primarily in the Mid-West, ultimately failed because of the inherent conflict between the socialists, who wanted to eliminate capitalism, and the Populists, who desired merely to reform it.

From the first years of its existence, as Grob points out, socialists within the AFL had been urging the Federation to endorse collective ownership and to engage in independent political action to achieve this end. Gompers' attack upon the socialists, and the consequent defection of some of their number from Federation ranks, is detailed in the reading.

Interest in Marxian socialism had developed in the United States soon after the Civil War. The two most important organizations espousing it during the late nineteenth and early twentieth centuries were the Socialist Labor Party and the Socialist Party of America. The SLP grew out of the Workingmen's Party of the United States, established in the post-Civil War period, and was composed largely of the foreign-born. It was more doctrinaire than was the Socialist Party of America, particularly after Daniel DeLeon, a fiery, brilliant, and dogmatic ex-college professor, became its head. The SLP's inflexibility was, in fact, a major factor contributing to the establishment of the Socialist Party of America in 1901. The latter organization was composed primarily of the native-born and espoused a far more moderate, long-range program than did the SLP. The Socialist party's leader, Eugene Debs, earlier had headed the American Railway Union, an industrial union patterned after the Knights of Labor and open to all white skilled and unskilled railroad employees. The ARU met disaster as a result of its defeat in the 1894 Pullman Strike and, soon thereafter, Debs transformed what was left of his union into a vehicle to spread socialist doctrine.

Members of both socialist parties had a hand in the creation, in 1905, of the Industrial Workers of the World, which was specifically established to challenge what its creators termed "the American Separation of Labor." The new organization, soon nicknamed "the Wobblies," is described in the selection by Henry Pelling. It was intended to be One Big Union, open to all skilled and unskilled workers, regardless of craft, religion or race. It never lived up to these hopes. The IWW pronouncement that the "working class and the employing class have nothing in common" smacked too much of class warfare and was too revolutionary a view for the average American worker. Its initial successes were in the West, among the migrant workers in the fields, logging camps, and mines. By 1912 it had also penetrated the eastern textile mills, appealing particularly to the immigrant factory worker.

The IWW strongly favored action on the job rather than at the ballot box. Political action had no meaning for a large portion of its members—women, migrants, aliens, southern Negroes—who were unable to vote. The organization also questioned the value of reforms gained through "the capitalist state" which, it held, looked after employer interests alone.

The Wobblies were often harassed and at best merely tolerated before World War I. The IWW's denunciation of the war as a capitalist plot, coupled with its reputed penchant for violence and sabotage, immediately branded it as disloyal and un-American. The organization's headquarters were raided; its leaders arrested en masse. The remnants that survived that onslaught were virtually destroyed during the post-war "Red Scare."

The Communist Party of America, the subject of the reading by Max Kampelman, was also spawned from the ranks of the socialists.

Its impetus came from the successful Bolshevik revolution of 1917. As Kampelman points out, the Party see-sawed in its attitude vis-a-vis the American trade unions, advocating a policy of "dual unionism" until 1921, and "boring from within" for the eight years that followed. As will be noted from the reading on the political left in Chapter 6, this vacillation continued in the years following the Depression: the policy of dual unionism reinitiated in 1928 was again abandoned in 1935 in favor of Communists working within existing unions. These shifts in Communist party line reflected decisions made in Russia, which had little reference to the conditions in this country, thus further weakening the effectiveness of a movement already highly suspect as being outside the mainstream of American political thought.

In the last reading in this chapter Foster Rhea Dulles describes labor's endorsement of Robert La Follette in 1924, prompted by the renewed hostility of government and courts toward unions following a honeymoon period during World War I. Although La Follette received the AFL's highly qualified endorsement, a number of the Federation leaders refused to support it.

As Eric Goldman succinctly describes it:

> In the election of 1924 the AFL flabbergasted thousands of progressives by acting like the AFL. Both the Republican and Democratic conventions had ignored labor so contemptuously that rank-and-file resentment ran high and the AFL executive committee endorsed the La Follette ticket. Before the week was out, headquarters began hearing from local AFL chiefs, who saw their carefully constructed arrangements with Democratic or Republican political machines endangered. Bit by bit Gompers whittled away the force of the endorsement until at election day AFL support amounted to little more than the Gompers' statement that "Bob La Follette is a great American."[1]

Gompers' inability to provide any real labor support for the unsuccessful La Follette campaign is a concrete demonstration of the hold which voluntarism had taken on the AFL. In a sense, by endorsing La Follette, Gompers was challenging his own policy. It is, perhaps, a tribute to his earlier efforts that he was no more successful than were any of the other pre-Depression challengers of voluntarism.

---

[1] *Rendezvous with Destiny*, rev. ed., New York: Vintage Books, 1956, p. 228.

Populists and Socialists

Gerald N. Grob

Clark University

GOMPERS' NEUTRALIST POLICY . . . was undercut in 1893 by an economic depression that renewed the labor movement's dream of concluding the illusive farmer-labor alliance. [Carnegie Steel's Henry Clay] Frick's victory over the Amalgamated Association of Iron and Steel Workers during the Homestead strike and the other disastrous defeats suffered by the Tennessee and Coeur d'Alene miners further disillusioned many workers with purely economic activity and turned them once more toward the political arena. Even the AF of L wavered in its support of pure and simple trade unionism and in 1893 adopted a resolution instructing its Executive Council to do everything possible "to effect and perfect an alliance between the trade and labor unions and the farmers' organizations to the end that the best interests of all may be served." The socialist delegates supported the proposed alliance because of the partial collectivism endorsed by the convention of the People's party at Omaha in 1892.

After the Omaha Populist meeting, however, the western rural Populists began to retreat from the radicalism of their platform. Expressing distrust of eastern urban radicals seeking to socialize the party, they turned to the free silver issue in the hope of attracting dissident Democrats and Republicans to the new party, as well as removing the stigma of extremism by supporting a historically-respectable program of monetary inflation. By placing more and more emphasis on the demand for the free and unlimited coinage of silver at a sixteen to one ratio with gold, the conservative faction within the People's party succeeded in playing down the more collectivistic planks of the Omaha platform.

Between 1893 and 1896 a fierce struggle ensued for control of the People's party. Socialists and unionists disillusioned with the apparent failure of trade unionism united on a semi-collectivist platform. Rural and western Populists, on the other hand, fought off left-wing attempts to socialize their organization, and in 1896 they succeeded in uniting with the silver Democrats behind Bryan on a free silver platform. Bitterly disillusioned with the fruits of their endeavors, the socialists either deserted or else gave only token support to the People's party during the campaign of 1896.

Excerpted by permission of the publisher from *Workers and Utopia*, © 1961, Northwestern University Press. Footnotes in the original have been deleted.

Meanwhile, the AF of L had endorsed free silver in 1893, but ensuing developments were to demonstrate that the proposed farmer-labor alliance had again failed. As the Populists continued to place more and more emphasis on the silver issue to the exclusion of all others, Gompers and his associates became less and less friendly toward the People's party. To these unionists, free silver was an unrealistic panacea that hurt the labor movement by diverting attention from more important problems. "If asked in regard to the matter [of free silver]," Gompers remarked, "I simply place my index finger upon . . . [the resolution adopted by the AF of L] and say not a word. . . . I believe that there are other and more important subjects which affect our wage earners more directly, more intensely, to which they should give their undivided attention. These middle class issues simply divert attention from their true interests."

In the face of the mounting discontent resulting from the economic depression, however, the leaders of the AF of L could do little except engage in a holding action and ward off attempts to commit their organization to a particular candidate or party. While accepting the convention's endorsement of free silver as official policy, they worked furiously to restrain the labor movement from becoming immersed in a single issue to the exclusion of bona fide trade-union activity. During the campaign of 1896, despite continued pressure, Gompers refused to come out in support of either Bryan or McKinley. "Since both of them are blessed with the same Christian name," he facetiously commented, "I cannot be charged with being partisan if I shout to you, 'Hurrah for William!' " In a circular issued on June 27, 1896, Gompers warned affiliated organizations against the dangers of engaging in partisan politics, and he pointed to the disastrous experiences of the National Labor Union. Consistently maintaining that the campaign, with its emphasis on the silver issue, was a dangerous digression, Gompers did everything within his power to prevent it from intruding on the legitimate work of the trade unions.

While Gompers succeeded in preventing the AF of L from making any commitment during the campaign, many prominent labor leaders and not a few unions came out in open support of Bryan. Although he emphasized the silver issue, Bryan enjoyed strength in labor circles because of the other planks in his platform, notably the endorsement of an income tax and the expressed opposition to government by injunction. In the end, however, Gompers' views prevailed. He recognized that the AF of L could not affect the course of the election. This being the situation, much could be lost by pledging labor's support in advance of the election results. Moreover, the silver issue, Gompers argued, was an unrealistic panacea and a detraction; and after the election he expressed his hope that the workers would return to their legitimate business after sobering down "from the political inebriety." Cognizant of the fact that the older antimonopolism and reformism had little in common with the new unionism, Gompers had clearly foreseen the incompatibility of a labor-farmer alliance based on the silver issue. After the campaign of 1896 had passed into history, the Federation resumed its efforts to strengthen the labor movement, and it succeeded in increasing its membership sixfold between 1897 and 1904.

The vision of an irresistible farmer-labor coalition, however, was not the only threat to the young trade-union movement during the 1890's. A much more serious challenge came from the socialists, who denied that trade unionism was an end in itself. While accepting unionism as historically correct and necessary, the socialists insisted that purely economic action was futile. Instead, they demanded the unification of economic and political action behind a socialist platform and the repudiation of established political parties as well as all reformist fads.

While socialist resolutions endorsing collectivism and independent political action were introduced regularly at the annual conventions of the AF of L, they were either defeated or else passed and almost as quickly forgotten (as in 1886). Nevertheless, the socialists played an important role in the Federation through their control of some unions and their representation in others. Adopting the policy of "boring from within," they sought to convert the labor movement to socialism by capturing control of the AF of L and its affiliates.

Between 1886 and 1890 the socialists, although critical of some AF of L policies, continued to view that organization as the best hope of uniting the workers behind a socialist program. The official organ of the Socialist Labor party, for example, while condemning the Federation's emphasis on the eight-hour movement and the lack of a radical political program, often commended it for its organizational work, and on occasion even spoke well of Gompers. Thus the lack of complete unity and agreement between trade unionists and socialists did not appear to be a barrier to effective cooperation between the two groups.

Yet in reality there were unbridgeable differences between the economic program of the trade unionists and the political emphasis of the socialists. But so long as the AF of L did not come out in unequivocal opposition to collectivistic ideas, the socialists were content to bide their time and continue their efforts to seize control and convert the Federation to a radical program. Sooner or later, however, the fundamental differences between the two groups were bound to make themselves felt. What the final results would be few ventured to predict.

The first major clash between the trade unionists and socialists, which came at the Detroit convention of the AF of L in 1890, grew out of a somewhat complicated situation in New York City. There the Central Labor Union had come under the domination of the Knights of Labor. A number of affiliated AF of L unions withdrew in February 1889, and organized the Central Labor Federation. When the new body applied to the AF of L for a charter, the Executive Council voted in June 1889, to grant the request. In the interest of harmony, the Central Labor Federation attempted to effect a reconciliation with the Central Labor Union. Between December 1889, and June 1890, a temporary union was effected, and the Central Labor Federation returned its charter to Gompers. But in June 1890, the *rapprochement* between the two New York organizations broke down, and Ernest Bohm, secretary of the Central Labor Federation, asked Gompers to return the charter. In refusing, Gompers replied that the Central Labor Federation had ceased to exist.

Controversy developed when the Central Labor Federation reapplied for a charter. Noting that the American section of the Socialist Labor party held membership in Bohm's organization, Gompers refused to grant the request. "I cannot bring myself to understand," he wrote to Bohm, "how a political Party as such can be represented in a central trade organization. Of the merits or demerits of the 'Socialistic Labor Party' it is not within my province to discuss but the representation of that party or any other political party in a purely trade union central organization is to my mind not permissible."

A bitter controversy followed, and partisans of the Socialist Labor party bitterly denounced the AF of L's president. "It seems to me," Gompers complained to Bohm, "that men in the labor movement can honestly differ with each other without finding it necessary to indulge in abuse and I cannot for the life of me understand why an expression of opinion should call forth the spleen manifested by you in your official journals, and which was given out officially by you for publication in the public press." Gompers then decided to refer the matter to the AF of L convention in December.

When the convention met in Detroit, Lucien Sanial was present to plead the socialist case. Denying that the Socialist Labor party was an ordinary political party in the accepted sense of the word, Sanial asserted that it was a working-class party whose unionizing activities predated the founding of the AF of L. "The Central Labor Federation," he continued, "has merely seen fit to declare—by the admission of the delegates of the American Section of the SLP, and by sending to this Convention, as its representative, one of those very delegates—its right to take independent political action with this economic labor party, which the members of its constituting organizations own and control; and in taking this step, deliberately and unflinchingly, it has at the same time virtually announced that the time is coming when Organized Labor in all parts of the country must and will recognize the absolute necessity of taking independent political action."

In opposition to Sanial, Gompers expressed his hostility to having a political party represented in a purely trade-union organization. Denying that he was attempting to drive the socialists out of the labor movement, Gompers affirmed his willingness to surrender his post to further the cause of organized labor. "But I can not and will not," he proclaimed, "prove false to my convictions that the trade unions pure and simple are the natural organizations of the wage-workers to secure their present material and practical improvement and to achieve their final emancipation.

For the better part of two days the delegates discussed the relative merits of the case. The defenders of the socialist cause, while generally conceding that the Socialist Labor party had made a tactical error in trying to graft itself onto the AF of L, felt that the Federation would make an even greater error in excluding Sanial. The trade unionists, however, continued to reiterate their opposition to the Socialist Labor party. "We do not refuse to recognize the Socialist Labor party as an integral part of the labor movement," Frank K. Foster stated as he summed up the position of the unionists. "We simply decline to permit it, as a *political organization*, to engraft itself and its methods upon the organizations we represent upon this floor. We do not disdain the proferred hand of fraternity, or the propaganda of principles upon which we are mutually agreed; but we do decline the admission of any organization or representation having for its object a political movement."

In the end the convention, by the emphatic vote of 1,574 to 496, decided to exclude Sanial. While denying that the hopes and aspirations of the trade unions and socialists differed markedly, the delegates refused to permit partisan politics to intrude into a purely trade federation because they feared that the admission of the Socialist Labor party delegate would inevitably open the gates to other political bodies, to the ultimate detriment of the labor movement.

Furious at its defeat, the Socialist Labor party renewed its attack upon Gompers. "Gompers' 'policy'—if such may be called the intricate web of an unprincipled and egotistic schemer, pandering to ignorance for the sake of position—can deceive no one whose sense of right is not blunted by corruption or obscured by prejudice," proclaimed the *Workmen's Advocate*. Deciding to write off the AF of L, the Socialist Labor party now embarked upon a campaign to win control of the dissension-ridden Knights of Labor. Party leadership was quickly assumed by Daniel DeLeon, a recent convert to orthodox Marxism. From a Columbia University lectureship in Latin American Diplomacy, DeLeon had initially become a devotee of Edward Bellamy's Nationalist movement and had then abandoned its utopianism for a more "scientific" socialism. More than any other man, DeLeon succeeded in fragmentizing the American socialist movement and completely alienating the young trade-union movement.

An individual of immense erudition, rare ability, and tremendous energy, DeLeon was fanatically devoted to the socialist cause. Morris Hillquit, an unfriendly but perceptive critic, commented that DeLeon "never admitted a doubt about the soundness of his interpretation of the Socialist philosophy or the infallibility of his methods and tactics. Those who agreed with him were good Socialists. All who dissented from his views were enemies of the movement. He never compromised or temporized outside or inside the Socialist movement." DeLeon, concluded Hillquit, "was the perfect American prototype of Russian Bolshevism."

To DeLeon the only sound remedy was the overthrow of an incorrigible capitalism by a revolutionary socialist movement. Attacking the trade union's emphasis on "bread and butter" policies, he charged that labor leaders had been bought off by the capitalists for the sake of small increases in wages. The correct policy, DeLeon argued, was a labor movement organized along industrial lines and affiliated with the Socialist Labor party. The test of any union policy was: "DOES THE CONTEMPLATED STEP SQUARE WITH THE ULTIMATE AIM [of overthrowing capitalism]?"

While DeLeon was emerging as the champion of a militant and dogmatic Socialist Labor party, Gompers was coming to the forefront of the trade-union movement and almost as quickly assumed the leadership in the struggle against the socialists. Gompers' conversion to an antisocialist position was a crucial event in the history of the American labor movement, and provides an excellent illustration of the process whereby many American labor leaders who began their careers as socialists could end up not only as staunch trade unionists, but also as vigorous opponents of socialism. Gompers, together with [Peter J.] McGuire and other union leaders, played vital roles in isolating the socialists from the working class.

Familiar with the writings of socialist theoreticians, Gompers had taken part in the furious conflicts of the 1870's between Marxism, then identical with a class-conscious trade unionism, and Lassalleanism, with its emphasis on political action. Throughout the 1880's Gompers continued to express friendliness toward socialist goals, but his preoccupation with the daily problems of the unions tended to relegate ultimate objectives into the background. His initial disillusioning experience with socialism came in the early 1880's, when the socialists in the Cigar Makers International Union refused to support a member of the New York legislature who had led the fight for the abolition of tenement-house cigar manufacturing. In that episode, the socialists heaped vitriolic criticism upon Gompers and [Adolf] Strasser for abandoning ultimate reform for immediate advantages. In testifying before a Senate committee in 1883, Gompers showed the marks of the fight. "Whatever ideas we may have as to the future state of society," he remarked, "regardless of what the end of the labor movement as a movement between classes may be, they must remain in the background, and we must subordinate our convictions, and our views and our acts to the general good that the trades-union movement brings to the laborer."

Gompers' study of history had convinced him that the labor movement's immersion in political and reform panaceas had proved its undoing, and he insisted upon concentrating on building the trade unions on a wider and more stable base. Yet he never advocated the exclusion of the socialists from AF of L and argued that the labor movement was broad enough to include men of all beliefs. The violent attacks of DeLeon and his followers, however, inevitably forced a subtle change in Gompers' moderate attitude. Convinced that the Socialist Labor party aimed at nothing less than control of the AF of L, Gompers' position began to harden. "After all," he wrote to a fellow unionist, "it is merely a difference of opinion as to the most practical methods to be employed in securing to the laborer his just rights; and until the advent of Prof. DeLeon in the Socialist movement we managed matters so that we could at least work together. This man's characteristics of intolerance to every one that does not adopt his policy, his venom and spite crop out at every opportunity [and] that makes it impossible for any one that has any self-respect to have any dealings with him or those for whom he speaks. He has simply widened the chasm between the different wings in the labor movement."

Meanwhile, the conflict between the socialists and trade unionists in 1890 had also precipitated a crisis within the ranks of the former. The decision by the Socialist Labor party to abandon the AF of L and work through the Knights of Labor had been resisted by a substantial proportion of socialists who, under the leadership of Thomas J. Morgan and J. Mahlon Barnes, decided to continue their efforts within the

AF of L to convert the labor movement to collectivism. But for a while it seemed as though DeLeon's prediction that the Federation was hopeless was justified, for in 1892 the convention, by a decisive vote of 1,615 to 559, rejected a proposition to endorse the governmental ownership of the means of production, transportation, and communication. Instead, the delegates adopted a mild resolution calling for public ownership of the telephone, telegraph, railroad, and transportation systems. To the socialists such a position was worse than futile.

The eclipse of the socialists within the AF of L, however, proved to be only temporary, and in 1893 they renewed their proselytizing activities. Circumstances augured well for the success of their efforts. The beginnings of an economic depression and the failure of a number of prominent strikes had given rise to widespread disillusionment in labor circles with the tactics and program of trade unionism. At the convention of the AF of L in 1893 the socialists, led by Morgan, introduced an eleven-point "political programme." Praising the action of the British unionists who had endorsed the principle of independent political action, the socialist resolution called for: "1. Compulsory education. 2. Direct legislation. 3. A legal eight-hour workday. 4. Sanitary inspection of workshop, mine, and home. 5. Liability of employers for injury to health, body or life. 6. The abolition of contract system in all public work. 7. The abolition of the sweating system. 8. The municipal ownership of street cars, and gas and electric plants for public distribution of light, heat and power. 9. The nationalization of telegraphs, telephones, railroad, and mines. 10. The collective ownership by the people of all means of production and distribution. 11. The principle of referendum in all legislation." The final section of the resolution called for the submission of the programme to the affiliated unions for their "favorable consideration." The unionists succeeded in deleting the word "favorable" by the narrow margin of 1,253 to 1,182, but the amended version was adopted by the overwhelming vote of 2,244 to 67.

The crucial section of the resolution was the tenth plank. If adopted, it would have unequivocally pledged the labor movement to the support of a frankly socialist program. "The extent to which this radical sentiment has permeated the Union labor movement of the United States," observed Morgan, "will be shown by the instructions of the Unions to their delegates to the next annual convention of the AF of L, and in the vote which will then be taken upon Section 10, of the programme, submitted for their consideration. This alone will be the vital test. Every other section is commonplace, and from time to time can be safely sandwiched into the political programmes of our masters, whenever the emergency demands, but not so with number 10. In no capitalistic platform has or will this section ever find a place; while in Europe, it is the foundation of the whole political labor movement, *but it is socialism!*"

Immediately following the convention of 1893 the affiliated unions began to consider the political programme. In a display of near-unanimity, union after union voted to endorse the principles embodied in the resolution. The miners, iron and steel workers, lasters, tailors, wood workers, cigarmakers, street-railway employees, waiters, shoe workers, textile workers, mule spinners, machinists, and the German-American Typographical Union all voted their approval, as well as at least eleven state federations and eight city centrals. Only the bakers rejected it completely, while the International Typographical Union and web-weavers union voted to strike out plank ten, with the former substituting a land resolution in its place. The carpenters approved plank ten, but with the amendment, "as the people elect to operate." "We sincerely hope," summed up the organ of the United Brewery Workers, "that plank 10 of the political programme [will] be adopted and that the sound principles of scientific Socialism will be officially recognized by the representative body of the Trades and Labor Unions of America."

But even while the socialists were joyously celebrating their coming triumph, events were transpiring that would conclude in the almost total emasculation of their programme. Gompers and McGuire, while publicly maintaining their silence, privately set to work to bring about the defeat of the resolution. "This is a time when it will require the exercise of our best judgment and the assertion that the trade unions shall not be made a plaything of nor diverted from their true sphere of action," Gompers wrote to a sympathetic McGuire. Both leaders regarded the defeat of the socialists as an absolute necessity, and they agreed that almost any means would be justified. "The men who worship other gods and simply use the trade union house of worship are summoning their forces, and the trade union movement will indeed pass through its most crucial test at Denver," Gompers wrote to [Frank K.] Foster. "There it will not be so much the question of a man or an officer as it will be the root and fundamental principles of the organization. If we successfully resist it this time I have little fear for the future. If those who do not understand the trade union movement together with those who are its enemies should divert our movement from its proper channel you may rest assured that it would mean a setback for our movement, and a deterioration in the condition of our fellowworkers for more than a decade." Therefore, concluded

Gompers, "I propose to take a positive stand at the convention regardless of consequence to myself; at least I propose to do my duty as I see it and I can only hope that our earnest, intelligent trade unionists will view the danger as I know it to exist."

At the beginning of December 1894, Gompers, McGuire, and other AF of L leaders met in Chicago and mapped out their strategy to wean delegates over to their side regardless of union instructions. Then at the Denver convention a few days later Gompers struck hard in his opening presidential address. Asserting that he favored non-partisanship in politics, Gompers denounced the proposed platform and warned that a "political labor movement cannot and will not succeed upon the ruins of the trade unions." On the fourth day of the convention the delegates took up the programme, and immediately voted to consider each plank separately. The unionists scored the initial victory when Strasser's motion to delete the first preamble (commending the English trade unionists for adopting independent political action) passed by a vote of 1,345 to 861. Thereafter the convention adopted all of the planks with the exception of the tenth one.

When the tenth plank came up for discussion, the unionists made their move. First Strasser offered an amendment calling for the "collective ownership by the people of all means of production and distribution *by confiscation without compensation.*" This proposal was clearly intended to drive a wedge into the ranks of the socialists by making the article so obnoxious that many who favored the original would be forced to vote against the substitute. Other amendments emasculating the original intent of plank ten quickly followed. With Gompers keeping a firm hand over the convention proceedings, the socialists found that their entire programme was being amended to death. In the end the delegates voted 1,217 to 913 to accept a substitute for the original plank offered by the International Typographical Union calling for the "abolition of the monopoly system of land holding and the substituting therefor of a title of occupancy and use only." The culmination of the proceedings came with a motion to endorse the amended programme "as a whole," whereupon the convention defeated the move by a vote of 1,173 to 735. As Gompers later admitted, the unionists had deliberately used ridicule to demolish the political programme In vengeance the socialists combined with the miners' delegation to elect John McBride as president of the AF of L—the only time between 1886 and his death in 1924 that Gompers failed to be re-elected.

Thus the socialists had tasted the bitter fruits of defeat largely because of the tireless efforts of a small coterie of union leaders led by Gompers and McGuire. Undoubtedly preconvention sentiment had seemed to favor endorsement of the programme. Yet was this an accurate estimation of the true feelings of the working class? Obviously such a question cannot be answered with any degree of certainty. Yet if the labor movement had favored endorsement of socialism, we should expect to find a bitter uprising against those leaders who had been instrumental in defeating the programme. There was, in fact, no such revolt. Some unions, including McGuire's own organization [Brotherhood of Carpenters and Joiners], endorsed the actions of their representatives. As a matter of fact, socialist strength at subsequent conventions declined drastically.

The final event in the isolation of the socialists from the main body of the trade-union movement came in 1895, when DeLeon, after failing to capture the near-moribund Knights of Labor, proceeded to organize his own union, the Socialist Trade and Labor Alliance. Designed to replace the AF of L and Knights of Labor, it was nothing more or less than a dual union attached to and under the domination of the Socialist Labor party. While the party was the vanguard of the socialist movement in the political arena, the Socialist Trade and Labor Alliance would be its economic counterpart. Such a move was necessary because, according to one follower of DeLeon, "there was absolutely no hope from the old leaders." Soon after its establishment, the Alliance embarked on a campaign to capture the national unions and force them to leave the AF of L.

While it never became an important factor in the labor movement, the Socialist Trade and Labor Alliance did convince many trade unionists that socialism was utterly bankrupt. Tolerant of ideological heterogeneity and differences over theory and tactics, these unionists could not forgive dual unionism, which in their minds was *the* unpardonable sin. Equating radicalism with schism, the trade unions became the socialists' most bitter foe.

DeLeon's disruptive tactics also completed Gompers' conversion to a militant antisocialist position. Heretofore Gompers had fought socialism on grounds of expediency; now he fought it solely on principle. Although always willing to work with individual socialists who remained faithful to their union, Gompers ceased to pay even lip-service to socialist ideals. After the socialists had failed in another of their proselytizing efforts soon after the turn of the century, Gompers, in perhaps the clearest and most incisive statement of his entire career, remarked:

> I want to tell you, Socialists, that I have studied your philosophy; read your works upon economics, and not the meanest of them;

studied your standard works, both in English and German—have not only read, but studied them. I have heard your orators and watched the work of your movement the world over. I have kept close watch upon your doctrines for thirty years; have been closely associated with many of you, and know how you think and what you propose. I know, too, what you have up your sleeve. And I want to say that I am entirely at variance with your philosophy. I declare it to you, I am not only at variance with your doctrines, but with your philosophy. Economically, you are unsound; socially, you are wrong; industrially, you are an impossibility.

The failure of the socialists to capture the AF of L was due to the interplay of several factors. It is clear that leaders like Gompers and McGuire proved themselves formidable opponents in the struggle with the socialists, but their efforts would probably not have succeeded without substantial support from other unionists and the rank and file. Above all, the fact remains that the American worker has been by tradition and by history inclined toward a capitalistic outlook, a phenomenon well recognized by such European scholars as Werner Sombart. This being the case, acceptance of a socialist ideology would have come into direct conflict with labor's outlook. It is true that on occasion socialists have enjoyed greater popularity, but such aberrations have generally proved to be short-lived. Thus at the Denver convention, as well as at other ones, the socialists were always unable to overcome the strength shown by the trade unionists, whose appeal to their followers was predicated largely, if not exclusively, on acceptance of industrial capitalism, within which labor could attain a higher standard of living. Leaders like Gompers were well aware of the capitalistic psychology of American workers, as well as the barriers imposed upon an organized socialist movement by the American environment. Like so many of his colleagues, he accepted what he felt he could not change. Undoubtedly such an attitude resulted in a political system that left the worker without any real choice, but this sacrifice, in the eyes of the trade unionists, was absolutely necessary if the labor movement were to survive. Perhaps Shaw was correct when he once remarked that trade unionism was not socialism, but rather the capitalism of the working class. In any event, the American labor movement, ironically enough, became one of the most bitter foes of socialism, a fact which played an important role in the failure of socialism to gain a foothold in the United States.

By the turn of the century, therefore, the socialists had been decisively defeated in their efforts to capture the AF of L. The high point of socialist hopes had come in 1894, and thereafter socialist strength within the Federation gradually diminished. While individual socialists like Max Hayes continued to play important roles within the Federation, and others left the fold to form the Industrial Workers of the World, the socialist movement as a whole was isolated from the main body of organized labor, and nothing that leaders like Eugene Debs or Victor Berger did could change this vital fact. Undoubtedly the failure of the socialists to play an important role in the United States was due to far more basic factors than their inability to capture the AF of L; nevertheless, the influence of this fact should not be minimized, especially when we consider the history of trade unionism and socialism in England, where events finally culminated in the establishment of the Labour party in 1906.

The Challenge of the IWW

Henry Pelling
Queen's College, Oxford

[IN THE EARLY TWENTIETH CENTURY] the AF of L was being challenged on its flank by the formation of a rival national labor organization. The Western Federation of Miners had for some time been hostile to the type of unionism represented by the AF of L. The concepts of craft exclusiveness and autonomy, and the attempt to secure mutual respect between employer and employee, seemed quite out of place in the mining camps of Colorado and Idaho, where law enforcement was so inadequate that labor disputes readily degenerated into civil wars. The Western Labor Union, which . . . was founded by the Western Federation of Miners, was designed to comprise all the workers of the West, "irrespective of occupation, nationality, creed or color." The new organization made little progress, but in 1902 it was decided to extend its scope, with the intention, as the union journal put it, of forcing "the Gompers brigade" to "keep step to the music of progress" or alternatively, of eliminating "this per capita tax eating gang from the councils of organized labor." The headquarters of the Western Labor Union were moved from Butte to Chicago and its name was changed to American Labor Union.

In 1904 the Western Federation of Miners was weakened by the complete defeat of its strike at Cripple Creek, Colorado, by a com-

Excerpted by permission of the publisher from *American Labor,* © 1960, the University of Chicago Press.

bination of forces led by the Mine Owners' Association and local Citizens' Alliances. Its members in the area were simply driven away and replaced by foreign immigrants and country boys. The miners' leaders turned more and more to the prospect of help from a strong new national organization. Meetings were held in Chicago to plan the formation of such a body, and a number of prominent Socialists were drawn in, including Eugene V. Debs, the former president of the American Railway Union, who was now the most popular spokesman of the Socialist Party of America. Daniel DeLeon and his Socialist Trade and Labor Alliance also found the new venture to their taste, and rallied to its assistance.

The delegates who met at Chicago in June 1905, to found the Industrial Workers of the World (soon abbreviated to IWW) represented almost all the forces of labor which, whether for temporary or for permanent reasons, resented the domination of the AF of L in the labor movement. They did not, however, include the highly conservative railroad brotherhoods. Debs and his colleagues represented the current of hostility to conservative unionism which existed in the Socialist Party of America—although it is true that many preferred to work through the AF of L and opposed this attempt to found a rival union organization. DeLeon, the Socialist Labor Party and the Socialist Trade and Labor Alliance were of course happy to find allies in the work of "smashing" the AF of L. The only union of any size which committed itself to joining the new body was the Western Federation of Miners; but one somewhat unexpected ally was the Amalgamated Society of Engineers, a tiny body consisting mostly of immigrants who were members of the British union of that name, and who were nursing a grudge against the AF of L, from which they had lately been unceremoniously expelled at the behest of their stronger rivals, the Machinists. Thus ethnic and sectional factors combined to add weight to a protest movement which, superficially at least, seemed almost entirely ideological in character.

The attitude of the IWW was stated boldly in the first sentence of the preamble to its constitution: "The working class and the employing class have nothing in common." Its object was to unite the workers in one centralized organization, without distinction of trade, skill, race, or ethnic origin. Initiation fees and dues were to be kept to the minimum so that no one would be excluded on grounds of poverty. The only division among the members was to be on industrial lines, for there were to be thirteen departments of the IWW covering all the possible occupations of the workers; but the IWW executive board was to have the authority to call any section of the organization out on strike. All this was accepted enthusiastically by the inaugural convention, but there was some difference of opinion on the value of political action, which some of the delegates thought was an undesirable diversion from industrial work. A clause indorsing the use of political action was carried by a majority.

In nearly all respects the IWW was the exact antithesis of the AF of L, as indeed it was designed to be. Centralization contrasted with the national-union autonomy of the older body; industrial organization cut across the craft basis of the AF of L unions; and the policy of low dues differed markedly from the high-contribution systems which Gompers and his colleagues favored. But the IWW had even more difficulty than the AF of L in deciding its attitude to politics, and this soon led to factionalism within its ranks. At the second convention in 1906, DeLeon and his group secured the defeat of those leaders of the Western Federation of Miners who opposed political action. This was a very damaging act, as it led to the withdrawal of the Western Federation of Miners from the IWW, which deprived it of the bulk of its membership. At the same time, Debs and several other prominent Socialists dropped out, being disappointed at the new turn of events. There were, however, two Western Federation leaders still left in, and both of them were men of distinct personality—William D. Haywood and Vincent St. John; and the IWW itself consisted not only of the dogmatic DeLeonites but also of an unruly band of western "hoboes," unskilled in the dialectics of Socialist theory but willing to follow any effective leadership. St. John, who had himself been something of a "hobo," mobilized the western elements and in 1908 was able to drive DeLeon out of the organization and to abolish the clause in the constitution which favored political action. DeLeon, refusing to accept defeat, established a rival IWW at Detroit with the political clause still retained, but this body never acquired any influence of note.

Under St. John, who was secretary-treasurer from 1908 to 1915, the Chicago IWW gradually attained national prominence, if not large membership. Most of its work was done either among the migratory workers of the West or among the unskilled immigrants of the eastern cities. In the West, the IWW recruited lumber workers and farm laborers and mobilized them for the violent battles into which western labor disputes almost inevitably degenerated. They engaged in campaigns for "free speech," and met the challenge of the vigilantes organized by the local property owners. In the East, their role was different: they provided an English-speaking leadership for groups of immigrant workers, notably for those in the textile factories, who found themselves neglected by the small and conservative AF of L union of their trade, the United Textile Workers. The largest and most important of their strikes was that at Lawrence, Massachusetts, in 1912, when under the leadership of Joseph J. Ettor and Bill Haywood some thirty thousand workers won wage increases and other benefits.

But the "Wobblies" (as the members of the IWW were commonly called) secured little permanent increase of membership as the result of their efforts. Their tactics and methods of propaganda, including the open advocacy of sabotage (a word derived from the French Syndicalists), were too extreme for all save the most desperate workers to accept. Haywood himself, who was a member of the National Executive of the Socialist Party, was deprived of that office by national referendum of the party for his advocacy of violence. Another factor which prevented the IWW from gathering real strength was the indiscipline of its members, who refused to acknowledge the necessity for central control. By 1914, Debs, who had continued to look upon the IWW with a good deal of sympathy, was at last convinced that it "stands for anarchy," and was prepared to advocate a fresh start in revolutionary unionism, based upon the two miners' unions, the Western Foundation and the United Mine Workers. Ten years after its foundation, the membership of the IWW was apparently hovering round about the 15,000 mark, which was less than one-hundredth of the membership of the AF of L.

The importance of the IWW was much more symbolical than actual. It was a protest against the AF of L's claim to speak for a working class which consisted to an increasing extent of unskilled workers, whether native or immigrant. Although some of its leaders were influenced by Marxism and by Syndicalism, it was nevertheless largely the product of the American environment. The Wobblies fit naturally into the mythology of the West, along with the cowboys and the miners with whom to some extent they overlapped; and their songs of the tough life they led, especially those composed by Joe Hill, who was executed after being convicted of murder in 1915, belong now to the tradition of American folklore. Nevertheless these characteristics did not save the IWW from condemnation and persecution as "un-American" during the first World War and afterward.

The Communist Party

Max M. Kampelman

WORLD WAR I STRENGTHENED the conservative leadership of the American labor movement. Critical groups, such as the IWW, the Socialist Labor Party, and the Socialist Party found their remnants clipped of strength in the AFL and often broken of heart—partly, of course, because of wartime prosecutions by the government.

On this scene the American Communist movement was born within the ranks of the Socialist Party. Influenced by Leninism and the success of the Bolshevik revolution of 1917 in Russia, a small dedicated band of militant radicals attempted to gain control of the Socialist Party and begin preparing the country for revolution. The deep inconsistencies between democratic socialism as expressed by the gradualist Socialist Party majority, and Leninist elitism, was early apparent, and the Communists were expelled. In September 1919 the Communist Party of America came into being. Its trade union policy was one of opposition to the American Federation of Labor and sympathy with the Industrial Workers of the World. A policy of "revolutionary unionism" espousing the overthrow of capitalism was enunciated. Unions were looked upon as "schools of communism." At ordinary strikes leaflets urging the worker to overthrow the government and establish Soviets were distributed. The revolution, however, did not come as quickly as expected and different tactics had to be used. With a more moderate appeal, unions established and run by Communists gained some following, particularly among foreign-born workers in the needle trades, food, and metals, and among laborers, thus illustrating what was called "dual unionism."

This line was followed until May 1920 when Lenin, for reasons that had nothing to do with America, published his pamphlet, *Left Wing Communism: An Infantile Disorder,* in which he urged Communists to go into existing unions and criticized the German Communists for not doing so. Benjamin Gitlow, writing of this period, said: "The publication of Lenin's pamphlet turned the trade union policy of our Party upside down." It was clear that the activity of the Communists in the trade unions was to be major. Gitlow, at the time an important functionary of the movement, described it as follows:

Excerpted by permission of the author from the *Communist Party vs. the C.I.O.,* New York: Frederick A. Praeger, Inc., © 1957 by Max M. Kampelman. Footnotes in the original have been deleted.

The Bolsheviks from the time of Lenin to the present have never given up hope of capturing the trade union movement of the United States. Our Party received more assistance, more advice, more decisions on the trade union question than on almost any other question. Lenin was particularly anxious to win over the American trade unions. It was Lenin who conceived the idea that it would be possible for the Communists in the United States, by hiding their identity, to form an opposition bloc in the trade unions, which would enable them to dislodge the reactionary forces in control of the American Federation of Labor.

In December 1921, the Workers Party was formed at a New York convention, and the Communists emerged from underground. Four years had passed since the October Revolution and there was no indication that the mass of American workers would accept Communist leadership. Led by William Z. Foster, a prominent labor organizer in steel and meatpacking, the Communists began a policy of penetrating the AFL. Foster had been a Socialist and a member of the syndicalist IWW. He had a reputation as a successful labor organizer, having led the great Steel Strike of 1919. The Communists dropped the policy of overtly promoting revolution and adopted the strategy of obtaining a place for themselves in ordinary trade union activity. In 1922 they formed the Trade Union Educational League (TUEL), intended as a rallying center for all progressive groups and individuals within the trade union movement.

The head of the TUEL was William Z. Foster and the managing editor of its first publication, *The Labor Herald*, was Earl Browder. It called itself "a left progressive bloc of all revolutionary and progressive elements in the trade union." It hoped to act as a revolutionary wing of the AFL and remain within it. This strategy was difficult to maintain. The Communist (Third) International had again proclaimed the Lenin thesis of "permanent revolution" and the impossibility of establishing lasting socialism in one country within a capitalist world. The League and its leaders were from the outset obliged to subordinate trade union policies to political objectives. The Workers Party became increasingly aggressive as a left wing opposition; it began to attempt to gain control of unions through active participation in union elections; it nominated its own opposition candidates. This lost the Party the support of non-Communist progressives, and left the TUEL and its leader, Foster, in 1923 exposed as Communist and nothing more. This, in turn, led to a great many expulsions from the AFL on the ground of dual unionism.

The TUEL now spearheaded an attack upon the AFL. The

League's program called for a reorganization of the labor movement through a program of amalgamation, under which craft unions were to be merged into industrial groupings. AFL reaction to the new policy was immediate. Drastic punitive measures against TUEL adherents were undertaken. Many unions insisted on loyalty pledges. TUEL members were removed from union offices and others were expelled.

To meet these attacks, Foster advised his followers to sign membership pledges against the TUEL so as to avoid expulsion. The Communists remained a conspiratorial minority group, a policy of "boring from within" began. This program lasted until 1928, when the Communists appeared with another dual labor organization, the Trade Union Unity League, designed to follow a more independent policy.

The La Follette Campaign of 1924

Foster Rhea Dulles
Ohio State University

EARLY IN 1921, the Supreme Court stated in *Duplex Printing Press v. Deering* that nothing in the [Clayton] act legalized secondary boycotts or protected unions from injunctions that might be brought against them for conspiring in restraint of trade. Later that same year, in the notable case of *Truax v. Corrigan,* any hope of legal relief for labor was even more effectively killed. Arizona had passed a law that sought to do away altogether with injunctions in labor disputes and the Supreme Court in effect declared it to be unconstitutional. In preventing an employer from obtaining an injunction, it was decreed, the state took away his means of securing protection and thereby deprived him of property without due process of law. With such encouragement employers resorted to injunctions even more frequently than in the days before passage of the Clayton Act. In 1928 the American Federation of Labor submitted a list of 389 that had been granted by either federal or state courts in the preceding decade, and this was obviously far from complete because of the large number unrecorded in the lower courts.

Perhaps the most revealing of all court decisions in this period was that in the . . . case of *Adkins v. Children's Hospital* which was

Excerpted by permission of the publisher from *Labor in America,* New York: Thomas Y. Crowell Co., 1949.

handed down in 1923. In invalidating a minimum wage law as a violation of constitutional safeguards of liberty of contract, it marked an abrupt reversal of the earlier trend toward sustaining such legislation, but it was even more significant because of a reassertion of the old concept that labor was a commodity. While the Supreme Court conceded "the ethical right of every worker, man or woman, to a living wage," it declared that the employer was not bound to furnish such a wage and that there was no warrant for the state to seek to establish it by legislation. Since in principle "there can be no difference between the case of selling labor and the case of selling goods," the court said, any attempt to compel the employer to pay a stated wage "is so clearly the product of a naked, arbitrary power that it cannot be allowed to stand under the Constitution of the United States."

Even Chief Justice Taft—the "injunction judge"—protested this conclusion and pointed out that individual employees were not on a level of equality in contracting with employers and were "peculiarly subject to the overreaching of the harsh and greedy employer." Associate Justice Holmes also dissented, with sharp criticism of the court's one-sided support of "the dogma Liberty of Contract."

Although both government and courts theoretically recognized the desirability of labor unions, even President Harding declaring that the right of workers to organize was "not one whit less absolute" than that of management and capital, they were consistently restricting the activity for which unions were formed. The one exception to such repressive policies during the 1920's was the passage and approval of the Railway Labor Act of 1926. This measure provided for the formation of unions among railway workers "without interference, influence or coercion," and set up special machinery for the settlement of all railway labor disputes. In upholding this law, the Supreme Court declared that the legality of collective action on the part of employes would be "a mockery if representation were made futile by interferences with freedom of choice." But rights upheld for railway workers were not extended to other classes of employes until the 1930's.

Confronted with legal restrictions on union activity and adverse court decisions, organized labor once again began to feel, as it had when it submitted its "Bill of Grievances" in 1906, that more direct political pressure would have to be exercised if it was to win any freedom of action in combatting the employers' antiunion campaign. The drive for a labor party that had first developed in 1919 when "Labor's Bill of Rights" was drawn up, gathered increasing force with further revelations of the Supreme Court's attitude. Even the AF of L was unable wholly to resist the pressure for some sort of unified political action.

This agitation had first come to a head in 1922 when a Chicago meeting of some 128 delegates from various farm, labor, and other liberal groups formed the Conference for Progressive Political Action. William H. Johnston of the powerful International Association of Machinists was a leading figure in this movement; the railway brotherhoods, smarting under the restrictions of the old Railway Labor Board and the revival of injunction law, backed it vigorously, and support was also forthcoming from twenty-eight national unions, eight state labor federations, several mid-Western farmers' parties, the Women's Trade Union League, and the Socialists. When two years later both the Republicans and the Democrats nominated highly conservative candidates, Calvin Coolidge and John W. Davis, these progressives offered an independent nomination to Senator La Follette of Wisconsin. On the condition that no attempt be made to run candidates for other offices than the presidency and vice-presidency (Senator Wheeler of Montana being given the latter nomination), La Follette accepted this proposal and the Conference for Progressive Political Action formally entered the 1924 campaign.

The platform, declaring that the principal issue before the country was the control of government and industry by private monopoly, was in large measure a carryover of the progressive principles of pre-war years. It called for public ownership of the nation's water power and of railroads, the conservation of natural resources, aid for farmers, tax reduction on moderate incomes, downward tariff revision, and remedial labor legislation. "We favor abolition of the use of injunctions in labor disputes," it was stated, "and declare for complete protection of the right of farmers and industrial workers to organize, bargain collectively through representatives of their own choosing, and conduct without hindrance cooperative enterprises."

The American Federation of Labor was at first opposed to the Conference for Progressive Political Action, but when both major parties ignored labor's demands, it took the unprecedented step of endorsing the La Follette candidacy. The Republican and Democratic parties, declared the executive council, have "flouted the desires of labor" and are "in a condition of moral bankruptcy which constitutes a menace and a peril to our country and its institutions." In spite of this attack on the major parties, however, the AF of L aligned itself with the Progressives of 1924 very cautiously. In keeping with his policy during the political flirtations of pre-war years, Gompers tried to make it clear that the Federation made no commitments except to support La Follette as "a friend of labor" in this single campaign and was not countenancing a third party as such. While recognizing the need for legislation to free labor from the restrictions represented by injunction law, he reaffirmed his faith in "voluntarism" by declaring that "we do not accept government as the solution of the problems of life."

Even with these qualifications and reservations, many AF of L leaders refused to go along with the action of the executive council. John L. Lewis and William Hutcheson, of the Carpenters, gave their support to Coolidge, and George L. Berry, of the Printing Pressmen, at the last moment shifted over to the camp of John W. Davis. Although the AF of L had so far departed from its traditional policy as to come out openly for a presidential candidate of a third party, its support was somewhat left-handed and only $25,000 was raised as a campaign fund.

La Follette secured nearly five million votes—a substantial indication of popular discontent with both Republican and Democratic conservatism—but he carried only his home state of Wisconsin. The labor vote had not been delivered and the progressives' failure was widely interpreted as labor's failure. "The radical movement of this year," wrote the Washington correspondent of the *Seattle Times,* "represented the first attempt on the part of organized labor, through its governing bodies, to secure separate political action. The radical failure seems likely to end the possibility, for a good many years, of labor endorsement of a third-party presidential ticket." There was "no such thing as a labor vote," the *New York Herald Tribune* stated in analyzing the election returns, and the *Washington Star* agreed that "the workingmen of this country have not joined the insurgency against the established parties." More succinctly and colloquially, the *Philadelphia Bulletin* simply stated that "labor's incursion into politics was a dud."

The AF of L apparently read very much the same meaning into the election. It promptly withdrew its support from the Conference for Progressive Political Action and reasserted its opposition to a third party. The entire movement collapsed. While in succeeding years labor continued to press for relief from injunctions, no further direct forays were made into politics. With even the Socialist vote falling off heavily, wage earners appeared ready to accept, with the rest of the country, the conservative political pattern that continued to characterize the national scene until the advent of the New Deal.

Chapter 6

The Change in Labor's Political Role

WHEN HERBERT HOOVER ACCEPTED the Republican presidential nomination in the summer of 1928, he spoke with great confidence. "We in America today," he said, "are nearer to the final triumph over poverty than ever before in the history of any land."[1] Five years later, as he turned the reins of government over to his successor, Franklin D. Roosevelt, he felt that "We are at the end of our string."[2] In the intervening years, the American economy had collapsed.

When Franklin D. Roosevelt took office, about one-fourth of the civilian labor-force—estimates run anywhere from 13 to 15 million—was totally unemployed and much of the rest was working short hours at reduced wages. Industrial output was about half of what it had been before the onset of the Depression. Farm prices, already falling during the 1920's, had hit bottom. Bankruptcies were commonplace.

The impact of the Depression cannot be measured solely in terms of statistics. As one historian has put it, "The depression of the mind was more severe than that of the economy. . . ."

> The evidence of the breakdown in morale was abundant. "I'm afraid," Charles Schwab of Bethlehem Steel said, "every man is afraid." The unemployed were drained of their vitality. Leisure became a misery. Young people grew aimless and apathetic, accepting the idea that they would never find jobs. The self-reliant lost their self-reliance. Fear and inactivity were the enemies of mental stability. "I cannot stand it any longer," a jobless Pennsylvanian wrote Governor Pinchot. A group of forty experienced stenographers called back to work in 1933 after at least a year of unemployment found that they could not face their employers for dictation without breaking down emotionally. . . .[3]

No one seemed to know what to do. The leaders of the AFL were as much in the dark as anyone else. Still committed to a policy

---

[1] Herbert Hoover, *The New Day*, Stanford, Calif.: Stanford Univ. Press, 2d ed., 1929, p. 16.

[2] Quoted in Eric Goldman, *Rendezvous with Destiny*, New York: Vintage Books, rev. ed. 1956, p. 250.

[3] Irving Bernstein, *The Lean Years*, Boston: Houghton Mifflin Co., 1960, pp. 331–32.

of governmental noninterference, their initial reaction to a proposal for unemployment insurance was negative. "Labor wants jobs, not a dole," they said. But the only suggestion they had to relieve the situation was to spread the then available jobs around among more people by means of a shorter work week. By 1932, after a close convention fight they had come out for unemployment insurance and expanded public works, and they continued to maintain their nonpartisan attitude in that year's election.

The dramatic change in government's attitude toward organized labor which came about during the New Deal period was foreshadowed in 1932 when the large number of Democratic Congressmen elected in 1930 helped to pass the Norris-LaGuardia Act. By its terms, the power of the federal courts to issue antistrike injunctions was severely limited. In addition, so-called "yellow dog" contracts, by which an employee pledged himself not to join a union as a condition of employment, were now no longer enforceable in the federal courts. In itself, of course, the Act was no solution to the problem of finding jobs.

President Roosevelt had no pat answers to the nation's problems when he took office. What he proposed to do was "to take a method and try it. If it fails, admit it frankly and try another. But above all, try something."[4] At first, he was inclined to believe, with the AFL, that a 30-hour week, coupled with some sort of provision for minimum wage standards, would help alleviate labor's distress. This idea was abandoned, however, as a result of the vigorous protest it elicited from the business community.

The President then backed the National Industrial Recovery Act of 1933, designed to help both businessmen and wage earners. This legislation permitted industries to establish their own codes of fair competition, and was intended to eliminate indiscriminate price and wage cutting. At the same time, section 7(a) of that Act guaranteed to workers the right to bargain collectively through representatives of their own choosing, free from employer interference. This was a landmark for organized labor. Although the NIRA was later declared unconstitutional, that same section was incorporated into the National Labor Relations Act of 1935, the so-called Wagner Act.

The President was not concerned solely, nor indeed primarily, with the welfare of organized labor as such. The initiation of public works projects and the enactment of the Social Security Act in 1935 were intended to benefit a much larger segment of the American pop-

---

[4] Quoted in Oscar T. Barck, Jr., and Nelson M. Blake, *Since 1900*, New York: The Macmillan Co., 3d ed., 1959, p. 449.

ulace. Nevertheless, the encouragement and support the union move-ment did receive during Roosevelt's administration constituted a marked departure from the government's previous attitude.

Some unions took full advantage of the changed environment. In the mining areas, for example, banners appeared everywhere carry-ing the message that "President Roosevelt wants you to join the Union." The AFL moved to organize workers in the mass production industries as well, but the results of those efforts were not spectacular. The Fed-eration's traditional craft-union orientation made it reluctant to organize those workers into industrial unions—labor organizations embracing all employees, unskilled as well as skilled, within a given industry. In-stead the Federation issued temporary charters to groups of newly organized workers with the idea of parceling them out to its member craft unions in due course.

Not all of the Federation leaders agreed with that policy. At the Federation's 1935 convention, the conflict over craft vs. industrial unions within the organization came to a head,

> . . . when the resolutions committee split eight to seven on the ques-tion of how to deal with the problem [of organizing the mass-produc-tion industries]. The majority took the view that it was necessary to safeguard craft jurisdictions at all costs; the minority favored aban-doning them in the mass production industries, so as to mobilize the workers on an industrial basis. In spite of eloquent speeches by the minority and the bitter scorn of John L. Lewis, their principal spokesman, who derided organization of the workers into "fifty-seven varieties" of crafts, the majority position was indorsed by the con-vention by 18,204 votes to 10,933. Two-thirds of the minority vote came from the Mine Workers and the Clothing Workers. At a later stage in the convention, Lewis and [William L.] Hutcheson of the Carpenters exchanged sharp words, and Lewis struck Hutcheson on the jaw—an act that symbolized the rift in the organization.
>
> After the convention was over, the minority leaders established a Committee for Industrial Organization (CIO), with Lewis as chair-man. In forming this body they claimed to be acting within their rights as members of the AF of L. But the executive council, realiz-ing that they would soon be trespassing on the chartered territory of other unions, at once demanded the disbanding of the committee. The rebels remained obdurate, and they were joined by the new unions founded by the AF of L in the auto and rubber industries, as well as by the Amalgamated Association of Iron, Steel, and Tin Workers. On complaint from various of its affiliates, the AF of L executive council in August 1936, found the unions belonging to the CIO to be guilty of "dual unionism" and gave them one month in which to withdraw from the CIO or be suspended from the AF of L.

The CIO unions did not respond to the ultimatum and were accordingly suspended. At this point, the American labor movement was effectively split in two.[5]

It was not reunited until 1955.

The heads of the new CIO[6] unions were certain that Franklin Roosevelt's reelection in 1936 was essential, for in large measure their organizations owed their existence to the New Deal. Thus, they were ready not only to endorse Roosevelt but, as the selection by Arthur Schlesinger, Jr., indicates, to contribute heavily in time and money to his campaign. Labor's involvement in the 1936 presidential election has often been cited as the beginning of an alliance with the Democratic Party that continues to this day.

The old guard AFL chieftains were reluctant to make so firm a commitment to Roosevelt, though some craft unions did cooperate with Labor's Non-Partisan League, the organization created by John L. Lewis to reelect Roosevelt. The selection by Walter Galenson relates their increasing hostility toward the League in the late 1930's.

Galenson also notes the division within the CIO that resulted from John L. Lewis' endorsement of Wendell Willkie's presidential candidacy in 1940. "Lewis and Roosevelt, Inc.," by James A. Wechsler, describes the early relationship between the two men, and the events leading up to Lewis' withdrawal from the Roosevelt camp.

When Lewis left the CIO he took Labor's Non-Partisan League with him. To replace it, the leaders of the CIO established the Political Action Committee in 1943, and selected Sidney Hillman to head the organization. The reading by Matthew Josephson describes Hillman's work in organizing the PAC and the effectiveness of his efforts in the 1944 election. The selection which follows, by Claire Neikind, describes the day-by-day activities of the PAC in the New England area in the 1948 election. As the author points out, the organization Hillman had created in 1943 had come a long way in five years.

In the selection by Walter Galenson in this chapter, it is stated that "the communists, veering between 'United Front' and independent political action, were too far removed from American realities to have any lasting influence. . . ." For a time, during the late 1930's, and into the 1940's, it was not clear that this would be the case. Their influence upon the American labor movement, particularly within the CIO unions,

---

[5] Henry Pelling, *American Labor,* Chicago: The University of Chicago Press, 1960, pp. 164–65.

[6] Once the CIO split from the AFL, the name of the organization was changed to Congress of Industrial Organizations.—Eds.

is the subject of the selection by Bernard Karsh and Phillips L. Garman.

Labor's efforts to rid itself of communist influence was inextricably involved with its attitude toward Henry Wallace's presidential candidacy in 1948. This is the subject of the first of three topics contained within the reading by Philip Taft. Taft also describes the creation, in 1947, of the AFL counterpart to the CIO's PAC, Labor's League for Political Education. Both the establishment of the LLPE and the stepped-up activities of the PAC in the 1948 elections can be attributed to the passage of the Taft-Hartley Act in 1947.

Once the LLPE was established, its representatives and those of the CIO's PAC often worked together. Thus when the AFL and CIO merged, in 1955, a merger of their political arms presented no insurmountable difficulties. The new organization, the AFL–CIO Committee for Political Education, and labor's contemporary political activities are the subjects of Part Two of this book.

Labor's New Role: The 1936 Election

Arthur Schlesinger, Jr.
City University of New York

THE MOST POWERFUL NEW ELEMENT in the coalition [that was being created by Postmaster General James Farley and President Roosevelt to insure Roosevelt's reelection in 1936] represented a major departure from classical Democratic politics—and one with which Jim Farley was little qualified to deal. This was organized labor, endowed by NRA and the Wagner Act with a new stake in the federal government and now determined to keep a friendly administration in Washington. In 1932 Roosevelt had not even bothered to make a major labor speech, despite pleas from [Teamster President] Dan Tobin, the head of the Democratic National Committee's Labor Division; nor had the labor vote made a distinctive contribution to the outcome. But by 1934 the federal guarantee of collective bargaining had transformed the prospects of the labor movement. "Labor knew this," Francis Biddle wrote Roosevelt in 1935, "and looked to you as their leader. This faith in you was very largely responsible for the swing in Pennsylvania last Autumn, particularly in the steel mills and coal mines, where employer

Excerpted by permission of the publisher from *The Politics of Upheaval*, Boston: Houghton Mifflin Co., 1960.

domination had been synonymous with Republican control." Organized labor promised to be an active factor in 1936 as it had never been in American history.

In the past the Labor Division was but one of a miscellany of the National Committee's ritualistic gestures toward special groups—more for show than for use. When it became evident that Farley, who displayed little appreciation of the possibilities of the labor vote, meant to hand the Labor Division over to Tobin again in 1936, the labor militants decided they would have to organize for Roosevelt on their own. This was not just to prevent the old line unionists from freezing the CIO leaders out of the campaign. It was also to make sure that the labor vote was mobilized in quantity—something the Labor Division, operating on traditional lines, had never been able to do.

Accordingly, in early April 1936, John L. Lewis, Sidney Hillman [of the Amalgamated Clothing Workers, CIO], and George L. Berry [of the Printing Pressmen, AFL] announced the formation of Labor's Non-Partisan League. The immediate aim of the new organization was the reelection of Roosevelt—"the greatest statesman of modern times," as Lewis called him. "President Roosevelt has undertaken and accomplished more for the workers than any other president in the history of the nation," Lewis said, "and labor owes him a debt of gratitude that can be liquidated only by casting its solid vote for him at the coming election." Hillman added, "We know that the defeat of the Roosevelt Administration means no labor legislation for decades to come." Beyond 1936, they contemplated continuing the League as the political arm of labor and as the basis for what Berry described as "the permanent establishment of a liberal party, if necessary, in the United States in 1940."

The League swung into action over the summer. David Dubinsky of the International Ladies' Garment Workers and Emil Rieve of the Hosiery Workers resigned from the Socialist party to join its campaign. Though Bill Green disapproved, a number of AFL craft unions took part. In New York, the League invented a new party—the American Labor party—to get support for Roosevelt and for Herbert Lehman from people reluctant to vote for them on the Democratic ticket. While the League did not generally attempt ward-and-precinct organizations, it worked through local trade union people in nearly every state to stimulate a sense of urgency. It went on the radio, passed out leaflets by the thousand, staged rallies (109 in Chicago alone), and spent nearly a million dollars. Lewis himself set the tone for the fight against the Republican candidate—"this little man out in Topeka, Kansas, who has no more conception nor idea of what ails America or what to do about it than a goat herder in the hills of Bulgaria." Landon, Lewis said, was "as empty, as inane, as innocuous as a watermelon that has been boiled in a washtub"; in another mood, Lewis saw him as a "bootlicker of plutocracy . . . as with quibble and quirk he seeks to cozen the American people."

Labor's greatest contribution to the campaign, however, was money. Lewis, Hillman, and Berry chipped in to keep the League going; and the United Mine Workers in particular became in the end the chief support not only of the Democratic party but of other campaign subsidiaries, such as the Progressive National Committee. The history of the financial transactions of the 1936 campaign remains obscure. According to one detailed account . . . Lewis originally proposed to hand Roosevelt a check from the UMW for $250,000. Roosevelt replied "No, John, I don't want your check, much as I appreciate the thought, just keep it, and I'll call on you if and when any small need arises." Lewis grumbled to his associates that they had been outsmarted; now there would be no limit to the amount for which they would be asked. Certainly, as the campaign proceeded, the Democrats subjected the UMW to a series of requisitions until the bill ran up to just under a half a million dollars (of which $40,000 was a loan, eventually repaid). With gifts from other unions the total labor contribution to the Democratic campaign was almost three-quarters of a million dollars. At a time when contributions from big business were falling sharply (bankers and brokers who had given about one-quarter of the funds received by the Democrats in 1932 in amounts over $1,000, gave less than one twenty-fifth in this same category in 1936), labor enabled Roosevelt and Farley to campaign in the style to which they had become accustomed.

Labor and New Deal Politics: 1936–40

Walter Galenson

University of California, Berkeley

IT SOON BECAME CLEAR that [Labor's Non-Partisan] League was CIO-dominated, and with the resignation of Berry as chairman in 1937, it became formally the political arm of the CIO. In September 1937,

Excerpted by permission of the publisher from *The CIO Challenge to the AFL*, Cambridge, Mass.: Harvard University Press, © 1960 by the President and Fellows of Harvard College. Footnotes in the original have been deleted.

William Green informed all AFL local bodies that the AFL considered the League as a CIO political machine, to which no cooperation was to be accorded. Nevertheless, some AFL unions continued to give the League their support, and at the 1938 AFL convention, the Hotel and Restaurant Workers' Union introduced a resolution condemning the Executive Council's action in withdrawing AFL assistance. George Meany, then a delegate from the New York State Federation of Labor, spoke strongly against the resolution. He said, among other things:

> I want to say now that the American Federation of Labor in that state [New York] today is nonpartisan and is going to stay non-partisan. . . . A labor party such as we see it in New York State is a class party, and there is no place in America for a party founded on class or caste lines . . . we are going to carry out the policies of Gompers and not bow to any political boss, no matter what party label he may bear, even if it bears the honored and sacred name of labor.

A few delegates rose to the defense of the League, but the resolution was defeated overwhelmingly. Charges of communist infiltration into the League were made by Meany and others, charges which were to be repeated with increasing vehemence in later years.

The CIO, on the other hand, affirmed its loyalty to the League, which was active in local elections in 1938, particularly in New York State, where the American Labor Party provided Herbert H. Lehman the margin of victory over Thomas E. Dewey in the gubernatorial election. At the 1939 CIO convention, John L. Lewis boasted:

> Let no public representative or citizens underestimate the tremendous power and influence now being exercised by labor in the political realm of the nation, and let no politician assume that he can ignore Labor's Non-Partisan League, nor ignore the mandates and the ideals and the objectives of organized labor, without being held to strict accountability in that inevitable day when elections come again.

But the split within the CIO during the 1940 election campaign rendered Labor's Non-Partisan League ineffective. Although most CIO leaders were pro-Roosevelt, Lewis controlled the League, and with the aid of the Communist Party, then in its "neutralist" phase, he carried on a campaign which had as its purpose the defeat of Roosevelt. The aftermath of the election was a bitter one. At a meeting of the CIO Executive Board, [Jacob] Potofsky of the Amalgamated Clothing Workers accused the Lewis forces of spending CIO money for Willkie. Allan S. Haywood, head of the New York State Industrial Council and a Lewis supporter, countered: "Some of your representatives, Brother Potofsky, have stated the [per capita tax] was held back for political reasons. No CIO money was spent for Willkie, not a dime." Potofsky retorted: "You work for the CIO, and you supported Willkie." The American Labor Party in New York was increasingly split over the communist issue.

Lewis would probably have liked to commit the CIO to a third party venture after 1940. The CIO convention of that year, held shortly after the elections, adopted a resolution authorizing the Executive Board to "give serious consideration to this problem looking toward the formulation of a program which would guarantee and assure an independent political role for organized labor." But the growing estrangement of Lewis from the CIO militated against the commitment of the CIO to any such goal. The CIO leadership, headed by [Philip] Murray and Hillman, who had given Roosevelt their unqualified support in 1940, continued to follow the pro-Democratic Party policy initiated in 1936. When Lewis withdrew from the CIO, he took Labor's Non-Partisan League with him, leaving a vacuum in the CIO which was not filled until the formation of the Political Action Committee in 1943.

Confirmed in its traditional nonpartisanship by the activities of Labor's Non-Partisan League and the American Labor Party, the AFL adopted a statement in January 1940, which termed acceptance of CIO endorsement by any candidate the "kiss of death," and warned: ". . . we caution the members of the American Federation of Labor not be misled by the endorsements or blacklists of the so-called Labor's Non-Partisan League. This league is a sham. It is merely a paper organization, a puppet of the CIO. It has been entirely discredited and its political power is nil. . . ." Committees was appointed to attend both Democratic and Republican conventions in order to present the views of the AFL on appropriate platform planks. Although the AFL as such maintained its traditional neutrality, there was a sharp division of opinion among its leaders. Thus, Daniel Tobin, who served as head of the Labor Committee of the Democratic Party, called the attention of the Executive Council to a public attack upon the New Deal issued by ten AFL officials, and complained that this had given rise to the impression that the AFL was opposed to Roosevelt. Upon a motion by George Meany, it was declared that the statement did not emanate from the Executive Council. On the other hand, William Hutcheson, like John L. Lewis, warmly supported the Willkie candidacy, and it is a commentary upon the nature of American politics that the two great antagonists of 1935, whose angry clash on the floor of the AFL convention had signalized the formation of the CIO, were once again united in opposition to the man for whom a substantial majority of American workers consistently voted.

The great Roosevelt victories of 1932, 1936, and 1940 effectively dampened the third-party sentiment that prevailed in some labor quarters, particularly among the unions with a socialist background. The garment unions, not to be denied, had their fling in the form of the American Labor Party locally while supporting the Democratic Party nationally. Against the third-party proponents, the Roosevelt supporters could argue that the Roosevelt Administration had brought to the American worker social benefits and protection of trade union rights that would have seemed utopian to the most ardent socialist at the depths of the depression.

It cannot be said that there was ever any chance for a third party during the nineteen-thirties. For one thing, the AFL was firmly and consistently opposed to any deviation from its traditional non-partisanship. For another, John L. Lewis, the only labor leader with enough prestige to lead the newly organized industrial workers into untried political paths, was fundamentally a conservative, who strayed into the Roosevelt fold in 1936 to his subsequent regret. The Socialist Party was, by 1932, a mere shadow of its former self, while the communists, veering between "United Front" and independent political action, were too far removed from American realities to have any lasting influence, and killed whatever organizations they touched.

But to conclude that the New Deal marked no change in the political attitudes of organized labor is to misread history. For the first time, American trade unions began to work systematically at the precinct level within the framework of the established political parties. For the first time, they tasted the fruits of electoral victories for which they could fairly claim credit, and these fruits, in the form of greatly enhanced legislative influence, were sweet indeed. The AFL of Samuel Gompers was a humble supplicant before the Congress of the United States on a very limited range of matters. The AFL of William Green, and the CIO of John L. Lewis and Philip Murray, were constant visitors in the halls of Congress, and it required the shock of the Taft-Hartley Act in 1947 to bring them to the realization that labor's political millennium had not yet arrived. Nonpartisanship in 1932 meant that the labor movement was at liberty to present its views to the national conventions of the Democratic and Republican parties, and to have these views generally disregarded. Nonpartisanship in 1940 meant a voice in the selection of many state and local candidates, invitations to meet publicly with the president of the United States and his Republican challenger, nationwide radio broadcasts by labor leaders, and attendance at trade union conventions by the highest officials of the nation, including the president himself.

In part, of course, the increased political influence of organized labor was a function of its numerical growth and its greater financial resources. But beyond this, there had come about an awareness by even the most oldfashioned of the AFL leaders of the augmented role of the federal government in the labor market, and the consequent acceptance of the need for institutionalizing the means of influencing government decisions. Political action had become a necessity, and in the light of what the two parties stood for, this implied pro-Democratic partisanship. A few staunch Republicans in the top leadership of the AFL managed for a time to ensure the preservation of the old Gompers slogans as official AFL policy, but in reality, the AFL, together with the rest of the labor movement, ceased to be neutral after 1936.

Lewis and Roosevelt, Inc.

James A. Wechsler
New York Post

IF IT WAS AN ACCIDENT that [Franklin D.] Roosevelt and [John L.] Lewis ripened as leaders during the same period, it was no accident that their paths crossed. For both were measured by their ability to confront the anarchy of 1932, to restore some order in the competitive chaos, to check the suicidal corporate "individualism" that had produced the panic. Roosevelt needed Lewis's strength to coordinate the confused discontent of the propertyless as a counterweight against the pressures of business. Lewis could not have built a labor empire without the benevolent neutrality and overt encouragement of the White House. They were drawn together not by any common vision of the Promised Land, but by common peril. If Roosevelt had been forced to rely on the flabby minds and stodgy spirits of the AFL craft unionists, he would have had puny resources with which to wage the New Deal struggle. If Lewis had faced a hostile, upper-class-conscious administration exclusively responsive to the voices of property, CIO might have been crushed in the pattern of "Little Steel."

So the two men were, in a sense, thrown upon each other's mercy, and their collaboration evoked terror among believers in the old order. This was the "unholy alliance," dedicated (so conservatives

Excerpted by permission of the publisher from *Labor Baron, A Portrait of John L. Lewis,* New York: William Morrow and Company, © 1944 by James A. Wechsler.

said) to the overthrow of the profit system. The earnest, genuine disclaimers by both men of any such intentions were treated as part of the plot.

Neither lost his identity in the combination. It was no Damon and Pythias affair, no one-for-all-and-all-for-one comradeship. Perhaps neither man was capable of such abdication. In 1933 word had raced through the mining camps that "John L. Lewis was having beer and sauerkraut with President Roosevelt every night, and to hell with the company guards." In December 1935 Lewis was telling an interviewer:

"Labor has gained more under President Roosevelt than under any president in memory. Obviously it is the duty of labor to support Roosevelt 100 per cent in the next election."[1]

As 1936 neared, there was every indication that the partnership was indissoluble. . . .

A Lewis aide, discussing [the 1936] election several years afterwards, says Lewis was disturbed by the size of the plurality, that he would have preferred a closer contest which would have emphasized Roosevelt's dependence upon labor. More probably what Lewis wanted was a demonstration of Roosevelt's dependence upon Lewis. . . .

In the tumult of the 1937 labor battles the first harsh words were spoken. While the Flint auto strikers held the fort and mediators commuted between Detroit and Washington, Lewis bluntly told newspapermen that the CIO demanded its pound of flesh for its gift to Roosevelt's campaign fund. His demand, whether morally justified or not, was couched in crude market language:

". . . for six months the economic royalists represented by General Motors contributed their money and used their energy to drive this administration out of power. The administration asked labor for help and labor gave it. The same economic royalists now have their fangs in labor. The workers of this country expect the administration to help the workers in every legal way and to support the workers in General Motors plants."

At his press conference the next day the President delivered a blow to the strikers' hopes in an oblique but unmistakable rebuke to Lewis. A few days later, however, when Alfred P. Sloan refused to meet with [Secretary of Labor Frances] Perkins and Lewis for peace sessions, the President rapped Sloan's knuckles, restoring some of the balance. The tension in Lewis-Roosevelt relations seemed momentary, and settlement of the strike postponed any final reckonings. . . .

---

[1] *Common Sense,* January 1936.

The "Little Steel" strike produced a more ominous exchange. The CIO's steel union was fighting for its life in the citadels controlled by Tom Girdler and Eugene Grace. The newspaper cliche—"violence flared"—was being tiresomely tortured, as the antiunion counteroffensive brought upheaval and death. The strikers were not Gandhiists and their actions did not faithfully comply with Marquis of Queensberry rules. Nevertheless, as the La Follette Committee hearings revealed, most of the initiative for violence and most of the atmosphere of terror was provided—without regard for expense—by the steel companies. In this setting, as blood soiled the streets of steel towns, the President delivered his celebrated condemnation of the opposing armies: "A plague on both your houses!"

The statement disheartened many of Roosevelt's followers, brought grief to the picket lines, criticism from the liberal journals. It might have been one thing to lament the fury of the conflict; it was another to blame both sides without apparent distinction between cause and effect. In the moments after Roosevelt spoke his line, Lewis sulked and raged.

"Which house, Hearst or du Pont?" he commented privately to newspapermen, undoubtedly aware that they would not observe the confidence.

Roosevelt, possibly regretful at the rejoicing which his words had brought to some of his oldest critics, characteristically seeking to "even up" the damage, amended his remarks a few days later. A "spokesman" for the White House explained that the "plague" referred on the one hand to those who refused to bargain collectively with labor, and on the other to those who practiced violence. Presumably this exempted Lewis and responsible CIO officials. Nevertheless labor took the view that those who would not negotiate and those who had unleashed the violence belonged to the same house: Girdlerism. The President's declaration was regarded as unfriendly and gratuitous.

In July, Lewis, publishing a statement of CIO aims in the *New York Daily News*, referred to Roosevelt as the "champion of industrial democracy." But through the summer months, as SWOC [Steelworkers Organizing Committee] fell back in "Little Steel," Lewis brooded over the Roosevelt rebuff, possibly blaming much of the setback on the White House stand.

He was scheduled to go on the radio on Labor Day. Some CIO officials urged him to be discreet in any references to the controversy. They argued that the CIO's prestige would be gravely impaired by any formal rift. Despite the President's harshness, they pointed out, his past blessings upon unionization efforts were still valuable assets.

While Lewis, ignoring this counsel, prepared an address containing an angry thrust at the White House, an invitation to confer with the President arrived. Then the President postponed the appointment, avowedly because of other urgent business, until after the date set for Lewis's radio address. The CIO president had to decide whether to soften his indictment, pending the opportunity to talk things over, or proceed with his original manuscript. He chose the latter course. Recalling the workers who had perished in the "Little Steel" strike and the scores who had been wounded, he recited this passage:

"Labor, like Israel, has many sorrows. Its women weep for their fallen and they lament for the future of the children of the race. It ill behooves one who has supped at labor's table and who has been sheltered in labor's house to curse with equal fervor and fine impartiality both labor and its adversaries when they become locked in deadly embrace." . . .

In May, Lewis was again seen passing through the White House gates and there were new flutterings of hope among those who feared an irrevocable break. The meetings, however, were apparently formless and fruitless; the participants shadowboxed. They were distrustful of each other; neither was endowed with excessive candor. Lewis began privately to refer to the conversations as "chit-chats," to express irritation and impatience when a White House summons arrived. . . .

Up till now the differences, in so far as there were coherent issues, had revolved around domestic problems. In crudest terms Lewis was saying that labor was not getting its money's worth out of Roosevelt. The investment of the 1936 campaign was not paying dividends, and mounting unemployment was jeopardizing the CIO's structure. In the General Motors and Little Steel crises Lewis implied a simple sell-out: labor's president had refused to come to labor's rescue. There were, as I have said, many who shared Lewis's resentment. Yet whatever the President's shortcomings from labor's viewpoint his conduct had to be evaluated on a wide, complex political canvas. As CIO president leading bold assaults on open-shop strongholds, Lewis could temporarily ignore the battalions of "public opinion"; as President of the United States, Roosevelt was caught in the crossfire of rival economic blocs. Lewis might legitimately decry the deeds of corporate tyranny and denounce John Nance Garner as "a whisky-drinking, poker-playing, evil old man"; but the sour-visaged Garner, denouncing the sit-down strikes and intriguing with the New Deal's enemies, was a constant reminder to Roosevelt of the antilabor passions that swept a large section of the people. It is not improbable that Roosevelt would have doomed himself politically by open alignment with the sit-down strikers, whether he sympathized with them or not. One wonders whether Lewis, flushed with organizing triumphs, appreciated the vast areas of American life in which CIO was anathema and his own name virtual incitement to riot. In a nation whose predominant psychology was middle-class, Girdler's "right to work" demagogy had more than a handful of adherents, and many of them did not belong to exclusive clubs. In a temporary crisis Lewis might casually damn the public. The President had to deny himself that luxury. . . .

When Willkie [in 1940] was nominated, Lewis went into a summer sulk. Administration politicos, striving for a reconciliation, hoped at least to prevent Lewis from endorsing Willkie. As autumn came it appeared that the latter purpose could be accomplished. Lewis was expected to invite a plague on both houses.

Not until the closing stages of the Willkie campaign, when newspapers reported a rumble of last-minute Willkie sentiment and Willkie advisers wistfully heard the same noises, did Lewis finally stir. He announced that he would deliver a nationwide radio speech on the night of October 25. It was to be carried by all three national networks, at an estimated cost of $65,000. The contents of the address were kept as impenetrable a secret as the identity of the financial sponsor. The dramatic build-up for the performance was brilliant. Not even top CIO officials were informed of what he would say, though the CIO's future might be shaped by the address. He was elusive when questioned, often answering in parables. Shrewder associates, however, finally deduced the worst from the trend of Lewis's unfinished remarks. He intimated that neutrality in the contest might not be enough, that what was required was an affirmative indication of labor's restiveness under the Democratic leadership.

A day before the broadcast President Roosevelt signed the Neely mine-safety bill for which the UMW had aggressively lobbied. The gesture was variously interpreted as the belated blowing of a kiss at Lewis and as an effort to drive a wedge between Lewis and the miners. By the time Lewis took the air he had assured himself a radio audience of tremendous size. His listeners heard him say:

"I think the reelection of President Roosevelt for a third term would be a national evil of the first magnitude. He no longer hears the cries of the people. I think that the election of Mr. Wendell Willkie is imperative in relation to the country's needs. I commend him to the men and women of labor . . . as one who will capably and zealously protect their rights, increase their privileges and restore their happiness.

"It is obvious that President Roosevelt will not be reelected for a third term unless he has the overwhelming support of the men and women of labor. If he is, therefore, reelected, it will mean that the members of the Congress of Industrial Organizations have rejected my advice and recommendation. I will accept the result as being the equivalent of a vote of no confidence and will retire as president of the Congress of Industrial Organizations at its convention in November."

Lewis had delivered the sermon at his own political funeral.

Sidney Hillman and the PAC

Matthew Josephson

AFTER THE GREAT "LABOR WAVE" of the 1930's there had come to the CIO, as in every popular movement for political or social change, a period of consolidation. To be sure, the momentum of the CIO's earlier days still generated big organizing drives during the war years under the leadership of Philip Murray, a steadier, less spectacular figure than Lewis, though by no means lacking in native ability and shrewdness. These operations were conducted along lines marked out previously and without the apocalyptic fervor of the sit-down strikes. Indeed, with the AFL pursuing industrial-union methods in the booming war industries, there was increasingly less real difference between the two rival federations. In the CIO the leaders were as a rule younger men; and more progressive young intellectuals, including economists, journalists, and lawyers, sought to make their careers in its constituent unions and central organization.

By the winter and spring of 1943, the younger element in the CIO showed much concern at the New Deal's setbacks and seriously discussed measures for the expansion of the CIO's political department, previously consisting mainly of Labor's Non-Partisan League, now vanished with Lewis. The Smith-Connally Act[1] gave point to their discussion. At the time of its passage by Congress, certain emissaries came to Philip Murray with the proposal that [Sidney] Hillman's[2] varied talents be pressed into service again in the political field. Meanwhile others discreetly approached Hillman too with the same idea.

Excerpted by permission of the author from *Sidney Hillman, Statesman of American Labor,* New York: Doubleday and Co., 1952.

[1] The Act governing labor disputes during World War II, which included a section limiting labor's political contributions.—Eds.

[2] President of the Amalgamated Clothing Workers of America, and long-time member of the CIO Executive Board under John L. Lewis.—Eds.

He himself had been saying that the 1942 defeats showed that labor must make renewed efforts to mobilize the country's voters during the war period. One day in July 1943, when the CIO Executive Board was meeting in Washington, Murray asked Hillman to lunch with him. It was on this occasion that the CIO president first proposed the scheme which was to bring Hillman back on the national stage. He said: "I have an idea that I would like to form a political action committee in the CIO, and I would like you to head the committee." . . .

Within a few days [Hillman] had organized a meeting of 127 Eastern labor leaders, associated not only with the CIO, but with various AFL and railway unions, and several state and city labor councils. It was his way to consult as many persons of different mind as possible before he made an important move. There was also the strong hope of forming a united front with AFL through the new political league. Hillman presided at this meeting, which was held in Philadelphia on July 11. Following a full and frank discussion of the proposed program of the Political Action Committee, a public announcement was made of its formation. Its declared purpose was not only to mobilize the millions of the CIO's cohorts for active participation in state and national elections, but also church and women's groups as well as farmers, consumers, and "community organizations" throughout the United States.

Sidney Hillman, it was now announced, had been named chairman and director of the PAC; the other members of the committee were Van Bittner, R. J. Thomas, Sherman Dalrymple, and David MacDonald. A statement of policy worked out at this gathering was issued by Hillman and reflected the highly practical spirit with which the labor men approached their task. The country faced a political crisis, he said. The election of many isolationist and conservative congressmen in November 1942 was a dire warning of what might happen in the presidential contest of 1944. Recalling the intense political reaction and post-war depression experienced in 1918–20, he said that one of the prime objects of the new committee was to see to it that our war veterans this time would not "go back to selling apples after peace came." He stated:

> We are opposed to the organization of a third party at this time because it would divide the forces of the progressives throughout the nation. We are here to mobilize our power for political action now—not to wait until a few months before the elections of 1944. . . .

Since the days of La Follette's Progressive Party movement in 1924, he had often thought about the problem of building a third party for labor. But in many sections of the country, state primary laws made it well-nigh impossible to organize a real third party. Moreover, during the long period needed for the building of an independent party, the risk of a breakdown of advantageous political relations were incurred. Now Hillman still believed that labor's "investment" in Roosevelt and his political apparatus was worthwhile; that a friendly alliance with the Roosevelt Administration represented the best way in which the interests of labor could be advanced in the immediate sense. As early as September 1943, he had sent up a few trial balloons in favor of a fourth term for Roosevelt, declaring that the CIO would support the wartime President if he ran again.

But the problem of organizing a broad class-conscious group that would function in the political field as an independent and coherent force still remained. There were so many clashing sectional forces in the labor movement itself; even in the AFL there was the Socialist minority; there was the rising Negro movement to be taken into account; there were old ties between union leadership and professional party machines; and there was even a vigorous pro-Communist minority moving in another direction. At this time, in 1943, we were the military allies of the Communist fatherland.

Hillman's improvisation, therefore, took the form of a nationwide political league which, while representing labor primarily, was *not* to be a third party or an independent national political party, and yet was also to be autonomous. That is, it was to function as full partner in a coalition, mainly with the Roosevelt Democrats, but it would also lend its strength to progressive Republican candidates for Congress. This was the overall plan and represented a sort of half-way stage between a third party for labor and an auxiliary of the old professional parties. In its details, in its development of a "grass-roots" organization affiliated with the network of thousands of CIO local union offices dotting the map of the United States, the PAC reflected Hillman's highly imaginative and inventive spirit. The PAC, he insisted, was going to pay its own way. Large sums of money would be needed. In the preliminary conferences with the CIO executives he had asked that seven of the biggest unions donate at least $100,000 each to the PAC treasury.

Appearing before the November 1943 convention of the CIO at Philadelphia after his Western tour, Hillman enjoyed again the long ovations of the union delegates. . . . Hillman, in a powerful speech, appealed to the delegates for support of the PAC, arguing that labor had lost much ground politically since 1942. In that year the picture had been dark; it had seemed almost as if we would lose the war. Now, he prophesied: "We will win the war." . . .

The upshot of this enthusiastic gathering was that by vote of the delegates Hillman got the $700,000 promised for the PAC. Not all the CIO chieftains were really eager to part with all that money, but Hillman was a hard man to stop when it came to fund-raising. As news of this got around the professional politicians in both parties began to have the jitters. The newspapers, magnifying Hillman's political "war chest" about tenfold, reported that he was being armed with a "slush" fund of $7,000,000. . . .

By 1944 the American people were feeling many of the discomforts attendant upon a great war in modern times. Wages were frozen, while great stores of consumer goods, especially beefsteaks, tires, and nylon stockings, were passing into the black market. Millions of workers saw their earnings fixed by agreements written for them in a room in Washington under the procedures of the powerful War Labor Board, an arrangement scarcely calculated to inspire them with a sense of participation in their own affairs. Meanwhile their sons and brothers were being called up to the Army day by day. Though the workers were fully employed and prospered somewhat, practical observers of the political scene reported that they felt themselves alienated from the Roosevelt Administration and were of a good mind to stay away from the polls.

It was at this psychological moment that Hillman inserted himself into the picture with the PAC "crusade"—indeed, he and Philip Murray were among the few outstanding labor leaders who offered strong support to the wartime government. Hillman, particularly, was instrumental in making labor a coherent, highly efficient force in the political field; he gave a voice to the common men who were doing most of the producing and fighting. He raised issues which the former New Dealers, absorbed in military and supply problems, were neglecting. What kind of peace would we have after the fighting was over? Would there be full employment and security after the war? Above all, the PAC pounced upon the issue of the soldiers' ballot—which the Republican-Dixie bloc in Congress had obstructed for a time. Soon the widespread discussion of human affairs inspired by the distribution of millions of bright little pamphlets by the PAC and by the busy marshaling of voters everywhere for registration in the primaries began to make itself felt in all parts of the country. Hillman said: "Everyone was gloomy when we started the PAC. Then liberals seemed to spring up from the ground everywhere!"

"One thing we know in the labor movement," Hillman said later, "is *organization*." The PAC showed his organizing hand everywhere. As he explained:

We got up an organization of fourteen regional centers in the United States and from these centers organized downward into states, cities, wards, and precincts. On a door-to-door basis we are registering voters, persuading them that unless the 1944 vote is a mandate for peace and full production, 1932 will seem like a picnic. . . .

As the PAC got under way there were many mocking comments in the press to the effect that it might do more harm than good to the cause it hoped to serve. Mr. Martin Dies,[3] at any rate, made ready to blast the whole organization with a few flourishes from his "Americanist" trumpet. But for him the PAC was to be no easy game.

Many months before primary elections were to take place in the Southern states CIO local union officers, in contact with the PAC's regional and national headquarters, had begun to canvass all their union members and urge them to register and vote. "Every worker a voter" was the slogan. In Martin Dies' own district in Texas (Jefferson County), where the poll tax severely restricted voting, usually to about 10 percent of the population, thousands of shipyard and oilfield workers in the towns of Port Arthur and Beaumont were rapidly lined up to pay their poll tax and register for the primaries.

No sooner did Mr. Dies hear of all this than he began his attack on the PAC, . . . in a torrential speech before the House on January 26. He had at that time an enormous influence in Congress, most of whose members stood in dread of his possible attacks on their "Americanism." Now he warned his fellow congressmen that "gigantic slush funds" were being raised by the CIO to defeat them. A few weeks later, agents of the Un-American Activities Committee appeared in New York and sought permission of the banks used as depositories by the PAC to examine the new organization's records and expenditures. . . .

For several days Hillman examined the question of what course to take toward Dies, with some of his advisers urging that he permit the PAC books to be examined while others argued strongly that the Un-American Activities Committee had no legal authority whatsoever to examine the PAC. There were, however, other standing committees of Congress empowered to investigate possible malpractice in election campaigns, before whom he could more properly appear. At length Hillman resolved to "fight back at Dies" and try to make the affair a popular issue. "I have wanted to do that all along," he said.

On February 19, in a statement to the press, he announced that

---

[3] Mr. Dies was the original chairman of the House Un-American Activities Committee.—Eds.

he had given orders denying access to the PAC's bank accounts by the agents of Dies, adding:

> Mr. Dies has no right to any of our records. The PAC . . . will refuse any demands he may make on it for records, files, documents, or materials. . . . It is high time that someone challenged Martin Dies' abuses of congressional power.

The PAC, he held, was an "educational movement" characterized by a "profound Americanism." Far from advocating any subversive ideas, he argued that

> it is mobilizing millions of Americans *to do their duty as American citizens at the polls.* It is a perversion of reason and common sense to hold that it is un-American or subversive to ask these millions of American citizens to give their support to a program of political education.

The CIO and its friends believed that a large vote would most accurately reflect the democratic will of the country. It was the Economic Royalists who desired that "as few as possible might vote"; it was they who were the real "un-Americans."

Up to then virtually no one had dared refuse to testify or furnish records to the Dies committee in fear of a citation for contempt of Congress.

Hillman's old antagonist in Congress, Mr. Howard Smith, had also threatened to take action against the PAC, charging that it had violated the Smith-Connally Act in expending union funds for election purposes and should be cited before a Federal Grand Jury. To forestall this, Hillman and his lawyers went to Attorney General Biddle and voluntarily submitted the PAC's record for examination by FBI agents. On March 4 it was reported that the PAC would be "cleared." Under existing law any labor organization could legally expend money in "educating" people on political issues or in persuading them to register and vote in the primaries. In this case, Biddle's report indicated, funds had not been paid out to politicians or their agents, but only for pamphlets and lecturers. . . .

Within the Un-American Activities Committee of Congress there was now much dissension between Dies and a minority group who held that he had not been authorized to move against the PAC. Nevertheless, he rushed forth with a large 215-page report on the PAC which charged (under congressional immunity) that Sidney Hillman aspired "to become the Red Chief" of America in place of Mr. Earl Browder(!). Hillman, the report admitted, had been "actively and effectively anti-

Communist" in the past, but now, it was alleged, he was building up the CIO-PAC by entering into a coalition with the Communists.

A terrible power of slander was lodged in the hands of Mr. Dies, and few men had faced him in public without being besmirched. Yet Hillman bluntly challenged him by declaring to the press: "When Mr. Dies calls men like Philip Murray and other members of the Political Action Committee Communists, he lies and knows that he lies." Dies had made no investigation. He was only "peddling the same shopworn smears." Recently the PAC had been broadcasting the actual attendance and voting records of congressmen like Dies. Was Mr. Dies, then, afraid of having his public record made known? Hillman's parting shot was a telling one and caused a sensation: "Dies is obviously aroused to a frenzy by the possibility of his defeat in the Texas primary election."

Mr. Dies had in fact grave cause for alarm. In his congressional district, embracing Orange and Beaumont, thanks to the current campaign run by the CIO and AFL local union officers, registration had risen 30 percent higher than ever known before in that region. The PAC workers in Texas had done their job thoroughly. Indeed, in a thousand precincts local union officers who acted as field representatives for the PAC recorded exactly how many union members had voted in the last election, how many had moved from their homes, and how many held residence permitting them to register. Thus in Jefferson County, Texas, the registration of the union workers in the new war industries reached figures astonishing to hack politicians.

In May came news that seemed miraculous beyond belief: Mr. Martin Dies had withdrawn from the Democratic primary contest for renomination in his old district, admitting openly that he had done this because of the jump in registration stimulated by the PAC. It showed, he said, that "the CIO has captured control of the Jefferson County, Texas, Democratic convention." In quick succession Representative Joe Starnes of Alabama and John Costello of California, two other members of the Un-American Activities Committee, were also defeated in their primary election contests. Sidney Hillman was elated. "This was the biggest thing the PAC had accomplished thus far," he said, "and made the whole effort seem worth while." . . .

Earlier there had been some rumors in high Democratic Party circles that the PAC was "too hot," that Sidney Hillman was stirring up too many factional feuds which were likely to injure the chances of the ruling party in the coming elections, and that President Roosevelt would have to speak to Sidney sternly about this. . . .

But by early June, when Hillman came to see him at the White House, the President had begun to cheer up and there was no more talk of "toning down" the PAC. . . .

In July 1944, . . . as preparations were being made for the opening of the Democratic National Convention at Chicago, Sidney Hillman and Philip Murray arrived on the scene with a large and imposing party representing the CIO, and opened headquarters of their own at the Hotel Sherman. The CIO-PAC was reported to have some 200 Democratic Party delegates in its pocket—though this was greatly exaggerated. Nevertheless, Hillman and Murray seemed determined that the spokesmen of organized labor should take a hand in the president-making of that season, or rather the vice-president-making—which proved to be the same thing.

The war in Europe was in its climactic phase, for the invasion of France had been recently launched; but who could tell how soon the end would come? Roosevelt, with much less hesitation than in 1940, had resolved to run again for the presidency and thus see the war through. None in his party opposed him. The third-term taboo had already been broken, and many persons and organizations (including the Amalgamated at its May 1944 convention) had favored "drafting" Roosevelt once more.

But those who saw the President in the winter and spring of 1944 were quite shocked at his changed appearance. It was not known to the public that in mid-April he had gone to rest at Bernard M. Baruch's estate in South Carolina for two weeks, during which he "looked like a case of walking pneumonia," and had been too weak and ill to return to Washington until four weeks had passed. Roosevelt's intimates and the party leaders were aware that he might well die in office during his fourth term. This led to some ferocious intriguing among the Democrats interested in the vice-presidential choice, all of it very distressing to the weary President.

Mr. Baruch, an old hand at inside politics, used every opportunity while the President convalesced, to urge the cause of his old political alter ego, James F. Byrnes, former senator from South Carolina and Supreme Court Justice, now serving as Director of War Mobilization. Vice-President Henry Wallace (then on a mission to China) should normally have been renominated, for he was supposed to hold great appeal for millions of liberal and labor voters. But powerful opposition to him had arisen among the Democratic Party's big-city bosses such as Edward J. Flynn of New York, Edward Kelly of Chicago, Frank Hague of Jersey City, and Robert Hannegan of St. Louis, the Democratic national chairman. The Southern politicians also were opposed to Wallace, and Roosevelt was "inundated" with advice from anti-Wallace Democrats that the incumbent Vice-President, if renominated, would "hurt the ticket" in a close election.

The party bosses leaned toward Byrnes, a Southern conservative with much political experience—though some, like Flynn, noted that, as a former Catholic converted to Protestantism, Byrnes would be objectionable to one large religious group. Roosevelt was depressed and, according to Flynn, hated to discuss or argue with anyone about who might succeed him at his death. In the end he agreed that Byrnes would be his first choice for Vice-President.

Hillman, hearing of the Byrnes movement, on several occasions in June made plain to the President that Byrnes was considered unfriendly to organized labor and would be ill-regarded by the Negro voters in the North.

It was at this period, in an off-the-record visit with Roosevelt on June 9, that Hillman learned that the names of others being definitely considered for the vice-presidency included Supreme Court Justice William O. Douglas, Senator Alben Barkley of Kentucky, and Senator Harry S. Truman of Missouri. Philip Murray strongly favored the renomination of Wallace. Truman, on the other hand, in view of the sectional conflicts within the Democratic Party, was a more conciliatory figure, coming as he did from a "border" state, and having an excellent record with regard to New Deal and labor legislation. . . .

By July 10, 1944, the situation (as far as we can piece it together from the incomplete and conflicting recollections of all parties concerned) was as follows: Roosevelt had Edward J. Flynn's reports from the field indicating that Wallace was unwanted by the Democratic Party bosses; he had meanwhile committed himself, in some measure, to sponsoring Byrnes, but had noted the vigorous objections of Hillman on behalf of the CIO and of Negro leaders and Catholics as well; and finally he had asked Flynn to get a group of the Democratic bosses together and "inject Truman into the picture" as the best possible alternative to Byrnes. On the evening of July 11, a committee composed of Flynn, Hannegan, Kelly, George Allen, and Frank Walker came to dinner at the White House and discussed the whole affair with Roosevelt. Justice William O. Douglas was mentioned as a possibility by the President, though without evoking enthusiasm. In the end Roosevelt is said to have handed Hannegan a little penciled note saying: "Bob, I think Truman is the right man." . . . .

On the night of Friday, July 14, the President boarded his private train for a destination on the West Coast, his movements being kept secret according to wartime regulations. The next day the train halted at Chicago, where preparations for the opening of the Democratic convention five days later were in full swing. Democratic Chairman Robert Hannegan went on board the train and received his last instructions from Roosevelt, who did not show himself in Chicago. He is said to have related afterward that Roosevelt said that, as to the final choice of Byrnes, Wallace, or Truman, he and the other Democratic leaders must first "clear it with Sidney." The phrase "Clear it with Sidney," picked up by the New York *Times'* Arthur Krock (through Byrnes and Baruch), was to echo and re-echo through the country (suffering increasing distortions) after the convention was over. What it definitely signified at the time was that a veto power was given to Hillman, as the CIO's political leader, only over the final choice for Vice-President at the convention. Roosevelt wanted labor's wholehearted support. . . .

The Republican propagandists, commanding about 85 percent of the country's newspapers, fastened on the phrase attributed by Arthur Krock of the New York *Times* to President Roosevelt in his orders to Hannegan on the vice-presidential choice: "Clear it with Sidney." But the words were soon converted into the slogan: "CLEAR EVERYTHING WITH SIDNEY," which was placarded all over the United States. Study of the propaganda technique used by the Republican supporters of Dewey and John Bricker has shown that the ideas they stressed mainly were: (1) the "menace" of labor's entrance into politics; (2) the use of "huge slush funds" by labor; (3) alleged communistic influences back of the CIO; (4) the vague irrational appeal of anti-Semitism, directed against Sidney Hillman in particular.

Our election-time "debates," to be sure, are usually pointed at the lowest common denominator among the voting population. But the contest of 1944 has probably never been surpassed for abusive violence of language, for hysterical appeals to prejudice, or for slanderous whispering campaigns used by the party of the "outs." For four months the name of Sidney Hillman scarcely ever left those verbal pillories erected for it in the front pages of the chain newspapers of Hearst, McCormick-Patterson, and Gannett.

Governor Dewey had begun mildly by offering his own "me too" version of a Republican New Deal. He ended by centering his attention on the alleged "Roosevelt-Hillman-Browder plot" to subject the United States to a Communist dictatorship. An example of one of the opposition party's slogans was:

> *Sidney Hillman and Earl Browder's Communists*
> *have registered. Have you?*

The nation was declared to be in instant peril of capture by "Sidney Hillman, the pants presser." President Roosevelt and Mrs. Roosevelt were pictured in our yellow press as surrounded by the gangsters of Murder, Inc. Mrs. Claire Boothe Luce, in mid-October, discovered that Hillman's PAC was spending dollars "like confetti" in order to defeat her in a Connecticut congressional district. "If my head is to roll in a basket," she exclaimed, "at least it's a more American head than Sidney Hillman's"—thus joining the brave company of those who aroused the passions of race hatred. Hillman's reply was that Mrs. Luce was overestimating both the PAC's resources and her own importance. He added gallantly: "I hope she carries her pretty head around for a long time—but not in Congress.". . .

Roosevelt had figured on a very close race. In the final weeks the PAC campaign all over the country wound up with a strong finish. Numerous political "experts" were all in agreement that Roosevelt's margin of victory, reduced to only 3,100,000 in excess of Dewey's 21,300,000 could not have been gained save for "the strength of Hillman's PAC drive." Republican newspapers saluted Sidney Hillman as the "Number One labor politician" who had emerged triumphant over bitter attacks, and "as the mobilizer of millions of labor votes that were Mr. Roosevelt's margin of victory." The great turnout, the rise of the PAC, the "Hillman Blitz" were "providential for Roosevelt."

From the PAC headquarters in New York, on the night of the election, Hillman spoke on the air, a few minutes after midnight, to the PAC workers throughout the country, announcing the news of certain victory for the party of Roosevelt. He was weary but elated as he congratulated them, saying that labor had come of age and a "phalanx of liberalism" had rallied to its cause. "This election was *cleared* with the American people!" he wound up.

Only two years before he had been, as many thought, at his political "nadir" when he left Washington. Now Roosevelt wired him on November 8:

> I cannot delay longer telling you how deeply I appreciate the splendid job which you did from start to finish. Hope to see you soon. Affectionate regards.

A fortnight later Roosevelt make his acknowledgements by letter more handsomely still:

> One thing I want to make perfectly clear to you, Sidney, is my appreciation. It was a great campaign and nobody knows better than I do how much you contributed to its success. I was glad to learn that the CIO in Chicago authorized the continuation of the

PAC. I can think of nothing more important in the years to come than the continuing political education and political energy of the people who do the jobs in this land, in the determination that the American nation shall do the great job it can do for all. I send you no condolences for the licks you took in the campaign. You and I and Fala have seen what happened to the people who gave them.

Hillman's reply, less modest than usual, was intended as a reminder to the sometimes overburdened President that labor would be a force to be reckoned with in the political arena:

Dear Mr. President:

Your letter was most heart-warming. As old campaigners you and I have come to accept the "licks" as a tribute to the effectiveness of the job. But I am delighted to learn that Fala too took them like the true thoroughbred that he is.

The enthusiasm, determination, and deep political understanding with which the CIO convention moved to put the PAC on a permanent basis is a good augury for the future. I came away from Chicago confident that we can look forward to the continuance of intelligent and effective participation in American political life by millions of the men and women who do the work of the nation. I know you believe with me that this is the best guarantee that we can move forward with assurance to attain the great goals which our people have set for themselves and for the world.

I do not need to tell you how greatly I have deemed it a privilege to have made some contribution to the recent campaign and how deeply I and my associates rejoice at the result.

Ringing Doorbells with PAC

Claire Neikind

Monday, September 27, 10 A.M.

JOINED HENRY MURRAY, New England CIO–PAC Director, at the Bondmore Hotel in Hartford. A stubby young man who chain-smokes cigars and refers frequently to notes on backs of envelopes, leaflets and old bills overflowing from all his pockets. He briefed me quickly on the Connecticut situation.

The big issue here, Murray says, is the election of Chester

Reprinted by permission of the publisher, *New Republic*, Vol. 119, October 25, 1948.

Bowles as Governor. Labor's help was significant in pushing through his nomination, and since in Connecticut a 5 percent shift decides Republican or Democratic victory, labor's turnout will decide whether or not Bowles will win.

A low vote in 1946 left Connecticut's liberal Representatives high and dry. Chief job this month is to get 70,000 CIO members registered, later to persuade them to vote for liberals.

7 P.M.

Dinner with UAW organizers for area. They point out their International union deeply concerned over Bowles's election, but struggle between right and left wings for control of Hartford CIO has prevented full attention to this until recently. Left is now defeated here, and Bowles campaign is getting full attention. UAW organizers believe his popularity is so great among workers that he might not only get in, but pull Truman ticket in with him, which otherwise would be doubtful.

Murray questions them on registration, which opened last week here. It's slow. They lay plans for this evening's Hartford CIO Council meeting to improve registration within remaining nine days.

8:30 P.M.

CIO Council meeting at headquarters of Royal local on New Park Avenue. Twenty-five officers of member locals present. Chairman Pat Ward, former Colt worker and candidate for reelection to state senate. Opens meeting by reading letter from national CIO, outlining its position on elections. It urges "intensive campaign on issues of living costs, housing, anti-labor laws, $1 minimum wage, extension of social security." Calls on locals to organize "block workers as footsoldiers of PAC." Delegates listen with sober concentration. Murray then speaks on urgency of Bowles campaign. "We've talked enough about our political strength . . . this is our chance to put up or shut up. . . ." "How right you are, Brother," someone sings out from the back of the hall. Meeting picks up momentum, delegates pass unanimous resolution pledging "everything humanly possible to elect Bowles," propose ways of providing at least 50 cars to carry registrants to city hall, and a hundred volunteers at PAC headquarters, to canvass by telephone and on foot.

Meeting ends with delegates clustering around Murray. One precinct rally needs a speaker; would he be free? The Negro voters need more attention; can he suggest anything? Something should be done about unionists' wives; what have other areas done about this?

Tuesday, September 28

Up at eight and over to PAC headquarters, in one-story frame building on New Park Avenue. A crew of girls are busy at phones, typed lists in front of them.

Murray first telephones Washington PAC office, to report progress and order 100,000 copies of new leaflet for Hartford area. Then produces from his bulging pockets copies of postcards and leaflets being used in Massachusetts to good effect, consults with Ward on possibility of adapting these to Hartford situation.

Then to Democratic headquarters in Bond Hotel. With Bowles's aides, Murray discusses citywide meeting of shop stewards at which Bowles is to speak on Friday. Selects copies of two Bowles speeches on housing and prices, to send to key CIO stewards all over state. Suggests list of possible speakers for Negro community. . . .

In New Haven we go to CIO headquarters for a talk to Scranton's Ed McCrone, CIO regional director, and Harold Senior, state CIO treasurer. Local unions working independently here, Steel, Amalgamated and Auto carrying out individual campaigns in their shops on registration. Murray points out this involves waste motion.

From there to New London, 50 miles away, for a meeting with AFL leader on Mrs. Chase Going Woodhouse's campaign. This is second most critical in state. Here is a 5 percent-margin district, with 64 towns and heavy farming vote, mostly Republican. She won in '44, with a 5,000-vote majority, because cities voted. She lost to a smaller Republican vote in '46, because cities didn't vote. With her excellent record in Congress, Mrs. Woodhouse is only Democrat outside of Bowles himself who has joint AFL–CIO support. . . .

Wednesday, September 29

Up at what I am certain was the crack of dawn. Breakfast conference with Stanley Petkas, Textile Workers organizer assigned to full-time PAC work in the state. Textile has put 10 or 12 such men in the nation's critical areas, with splendid results. Petkas is rightfully proud. "We have 10,000 textile workers in this state and we've checked every one of them for registration and even some across the state line," he reports. "In Stonington this week I found one shop of 330 workers with 15 unregistered. We registered them, all right.

"We've raised $13,000 for the PAC dollar drive, three to four times better than we did in '46. We've even taught the Democratic party its business. In some cases, while checking our own lists, we found slews of regular Democrats, not workers, unregistered. We turned them over to the Democrats and lit some fires under them. What the hell is the matter with those guys?"

He reports, too, that Textile and other CIO unions were right in the heart of primary politics for the first time in Connecticut labor history in towns like Putnam, Killingly, Stonington, Jewett City, Willimantic. "It'll take some doing to put an antilabor man over on us from now on.". . .

Thursday, September 30

Off early for Providence, Rhode Island, Murray having arranged to return to Connecticut the following week to lay plans for vote-getting after registration is completed.

In Providence, a conference with Frank Benti and Antonio Di Pinto, president and secretary, respectively, of the Rhode Island CIO, makes it clear this state is a model for CIO-PAC action. It has the highest per capita organized labor membership in the country, and there isn't a political leader here who doesn't know it. Labor political action began to get results in '44. Since then Rhode Island has been one of the most consistent pro-labor states in the nation. . . .

1 P.M.

We leave Providence and head for Massachusetts, where organized labor is fighting for its life. On our way to Fall River, Murray explains the situation. There are three anti-labor referenda coming up, one of which makes it a criminal offense to sign a contract containing *any* form of union security, from union shop to maintenance of membership. The three together practically legislate unions out of existence.

As we drive into Fall River, we see a soundtruck on the main street, with an enormous "Register Now" sign and a loud horn blaring. At the City Hall, long double lines of would-be voters wait patiently, stretching from the third to the first floor and out into the street. This is a textile town, and we head for the Textile Workers office. We meet Dolores Marconi, educational director, flushed with excitement and finding it hard to sit calmly in her chair.

She tells us Fall River has already broken all registration records and there is still another day to go. This was accomplished after monumental job done of checking registration lists of 52,000 against police lists of 81,000 residents, and checking the balance against CIO membership. In this case, PAC went after *all* working-class unregistered voters, whether CIO members or not. They sent 40,000 postcards, went doorbell pushing, organized block workers, and have already shoved up registration from 52,000 to 59,000, and expect at least 1,000 more. "Our campaign is the talk of the town," Dolores says happily. . . .

6:30 P.M.

We reach the Hub toward evening, the flivver groaning in every joint. Dinner with Bill Belanger, regional Textile director, and Cyril O'Brien, state PAC organizer. Belanger, a French American who radiates competence, is wildly elated. Registration in Boston, Worcester, Springfield, Cambridge and almost every other industrial center is breaking all records. With a half-million organized workers in the state, and the AFL and CIO united for the first time in Massachusetts history, he is sure the anti-labor bills will be licked.[1]

We listen to the United Labor Committee's radio program, which goes over 12 major Massachusetts stations every night. Made with first-rate volunteer labor from the American Federation of Radio Artists, the "Ballots and Ballads" programs sound really professional.

Belanger tells us of the pioneering political job being done. "This is big-league stuff," he says. Key labor leaders are learning the a, b, c's of political ward organization, breaking down registration lists, organizing ward and precinct captains, building permanent organization. . . .

Friday, October 1

In the afternoon we visit one of the aides of Democratic candidate for Governor, Paul Dever. Three telephones on his desk ring constantly, workers popping in and out, general air of jubilation pervades loft headquarters. "In the bag, in the bag? Nothing's in the bag until November 2," he says nervously. I learn later he always says everything nervously. "But it looks good, it looks good. Labor's doing OK," he tells Murray, "but you fellows better realize there's many a slip between a registered voter and a voter."

Dinner with Belanger and AFL state chief Ernest Johnson. There is still some wariness between them. . . . AFL and CIO here never political bedfellows before, but every sign of excellent cooperation and mutual admiration. They discuss next stage in campaign— deeper education on referenda and intensive efforts to get workers to polls. . . .

---

[1] Belanger was the subject of a later *New Republic* article, November 22, 1948, entitled "The Man Who Elected Truman."—Eds.

Saturday, October 2

To Worcester, where AFL–CIO cooperation was late in starting but now is rolling. We learn that of the 20,000 unregistered voters, 10,000 have been picked up this week. Recent meeting of 600 shop stewards, roaring with enthusiasm, started action, and everyone confident of success. Point out in Roosevelt year, 1940, there were 100,000 registered. Now there are 107,000, and more to come. "We can't miss," the CIO man tells us. Expects that drive will not only vote down anti-labor bills, but will carry Democratic gubernatorial candidate Dever and local congressional candidate Donahue. . . .

At last on my way back to New York, I compare the labor picture in New England as I knew it in 1944, and the picture I've seen this week. In 1944 the work was sporadic, superficial, resting on Roosevelt. The work now is mature, self-reliant; labor is digging in for a long siege.

The Impact of the Political Left

Bernard Karsh and Phillips L. Garman
University of Illinois

THE LARGEST GROUP OF RADICALS in the labor movement during [the New Deal] period belonged to organizations affiliated with the Communists' Trade Union Unity League which in 1934 claimed a membership of 125,000 of whom 30,000 were said to be members of the Needle Trades Industrial Union. In addition to the Needle Workers, the TUUL had established an Automobile Workers Union of Detroit, the Independent Shoe Workers of New York, the Amalgamated Food Workers of New York, the National Textile Workers Union, the Marine Workers Industrial Union, and others. With the exception of the Needle Trades Industrial Union which was firmly established in the New York fur industry, the membership claimed by the TUUL was almost certainly greatly exaggerated and may not have been much more than actual party members working in these industries. Their unions, as trade unions, were hardly more than vantage points from which party

Excerpted with permission of the copyright owners, the Regents of the University of Wisconsin, from Milton Derber and Edwin Young, eds., *Labor and the New Deal*, Madison, Wis.: University of Wisconsin Press, 1957. Many of the footnotes in the original have been deleted.

organizers and propagandists could seek to recruit members to their small cadres. With few exceptions, particularly among the fur workers in the Needle Trades Union, they achieved no employer recognition and did not carry on collective bargaining activities. Yet, as tiny as they were, they constituted a very vocal minority, constantly putting forward their program, publishing newspapers, bulletins, leaflets, pamphlets, etc., and just as constantly holding meetings and conducting training schools. . . .

TUUL policy was one of dual unionism, including disruption of AFL unions under any and all circumstances; the party's mechanical control over the mass organizations in which it had influence, again with the possible exception of the Needle Trades Union, prevented these organizations from becoming unions in any real sense but made them simply party units under another name. During these years the Communist parties throughout the world followed a policy of extreme verbal (and sometimes physical) aggression against democratic and socialist forces. The latter were presented as "social fascists," against whom all means, including violence, were in order. The general consequence of this ultra-left period was organizational isolation which separated the Communists from the main body of trade union members and therefore from any significant influence among them. Nevertheless, it was during this period of ultra-left propaganda and organizational isolation that an "organizational weapon" was formed that would maintain its strength when thrown into active combat.

The long period of isolation and internal orientation served to consolidate the leadership of the movement, to test and train the cadres in party and trade union theory and in organizational strategy and tactics, and to intensify the commitment of individual members. It was during this period that the Communists developed to a greater extent and with more perfection the tactical use of the fraction and faction, the caucus, parliamentary maneuverings, and centralized control over rank and file party membership in the unions. The basis for later effective penetration of the mass unions stemmed from this apparently irrational period of "social fascism," "united front from below," splits and purges. After 1935 the . . . period of "united front from above" became the principal organizational strategy of the worldwide Communist movement, not only with respect to trade union work but in all of its far-flung activities. The party could now support any and all whose purposes it could use for its own ends. In the American scene, the TUUL was dissolved and the old aggression was relaxed against the "reactionary" trade union leaders of the AFL and then the CIO.

This change in basic party position on the trade union front in the United States meant that the Communists could now endeavor to work within the framework of the existing unions. However, with the emergence of the CIO, the Communists turned their attention to these new unions and new situations, largely ignoring the older established AFL unions in favor of the "wave of the future" represented by the CIO.

Their earlier training in the TUUL unions and in party and trade union theory and tactics was now directed toward the centers of mass production industries and the unions which were being forged there. Their previous isolation had fashioned a "combat weapon" which was put at the disposal of John L. Lewis and the CIO. Among the radicals in the trade unions, the Communists were the largest, the most disciplined and homogeneous group. Unlike the Socialists and the other splinter groups of the political left, their ranks were undiluted by conflicting dogmas and internal struggles for power.

The Socialist party during the early New Deal period was caught up in an internal struggle for supremacy between the "old guard" and the new young "militants" who sought to advance a more revolutionary program. In 1934 this internal conflict erupted when large numbers of the militants of the party left its ranks in disgust. A split occurred at the 1936 Cleveland convention when some 40 percent of its membership, largely the "old guard," walked out of the SP. Shortly thereafter, Norman Thomas, the Socialist party leader, called for an "all-inclusive party."

> He invited into the Socialist Party all independent, unaffiliated, affiliated, and dependent radical homeless, the splinter groups, factions, fractions, droplets, and kibitzers. He hoped in this fashion to achieve a unity of left-wing forces against fascism. Gitlowites, Zamites, Fieldites, Trotskyites, Lovestonites and all streamed into the party, and each group of intellectual pitchmen set up its own stand. A host of previously isolated one-ring circuses was now operating under one huge billowing tent. And the result was bedlam.[1]

Only the Communists remained out, though they too agreed with the SP leadership on a program for joint work in the trade unions. But unlike the Communists, the "all-inclusive" Socialists constituted a heterogeneous amalgam of disparate radical groups, each professing a different "Socialist" ideology and each seeking to impose on their new allies their separate programs and ideological formulations.

---

[1] Daniel Bell, "The Background and Development of Marxian Socialism in the United States" in Donald D. Egbert and Stow Persons, eds., *Socialism and American Life* (Princeton: Princeton University Press, 1952), I, 382.

Further, many trade unionists, such as those found in the needle trades and even in the AFL's Machinists Union, were unaffiliated with any radical group though they privately or publicly professed a generally Socialist ideology. The result was that the Communists remained the largest "undiluted" and "untroubled" radical tendency. Thus, they could mobilize with much greater efficiency their small numbers than could the rest of the political left.

Radicals in the CIO

Following the dissolution of the TUUL and initial efforts to enter the AFL, its directing personnel was offered to Lewis and the new CIO. He felt he could use, if not their philosophy, at least their experience. In trying to secure a mass following for their TUUL unions, they had learned to make speeches, write leaflets and reports, run mimeograph machines, set up and man picket lines, organize violence to resist violence, and hold the chair in turbulent meetings. They were familiar with all the other mechanics indispensable when workers almost completely unfamiliar with union procedures were crowding into halls, and demanding guidance. Further, they displayed a willingness to subject themselves to all of the physical hazards of a picket line attacked by police or National Guardsmen, and a dedication to their ideology had given them a reputation for self-sacrifice and almost boundless energy. Also, they were a relatively mobile force, submitting to the party's requirement that they often pick up roots and plant them in some new and faraway community for the purpose of "colonizing" a factory or a mill.

And when the old-line AFL leadership or employers denounced Lewis and his radical support as "reds," they rubbed a good many rank and file unionists the wrong way. For it must be remembered that in the mid-thirties the Communist party was not viewed with as much distrust as it later aroused in the labor movement. It was still regarded as a legitimate radical party rather than a monolithic and totalitarian arm of the Russian dictatorship, and even the splinter Marxist groups still considered it part of the radical community. It would be several years yet before this attitude toward the Communists would change. Furthermore, the indefatigable work of the Communists, literally pouring themselves into every task no matter how small or menial, had given them the reputation of being totally dedicated to their trade union work and of being bearers of the gospel of the promised land.

From 1935 to 1941, John L. Lewis was publicly idolized by them as well as by other radicals and large numbers of liberals. He and his lieutenants hired known and unknown radicals of every hue as organizers for the new CIO unions. He even welcomed the aid of a group of radical unionists whom he had previously driven out of his own United Mine Workers Union because they had opposed his dictatorial regime. . . . At this time, there was very little comfort and less glory in organizing for the CIO. Those willing to take the risks associated with the job were, in large measure, men who were moved by a conviction that unionization of the mass production industries was a step toward a larger social end.

Lewis was well aware of the degree and proportions of the Communist power within the CIO, but he was confident that he could control it. To charges of harboring Communist organizers, he would answer, "I do not turn my organizers or CIO members upside down and shake them out to see what kind of literature falls out of their pockets." Or again, speaking of Communists, "If they are good enough for industry to hire, they're good enough for us to organize." When ILGWU President [David] Dubinsky once protested against Lewis' use of known radicals, Lewis is reported to have quipped back, "Who gets the bird, the hunter or the dog?"

The effectiveness of the political radicals varied in different situations. By and large, they were most successful among the new industrial unions except in the needle trades where many Socialists were used as organizers. The radicals met with little success particularly where the AFL and already established CIO unions had strength and competent leadership. And where unions originated as organizing committees and remained for a relatively long period of time under the control of Lewis or Sidney Hillman, the Communists were less successful in establishing themselves permanently. But in those situations where there was little or no legacy of unionism or where independent leadership had made considerable headway prior to the CIO, the Communists met with greatest success. Of the eleven unions expelled in 1949 and 1950 from the CIO for Communist domination, only a few had histories which preceded their affiliation with CIO. The Mines, Mill, and Smelter Workers had a long legacy of radicalism growing out of the Western Federation of Miners and the IWW, and the Fur and Leather Workers had been controlled by Communist leadership since the middle 1920's. The Electrical, Farm Equipment, Food and Tobacco, Public Workers, Office and Professional, the American Communications Association, Fishermen and Allied Workers, and the National Union of Marine Cooks and Stewards were all new unions, created during the early days of CIO. Still other new CIO unions were found with Communist leadership at their top levels. Thus, the Transport Workers Union was for many years under Communist domination, and it was not until 1948 that its international president, Mike Quill, decided to take measures to oust them. And the National Maritime Union was likewise under Communist domination from 1938, shortly after it was organized, until its president Joe Curran broke with Communists in 1948 and succeeded in ousting them from control. The CIO's United Furniture Workers was slated for expulsion from CIO in 1949 when its international president succeeded in defeating the Communists who controlled the secretary-treasurer and the general executive board. The Communists had been established as the dominant force within the West Coast Longshoremen's Union before Lewis appointed Bridges as organizing director for CIO on the West Coast. It was into situations such as these that the Communists poured their strength and resources and were most successful. . . .

Various estimates have been made of the ultimate strength of the Communists within the CIO. At minimum they controlled unions containing about 25 percent of the CIO's total membership and at maximum they wielded powerful influence in unions having another 25 percent. They completely controlled the third largest CIO union, the United Electrical Workers, which for many years was the main industrial base of the party. The UE was formed in 1936 from a number of independent, IBEW, and AFL federal locals which had originated as company unions. . . . In addition to their strength in the national unions themselves, the Communists wielded powerful influence in the national headquarters of the CIO where Lee Pressman had become almost indispensable to Murray and other Communists controlled some of the organization's service arms. Further, many of the CIO's state and local subordinate bodies were controlled by them. It was not until the late 1940's, after [Walter] Reuther's victory over the Communists in auto, the pressure of [James] Carey, [Emil] Rieve, and others, and the onset of the "cold war," that Murray became convinced that Communist activities and influence in CIO were inimical to the basic interests of the organization. He succeeded in defeating them by setting the stage for their expulsion and aiding those unions not fully under their control to rid themselves of Communist leadership.

Political Activity of Organized Labor: 1948–55

Philip Taft

Brown University

Third Party

IN AN EFFORT to keep its factions united, the CIO Executive Board voted against its officers affiliating with Americans for Democratic Action, a liberal group sponsored by Mrs. Eleanor Roosevelt among others. The same rule was applied to the Progressive Citizen's Committee, which was an outgrowth of the National Citizen's Political Action Committee originally formed by Sidney Hillman. The National Citizens PAC was showing increasingly its "party colors" and was following the Communist line on important issues. A more serious problem confronted the CIO when Henry Wallace announced his candidacy for the Presidency on a third party ticket. Reactions to the announcement differed. *The Daily Worker*, the journalistic spokesman for the Communist party, headlined it as "A Historic Candidacy," while Jack Kroll[1] declared: "It has been the policy of the CIO Political Action Committee not to support a third party."

Unions controlled by the Communists and front organizations quickly fell in line. Sidney Hillman's intervention in the affairs of the American Labor party was revealed as a serious error in judgment. Officers of the Amalgamated Clothing Workers resigned from New York's American Labor party, and one of its leaders declared that "a third party must inevitably play into the hands of labor's enemies." The CIO Executive Board by a vote of 33 to 11 decided "it was politically unwise to inject a third party into the political scene of 1948." The CIO Political Action Committee voted by 9 to 2 against a policy of partisanship. One of the minor consequences of the anti-third party position of the CIO was the resignation of Lee Pressman[2] as counsel for the Steelworkers' Union and of the CIO. . . .

In 1948, Van A. Bittner and [William] Green testified on behalf of their respective organizations before the Republican and Democratic parties. Both labor programs were in essential agreement. Their

---

Reprinted by permission of the publisher from pages 612–17 of *Organized Labor in American History*. Copyright © 1964 by Philip Taft, New York: Harper and Row, 1964. Footnotes in the original have been deleted.

[1] Director of CIO-PAC after Hillman's death.—Eds.

[2] Pressman, who later admitted he had been a Communist, was a leader in the Wallace third party, the Progressive Party of America.—Eds.

most important plank was the repeal of the Taft-Hartley Act. In addition, they called for higher minimum wages, improvements in social security, fair employment practice legislation, and tax revision. It was a clear indication that those who controlled official CIO policy at this time were in close agreement with the AFL on political, economic, and social questions. However, the AFL and CIO differed on endorsing candidates for the Presidency. The AFL reiterated its traditional nonpartisan position, although George Harrison, a member of the executive council, headed labor for Truman and Barkley. Daniel Tobin, who had served three times as the head of the Democratic party's labor committee, belatedly and unenthusiastically endorsed Thomas Dewey for the Presidency.

The CIO Executive Board, by a vote of 35 to 12, on August 21, 1948, endorsed Truman and Barkley. The issue split the organization and was the forerunner of action against the Communists. The opponents clothed their arguments with references to Truman's antilabor actions, but it was the Marshall plan, bitterly opposed by the Cominform, which was the true cause for the opposition. It should be recalled that the attacks of the Communist-controlled unions on Roosevelt during the Hitler-Stalin pact were also usually explained by reference to domestic issues.

Labor's League for Political Education

Until 1947 the AFL had followed its traditional political policies; it published and distributed the voting records of members of Congress and periodically elected a Nonpartisan Campaign Committee, made up of the permanent officers of the AFL and several members of the executive council, to influence the election of labor's friends and defeat its enemies in the congressional elections. It maintained no permanent political department, nor was this task entrusted to a member of the staff. In fact, the AFL devoted only a minor fraction of its energies and resources to political activity. Largely as a result of the passage of the Taft-Hartley Act, the sixty-sixth convention of the AFL recommended the "immediate establishment of 'Labor's Educational and Political League.'"

The league was directed to acquaint the workers of the country with the economic and political views of the AFL, to prepare and disseminate information on the attitude of candidates for nomination or election to federal office, raise funds, and employ a staff for carrying out its duties. A conference of international presidents was called on December 5 and 6, 1947, to make final plans for launching the league.

Vice-President Matthew Woll, George Harrison, and Charles McGowan prepared a program.

In explaining the need for an intensified political program by the AFL, President Green informed the conference of international presidents that he had been surprised by the strength of antilabor feeling in Congress and by the overriding of President Truman's veto of the Taft-Hartley Act. Vice-President Daniel Tobin stressed that suggestions and amendments were welcome. The executive council recommended that Labor's League for Political Education be governed by a national committee consisting of the members of the AFL Executive Council and all national unions affiliated with the AFL. The national committee was to choose its officers annually. An administrative committee was appointed and authorized to select a national director and the necessary staff. Secretary-Treasurer George Meany assured the delegates that the league was "by no means a departure from the old political philosophy of the AF of L of 'defeating your enemies and rewarding your friends' . . . that policy is just as valid today as when it was initiated many years ago by Samuel Gompers and those associated with him in the founding of this Federation." Meany added that the formation of the league was an "attempt to give effect to that philosophy in line with present conditions." In his view, it was no longer sufficient "to send Central Labor Unions and Local Unions the voting records of Congressmen or representatives in the various State Legislatures. He declared we have gotten beyond that point. He stated we have got to do something more than that; we have got to make our people politically conscious; develop them politically in their own self-interest, not for the purpose of attempting to run the country but for the purpose of protecting ourselves."

The administrative committee tentatively selected Senator Burton K. Wheeler as director, but objections by some members, as well as newspaper reports that Wheeler had reservations on the Marshall Plan and that he regarded his office as a policy-making one, put an end to his consideration. After going over a long list of names, Joseph Keenan, secretary of the Chicago Federation of Labor, was appointed. The Department of Political Education, under the chairmanship of George Harrison, was in charge of endorsements. Other committees dealt with finances and public relations; one was also established to mobilize women voters. Counsel advised that union-contributed funds could be used for education but not for political campaigning. Later, a League for Political Education was established in every state. A news service was supplied, and voting records of candidates were circulated. In 1948 more than $115,000 was donated by the unions for the educational funds, and a larger sum for political action was raised by voluntary contributions of individuals. Expenditures for political education by unions were held proper. Educational work by the league was financed after 1951 by the AFL. Neither the AFL nor the league endorsed Presidential candidates in 1948, although George Harrison, chairman of the Department of Political Direction, was active in behalf of the Truman-Barkley ticket.

As the campaign rolled on, John L. Lewis sought to settle an old score with President Truman. He denounced him as "totally unfit . . . careless with the truth, elastic in his principles . . . a malignant scheming sort of an individual who is dangerous to the United Mine Workers of America and dangerous to the United States of America." George Harrison described Lewis' statement as designed to aid the election of Thomas Dewey. Undaunted by Lewis' opposition and the defection of several labor leaders to the Republican party, Jack Kroll, the director of the CIO Political Action Committee, forecast on the basis of spot polls in factories a victory for Truman. Following the 1948 election, Labor's League for Political Education was voted permanent status.

On the basis of data reported to the Clerk of the House of Representatives, national labor organizations spent $1,291,343 in the 1948 Presidential campaign, but the total does not include the funds raised by local groups. The largest amount, $513,003, was spent by the CIO Political Action Committee. Labor's League for Political Education was second, with an expenditure of $343,293. Of the political committees sponsored by each of eleven unions, the largest expenditure— $240,532—was reported by the International Ladies' Garment Workers' Union.

Labor's League for Political Education raised over $600,000 for its educational fund in 1948–49, and under $500,000 in 1950–51. These funds were used for writing and circulating printed material, for radio and television programs, and for organizing state and local groups. Both PAC and LLPE continued their activities after the 1948 campaign. The CIO pointed to the broad character of PAC's program. "Stress has been laid during the work of your Political Action Committee, on the inclusive nature of the CIO program which embraces matters of broad concern such as valley authorities, aid to education, housing, health, farm programs, civil rights, and other subjects." A similar view was voiced by the LLPE Department of Political Education. It believed that labor had to support candidates who were concerned with and would support programs to increase the incomes of farmers and low-paid wage earners, as well as development programs for the western states which could be "the greatest single bulwark against unemployment." . . .

Representatives from both the AFL and CIO appeared before the platform committees of the Democratic and Republican parties in 1952 and presented their views. According to the CIO, 107 of its members attended as delegates to the Democratic convention.

AFL and CIO delegates worked closely together. A joint coordinating committee was organized with George Harrison, James McDevitt, director of Labor's League for Political Education, Jack Kroll, director of PAC as members. Vice-President Alben Barkley, who sought the Presidential nomination, withdrew after the coordinating committee refused to support him.

Not all labor officers were happy at the display of power politics. AFL Vice-President Charles Macgowan described the rejection of Barkley "as a tragedy." John L. Lewis wired Sam Caddy, a district officer of the Miners' Union and a delegate from Kentucky, that Barkley should be placed in nomination. The *United Mine Workers Journal* noted that no "one familiar with the tactless political leadership of the CIO is ever surprised over their foolhardy movements and endorsements. The CIO has demonstrated over and over again its lack of gratitude in making political choice. The CIO's dirty political campaign brought about the defeat of Senator Wheeler . . . plus their 'commie' wing vote against La Follette . . . for re-election to the Senate—simply because they would not champion 'commie' sponsored legislation—is a lasting stigma that the CIO can never live down.

"For the AFL to sit idly by and let their own George Harrison, representing and publicly speaking for the AFL, join with Kroll and Reuther in turning thumbs down on Barkley is indeed a mighty despicable performance." The AFL renounced tradition and endorsed the Democratic Stevenson-Sparkman ticket.

The 1952 campaign demonstrated more clearly the increased fragmentation of labor's political effort. Thirty-five political labor organizations reported to the Clerk of the House of Representatives that they had spent a total of $2,070,350.19 in the campaign, the largest sum by the CIO PAC, which spent $505,721.70; the International Ladies' Garment Workers' Union, $265,345.10; and Labor's League for Political Education, $249,257.92.

Committee for Political Education

At the merger of the AFL and CIO in 1955, the Committee on Political Education was "vested with the duty and responsibility to assist the

Executive Council in meeting the need for sound political education
. . . encouraging workers to register and vote, to exercise their full
responsibility of citizenship and to perform their rightful part in the
political life of the city, state, and national communities." The committee is a permanent division and carries on the functions of PAC
and LLPE. It is a commentary on the wisdom of the political policy
followed over the years by the American labor movement that the
merger convention affirmed the "need for a continuing and expanding
nonpartisan program of political education" and "labor's traditional
policy of avoiding entangling alliances with any other group and of
supporting worthy candidates regardless of their party affiliation."

Part Two

Labor and Politics Today

Chapter 7

The Committee on
Political Education

ORGANIZED LABOR owes a curious debt of gratitude to the Taft-Hartley Act, one which it does not ordinarily acknowledge. Through a strange and ironic contradiction, the Taft-Hartley Act, enacted to restrict and weaken the scope of union activity, actually advanced and intensified labor's political growth and development.

Until 1947, labor had a sincere interest in politics, but its actual political effort tended to be diffuse and ephemeral. Even during this period, there was a distinction between the political activities of unions affiliated with the AFL and those affiliated with the CIO. For the most part, the leaders of AFL-affiliates merely mouthed slogans and made minor financial contributions, repeatedly declaring their intent to "reward their friends and punish their enemies." Even the CIO leaders, however, claiming close affiliation with President Roosevelt and occasional election victories for the CIO-PAC, could point to little in the way of an intense or sustained political effort on their federation's part. Other than in New York City, local, state and even most national union organizations did little to educate and involve their members in politics or to cultivate political alliances. Union political activity was a hit or miss effort, culminating in pleas by union leaders exhorting members to get out and vote on election day.

With the passage of the Taft-Hartley Act over President Truman's veto, organized labor began to realize that its stake in politics was substantial and permanent, involving the possible loss of all of the gains labor had made since the Great Depression. For example, section 14(b) of the Act which enabled states to forbid union shop agreements was widely viewed by labor as nothing less than a declaration of war against organized labor itself. This became particularly clear when the advocates of so-called "right-to-work" laws in the states often joined forces with those who opposed the minimum wage, improvements in unemployment compensation, and, in some areas, the introduction and enactment of civil rights legislation.

As a defensive measure, unions found themselves forced into intensive political action. The AFL established Labor's League for Political Education, its counterpart to the CIO's PAC. Both CIO and AFL union leaders worked hard for the reelection of President Truman, although in the last analysis a swing in the farm vote made a substantial contribution to his victory. By 1952, both the CIO and the AFL endorsed the Presidential nominees of the Democratic Party, and organized labor as a whole spent over two million dollars on politics that year.

In one state after another in the years that followed, unions began to fight back against the "right-to-work" advocates. Labor worked hard to defeat right-to-work campaigns in Ohio, California, and Oklahoma. In Louisiana and Indiana, unions managed the repeal of these laws. Of far more long-run significance, however, was the fact that these campaigns, even more than election campaigns, created a need for substantial political machinery, demonstrated the gains to be made from its use, and forced the education of union members on a whole range of political and social issues.

In these decisive, important battles certain basic lessons were hammered home. First, that without education of union members and their families on the issues no campaign was likely to be effective. Second, that voter registration is the first key to victory in the election booth, requiring not only intensive registration campaigns but efforts to amend state laws that make registration peculiarly difficult or inconvenient for working-class people. And third, that political effectiveness requires skill, practical support, money, and day-in, day-out attention and work.

Part Two of this book shifts from the chronological to the topical approach in order to permit systematic analysis of the various facets of labor's contemporary political activities. Among the issues discussed in the chapters which follow are: What are the concerns and methods of the labor lobby, and what accounts for its successes and failures? How does organized labor go about electing candidates it favors, and does it use different techniques when working on the local level as opposed to national politics? How does labor raise money for political purposes, and how is it spent? How do union members view political activity by their union, and what about the "labor vote"?

The sustaining force in most of these activities is the AFL–CIO's COPE-Committee on Political Education. This chapter is concerned with COPE. The purpose, establishment, activities, and organization of COPE are dealt with in the first reading. It is the Committee's own description of its purpose and means of operation.

Contemporary COPE activities, points of pressure and plans for the future are described by Mary Goddard Zon. Her article is a selection from a considerably longer study that was prepared by COPE's research department as a report to the AFL–CIO Executive Council. The concluding selection in this chapter is a contemporary example of labor's means of rating candidates—a box score of right and wrong votes on various issues, as seen through the eyes of labor's leaders. For comparison, a much earlier example of this same kind of rating technique was described in the selection by Harwood Childs in Chapter 4.

The immediate objective of COPE is to increase the efficiency of labor's political efforts. It concentrates on getting as many union members, their wives and families, and working-class and minority group citizens registered as is possible. By telephone, by personal call, now even by the use of computer tabulations of voters and precinct voting behavior, many segments of the trade union movement are geared for enlistment of their membership and their membership's families and friends in the political wars. In a few states it can almost be said that organized labor is the political spine of the Democratic Party.

Labor's overall strength and political effectiveness should not be exaggerated, however. There are many states where union membership is inconsequential and labor's influence negligible. There remain unions which even now do not engage in politics in any whole-hearted or systematic way. Even in some of those states where labor is organized and active, the old-line politicians of both parties view labor's political participation with great disfavor, as they vie with the newcomers for party control or electoral victory. Some campaigns are inept, and others for any one of a number of reasons fail to touch the voters.

In summary, labor's political effort has matured and grown substantially since 1947. But much more is possible than now occurs, and COPE leaders, more than most, know it well.

While one should not overestimate COPE's effectiveness, neither should it be minimized. For example, in recent years businessmen have been urged with increasing frequency to give up the idea that "business and politics don't mix," and to engage in political activity on their own behalf. In 1963, the National Association of Manufacturers sponsored the creation of the Business-Industry Political Action Committee as one vehicle to promote these efforts. It was announced that BIPAC would inform citizens on important political issues, summarize and evaluate the records of office-holders and candidates, and raise money for campaign contributions. One of the original sponsors of BIPAC said that he had "always admired the COPE operation" and frankly stated that the new organization would function in much the same way as COPE itself. Thus the business community, a major opponent of organized labor, testifies to the efficacy of the present COPE effort.

What Is COPE?

COPE IS THE NAME taken from the initial letters of the Committee on Political Education of the AFL–CIO. The Committee was established by the First Constitutional Convention of the AFL–CIO in December 1955.

COPE is nonpartisan and has the responsibility spelled out in the AFL–CIO Constitution of "encouraging workers to register and vote, to exercise their full rights and responsibilities of citizenship, and to perform their rightful part in the political life of the city, state, and national communities."

The national Committee on Political Education is made up of the members of the Executive Council of the AFL–CIO. Its chairman is George Meany, and William Schnitzler is secretary-treasurer. National director is Alexander E. Barkan.

Why Is the AFL–CIO in Politics?

Labor unions have historically participated in the government of their communities, their states and their nation as all good citizens do. Politics is the process by which governments are elected.

Many gains made by organized labor at the bargaining table have been attacked in state legislatures and in Congress by reactionary groups who could not achieve their objectives through negotiation.

It is also true that as our society has become more complex, many of the needs of union members can only be met by legislation in the general welfare.

Finally, many of the aims of the AFL–CIO, designed to advance the general welfare of *all* citizens of the country, can only be achieved in the legislative halls.

In each of these cases, good government comes through the election of good officials—men and women who seek public office to help make their communities, their states and their nation better places for the people who live in them. It is the aim of the AFL–CIO to help the candidacies of such people.

What Is the COPE Program?

The AFL–CIO is committed to programs to maintain a prosperous nation in a peaceful world. It is concerned with improving the security and freedom not only of union members, but of all people. It supports programs to provide better education, to protect the rights of all individuals, to provide full employment at a decent wage, to achieve social and economic justice, to establish sound and fair labor relations, to develop better housing, to expand social insurance programs for the ill, for the elderly, for the unemployed and those injured on the job, to provide fair tax laws, to ease the burden of poverty, to protect consumers, to protect and develop our resources, to help solve the pressing problems of urban life, to support foreign trade and aid.

How Are Candidates Endorsed?

Candidates for President and Vice-President of the United States are recommended to AFL–CIO members by the General Board of the AFL–CIO which represents all the affiliated unions. The endorsement is based on the records of the candidates and the platforms of their parties. These are the only endorsements made at the national level.

Candidates for local, state, and other federal offices are recommended to the membership in the appropriate area by state and local COPE bodies, representing affiliated unions at the local and state level. The basis for the endorsement is the record and the program of the candidates compared to the policies of the AFL–CIO.

How Does COPE Work?

COPE believes that an educated and informed electorate is essential to the democratic process.

COPE reports facts about issues and candidates. It publishes voting records of elected officials to help AFL–CIO members inform themselves in order to vote intelligently.

COPE carries on extensive drives to help people register and vote so that the result will truly reflect the decisions of the majority of the people.

Is COPE a Political Party?

COPE is not a political party, nor is it committed to the support of any particular party. From the first convention of the AFL–CIO to the most recent, COPE has been instructed to work in support of candidates who support issues of concern to the AFL–CIO regardless of the party affiliation of the candidate.

The policies of COPE are determined by its national committee in line with the policies and programs adopted by the AFL–CIO conventions.

Does COPE Tell Union Members How to Vote?

No organization can tell anybody how to vote. The secret ballot is a fundamental protection of a free electorate. COPE can only provide union members with the facts about issues and candidates in the sure knowledge that informed union members, like other good citizens, will make their own choice in the voting booth.

Where Does COPE Get Its Money?

COPE is instructed by the AFL–CIO convention to conduct a campaign to solicit voluntary contributions from the members of affiliated unions, for use in federal elections.

Does COPE Work with Other Groups?

COPE cooperates with other groups and organizations that have the same aims and ideals as the AFL–CIO. It will work with other citizens who share the concerns union members have for programs to promote the general welfare.

Committee Setup

COPE operates on national, state, county, city and Congressional District levels.

State COPE

The President and the Secretary (or Secretary-Treasurer) of the AFL–CIO state central body are automatically chairman and secretary (or secretary-treasurer) of the state COPE.

State COPEs make endorsements for such statewide offices as U. S. Senator, governor, and other officers elected to serve the state as a whole.

Congressional District COPE

Where there is only one COPE in a Congressional District, it must of necessity be a Congressional District COPE. Where there are two or more COPEs in a Congressional District, each COPE should appoint a delegation to meet with representatives of the other COPEs in order to plan overall operations throughout the district.

ORGANIZATION CHART
OF
COMMITTEE ON POLITICAL EDUCATION

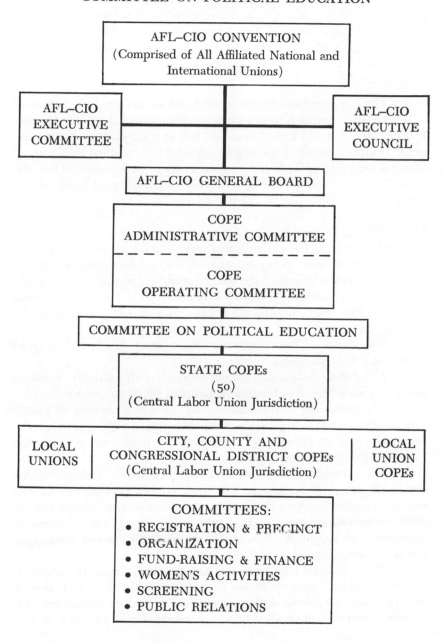

AFL–CIO CONVENTION
(Comprised of All Affiliated National and International Unions)

AFL–CIO EXECUTIVE COMMITTEE

AFL–CIO EXECUTIVE COUNCIL

AFL–CIO GENERAL BOARD

COPE ADMINISTRATIVE COMMITTEE

COPE OPERATING COMMITTEE

COMMITTEE ON POLITICAL EDUCATION

STATE COPEs
(50)
(Central Labor Union Jurisdiction)

LOCAL UNIONS

CITY, COUNTY AND CONGRESSIONAL DISTRICT COPEs
(Central Labor Union Jurisdiction)

LOCAL UNION COPEs

COMMITTEES:
- REGISTRATION & PRECINCT
- ORGANIZATION
- FUND-RAISING & FINANCE
- WOMEN'S ACTIVITIES
- SCREENING
- PUBLIC RELATIONS

Local Union COPE

It is suggested that each local appoint a local union Political Education Committee of at least *five* to serve (1) the local union on matters of political education, and (2) as representative delegates to the City, County or Congressional District Committee on Political Education. *These delegates should be persons who are definitely interested in political action, and who are willing to devote time and energy to these activities.*

The organization chart (p. 205) shows the general pattern of COPE organization as is generally in use throughout the United States. It *is not intended* that COPE must use this as a set pattern. Conditions in all localities vary and the organization of COPE must be arranged to suit the particular needs and circumstances of each state and locality. The chart presented here *is offered only as a suggested* basis for the formation of COPE.

Committees

The delegates from the various local unions make up the COPE committee and from these delegates, the officers, subcommittee chairmen, and subcommittee members are elected and/or appointed. These officers are *Chairman* and *Secretary-Treasurer*. The *Executive Council* should include subcommittee chairmen, and should function as the steering committee.

The *Finance Committee* functions to raise funds and to audit disbursements of all funds.

The *Public Relations Committee* handles all publicity, speakers bureau, news releases, radio and all political education material.

The *Screening Committee* checks on voting records of candidates; recommends action by the Executive Board as to endorsements, etc.; interviews all prospective candidates for public office whom the league might support or oppose.

The *Women's Activity Committee* coordinates women's activities in all phases of campaign; sets up Women's Divisions of COPE; sets up women's precinct committees; furnishes women as speakers to other organizations, etc.; creates interest in voting among wives of members, and neighbors; furnishes volunteers for clerical work, telephone contacts, etc.

The *Registration and Precinct Organization Committee* appoints precinct captains; sets up teams in every precinct to visit homes of members and friends to explain issues and record of candidates; sets up index card system on all voters in precinct; checks membership lists against voting lists; notifies locals of members not registered; explains election laws to members through local union meetings and literature; in general functions to register and otherwise qualify the members, their families and friends to vote; furnishes workers for polls on election day.

Contemporary COPE Activities

Mary Goddard Zon

AFL–CIO Committee on Political Education

THERE ARE NOW more American trade unionists actively involved in political affairs than ever before in the history of the nation.

It is the constant and continuing purpose of the AFL–CIO's Committee on Political Education (COPE) to broaden the base of the electorate. As each American citizen benefits from assuming an active and responsible role in political decisions, so the nation benefits from a dedicated and informed electorate.

This job will never be finished. Each year thousands of youngsters reach voting age. Each year millions of families change residence and face the problem of reregistering under different and sometimes restrictive laws. As technological discoveries affect employment opportunities, our members are often forced to move in order to find work. As the nationwide residential pattern shifts from the city to the encircling suburbs, our members move across city, county, and sometimes state lines.

The problem of maintaining contact with our mobile membership is growing in complexity. Only a small fraction of the total can be reached at regular union meetings. We are exploring new techniques for communicating with our members and providing them with the tools they seek and the information they demand as the basis for mature political judgment. . . .

There has not been, and is not now, complete unanimity in labor's political efforts. The debate continues within the labor movement as to the scope of political activity appropriate to a labor organization, and answers differ from time to time, from place to place, and from

Reprinted by permission of the publisher from "Labor in Politics," *Law and Contemporary Problems*, copyright © by Duke University, 1962, Vol. 27, Spring 1962.

union to union. There are still those who believe that labor has no proper concern with a political question not directly and immediately related to wages, hours, and working conditions. The more widely held view is that there is no political question which will not, in the end, have such an effect.

Until the formation of the Political Action Committee (PAC) by the CIO in 1943, political activity on the part of most trade unions in this century consisted mainly of lobbying and supporting candidates by endorsement at union meetings and in publications. The PAC introduced the concept of grass roots organization, including collections of small, individual, monetary donations, registration drives, massive distributions of literature on issues and candidates, election-day organization, rallies, and all the rest. In 1947, the American Federation of Labor created Labor's League for Political Education (LLPE) along the same general lines.

Both PAC and LLPE learned painfully and expensively that there are no easy short cuts to political success. In nonfederal elections, where it is legal for a union to contribute from its treasury, such a contribution, while relatively easy to obtain, is not worth half a contribution of the same amount from individual donations. A man who gives a dollar to a political campaign has a personal stake in the outcome of the election. He will very likely vote, and he may do more in terms of working in the campaign or just talking about it. Labor learned that filling Madison Square Garden for a political rally, filling the air with exhortations from sound trucks, grinding out miles of mimeographed press releases, and buying prime time on radio and television do not win elections. Nothing takes the place of personal contact.

PAC and LLPE achieved a large measure of cooperation even before the AFL and CIO merged in 1955. Starting in 1950, United Labor Committees in more than twenty states coordinated the efforts of these two groups and, in some instances, brought them together with the United Mine Workers, the Railroad Brotherhoods, and various farm organizations. In other areas, cooperation on endorsement of candidates and legislative programs was achieved informally. Infrequently, one or another of the labor groups was at variance with the rest, and labor support was split between opposing candidates. The situation still occurs occasionally with regard to an individual union within the AFL–CIO; and, in a number of instances in 1960, the Teamsters and the United Mine Workers opposed candidates supported by the AFL–CIO.

The Committee on Political Education was established at the December 1955 convention, merging the AFL and CIO. Physical merger of the two national staffs was not completed until the spring of 1956, and merger of the state organizations was not completed until 1961. The 1960 election was the first presidential election in which national and state merger was sufficiently advanced to judge the organization as a cohesive unit.

The AFL–CIO's concern with politics was defined by George Meany to a COPE conference in May 1962 as "labor's most important activity at this time," encompassing legislative programs which will "advance the interests of the entire people." [1]

New Trends

A study of the 1960 election returns directs attention to four conclusions of particular interest in COPE's assessment of its performance in that election and in planning for elections to come:

1. Our population is increasingly centered in metropolitan areas; but, while the population of many central cities has dropped or remained the same, a population explosion has occurred in the surrounding suburbs.

2. The minority vote (Negro and Spanish-American) is increasingly concentrated in northern cities. Negroes have moved from the South in large numbers and have found homes in the central cities recently abandoned by whites of the same or a slightly higher economic group. There are new leaders in the Negro community and better educational opportunities are reflected in a new, sophisticated view of the issues.

3. The Republican Party is a real and growing factor in southern politics. A half million more southern voters turned out for Nixon in 1960 than for Eisenhower in 1956, his best year. The 1961 election of Republican John Tower to the Senate from Texas demonstrated that the 1960 Republican strength cannot be attributed to the religious issue, although religion undoubtedly played a part in this area.

4. A new pattern may be emerging with regard to the relationship between presidential and congressional voting. Kennedy, trailing the Democratic slate in many areas, was less able than Eisenhower to extend coattails to other candidates. (While Eisenhower led his ticket, his popularity did not extend to other Republican candidates.)

A. The Suburban Vote

Historically, trade union membership has centered heavily in cities and often in certain clearly defined sections within the cities. While it is

---

[1] *AFL–CIO News,* May 5, 1962, p. 1, col. 2.

still possible to identify "labor precincts" in some cities, the trend is toward dispersal. The city remains as the major location of employment, but trade union members live and vote in increasing numbers in areas outside the city.

In 1958, 73.8 percent of the total number of industrial employees worked in 212 metropolitan areas. In 1959 and again in 1960, sixty-nine percent of all housing starts occurred in these areas. But the auto worker in Detroit may now live in Macomb or Oakland county. The carpenter in Manhattan may live in New Jersey or on Long Island. The packinghouse worker in Kansas City may live in Johnson County.

The 1960 election returns illustrated the impact of new voters on the suburban voting pattern. When the suburbs were reserved for families with higher than average income, they provided a predictable majority for conservative candidates. New families moving into established communities in small numbers usually adopted the political coloration of their new surroundings, even if they had voted differently in their old, city residence.

Now whole suburban towns spring up and are entirely populated in weeks or months. Since most of the residents of the new community moved from the same city at about the same time, they are not subjected to social pressures any different from those they left.

Liberal successes in a number of suburban areas in 1958 gave advance notice that the suburbs were no longer "safely" conservative. In 1960, Kennedy's vote rose dramatically over the 1956 Democratic vote in the suburbs of Baltimore, Boston, Buffalo, Chicago, Cleveland, Detroit, Minneapolis-St. Paul, New York, Philadelphia, Pittsburgh, and San Francisco. . . .

Our members are numbered among the most mobile in the voting population. The implications for COPE are clear. Local COPEs, structured under city or county central bodies, must work out entirely new techniques to locate their members for the purpose of registration, get-out-the-vote, and educational programs.

National COPE has undertaken a pilot project in one such area. It has two main objectives—to develop organizational techniques coordinating the activities of existing COPEs across geographical or political boundaries and to identify issues which may have been unimportant to our members as city dwellers but are important to our members as suburban home owners.

About 100 union leaders and COPE representatives from twenty-one states and thirty major cities attended a conference in May 1962 to study the problems of the 1962 registration drive as it relates to major cities and their suburbs.

B. *Minority Groups*

The nonwhite population of major cities has increased tremendously over the past ten years. Between 1950 and 1960 the increase in Chicago was 64.4 percent; in Los Angeles, 97.2 percent; in Cleveland 69.3 percent; in San Francisco, 66.8 percent; in Milwaukee, 189 percent; in Dallas, 129 percent; in San Diego, 143 percent; in Buffalo, 94.7 percent.

Not only are there more nonwhite Americans of voting age than ever before, concentrated more and more in major cities, but, particularly in the Negro community, there is a new political climate. The "Negro vote" has slipped out from under the control of old-line leaders. American Negroes cannot be bought. They want information, not dictation. They demand action and will not accept promises. They eagerly accept the responsibilities of citizenship, even when the simple exercise of the franchise may entail humiliation and physical danger, as it sometimes does in the South. In 1960, COPE planned its campaign with minority groups with respectful attention to these facts.

In this situation, COPE is fortunate in having its credentials in order. Tempers may be short, but memories are long. Trust and respect are the treasure piled up by COPE over years of fighting unpopular battles for civil rights and equal economic opportunities for all Americans.

The heavy Democratic majorities scored by Negro and Spanish-American voters can be counted as the deciding factor in several crucial, industrial states in the Northeast and Midwest. Negro voters are credited with swinging South Carolina to the Democratic column and were important to Democratic victories in North Carolina and Texas.

Under COPE direction a task force of volunteers worked in ninety-seven cities, towns, and villages in seventeen states. Approximately 9,100 workers participated in this campaign. More than ten million pieces of literature were distributed, including special literature directed to Negro and Spanish-speaking voters.

Minority voters gave President Kennedy lopsided majorities in northern industrial cities: 81.2 percent in Hartford; 72 percent in New Haven; 78 percent in Chicago; 74.4 percent in Baltimore; 81.1 percent in St. Louis; 77.3 percent in New York; 60.6 percent in Cleveland; 77.1 percent in Pittsburgh; 73.7 percent in Milwaukee. . . .

We believe that this great reservoir of liberal votes has still barely been tapped. In New York City where Puerto Rican voters gave Kennedy an eighty-eight percent majority, it is estimated that only twenty-two percent of the potential actually voted. This was after a hard-driving, round-the-clock registration drive conducted in connection with a general "crash" registration program discussed below.

A similar situation exists with regard to the Latin-American vote in several southwestern states and potential Indian voters in the Southwest and in the Dakotas. The Negro vote will be a tremendously important factor in those congressional districts in the South where there is a hope of electing liberals in the 1962 primaries.

C. Southern Developments

Nixon made the most dramatic gains of his 1960 campaign in the South—where trade union membership is smallest.

The broad base of Republican support in this area rests with conservative, anti-civil rights, anti-union, states'-rights Democrats. Over the years, this affinity has been reflected in Congress by the Republican-Dixiecrat coalition.

With a few striking exceptions, old-line organization Democrats have held tightly the reins of political control in a one-party situation where serious contests, if any, occurred in primary elections. The primaries were regarded as a private, party affair, and the rules were designed to limit the franchise to voters who could be relied on to perpetuate the system. (25.6 percent of the citizens 21-years-old and older voted for President in Mississippi in 1960; 30.9 percent in Alabama; 34.4 percent in Virginia.)

The 1960 senatorial primary in Tennessee was typical of the liberal-conservative struggle in a one-party state. Senator Estes Kefauver won renomination against bitter, heavily financed opposition, marked by the irresponsible use of scurrilous literature designed to inflame voters on the segregation issue.

This campaign provided a clear example of what COPE can achieve against the organized forces of big business when the basic work of getting our members registered and voted is pitted against a flood of corporation money (in this instance the drug industry).

Particular emphasis was placed on the COPE drive among minority groups. Women's Activities Departments functioned efficiently in major cities. The proportion of AFL–CIO members registered increased from fifty percent in April, when the drive started, to eighty percent on July 15.

The *Chattanooga Times* reported,[2]

> Kefauver showed strength in many areas where he normally would have expected to be swamped if the segregation sentiment had prevailed. . . .

---

[2] *Chattanooga Times,* Aug. 5, 1960.

The returns in those areas indicated that organized labor exerted more influence than usual on the voters.

The long-range prospect of a real choice between political philosophies is exciting to southern liberals. A number of important Texas Dixiecrats have announced their affiliation with the Republican Party, and one ex-Democrat is the 1962 Republican candidate for governor. Congressional incumbents, with impressive seniority at stake, cannot be expected to join a large-scale shift of affiliation or to encourage it; but they may not, in the end, be able to prevent it. The Republican Party is already a factor to be reckoned with in Florida. The North Carolina legislature eliminated the state's only Republican district in redistricting, but Democratic incumbents in the same area of the state are nervously studying the Republican strength in the counties which were added to their districts. . . .

Growing industrialization in the South may have long-term implications. While unionism in the South is still relatively limited, southern trade unionists are exhibiting a willingness to exert and tax themselves to build politically and legislatively to an extent which should be an inspiration to their stronger, more numerous brothers in other areas.

A thoughtfully conceived "Program of Progress" has already been adopted by the Alabama, Mississippi, and Louisiana COPEs and is under study in other southern states. The program lists a number of specific legislative goals for each state, and details the organization required and the activities prescribed to attain those goals. In each state convention to which the program has been presented the delegates have voted overwhelmingly to assess themselves a sizable per capita payment to put the program into effect.

In the three states operating under the "Program of Progress," COPE has attained a new maturity and a new respect in the community. In 1961, in Mississippi, for example, candidates for the state legislature publicly sought COPE endorsement for the first time in history.

D. *Congressional and State Elections 1960 and 1962*

The historical American pattern of electing a large congressional majority to support a new President has been suspended for the past three presidential elections. Eisenhower got a bare majority in 1952 and lost the Congress in 1956. Democrats lost two Senate seats (one to a COPE-supported Republican in Delaware) and twenty-one House seats in 1960. Nineteen of the twenty-one had been traditionally Republican until the 1958 Democratic sweep, which extended to midwest farm areas, and ten were in sections where anti-Catholic sentiment was strongest. But, whatever the mitigating factors, supporters of liberal legislation have no grounds for complacency in a realistic appraisal of the 1962 Senate, House, and gubernatorial elections.

The party in power has lost congressional seats in every off-year election in this century except the 1934 election. While COPE is non-partisan and supports liberal candidates of both parties, it is a simple fact that many more Democrats than Republicans qualify for COPE support. The success of liberal legislation in the immediate future will depend on the ability of Democrats to hold the seats they have and, if possible, to increase their margin.

Present liberal majorities in both houses of Congress may best be gauged by close votes on vital issues. Temporary unemployment compensation legislation passed the Senate in March 1961 by a margin of two votes. The Rules Committee change in the House passed by five votes on January 31, 1961. By August 1961, the Republican-Dixiecrat coalition had reformed to defeat the President's aid-to-education recommendation in the House by seventy-two votes and in the Senate by five votes.

E. COPE's Score in 1960

Candidates endorsed by state and local COPEs for state or federal office fall into one of two categories: (1) those with a reasonable chance of winning who are given maximum assistance by their respective COPE organizations, and (2) candidates with almost no chance of success who are endorsed as a protest against their opponents.

In the first category, fifteen out of nineteen senatorial candidates, fourteen out of nineteen gubernatorial candidates, and 157 of 258 House candidates who were endorsed by COPE won election—or 73.7 percent.

Fifteen Republican candidates for the House of Representatives, one Republican candidate for the United States Senate, and one Republican candidate for governor were endorsed by COPE in 1960. A preliminary survey of endorsements for lesser offices (state legislature, state offices other than governor, and so on) indicates that the total number of labor-backed Republican candidates in that election exceeded 400. . . .

Labor Expenditures in Political Campaigns

Labor expenditures have always been relatively minor when compared with the total expenditures in any given political campaign. In the

1944 campaign, the total of labor contributions, including individual and treasury contributions, accounted for only 7.7 percent of the total spent by both parties in the election. (The National Citizens Political Action Committee was ruled not to be a labor union and, therefore, eligible to receive treasury contributions.)

Another interesting arrangement of the same figures revealed that 242 individuals representing sixty-four well-heeled families made direct contributions of nearly $1.3 million, compared to the union contributions of $1.6 million, representing millions of workers.

With minor deviations, the ratio has remained approximately the same through the years. Since treasury contributions to federal elections have been outlawed, the mechanics of collecting voluntary, individual contributions have steadily improved. There is still vast room for improvement.

The collection machinery is cumbersome, since it is necessary to record each dollar contribution and retain a receipt. Most large unions are in charge of their own collections. Receipt books are sent from national COPE to the various national and international unions. There they are remailed to local unions where the shop steward is expected to take charge of collections in addition to his other duties. At this point collections are turned over to volunteers. It has been found that the number of union members who refuse to contribute when they are asked is negligible. The number who are never asked, however, is enormous. As a result no more than a small fraction of the goal of $1 per member has ever been achieved.

Constant and continuing charges of labor "slush funds" and "war chests" find credence with our opponents and implant blissfully unrealistic notions of financial assistance in the minds of candidates. A COPE-endorsed candidate for the Senate in New England in 1958, when publicly accused of accepting a $25,000 contribution from the United Automobile Workers, telegraphed Walter Reuther, "Please deny story or send money."

Today maximum COPE contributions are normally $10,000 in a senatorial campaign and $2,500 in a House race. Some individual unions retain a part of the voluntary COPE dollar and make separate donations from these funds, so that the total union contribution to a single candidate may exceed these figures.

COPE expenditures in 1960 totalled just under $800,000, less than five percent of the money spent on the campaign. All union expenditures totalled slightly more than $2 million. (This includes Teamster contributions which, in some instances, went to candidates opposing candidates supported by COPE.)

Two million dollars in labor expenditures represents contributions from approximately two million trade unionists. At the same time, 3,400 wealthy people contributed over $5 million to the 1960 campaign in chunks of $500 or more.

COPE Plans for 1962

COPE's plans for 1962 center in the following areas:

1. A careful selection of areas of concentration.
2. Extension of the successful 1960 registration and get-out-the-vote campaign.
3. Expansion of educational facilities on issues and on the records of candidates for public office.

A. Selection of Areas of Concentration

Because the margin is so slim and the stakes so high, it is more than ever necessary to pick areas of concentration with the utmost care. COPE must husband its resources and pinpoint its efforts to achieve maximum support for liberal incumbents in danger of defeat and liberal candidates with the best chance of defeating conservative incumbents.

The conservative forces can count as accurately as we can. In some instances they have generously announced which liberals they have marked for political extinction. In March 1961, Republican National Committee Chairman Thruston Morton announced the creation of a special task force to study ways to build Republican strength in cities with a population of 300,000 or more.

The political activities of business are on the increase. In many instances, industry is going beyond management and reaching out to the workers, our own union members, with courses of instruction on political techniques and indoctrination on management's view of political issues. In a clear attempt to find a chink through which to drive a wedge, the Chamber of Commerce ordered a study of the attitudes of union members toward their leaders and the attitude of the general public toward unions and union problems. This privately circulated study by the Opinion Research Corporation reached two conclusions of great interest to us:

1. There is room for improvement in the relationship between our leadership and our membership to a sobering degree.
2. While the general public will not tolerate a threat to the fundamental right to bargain collectively, the public image of trade unions has been seriously damaged by unfortunate publicity in recent years.

The National Right to Work Committee has redoubled its efforts in support of so-called "right-to-work" legislation and referenda and has embarked on a nationwide "educational" campaign in an attempt to reach school, civic, and religious groups.

On September 19, 1961, the Chamber of Commerce announced the creation of a "Special Committee for Voluntary Unionism" to work for passage of state "right-to-work" laws.

In such states as California, Ohio, and Washington, where so-called "right-to-work" referenda were blamed for the poor showing of conservative candidates in 1958, more sophisticated conservatives may be inclined against such frontal assaults in favor of more subtle and devious attacks. . . .

B. Registration Campaign

In any election as close as the 1960 presidential election, every group which participated to any degree in behalf of the winning candidate can claim with some justice that it was the deciding factor.

However, there is general agreement that President Kennedy could not have won in the important industrial states which provided the bulk of his electoral vote without the tremendous outpouring of new voters resulting from the AFL–CIO registration program. While some segments of the press credited city "machines" with "delivering" the vote for Kennedy, anyone familiar with American politics knows that the shadowy remnants of these once-powerful organizations are historically uninterested in extending the franchise to new, untested, uncontrolled and uncontrollable voters. This points up one of the principal, philosophical differences between the old-line, out-moded political machines and the AFL–CIO's Committee on Political Education. We believe without qualification that Americans can be trusted to vote and that our function is to assist our members into the voting booth through the labyrinth of legal voting requirements and through the smoke screens beclouding the issues. . . .

The total presidential vote of 68,836,385 was the highest in history, both numerically and by percentage of the potential vote. Kennedy's vote exceeded Nixon's by 119,450; but, like Truman in 1948, he polled less than fifty percent of the total presidential vote including that for minor candidates.

Seldom has an election contained more compelling illustrations of the old thesis, "Your vote is the one that counts." A switch of 27,546 votes in Illinois and Texas would have given the election to Nixon. A switch of 38,442, variously distributed between the states of Alaska, California, Montana, Washington, and Wyoming, would have given Kennedy a landslide electoral vote of 345 to 168.

In August 1960, the Executive Council of the AFL–CIO voted to undertake a nonpartisan crash registration program. This program was under the direction of President Meany's office and operated largely through the COPE structure with state and local COPE personnel and volunteers in charge of field operations. Where possible, other non-partisan citizens groups were assisted in their registration drives. The crash registration program originally centered in fourteen key states and, to a lesser extent, was expanded to include an additional fourteen states. Thousands of volunteers participated.

COPE produced a record amount of registration and get-out-the-vote material which found gratifying acceptance, not only in the labor movement, but generally. One hundred and twenty-two television films containing ten-second spot announcements were distributed to stations covering more than ninety percent of the television market outside the South. Four hundred and fifty-six radio stations used COPE record-ings of six registration and get-out-the-vote spot announcements. Three radio scripts designed for local delivery and three sample leaflets for plant-gate distribution were sent to each state and local COPE.

State and local COPEs were provided with 630,000 posters, of which 140,000 were printed in Spanish. Three hundred labor papers received three different registration mats. A thousand mats for use in regularly placed department store advertising were sent to the adver-tising managers of the nation's leading retail stores. . . .

C. 1960 Registration Results

Industrial states showed dramatic registration gains over 1958, and, in most instances, over previous records scored in 1956. In spite of a pop-ulation drop in major cities over the previous four years, 1960 registra-tions held and often exceeded the 1956 figure in these areas.

Illinois registrations increased 450,000 over 1958 and more than 280,000 over 1956. In Cook County there were more than 100,000 new registrants over the 1956 figure. (Kennedy carried Illinois by 9,801 votes.) Maryland registration jumped by some 139,000 over 1956. (Kennedy carried Maryland by 78,282 votes.)

In 1960, Michigan registered 200,000 more voters in Wayne, Oakland, and Macomb counties than in 1956. That was one new voter for each fifteen persons who voted in Michigan in 1956. The new voters were registered mainly in heavily Democratic Wayne County and in the predominantly Democratic communities of southern Oakland and Macomb counties. These three counties cast more than two-thirds of the state's total vote. (Kennedy carried Michigan by 70,000 votes.)

In Missouri, registration in St. Louis County jumped to an all-time high of 707,000, including 85,000 voters who registered on a single day when the Citizen's Non-Partisan Registration Committee had 407 workers in the field. (Kennedy carried Missouri by 26,000 votes.) New Jersey registration increased by about 227,000 over 1956, with major gains scored in industrial cities and surrounding suburbs. (Kennedy carried New Jersey by 22,000 votes.)

New York City showed a spectacular gain of 958,000 new registrants over 1958 and 332,000 over 1956, the previous presidential election year. That gain was produced chiefly through the efforts of the Greater New York Committee on Registration (COPE). Erie County (Buffalo) scored an increase of 70,000 and Onandaga County (Syracuse), 20,000 over 1956. Long Island trade unionists worked diligently to reach members who had moved to suburban Nassau and Suffolk counties. These two counties showed a registration gain of 131,000 over 1956. (Kennedy carried New York by nearly 400,000 votes.)

Two hundred and sixty-six thousand new registrants were added to the rolls in Pennsylvania over the 1956 figure. (Kennedy carried Pennsylvania by 128,000 votes.) . . .

While many other forces were at work in the 1960 presidential election, it is a simple fact that President Kennedy could not have been elected without the broad base of the continuing COPE registration program. The AFL–CIO crash registration program, which was superimposed in selected areas on the regular COPE organization, provided the extra push in important industrial areas; but, in the excitement over electoral votes, some equally striking gains in smaller states went almost unnoticed.

In Delaware, for instance, registration increased by 58,000 (nearly one-third) over 1956. In Wilmington alone, registration was up 33,000. Maine registration rose 52,000 over 1956; Rhode Island, 32,000; Tennessee, 200,000; Utah, 39,000.

D. *Women's Activities Department*

No last-minute drive, no matter how well financed or ably conducted, can replace the steady, laborious constant work of checking registration lists, assisting the unregistered to qualify, and finally, urging and helping registered voters to vote on election day.

This responsibility rests mainly with the Women's Activities Department (WAD). In every area where the effectiveness of COPE participation is demonstrable, there was such a WAD program, working with the support, and, in some instances, the active participation of the COPE officers involved. In 1960 there were 440 WADs as compared to 288 in 1959. In many instances men volunteered for this work. (In Meriden, Connecticut, the Civil Liberties Union president, unable to enlist women, set up a "Male WAD" in which twenty men contributed 425 voluntary hours to process the names of nearly 4,000 potential voters.) Other areas have found additional manpower among retirees.

In every section of the country devoted men and women members of the AFL–CIO and wives of members worked long hours at no pay to achieve the successes in industrial centers which resulted in the election of the labor-backed candidate for President.

More than one million supervised telephone calls were made by WADs from COPE offices into union homes and union neighborhoods reminding trade union members to register and to vote on election day. Mailings by WADs from COPE offices totaled well over a million. In San Diego, California, 10,000 volunteer hours were contributed during the 1960 campaign. A Kansas group piled up 1,309 hours in a single week. . . .

In 1961 the Women's Activities Department maintained most of its existing organizations and added new, local WADs. Off-year interest was sustained at a high level by the formation within these groups of "letter lobbies" to study and express themselves on federal and state legislation. At the same time, in preparation for 1962, the work of indexing and processing membership and registration lists continued.

E. Area Conferences

At the annual COPE Area Conferences members of the staff of the national AFL–CIO go into the field to meet with trade union leadership and rank-and-file membership from every state in the union.

A format has been devised which permits a maximum of interchange between national COPE and the delegates. The information gleaned by the national staff from group discussions and reports on the part of the delegates is no less important than the material developed in Washington for instructing the delegates on issues and techniques. Visual materials and other techniques of presentation are used which can, in turn, be adapted for use by local COPEs.

Sixteen area conferences were held in 1961. They were attended by a total of 5,683 delegates from fifty states. The 1962 conference discussions center around the important elections taking place in each area in November 1962. Techniques of organization and issues are explored as they apply locally, with new emphasis on suburban problems.

Reapportionment

The implications of the Supreme Court's decision in the Tennessee reapportionment case[3] are salutary for labor. State legislative and congressional districts based on unequal divisions of the population have worked to devalue urban and metropolitan votes, including, of course, the votes of most trade union members.

President Eisenhower's Committee on Intergovernmental Relations reported, in June 1955,[4] that in a majority of states "city dwellers outnumber the citizens of rural areas. Yet in most states the rural voters are overwhelmingly in control of one legislative house, and overweighted if not dominant in the other. . . ."

Rural-dominated legislatures in many states have drawn congressional district lines in such a way as to repeat, as far as possible, the same pattern in the United States House of Representatives. As a result, the votes of a hundred or a thousand union members living in an urban district may have a par political worth no greater than a single vote in a rural district.

Labor has consistently supported proposed national legislation to require state legislatures to apportion United States Representatives' districts on the basis of population. State AFL–CIO officials have made the same appeal doggedly, year after year, before state legislative committees. The Supreme Court remanded the case of *Scholle v. Hare*[5] to the Michigan Supreme Court for a reexamination of the fairness of the state's apportionment on April 23, 1962. (Augustus Scholle is president of the Michigan AFL–CIO.) Resolutions have been passed on this subject repeatedly at state and national labor conventions, and reapportionment has been the subject of countless pamphlets, leaflets, and articles in the labor press.

Curiously, this was an issue which never before really caught the imagination of the membership. Even sophisticated unionists, quick to recognize and take vigorous action against a fast count in other areas, have been, in the main, singularly unmoved. If the courts had not opened an avenue of relief, it would be difficult to estimate when, or if, reapportionment might have emerged as a full-blown, mass-supported issue in labor ranks. This lethargy may have been attributable to despair of redress, since more concern has been evidenced in the months following the decision than in all the years preceding it.

---

[3] Baker v. Carr, 369 U.S. 186 (1962).

[4] *Commission on Intergovernmental Relations, A Report to the President* 38 (1955).

[5] 369 U.S. 429 (1962).

Although no formal arrangements or announcements have been made, it can be assumed that labor will play a role proportionate to its interest in future reapportionment actions.

Labor's Role in American Politics

The American labor movement has changed the face of American politics. By insisting that it is every American's right and duty to participate in the political process, COPE (and PAC and LLPE before it) broke the ground for the citizens' groups which have become the rule, rather than the exception, in the nation's political life.

By insisting that campaigns be fought on issues, instead of personalities or party loyalties, COPE has directed a clear, bright light of publicity on the legislative process. It is no longer possible for a congressman to claim that he has supported a liberal measure when he has, in fact, voted to gut it by amendment before voting for passage. By the careful compilation and wide distribution of the records of public officials, COPE has made the politician's performance match his promise.

We have not attained, and cannot hope to attain, perfection in politics any more than in any other field of human endeavor. We can and do honor our priceless heritage and work unceasingly to be worthy of it—as Americans and as trade unionists.

How Labor Keeps Score

[THE VOTING TABLE which follows is a typical example of how unions inform their members of the voting records of Senators and Congressmen. It shows the position of every U. S. Senator on 10 key votes of significance to labor during the 1st session of the 89th Congress, 1965. This particular tabulation was made by the Legislative Department of the International Association of Machinists.]

KEY TO SYMBOLS

R   Voted Right or was paired Right from labor's viewpoint
W   Voted Wrong or was paired Wrong from labor's viewpoint
O   Did not vote
E   Took office after vote on issue

Reprinted by permission of the International Association of Machinists from *The Machinist*, November 4, 1965.

1. *Appalachia Program*—Nation's new regional program to re-develop poverty-stricken areas in 11 states was approved in Senate Feb. 1, 1965. Key element is construction of 3,350 miles of roads to open mountain areas to job-producing industries. Senate voted approval 62 to 22. A vote for the program was a Right "R" vote.

2. *Manpower Training*—Because the 1962 Manpower Development and Training Act has been effective in helping train the unemployed for jobs, Congress extended the program five years and broadened it. Key Senate vote was on an attempt by Sen. Winston Prouty of Vermont to limit program to two years. This was rejected 35 to 49 on Mar. 16, 1965. A Right "R" vote was a vote against the Prouty amendment.

3. *Federal Aid to Schools*—After decades of controversy Congress this year voted Federal aid for elementary and high schools. Aid goes to school districts according to number of pupils from low-income families. Some new facilities in poverty areas will be shared by children attending church and other private schools. Senate voted approval 73 to 18 on Apr. 9, 1965. A vote for the measure was a Right "R" vote.

4. *Voting Rights*—Congress authorized Federal machinery for registration of Negroes and other minorities in states and districts where their voting rights have been denied. Key Senate vote was on a motion by Sen. Philip Hart of Michigan to invoke cloture and end a filibuster. Vote for cloture on May 25, 1965 was 70 to 30. A Right "R" vote was a vote for the Hart cloture motion.

5. *Medicare*—Long-sought measure providing hospital insurance for the aged under Social Security and a supplemental medical insurance plan passed Senate July 9, 1965. Vote was 68 to 21. A vote for the bill was a Right "R" vote.

6. *Rent Supplements*—Congress approved a plan to put poorly-housed low-income families into better quarter. Tenants will pay 25 percent of their income for rent and Government will make up balance. Key Senate vote July 15, 1965 was on motion of Sen. John Tower of Texas to kill plan. Motion was rejected 40 to 47. A Right "R" vote was a vote against Tower's motion. In closing days of session House voted down funds for plan, so it cannot start this year.

7. *Fair Reapportionment*—Senate defeated so-called Dirksen Amendment. This would have upset U.S. Supreme Court's decision that both houses of state legislatures must be apportioned on a population basis as required by the U.S. Constitution. Measure was rejected 57 to 39 August 4, 1965, failing to get two-thirds majority required for a Constitutional amendment. A Right "R" vote was a vote against the amendment.

8. *Urban Affairs Dept.*—To give city dwellers a spokesman in the Cabinet Congress voted to establish a new U.S. Department of Housing and Urban Development. Senate approved bill 57 to 33 on August 11. A vote for the measure was a Right "R" vote.

9. *Anti-Poverty Funds*—The Senate defeated an attempt to cut about one-third from the $1.65 billion proposed for the current year's war on poverty. The vote Aug. 17, 1965 on an amendment by Sen. Peter Dominick of Colorado was 40 to 51. A Right "R" vote was a vote against the Dominick cutback.

10. *14(b) Repeal*—A filibuster led by Sen. Everett Dirksen of Illinois blocked consideration of the bill to repeal the Taft-Hartley Act's Sec. 14(b). To break the filibuster and bring the bill to the floor for debate, a cloture vote was attempted. The attempt failed October 11, 1965 by a vote of 45 to 47. A vote to cut off the talk was a Right "R" vote.

KEY TO QUESTIONS

1—Appalachia Program	6—Rent Supplements
2—Manpower Training	7—Fair Reapportionment
3—Federal Aid to Schools	8—Urban Affairs Dept.
4—Voting Rights	9—Anti-Poverty Funds
5—Medicare Program	10—14(b) Repeal

	1	2	3	4	5	6	7	8	9	10
ALABAMA										
Hill (D)	R	R	R	W	R	W	W	W	W	W
Sparkman (D)	R	R	R	W	R	R	W	W	O	W
ALASKA										
Bartlett (D)	R	R	R	R	R	R	W	R	R	R
Gruening (D)	O	O	R	R	R	R	W	R	R	O
ARIZONA										
Fannin (R)	W	W	W	W	W	W	W	W	W	W
Hayden (D)	R	O	O	W	R	R	O	R	R	W
ARKANSAS										
Fulbright (D)	O	R	R	W	R	R	W	O	R	O
McClellan (D)	W	W	R	W	R	W	W	W	W	W
CALIFORNIA										
Kuchel (R)	R	W	R	R	R	W	W	R	W	R
Murphy (R)	W	W	W	W	W	W	W	W	W	W
COLORADO										
Allott (R)	W	W	R	R	W	W	W	W	W	W
Dominick (R)	W	W	W	R	W	W	W	W	W	W
CONNECTICUT										
Dodd (D)	R	O	R	R	R	R	R	R	R	R
Ribicoff (D)	R	R	R	R	R	R	R	R	R	R

	1	2	3	4	5	6	7	8	9	10
DELAWARE										
Boggs (R)	w	w	R	R	R	w	R	R	w	w
Williams (R)	w	o	w	R	w	w	w	w	w	w
FLORIDA										
Holland (D)	R	w	w	w	w	w	w	w	w	w
Smathers (D)	R	R	R	w	R	R	w	R	R	w
GEORGIA										
Russell (D)	R	o	o	w	o	w	w	w	w	w
Talmadge (D)	o	R	R	w	R	w	w	w	w	w
HAWAII										
Fong (R)	R	w	R	R	R	w	w	R	w	w
Inouye (D)	R	R	R	R	R	R	R	R	R	R
IDAHO										
Church (D)	R	o	R	R	R	R	w	R	o	R
Jordan (R)	w	w	w	R	w	w	w	w	w	w
ILLINOIS										
Dirksen (R)	R	w	R	R	R	w	w	w	w	w
Douglas (D)	R	R	R	R	R	R	R	R	R	R
INDIANA										
Bayh (D)	R	R	R	R	R	R	R	R	R	R
Hartke (D)	R	o	o	R	R	R	R	R	R	R
IOWA										
Hickenlooper (R)	w	w	w	w	w	w	w	w	w	w
Miller (R)	w	w	R	w	w	w	w	R	w	w
KANSAS										
Carlson (R)	w	w	R	R	R	w	w	w	w	w
Pearson (R)	w	w	R	R	w	w	w	w	w	w
KENTUCKY										
Cooper (R)	R	w	R	R	R	w	w	w	w	R
Morton (R)	R	w	w	R	w	w	w	w	w	w
LOUISIANA										
Ellender (D)	w	w	R	w	w	R	w	w	w	w
Long (D)	R	o	R	w	R	R	w	R	R	R
MAINE										
Muskie (D)	o	R	R	R	R	R	R	R	R	R
Smith (R)	R	w	R	R	R	R	w	R	R	R
MARYLAND										
Brewster (D)	R	o	R	R	R	R	R	R	R	o
Tydings (D)	R	R	R	R	R	R	R	R	R	R
MASSACHUSETTS										
Kennedy (D)	R	R	R	R	R	R	R	R	R	R
Saltonstall (R)	R	o	R	R	R	w	w	R	w	w
MICHIGAN										
Hart (D)	R	R	R	R	R	R	R	o	R	R
McNamara (D)	R	R	R	R	R	R	R	R	R	R

	1	2	3	4	5	6	7	8	9	10
MINNESOTA										
McCarthy (D)	o	R	R	R	R	R	R	R	o	R
Mondale (D)	R	R	R	R	R	R	R	R	R	R
MISSISSIPPI										
Eastland (D)	w	w	w	w	w	w	w	w	w	w
Stennis (D)	w	R	w	w	w	w	w	w	w	w
MISSOURI										
Long (D)	R	o	R	R	R	R	R	R	R	R
Symington (D)	R	R	R	R	R	w	w	R	R	R
MONTANA										
Mansfield (D)	R	R	R	R	R	R	w	R	R	R
Metcalf (D)	R	R	R	R	R	R	w	R	R	R
NEBRASKA										
Curtis (R)	w	w	w	R	w	w	w	w	w	w
Hruska (R)	w	w	w	R	w	w	w	w	w	w
NEVADA										
Bible (D)	R	R	R	w	R	w	w	w	R	w
Cannon (D)	R	R	R	w	R	w	w	R	R	o
NEW HAMPSHIRE										
Cotton (R)	w	w	R	R	R	w	w	w	w	w
McIntyre (D)	R	R	R	R	R	R	R	R	R	R
NEW JERSEY										
Case (R)	R	R	R	R	R	R	R	R	R	R
William (D)	R	R	R	R	R	R	R	R	R	R
NEW MEXICO										
Anderson (D)	R	R	R	R	R	w	R	R	R	o
Montoya (D)	R	R	R	R	R	o	R	R	R	R
NEW YORK										
Javits (R)	R	R	R	R	R	R	R	R	R	R
Kennedy (D)	R	R	R	R	R	R	R	R	R	R
NORTH CAROLINA										
Ervin (D)	R	w	R	w	w	w	w	w	w	w
Jordan (D)	R	R	R	w	R	w	w	R	w	w
NORTH DAKOTA										
Burdick (D)	R	R	R	R	R	R	R	R	R	R
Young (R)	w	w	w	w	w	w	w	w	w	w
OHIO										
Lausche (D)	R	w	w	R	R	w	w	w	w	w
Young (D)	R	o	R	R	R	R	R	R	R	o
OKLAHOMA										
Harris (D)	R	R	R	R	w	R	w	R	R	R
Monroney (D)	R	R	R	R	R	R	w	R	R	w

	1	2	3	4	5	6	7	8	9	10
OREGON										
Morse (D)	R	O	R	R	R	R	R	R	R	R
Neuberger (D)	R	R	O	R	R	R	R	R	O	R
PENNSYLVANIA										
Clark (D)	R	R	R	R	R	R	R	R	R	R
Scott (R)	R	W	R	R	R	R	W	R	W	O
RHODE ISLAND										
Pastore (D)	R	R	R	R	R	R	R	R	R	R
Pell (D)	R	R	R	R	R	R	R	R	R	R
SOUTH CAROLINA										
Russell (D)	E	E	E	W	R	W	W	W	W	W
Thurmond (R)	W	W	W	W	W	W	W	W	W	W
SOUTH DAKOTA										
McGovern (D)	R	R	R	R	R	R	R	R	R	W
Mundt (R)	W	W	R	R	W	W	W	W	W	W
TENNESSEE										
Bass D)	R	R	R	R	R	R	R	R	R	R
Gore (D)	R	R	R	R	R	W	R	R	R	O
TEXAS										
Tower (R)	W	O	W	W	W	W	W	W	W	W
Yarborough (D)	O	R	R	R	R	R	R	R	R	R
UTAH										
Bennett (R)	R	W	W	W	W	W	W	W	W	W
Moss (D)	O	R	R	R	R	R	W	R	R	R
VERMONT										
Aiken (R)	R	W	R	R	R	R	W	R	W	W
Prouty (R)	R	W	R	R	R	W	W	R	R	W
VIRGINIA										
Byrd (D)	W	W	W	W	W	W	W	W	W	W
Robertson(D)	W	W	W	W	W	W	W	W	W	W
WASHINGTON										
Jackson (D)	O	R	R	R	R	R	R	R	R	R
Magnuson (D)	R	R	R	R	R	R	R	O	R	R
WEST VIRGINIA										
Byrd (D)	R	R	R	W	R	W	W	R	R	W
Randolph (D)	R	O	R	R	R	R	R	R	R	R
WISCONSIN										
Nelson (D)	R	R	R	R	R	R	R	R	R	R
Proxmire (D)	W	R	R	R	R	R	R	R	R	R
WYOMING										
McGee (D)	R	R	R	R	R	R	R	O	O	R
Simpson (R)	W	W	W	W	W	W	W	W	W	W

Chapter 8

The Labor Lobby

THE COMBINATION of governmental principles, tradition, and diversity in the United States has made public officials especially alert to the voices of the people. Channels for effective political action have been kept open by the Constitution, the nature of the party system, and a social environment that permits interest groups to form and flourish. But government officials, party leaders, and legislators only hear the opinions of articulate citizens or their representative pressure groups. Today, as always, a group must work at effectively influencing the decisions that bear on its success or failure and the happiness or misery of its members. This work is most commonly done through the process of lobbying.

Lobbying is most accurately defined as all substantial and compensated attempts to influence governmental decision. It is a word and an activity that has an unfortunate connotation for most people, who feel that it is a somehow nefarious or illegitimate attempt to subvert the public welfare for private gain. Such reactions undoubtedly have their roots in the covert and even overt bribery undertaken by lobbyists of a century ago, a practice which is rare now but occasionally still revealed in minor scandals over secret campaign contributions or gifts of deep freezers or vicuna coats.

Upon careful analysis, however, pressure politics and lobbying are part of the bloodstream of the democratic process, necessary as an outlet for people's grievances and claims between elections. Moreover, lobbying has not one but several roles, most of which are desirable and fully legitimate. It fulfills not only the protective and promotional function with which the word lobby is usually associated, but also a representative and an educational role.

In its representational aspect, lobbying is an extension of territorial representation. In a society characterized by population growth, a steady increase in the complexity of issues presented for public policy decisions, and extreme specialization of labor, representation based upon territory is often inadequate to reflect the desires of the citizen as an individual and as a member of an occupational group. Lobbying meets the need for more complete representation. It provides a means to merge the common interests of individuals and groups living in different constituencies.

It unifies minority interests, often widely scattered geographically, which may otherwise have no voice at all. Through the lobby, all of the varied interests affected by governmental action can obtain a voice in regard to that action and, thus, transcend the limits of our traditional individualistic conception of political representation.

In his educational role the lobbyist functions as the advisor of legislators. He is often better informed on highly technical matters than are the legislators themselves. By marshaling arguments for and against measures, lobbyists add expertise to the legislative process, help to clarify issues, and provide an essential avenue of communication between lawmakers and constituents. Nor is lobbying to be despised because lobbyists are usually spokesmen for special interests. The chief danger arises when a few powerful organizations are able to silence voices of opposition by sheer force of numbers or superior powers of persuasion. However, this problem does not often arise. Usually the lobbying process educates legislators and often the public as well when all interested groups have an opportunity to present their case.

Finally, the lobbyist is, of course, the protector and promoter of the special interest or pressure group he represents. He attempts to improve the group's position and to defend an advantageous position vis-a-vis other economic, social, or political groups in the society. Some groups attempt and achieve a veto power over legislation or appointments, sometimes even seeking the creation of new executive agencies or legislative committees to guard and promote their interests. By such means the pressure groups and the lobbyists who represent them have gained considerable power in American society, and have become a respectable adjunct to the representative process in American government.

Early in its history, organized labor, like every other numerically significant group in our society, turned to pressure politics and lobbying of government officials to seek benefits for workers and protection of its own institutional interests. Chapter 2 described how the early trade unions and other labor interests turned to state legislatures to achieve the ten-hour day. In the post-civil war period, the eight-hour leagues, the National Labor Union and the Knights of Labor intensified these lobbying efforts. The Knights established the first permanent labor lobby in Washington in 1886. The achievements of the early labor lobbyists were scant, however, reflecting the pro-business mores of those times, as well as labor's early lack of institutional respectability. The labor lobbyist of the nineteenth and early twentieth centuries found achievement and acceptance much harder than does his counterpart of today.

The present chapter opens with a short excerpt from Lester Milbrath's study of *The Washington Lobbyist,* describing the daily routine of the average lobbyist and analyzing the ways in which the life and background of the labor lobbyist is apt to differ from lobbyists in general. Gus Tyler, in "A Legislative Campaign for a Federal Minimum Wage (1955)" shows the labor lobby working with great effectiveness to achieve a goal of benefit for specific unions and for workers generally. His detailing of methodology—grass-roots pressure, strong central coordination on policy and steady educational work with legislators —is extremely valuable.

The two readings that follow, one by Sar Levitan and the other by Alan McAdams, are two complementary studies of the same subject: labor's efforts to prevent the passage or weaken the force of legislation designed to reform certain internal union practices. The failure of the labor lobby in this case led to the passage of the Labor-Management Reporting and Disclosure (Landrum-Griffin) Act of 1959.

When analyzed in conjunction, these readings raise some provocative questions. The structure of American government makes it far easier to prevent legislation than to obtain its passage. Overlapping terms of office, federalism, checks and balances, all hinder the electorate's expression of an effective mandate. Delay in legislative committees and parliamentary maneuvering on the floors of Congress often hinder or prevent congressional action. These factors are particularly disadvantageous to the labor movement. Unions normally are politically aggressive, seeking social change and new legislation. The restraints in the legislative process make it inherently conservative, posing a severe handicap to such aggressive groups. Yet twice since World War II, labor has been unable to prevent major legislation (the Taft-Hartley and Landrum-Griffin Acts) that it considered adverse, but during the same period has been able to gain other affirmative legislation (such as increases in the minimum wage) that it desired.

What factors explain a lobby's success or failure? Organizational cohesiveness, a clear demonstration of strength at the polls, successful identification of the group's own desires with the "general welfare," or the general public's attitude toward a particular pressure group at any point in time—any one or all of these, and perhaps other variables as well, may be the key in a given situation. Whatever the answer, and whatever labor's success in gaining any particular objective, the labor lobby is the most important organized group today speaking in behalf of a substantial majority of Americans, particularly those who support welfare-state objectives. President Lyndon Johnson recognized this in his remarks when he signed the Older Americans Act in July 1965:

> The legislative efforts of the AFL–CIO have done more good for more people than any other group in America.
>
> It doesn't just try to do something about wages and hours for its own people. No group in America works harder in the interests of everyone.
>
> It helps young and old and middle-aged. It's interested in education, in housing, in poverty programs, and does as much good for millions who have never belonged to a union as for its own members.
>
> That is my conception of an organization working in the public interest. I've wanted to say this for a long time because I believe that the American people ought to know the remarkable contribution which organized labor makes to the promotion of sound legislation.

The Labor Lobbyist

Lester W. Milbrath

Northwestern University

[L]OBBYISTS SPEND MOST OF THEIR TIME receiving and sending communications. Most of this they do from the seclusion of their own offices. Some communications are passed via personal conversation with members of Congress or other governmental decision-makers, but these consume little time. Very few are transmitted or facilitated through entertainment.

Most lobbyists spend at least some time traveling about visiting local groups attempting to improve communication with the people who support them and to stimulate a flow of communications from the grass roots to governmental decision-makers. A particular lobbyist's allocation of time is determined partly by the demands and the boundaries of the political influence system within which he operates and partly on his personal predilections, skills, and the demands of the moment.

Whom the Lobbyist Sees

It is in the nature of his job that the lobbyist sees and communicates with governmental decision-makers. Usually people think that mem-

Excerpted by permission of the publisher from *The Washington Lobbyists* by Lester W. Milbrath, copyright © 1963, Chicago: Rand McNally & Co.

bers of Congress are the only targets of lobbying. In actual fact, however, most lobbyists are as concerned with decisions made in the executive branch as with those made in the legislative branch. This is especially true of groups or firms whose activities come under the jurisdiction of independent regulatory commissions. Lobbyists must develop contacts and carry on communications with persons in any branch of the government making decisions of importance to them or their groups.

We noted above that lobbyists spend only limited time with officials; they tend to spend more time with the staff aides to decision-makers: administrative assistants, legal counselors, legislative counselors, clerks, private secretaries, and so forth. In many instances, such aides are very close to official decision-makers and participate significantly in their decision processes. Aides have more time to listen to the pleas of lobbyists. The lobbyist frequently presents his case in full to a staff assistant first and later covers only the high spots in the few minutes allowed for personal conference with the official. In many offices, the various aides each concern themselves with a specialized subject matter area. A lobbyist with a problem in a given area—e.g., agriculture—works most closely with the aide who is responsible for that area. So useful are these aides, these brokers in communication, that many lobbyists say that in certain cases they prefer to confer with a trusted aide than with the decision-maker himself.

Another group of aides are the staff assistants to congressional committees. Staff members carry on the administrative and clerical functions of the committee, conduct research, and indirectly participate in the decision process. Their power comes from their ability partly to control the flow of information and communications to the committee: they do research, plan and administer hearings, question witnesses, write committee reports, give advice, and listen to lobbyists. So absorbed are these staff persons·in the committee's decision process that they cannot be considered impartial; therefore, most committees have both a majority party and a minority party staff. The chairman of the committee appoints the majority staff, and the ranking minority member appoints the minority staff. The lobbyist's most useful and open point of access to the committee's decision process is through the committee staff. Many staff persons also realize that they can get useful assistance, information, and advice from lobbyists. It is not uncommon to find close personal relationships between lobbyists and staff members. Although no figures directly indicate this, it appears that committee staff members have more communication with lobbyists than any other set of political role-players on Capitol Hill.

Lobbyists are not concerned solely with communications to decision-makers or aides close to them. They also interact frequently with fellow lobbyists, persons in political parties, members of the press, or ordinary voters. Lobbyists often act in concert to try to influence governmental decisions. Several groups interested in the same policy may regularly exchange information and plot joint strategy. Each organization may send a delegate or the entire staff to a conference. Groups may work in harmony on some issues and go separate ways on others. For example, the railroad brotherhoods and the Association of American Railroads may cooperate on a policy that affects the overall prosperity of the railroad industry, but may oppose each other on labor-management questions. Regular working sessions create close personal relationships between individual staff members of different organizations and facilitate a great variety of informal communications.

Most lobby organizations have regular staff sessions. Some staffs meet daily in the morning to check signals, exchange information, and plan their activities for the day. In addition, many informal conferences are held to clarify points, pass on information, agree on the wording of a draft, plan strategy, and so forth. Some staffs are as small as one or two persons; others are as large as ten or fifteen.

Lobbyists also interact regularly with the members and officers of their own organizations. Some of the officers may live in Washington or visit there regularly; some organization members visit Washington; some lobbyists take trips to the local units. The above is not a total cataloging of persons lobbyists see, but it covers the types of persons with whom they regularly interact.

. . . .

Officers of Organizations

The elected officer of an organization who registers as a lobbyist is somewhat similar to the trade association executive. Both administer the organization and represent it before the government and the press. Both handle errands and grievances for members. Yet certain differences warrant placing them in separate categories.

Many officers represent labor unions. In business, when a man is elected to an office in his trade association, he usually continues to run his own business and devotes only partial attention to the affairs of the association. In labor organizations (and, to a certain extent, farm organizations), however, when a man assumes high office in his union, he quits his job in the factory and devotes full time to the affairs of the union. From this basic distinction flow many related factors. Most officers who register as lobbyists have long tenures; they are older than most lobbyists; they are generally paid less than trade association executives (their salaries cannot be too much higher than those of members on the assembly line.) [Some union] officers believe they belong in the lower-middle class, whereas most lobbyists consider themselves in the upper-middle or upper class. Some officers are relatively poorly educated. They are more likely to be Democrats than are other lobbyists.

Moreover, officers generally represent organizations with considerable power at the polls. As such, they place more emphasis on grass-roots political activity and devote more time to stirring up and manipulating the local membership. Unlike trade association executives, most officers have been or are now involved in partisan politics; most have campaigned at one time or another; and most have made political contributions. In fact, they contribute more frequently than any other lobbyist group. They also place slightly greater emphasis on collaboration with other organizations in their lobbying activities than do trade association executives. In part, this results from the fact that labor organizations often advocate broad programs which require and attract collaboration from a variety of groups; but lobbyists for organizations with considerable power at the polls also favor pooling the resources and influence of several groups.

Officers of organizations, more than trade association executives, are charged formally and explicitly with policy development, though the board of directors generally has the final word on policy. It would be erroneous, however, to conclude that these officers have more impact on policy in their organizations than trade association executives have in theirs. Undoubtedly both types of role-players are centrally concerned with policy development.

A Legislative Campaign for a
Federal Minimum Wage (1955)

Gus Tyler
International Ladies' Garment Workers' Union

ON JANUARY 6, 1955, President Eisenhower, in his State of the Union speech, urged a modification of the existing Fair Labor Standards Act, commonly referred to as the minimum wage law:

Excerpted by permission of The Eagleton Institute of Politics, copyright © 1960 by Rutgers, The State University.

In the past five years, we have had economic growth which will support an increase in the federal minimum wage. In the light of present economic conditions, I recommend its increase to ninety cents an hour. I also recommend that many others, at present excluded, be given the benefits of a minimum wage.

The President's message was a green light to the American trade unions to resume their campaign for a higher and more broadly based minimum. The last revision of the minimum wage law had taken place in 1949, leaving a six-year gap without change. The change in 1949 from 40 cents to 75 cents an hour seemed inadequate to labor at the time and appeared doubly unsatisfactory in the inflated-cost economy of 1955. Eisenhower's statement placed the subject on the legislative agenda of the new 84th Congress. In the elections of 1954, the Democratic party had won control of both houses of Congress, carrying in with them a slightly enlarged contingent of labor-endorsed candidates. Both the AFL and CIO, at their separate conventions, had passed resolutions urging an increase in the minimum wage from $.75 to $1.25 per hour and an extension of the act to include several million American workers not covered by existing federal law.

This concurrence of circumstances—labor's desire to move, the new complexion of Congress, the Presidential message—placed revision of the Fair Labor Standards Act (FLSA) high on the unions' list of "must" legislation for 1955.

To four union presidents, however, FLSA revision was not simply desirable but necessary: these were David Dubinsky, president of the International Ladies' Garment Workers' Union (AFL); Jacob Potofsky, president of the Amalgamated Clothing Workers of America (CIO); Emil Rieve, president of the Textile Workers Union of America (CIO); and Alex Rose, president of the United Hatters, Cap, and Millinery Workers (AFL).

The industries covered by these four unions were all producers of light products, easily transported for sale in nationally competitive markets. Low-wage producers, operating in these industries at the federal minimum, constituted a constant threat to the organized sector, tending to produce unemployment, wage cuts, or wage freezes in the unionized areas. A higher minimum wage, in such industries, was a primary need to close or shorten the competitive gap, to preserve employment in unionized plants, to lay the groundwork for future increases in union contracts.

A Committee Is Born

For these reasons, the four unions mentioned above hastened to move toward a higher minimum wage. But to do so as an organized group it was necessary to create a joint committee, since the unions involved were divided between AFL and CIO. At that time, American trade unions were working on a no-raiding pact as a prelude to unification, thus it was not difficult for the four unions in the minimum wage drive to set up an *ad hoc* committee across federation lines. Established informally in Miami talks among the four presidents, the *ad hoc* committee was soon formalized into the Joint Minimum Wage Committee, headquartered in Washington, D.C., and assigned prime responsibility for the legislative effort to raise the minimum wage. . . .

The AFL and the CIO assigned members of their legislative staff to work with the Joint Committee. Three of the four major national unions assigned two staff members each: one to reside and work in Washington as the regularly registered legislative representative; the other to meet with the committee on a weekly or biweekly basis as a liaison with the national unions and their locals.

[Arthur] Goldberg, [then a Washington attorney, and labor economist Jack] Barbash, and the assigned representatives comprised the operational subcommittee for the minimum-wage drive. They met almost daily to compare reports, measure progress, map visits with members of Congress. About once a week, the national representatives of the union would gather in Washington in an enlarged committee, together with the AFL and CIO representatives and the coordinators of the committee. This group mapped overall strategy.

Funds for the operation of this committee came from the interested unions. The total budget of about $20,000 was spent largely for rent (offices and meeting places), phone, mail, secretarial and clerical staff. The legislative representatives were paid by their respective unions and so reported to Congress under the Regulation of Lobbying Act.

Getting Started

At its first session, members of the Joint Committee agreed that the immediate problem was to "get the campaign off the ground"—to make the issue important. Unless minimum wages loomed large in the eyes of Congress—and its leadership—the proposed legislation could dissolve in the vast crush of legislation that regularly crowds Capitol Hill. . . . To get a bill through, it is necessary to work up a heavy head of steam and to do it *early*. The Joint Committee began at once to build up pressure.

First, the committee urged as many Congressmen and Senators as possible to submit bills providing an upward revision of the minimum wage. In Washington, the urging was done through visits to

Senators and Representatives. At the "local union" level, it was done by letters to Congressmen.

Second, the committee planned a visit to President Eisenhower by presidents of international unions to give the drive the publicity that comes with "summit conferences."

Third, the committee planned interviews between top union leaders and the House and Senate leadership. These conferences informed both Lyndon Johnson (D-Tex.), majority leader in the Senate, and Sam Rayburn (D-Tex.), speaker of the House, that the unions were not carrying on routine agitation for just another measure but meant business in the matter of the minimum wage.

Finally, the regular legislative offices of both AFL and CIO gave the same message to Congressmen in general.

The private Presidential conference had one positive value: it produced press coverage to help get the campaign "off the ground." But it failed to persuade Eisenhower to become an active campaigner for minimum-wage reform or to move beyond his 90-cent line. Indeed, after the conversation with Eisenhower, the committee concluded that he might very well make 90-cents a party measure and might even veto a bill for more than 90 cents.

The third move—conferences with Senate and House leadership —received no publicity and none was desired. The intention in the "legislative" parleys was to inform Johnson and Rayburn of the importance of minimum-wage reform, to find out how much the Congress could yield, and whether the yield would be forthcoming at the first session of the 84th Congress.

Both Johnson and Rayburn recorded their concern for wage reform as one of labor's top "must" items, added that they would try to schedule action for the first session, were pessimistic about extended coverage or even a minimum of $1.25, but saw possibilities for something above 90 cents an hour.

The fourth move—a high priority for minimum-wage reform by AFL and CIO—was conveyed to the Senate and House leadership not simply by the interested unions but also by the top legislative staffs of the labor federations "on the hill." . . .

By mid-March, the committee's focus was fixed: to work up public interest in a minimum of $1.25 as ultimately desirable and justifiable but to settle for something between 90 cents and $1.25, and to build up testimony for extended coverage with the understanding that action on coverage would probably have to be postponed. While the committee constantly reevaluated this decision—as is inevitable in a bargaining situation—the original focus provided a basis for day-by-day operation, a handy brief for the Congressman who would say bluntly: "Don't tell me what you would like to have; tell me what you will settle for." . . .

Measuring Congress

Through February and March, the Joint Committee quickly gathered information to provide a political profile of Congress as a whole. The information came from direct conversations with Senators, answers to letters from constituents, analyses of voting records. Early in April, the Joint Committee scrutinized each Senator and put him into one of five categories. Category One: those known definitely to favor a minimum wage of at least $1. Category Two: those inclined to but not pledged to a minimum of $1. Category Three: unknowns and neutrals. Category Four: those inclined to vote against a minimum of $1. Category Five: those flatly opposed to a $1 minimum.

In the mathematics that, at a given stage, tends to dominate democratic politics, the results revealed:

Category One 23
Category Two 17
Category Three 23
Category Four 22
Category Five 11

Thus, only 40 Senators out of 96 were likely to vote for a minimum of $1 or more an hour: a clear minority.

The decisive area of conflict was the no-man's land of Category Three with its 23 Senators, all Republicans or Southern Democrats. Here were the votes to provide the needed majority: nine of these were required to attain the magic count of 49. By early April, the target in the Senate was plain: to win nine converts among the "unknowns and neutrals."

In the House, where the Labor Committee appeared as the prime obstacle, an attitude analysis indicated something close to a majority for at least $1. An early April count showed 132 members as favoring at least $1 an hour with another 58 members strongly inclined to accept a dollar minimum. This added up to 190 votes with 218 needed for a majority. In the "neutrals" category were 144 representatives with an additional 14 totally unknown. From these 158 representatives, the Joint Committee sought 28 votes.

It appeared that the problem in House and Senate could be reduced to 37 Congressmen to be won over. As the weeks and months went by, this figure constantly underwent revision. "Safe" votes slipped away; "bad" votes turned "good"; definite votes became indefinite and vice versa. Nevertheless, the Joint Committee never ceased counting noses—and making profiles. . . .

The Joint Committee worked toward an ideal objective: a pledge from a majority of the members of House and Senate to vote for a minimum wage of at least $1.00 an hour. This was the goal, although the Committee knew that an absolute majority is rarely necessary since at the final vote a certain number of Congressmen are almost always absent. Nevertheless, a "safe" majority was regarded as the aim.

Creating a Climate of Opinion

A major strategy decision before the committee was the question of whether to concentrate on the convertible doubtfuls or to "work on" the entire membership of both Houses. The argument for the first line of strategy rested on the belief that with limited resources it was advisable to pinpoint the fire, to visit and revisit, to stimulate petitions and letters to the "in-between" Congressmen who might be won over. This appeared to be the most efficient method at first glance. On further consideration, however, the second line of strategy—creating a climate of opinion that would permeate the whole Congress—was deemed more advisable. The reasons behind this decision shed light on the committee's view of the way Congress operates.

First, many Congressmen who were committed to the higher minimum wage were sometimes unprepared to present a strong factual case before committee and colleagues. It was deemed advisable to provide these "friends" with ammunition.

Second, many Congressmen who would themselves "go along with" a higher minimum did not feel the issue strongly enough to cause the "friend" to make more friends. A lively stream of communications from back home—especially if the communications were individual and personal—might induce a friend not only to vote for the bill but to work for the bill: to get it reported out and to get others to vote right.

Third, some friendly Congressmen asked to have much mail from home so that they could "explain" their vote to others in their constituencies who might ask why the vote was cast. A Congressman who doubted it was "safe" to vote for a higher minimum might feel on safer ground if he could declare publicly that as a representative he felt it his duty to reflect the will of the voters as expressed in the flow of mail.

Fourth, the degree of urgency felt by the collective membership of House and Senate would influence the House and Senate leadership who are always on the alert to find out what issues have vote appeal. The volume of interest registered by the folks back home is sometimes viewed as an indicator of public sentiment. The greater the total volume, the greater the concern of the leadership.

Fifth, a general groundswell would strengthen the hands of House and Senate leadership in delivering a favorable vote on minimum wages. . . .

Sixth, the Joint Committee was finally persuaded to use the broadside, rather than the pinpoint, attack by two other considerations: (1) the trade-union structure is such that it is, in a national campaign, much more difficult to try to influence individual Congressmen than to express a nationwide opinion of all of Congress; (2) in preparation for future elections, it was considered advisable to involve as many union members as possible in order to convert the minimum-wage effort into one great class in civics. . . .

The "Community Approach"

It is standard operating procedure for unions—like any other interest group—to urge their affiliates to write to Congress supporting the passage of legislation endorsed by the group. Such calls result in greater or lesser mail pouring or trickling into Congressional offices, usually identical in wording, often printed and mimeographed. The impact of mass-produced mail, where the citizen does nothing more than sign his name, is minimal.

The Joint Committee discouraged this kind of standard campaign. The central effort of the Joint Committee was to get "*communities*" to communicate with Congressmen rather than trade unionists alone. The Joint Committee assumed that a higher minimum wage should interest the "community," and that the role of the unions was to motivate the community to voice that interest. . . .

In a similar way, the trade unions tried to get their local organizations to stimulate, coordinate, express a body of opinion existing in their communities. In addition, however, the local unions were given an educational job; that is, *creating* a body of opinion.

The basic machinery for this operation was composed of the major *national* unions affiliated with the Joint Minimum Wage Committee. These *national* organizations prepared directives for their *local* affiliates. These directives were, in the first instance, made the responsibility of the staff and officers on a regional and local basis. In most cases, the staffs were called to regional conferences by the national unions. These conferences were generally joint affairs, where regional staff and officers of the four major national unions met together to be briefed on the issue, to work out the master plan of operation, to suggest the best methods for carrying out the plan at the local level. . . .

Because the Joint Committee looked upon the union affiliates as "community organizers" in this campaign, much of the briefing to locals dealt with the reasons why "others" should back the legislation. "Others" referred to workers who would not feel the direct impact of the minimum-wage change because their wages were far above legal minima. The appeal to the higher-paid worker was triple: to halt the relocation of plants in search of cheaper labor, to stimulate fuller employment through increased purchasing power, and to raise the *prevailing* pay by raising the *base* pay. (In some cases, the minimum wage and the average wage contained in the contract were pegged to a percentage or a set number of pennies above the federal legal minimum.)

"Others" also included nonlabor groups such as farmers, retailers, bankers, doctors, local editors, social workers, and so forth. Prime among these "others" was a group normally found opposed to the unions in economic matters; namely, the employers.

"Approach employers," exhorted a textile union booklet. "Employers constantly cry they need wage cuts to meet cheap wage competition. Here is the opportunity *for them* to do something constructive. A $1.25 minimum wage would eliminate the threat of low wage competition in the textile industry."

The appeal to the nonlabor groups was couched in terms of the worker as consumer, patient, client, bank depositor, taxpayer. As a consumer, with extra dollars at the end of the week, the worker could approach his retailer, his doctor, or dentist. As a market for fruits and vegetables, he could establish a common ground with the farmer. As a holder of a saving account, he could approach his local banker for backing, especially in small towns. As a taxpayer, he could talk with city officials, teachers, policemen, firemen, employees. In brief, the unions embarked on a campaign to inform the community how the circumstances of the wage earner conditioned the circumstances of many others in the community.

At the local level, labor, as a "special interest group," played the role of prime mover in a "public interest" action. The campaign depended for its margin of success on labor's ability not to raise a *separate* and *distinct* voice but to *merge* into an integrated community movement. . . .

Organization by Congressional Districts

In this campaign of resolution, letters, petitions, and later, visits to Congressmen, there was a minor obstacle of major consequence: the people did not know the name of the Congressman. (In many cases, though less frequently, they did not know the name of the Senators.)

To overcome this difficulty, the national unions took two steps. First, unions sorted out their locals by *Congressional districts*, concentrating on finding a few staff, officers, or active members who could be classified by their political units. Such paper work became necessary because unions are organized along *trade* rather than *political* lines, with locals and departments shaped for collective bargaining, rather than legislative, purposes. This basic clerical job by the national unions provided an exercise in political geography, a means of knowing in which Congressional districts the unions had headquarters, locals and members. The material from the several unions of the Joint Committee was collated for combined operations.

To help the individual member know the name of his or her Congressman, the unions drew maps of the key states, showing the geographic boundaries of Congressional districts. Often, this was supplemented or replaced by a listing of towns, indicating which municipalities or villages were in the districts.

This technical matter—the fact that the trade unions do not have their entire membership carefully broken down by Congressional districts—was one of the great reasons for the original decision to conduct a broadside rather than pinpointed campaign. For unions in mass-production industries, located in metropolitan areas, with workers pouring into and out of factories daily from and to a widely scattered area, the magnitude of the simple clerical job of locating total membership by political units is prohibitive, especially in lower paying trades where turnover is rapid.

By providing maps and town directories, the unions enabled every interested member to locate his district. Several thousand union members learned the names of their Congressmen and as a result, several hundred Congressmen learned the names of some of their constituents—and what was bothering them. . . . [As a result of this type of grass-roots operation, many city governing bodies, some employers, and a number of newspapers announced support of a substantial increase in the minimum wage.]

The Easter Talks

As the Easter recess approached, the Joint Committee felt it important that local delegations speak directly to their Congressmen. In recent years, the spring "break" is the period when Congressmen go back home to put their ears to the ground, to get the rustle of the grass roots. They are then receptive to delegations. It is also a means to communicate directly with Congressmen at bargain rates: a home-town visit is much less costly than a Washington junket.

Mimeographed instructions were issued by Washington to local unions on how to arrange and conduct Easter conferences. On March 29, for instance, the CIO Legislative Department put out a four-page mimeographed booklet entitled: *Organizing a Delegation to See Your Congressman or Senator at Home during the Easter Recess.* The purpose was clearly to push for minimum-wage reform. "In CIO's judgment," read the booklet, "this Easter recess should be used *primarily* for the minimum-wage campaign."

A quickie guide of "do's and dont's" was provided for Congressional conversations, a compound of Emily Post and Dale Carnegie.

> *Don't get into a quarrel with your Congressman.* . . .
>
> *Don't let the Congressman dominate the conversation but don't bore him or the rest of your group by making speeches.* . . .
>
> *Don't make vague, general statements about the need for a higher minimum;* be specific. . . .
>
> *Offer your help to the Congressman.* . . .

In keeping with the tone of the entire campaign, the local committees were advised to organize a "broad" delegation. "Some employers will be glad to join you. After all, they may be just as anxious as you to protect union wage scales. The local mayor or councilman may join you. Make the group as representative of the community as possible. This will help prove that it is to the public benefit to pass good minimum wage legislation."

The Easter conversations produced visible results.

The *Morning Call* of Allentown, Pennsylvania, reported on April 7, that Representative Karl C. King (R, Bucks and Lehigh districts) had told management and labor groups that he "wouldn't mind going along up to $1 an hour . . . if a proposal for up to $1 should be placed before the floor."

On April 18, the Lewistown, Pennsylvania, local press quoted Representative Richard M. Simpson, a leading Republican, as telling a joint labor and management delegation:

> I am not in a position to tell you I will get you $1.25 as a minimum wage, but I will support an increase from the prevailing 75 cents per hour to as near the $1.25 minimum as possible. I am sure it will be between 90 cents, which is now being proposed by the administration, and the $1.25 you seek.

Some Congressmen openly referred to their Easter conversations as factors in helping them to make up their minds. Thus Albert Morano (R-Conn., Fairfield County) announced that "during the Easter recess [he] had the opportunity to talk with many . . . constituents about a matter that is currently before the Congress of the United States; namely, the federal minimum wage bill of more than one dollar." . . .

The Senate Votes

On June 7, the Senate Labor Committee approved the Douglas bill for $1 by a voice vote after several alternatives had been rejected. A proposal for $1.25 an hour, and extended coverage, submitted by Senator Lehman (D-N.Y.) was defeated by voice. A straight proposal for $1.25 submitted by Senator Ives (R-N.Y.) was defeated 5 to 9. Senator Allott (R-Colo.) proposed a 90-cents minimum that received only two committee votes: Allott and Smith (R-N.J.).

The next day, the bill came to the Senate floor in the care of the majority leader. As the Citizens' Committee described the action:

> And 75 minutes later it was all over in a shouted vote (by a couple of dozen on hand) for $1. Douglas managed unheated pass-the-buck debate. Smith offered a last minute administration compromise: 90 cents in 1956, 95 cents in 1957, $1 after 1957. Only Allott and Senator John J. Williams (R-Del.) stood openly beside him.

The way in which the bill glided through the Senate was disappointing esthetically to some of the Joint Committee representatives who had come to the chamber to hear a classic debate. Senator Douglas was on the platform, prepared to present and defend his report. Several Senators were in the cloak room, trying to draw together a coalition of Eisenhower (90 cent) Republicans and Southern Democrats to block the committee proposal of $1. The galleries were ready for a Donnybrook: a tough debate and a tight roll call. But it never happened. Johnson, without vocal opposition from Republican Leader William Knowland (R-Calif.), interrupted the debate and neatly passed the bill. When a few of the cloak-roomers hurried back to the chamber to get into the fight, they found it was all over.

Old legislative hands saw more in this oiled handling of the bill than appeared on the surface. Apparently, there was a majority on the floor in favor of $1. But in a record vote—with each man's name called and recorded—the $1 minimum would have run into difficulty. There were the Southern Democrats who favored the $1 minimum but who preferred, because of constituent opinion, not to go on record for it. There were Republicans who preferred, because of their ties with the White House, not to oppose the administration in its efforts to hold the line at 90 cents. The live vote—a general shout at the moment when the chamber itself was hardly full—produced the necessary majority with embarrassment to none. . . .

Initiating House Action

The minimum-wage sponsors feared that if the House Labor Committee ran its education hearings into June, took added time to write an education bill, and only then began minimum-wage hearings, the House Committee would not be in a position to bring in a bill before adjournment.

Although the Democratic leadership in the House, through Speaker Rayburn, indicated a genuine interest in passage of a minimum-wage bill in the 1955 session, although mail poured in from all over the country, and although both national and local newspapers gave the matter increasing attention, the House Labor Committee had not by May 1 set a definite date for hearings on minimum wages. The Joint Minimum Wage Committee decided upon drastic and dramatic action: to let Congress hear from the country in person. . . .

In the give and take between delegates [brought to Washington to speak for labor] and Congressmen, the latter were interested not only in first-hand experiences but also in the effect of various proposed minima on the economy of the country or of the area involved. Delegates were briefed both on content and style, what to say and how to say it, and Congressional courtesy.

The Joint Committee believed the delegations "exercise a powerful persuasive influence . . . in our favor." It reported enthusiastically to the affiliate unions "the fact that these working men and women have expended time and money to take the trip is very impressive. We have been astonished by the commitments on minimum wage by many Congressmen whom we have previously regarded as hostile or doubtful."

The Farm Bloc

The delegations were particularly interested in three groups of Representatives: Republicans, southern Democrats, and a third group, not hitherto discussed, the "farm bloc." The last group cut across party and regional lines. Individual Representatives from the "farm" areas were not usually industrial-minded. Some felt that high wages placed an undue burden on the farmer when he went to purchase manufactured goods. Others felt that a minimum-wage push would reach into farm areas to disturb existing wage structures in their districts. Early in the minimum-wage campaign, the national legislative representatives of the federation addressed themselves to the farm bloc.

For a number of years, both AFL and CIO had been supporting legislation to maintain price levels and regular incomes for farmers. Congressmen from urban and industrial areas, representing heavily unionized towns and cities, had voted for such legislation. In the 84th Congress, the trade-union leadership dramatized its traditional support for these measures with publicized telegrams to Harold Cooley, chairman of the House Agricultural Committee.

A telegram from Walter Reuther to Harold Cooley set off fireworks in the House. Representative Leslie Arends (R-Ill.) charged that "labor leaders hoped to gain support of Southern Democratic farm members in their fight for a $1.25 minimum wage law in return for support of the farm bill."

Cooley retorted that "such labor leaders as Walter P. Reuther had endorsed the farm bill because he was aware that a strong farm economy was a part of a national prosperity."

Representative Victor Anfuso (D-N.Y.) felt it was perfectly proper for labor and farm elements to aid one another. On May 3 Anfuso took the floor to "appeal for a deal between farm and city members to win high rigid price supports for farmers and a higher minimum wage for labor."

Some measure of the importance of labor's backing for the price support legislation can be obtained from the statement of James G. Patton, president of the National Farmers Union, before the Senate Labor Committee (May 9): "I wish to state here that passage last week by the House of HR 12 repealing sliding-scale farm price supports is in large measure due to the support and friendly backing given us by labor organizations and by Congressmen elected from city districts."

When delegations from southern states reported on their Congressional interviews, May 22, J. W. Holder, secretary of the North Carolina CIO, stated that Representative Cooley "gave us a warm reception. He said he would vote for $1 an hour or more."

The reports of delegations during the first three weeks in May indicated great sympathy for a $1 minimum among House members. The problem still was the Labor Committee.

The Party Struggle

By mid-May, the pressures on this committee were considerable. The leadership of House and Senate were beginning to talk about adjournment, setting it somewhere between July 15 and August 15. Unless the House Labor Committee moved quickly on minimum wages, the Democratic Congress would have to end its first session without having passed a single major piece of "labor" legislation.

The Republicans were beginning to exploit the situation. When Senator George D. Aiken (R-Vt.) was interviewed by a CIO delegation he "told them he couldn't do anything; the place to take their problem was to Graham Barden in the House who, Aiken was careful to point out, is a Democrat."

Similarly, Republican House Leader Joseph W. Martin (Mass.) wrote to a constituent that he was "in favor of an increase, but as yet [he did] not know what figure would be reported out of the committee. The situation is controlled by the Democratic majority on the Education and Labor Committee."

On May 23, Drew Pearson wrote:

> Most significant factor about Barden's opposition is that the Republicans are quietly helping him—and getting a big laugh out of it. For their secret help to Barden puts all the blame on the Democrats and may even alienate part of the labor support hitherto steadfastly behind the Democrats.

Outside Congress, "liberal" commentators in the press pounded the Democratic party, primarily Barden, and secondarily Johnson and Rayburn for the Labor Committee impasse. . . .

The second week in May, the "liberal" wing of the Democratic delegation on the House Labor Committee caucused to break the deadlock. According to a United Press International dispatch of May 21, later confirmed by Democratic committee member Roy W. Wier (Minn.) "he and his Democratic supporters got tired of Barden dragging his feet about 10 days ago and held a strategy huddle in Wier's office. 'We decided to serve notice that we wanted an end to it,' he said."

This rare maneuver—the planned revolt of a committee against its chairman—was scarcely a secret. On May 20, Drew Pearson reported that "if Barden doesn't stop his filibustering tactics against two vitally important bills—federal aid for school construction and minimum-wage liberalization—some of his colleagues may start an open rebellion." Pearson also quoted Lee Metcalf (Mont.), Democratic member of the committee, as declaring that he had "every intention of asking for a vote in the near future on the minimum-wage bill, for which the distinguished chairman [Barden] seems to show small enthusiasm."

The Democratic revolt was sparked by two purposes: to get action on wages and to display the fact that 15 out of 17 Democrats on the House Labor Committee wanted to act and that Barden was able to delay action only by getting the unanimous backing of the 13 Republicans on the committee. . . .

Barden resented bitterly that members of his committee had

leaked information to the press about insurgencies and caucuses and the chairman's "dragging his feet." He also observed that:

> there can be no doubt in anybody's mind that knows the sentiment of the House, and the feeling of the committee, that the people of the country want the minimum wage dealt with. I have no purpose here in Congress except to serve my nation and my people. There has been no doubt in my mind and certainly not in many others no honest doubt, I would say, but that was the next order of business.

Barden spoke his piece, had it recorded, and made it available to the press.

Within a week, in line with Barden's promise, hearings started on the minimum wage. . . .

The House Acts

By mid-July, . . . the House Labor Committee was ready to report out the bill. A motion in committee to set the minimum at 90 cents was reportedly lost as a result of a tie vote. A subsequent proposal for a $1 minimum carried the committee narrowly. Coverage and modification of the Puerto Rican and Virgin Islands clauses were omitted from the House bill. Barden explained: "I do not think that there is anybody on the committee but what knows if you take the whole Wage-Hour bill that you will be here in December, let alone go through in July or August."

The bill ran into minimum difficulty in the Rules Committee, perhaps a reflection of a desire of the House leadership, mainly Speaker Rayburn, to enact at least one major labor bill before adjournment.

On July 20, the bill came before the House. Barden moved to have the "House resolve itself into the Committee of the Whole on the State of the Union for the further consideration of the bill." When the House changes its name to the Committee of the Whole, it generally casts its vote without roll call. This makes it easier to find out where a majority or minority stands before putting the final vote for the record.

Barden's motion was passed. The rules of debate covering this bill were then read, limiting amendments to two subjects: (1) the exact amount of the minimum; (2) the effective date. This eliminated any and all amendments on Puerto Rico or on coverage.

Several motions came before the Committee of the Whole. The first of these, submitted by Republican Sam McConnell, proposed a 90-cent minimum. The floor fight on this amendment had the curious effect of putting Barden, who favored 90 cents, at the head of the

Democratic majority against McConnell. Barden resolved the difficulty by yielding the floor to his Democratic committee colleagues who favored a minimum of $1.

The vote on the 90-cents amendment—a teller vote without a roll call—showed 188 against and 145 for.

McConnell offered a second amendment for "not less than 90 cents an hour after December 31, 1955 and not less than $1 after December 31, 1956." This motion was narrowly lost by a similar vote, without roll call, of 173 against and 168 for, a difference of five votes.

A motion by Roy Wier for a minimum of $1.10 an hour was lost 198 to 93.

Then the original Labor Committee motion for $1 was put to a roll-call vote. This passed by a huge majority: 362 for and 54 against.

It is interesting to note that in the first three amendments the total vote cast was between 291 and 341, although there are 435 members of the House of Representatives. When the roll call took place 416 votes were cast. This indicates that almost one hundred Representatives who were absent or who abstained during the votes on the amendments voted for the $1 "for the record."

Who were the absentees during the early tallies? Some of these were Southern Democrats who did not want a roll-call vote on 90 cents. If there had been such a roll call, these Democrats would have had to vote for the 90 cents and, perhaps, even caused its passage—to the distress of the Democratic House leadership, the unions, some of their low-wage constituents, and, in a few cases, of their own convictions. The way out of this dilemma was to abstain and by abstention defeat the 90-cent motion and thereby avoid a roll call on this issue.

Other abstainers were Republicans from industrial areas who also wanted to avoid a roll call on 90 cents. Had there been such a roll call, these Republicans would have been torn between area pressures and loyalty to Eisenhower. The way out, as for the Southern Democrats, was abstention. . . .

[The final bill, which had been passed by both Houses following a House-Senate Conference Committee Report] was referred to the President of the United States for his signature. He was expected to sign it because it appeared that a veto could be overridden and because, if the veto stood, there might be no change in the minimum, a potentially disastrous development for the Republican party.

The Joint Minimum Wage Committee, nevertheless, felt that the ranks ought to be alerted to communicate directly with the White House. Local unions rushed to their mimeograph machines to arouse the membership. One local union ground out a leaflet entitled *The*

Last Hurdle. It showed a horse, tagged "minimum wage," approaching a final hurdle, marked "President's Signature." "The Congress of the U. S. has passed a Minimum Wage Bill of $1 an hour," read the leaflet. "It now remains for the President of the U. S. to sign the bill to make it into law. Let us put on that final burst of speed that will enable us to cross the line a winner. Write to the President of the U. S., White House, Washington, D. C., urging him to sign the minimum wage bill."

The final words read: "Don't delay! Do it now!"

How much mail arrived at the White House on this issue the Joint Committee never knew. But, if the reports of the locals were accurate, the President received as much mail as all of Congress in the previous month.

On August 12, 1955, the bill was signed and became law.

Union Lobbyists' Contributions to Tough Labor Legislation

Sar A. Levitan

Upjohn Institute for Employment Research

CONGRESSMAN JOHN W. McCORMACK, Democratic majority leader of the House of Representatives, referred to August 14, the day the House passed labor reform legislation, as "Black Thursday for labor." It is commonly agreed that the passage of the Landrum-Griffin bill by the House was the worst defeat for organized labor on Capitol Hill since the enactment of the Taft-Hartley Act 12 years ago. The setback was even more pronounced than in 1947, in view of the increased union activity during the past decade and the results of the 1958 Congressional elections.

Whether McCormack's dark forebodings are justified is, of course, a matter for conjecture. But to set the record straight, McCormack might have added that the spokesmen for organized labor were as much responsible for the House-approved labor reform bill as were any of its proponents.

Of course, this generalization is necessarily an oversimplification. The pressures on House members to enact labor reform legisla-

Reprinted by permission of the publisher from the October 1959, issue of *Labor Law Journal*, copyright 1959, Chicago, Ill.: Commerce Clearing House.

tion in terms of personal lobbying, mail, and telegrams were possibly unprecedented in the annals of Congress. A Congressman cracked that at least one union had gained by the proposed legislation—Western Union.

Employer groups, sensing the climate favoring legislation to rid unions of racketeers, pressed hard for "tough" legislation. Their goal was by no means limited to the elimination of union abuses, but to the weakening of the power of unions in collective bargaining. To achieve this end, supporters of this legislation organized a coordinated and sustained grass-roots campaign aimed at convincing legislators that the public desires a "tough" labor reform law.

Under the circumstances, labor had some difficult choices to make as to the tactics it should use to overcome the pressures for restrictive legislation. Granted that some labor leaders find government regulation distasteful, the question arises as to the degree to which labor spokesmen should have cooperated with their friends in Congress, who insisted upon some unpalatable measures. Labor gambled by refusing to compromise and, as a result of unwise lobbying tactics, lost sufficient middle-of-the-road support. Union spokesmen also showed that they had failed to learn from their 1947 experience. Again, they resorted to crying "Wolf!" Instead of arguing the issues on their merits and organizing backing for their cause, they resorted to threatening Congressmen with defeat in 1960 for failing to vote the "right" way. This made it possible for the employer-supported bill to win the day.

Labor Slow to Recognize Facts

Ever since the beginning of the McClellan disclosures, union spokesmen have continued to vacillate concerning the proper position that labor should take with regard to proposed labor reform legislation. Labor spokesmen have been slow to acknowledge the facts of life. The McClellan investigations were preceded by several other Congressional hearings dealing with internal union affairs. In 1948 and 1949, House committees held extensive hearings on the lack of democratic procedures in the United Mine Workers and other unions. Four years later, Congressman Clare Hoffman of Michigan disclosed many of the facts about James R. Hoffa and his activities in the Teamsters Union that the McClellan Committee later highlighted. Between 1953 and 1955, Senators Irving Ives and Paul Douglas undertook, with full labor cooperation, an investigation of the administration of welfare and pension funds and found misuse of funds in the case of the Laundry Workers, Distillery Workers, and Allied Industrial Workers. Their investigation showed that the leaders of these unions had diverted health and welfare funds for personal aggrandizement. Investigations by the New York Legislature showed that the Longshoremen's Association was dominated by racketeers, which prompted the AFL, under President George Meany, to expell the union.

Despite all these public disclosures, it is somewhat puzzling that labor was surprised by the McClellan Committee findings. George Meany stated that he was not cognizant of one tenth or even one hundredth of the corruption that was going on in labor.

For the first year, while the McClellan investigations were going on, the AFL–CIO line was that McClellan disclosures were one-sided and overdramatized. Anyway, the AFL–CIO spokesmen asserted, there is no more "sin" in labor than in other sectors of the American economy. As late as March 1958, George Meany appeared as a somewhat unfriendly witness before the Senate Subcommittee on Labor. The weight of his argument was that labor had adopted self-regulating codes of ethics and that, given time, labor would clean its own house. He would not agree that any thorough legislation to assist labor to clean its house was necessary. In response to a query by Senator John F. Kennedy as to whether Meany would support the legislation recommended by a number of well-known college professors commonly regarded as friendly to labor, the president of the AFL–CIO replied curtly: "God save us from our friends."

However, labor could not ignore the general clamor for legislation to guarantee the rights of union members which was stimulated by the McClellan disclosures. Many friends of labor in academic and public positions were convinced that legislation was needed to protect the rights of union workers. It seemed only fair that the government, which sanctions compulsory union membership, should also guarantee the rights of workers who are compelled to join unions as well as the rights of workers who join unions voluntarily.

Package Deal with Reservations

The spring of 1958 thawed labor's icy attitude toward labor reform legislation. In May 1958, President Meany put in a repeat performance before Senator Kennedy's labor subcommittee. This time he endorsed legislation regulating internal union affairs. This legislation embraced the publication of detailed financial reporting by unions, regulation of union trusteeships, and elections of union officers. However, Mr. Meany's endorsement contained a price tag. He accepted these regulations when they were wrapped as part of a package containing long-sought amendments to the Taft-Hartley Act.

Many friends of labor believed that the AFL–CIO approach was ill-advised. It was felt that as a matter of tactics labor leaders might achieve greater success in securing favorable labor-management legislation and in realizing other labor programs if they would first gracefully cooperate in enacting sorely needed legislation affecting internal union affairs. Labor rejected this approach and, for a while, it appeared that the tactics of the AFL–CIO had borne fruit.

Once labor endorsed the principle of government regulation of internal union affairs and helped draft a bill to its liking, the greatest deliberative body acted with speed. Attempts by Senator William Knowland and others to amend the labor-approved bill were rejected. On June 17, 1958, the Senate approved, by an overwhelming vote of 88 to one, a labor reform bill to the AFL–CIO's liking, including the "sweeteners" requested by the unions. This final one-sided vote is rather misleading. It merely reflected the Senate's conviction of the need for legislation. On several key votes during the debate, the vote was more evenly divided.

The opposition was slow to rally its forces while the Senate considered the labor reform bill. But once the measure reached the House, its opponents gathered their forces for an attack. House action was delayed by a strange combination of forces. Employer groups and powerful forces within Congress wanted to use the McClellan disclosures as a base for a campaign to restrict the powers of unions. In this the conservatives were aided by potent groups within labor who continued to oppose any legislation.

John L. Lewis openly contended against any government legislation regulating internal union affairs. Also, a number of Washington lobbyists for powerful unions, which officially supported the Senate-approved Kennedy-Ives bill, were lobbying in the House against its enactment. Other labor lobbyists, including spokesmen for the AFL–CIO, had on their list higher priorities which they were pushing. These included legislation regulating the disclosure of pension and welfare funds and also aid to depressed areas.

In the House Committee on Education and Labor, which had to pass on the Senate-approved bill, Lewis' wishes were persuasive with a number of members. The more discreet opposition of other union spokesmen was sufficient to dampen the enthusiasm of additional members. Added to Republican and southern Democrats, including the powerful chairman of the committee, the opponents of the Senate-approved bill constituted a majority.

The gathering momentum of opposition on the part of employer groups and the outright or clandestine opposition on the part of some labor spokesmen were sufficient to bottle up the Kennedy-Ives bill in the House Education and Labor Committee. When it became apparent that the House Education and Labor Committee was not going to act on the legislation, Speaker Sam Rayburn called up the Kennedy-Ives bill for House consideration under suspension of rules. This procedure requires a two-thirds affirmative vote to approve the bill, with debate limited to only 40 minutes. The supporters of the bill could not even gather a majority for its approval. Sixty-one Democrats and 137 Republicans voted to reject the bill, while 149 Democrats and 41 Republicans voted for passage of the Kennedy-Ives bill.

This, as it turned out, was the last opportunity for labor to secure a labor reform bill which, at least officially, was fully to its liking.

Labor's Refusal to Compromise

To be sure, the Senate Labor Committee, which is composed of the majority of members generally friendlily disposed toward labor unions, approved early in the winter of 1959 a new bill very similar to the one that had been rejected by the House the previous year. But by this time the opposition to "soft" legislation had hardened considerably— a fact which the normally pragmatic labor spokesmen either refused, or failed, to recognize. Even though the November 1958 election changed the composition of the Senate in labor's favor, the new Senate reflected the country's mood for the need of legislation to restrict abuses of union power. Consequently, the Kennedy-sponsored labor reform legislation had much tougher sledding through the Senate.

In the course of the debate, 52 amendments were introduced. While the most objectionable features—from the point of view of union spokesmen—were defeated, the proponents of stronger legislation, both with reference to internal union affairs and to provisions dealing with the questionable union tactics in collective bargaining, won the debate and scored some notable victories. The AFL–CIO expressed categoric opposition to the Kennedy reform legislation as it emerged from the Senate. The labor federation denounced the bill as unacceptable and punitive. Labor insisted that it would support only the bill which was originally approved by the Senate Labor Committee and would not accept any amendments.

Labor leaders were apparently most incensed by the bill's provision guaranteeing members' rights. This measure is based upon the assumption that a conflict of interest may exist between members and union officials, and that the former need the protection of the law to safeguard them from abuses by power-grasping leaders.

Labor had a chance to recoup its losses when the Senate-approved bill was sent to the House Committee on Education and Labor, which, like its Senate counterpart, is composed of a majority favorably disposed to labor's causes. But mounting pressure for stricter labor reform legislation ruled out the possibility that the committee would adopt in toto the bill favored by labor. However, the AFL–CIO's rigid position left no room for compromise. The federation spokesmen persisted in an all-or-nothing attitude, and were apparently not averse to threatening dire consequences to any member who strayed from the straight and narrow line. In this the AFL–CIO was joined by the Teamsters, or vice versa. John L. Lewis continued to play the old record of opposition to any legislation. The 20 Democrats on the committee were divided into several diverse camps while the Republican members on the committee wanted a stronger measure than the Senate-approved bill. Added to the ten Republicans were two southern Democrats and several liberal northern Democratic members who followed the Miners' line of opposition to any legislation, which at times was hardly discernible from the AFL–CIO's and Teamsters' approach. This combination constituted a majority of the members of the committee, and for a while it appeared that the committee would be unable to report out any bill.

The pressures for the need of legislation were, however, too powerful. After five weeks of wrangling, the House committee reported out the Elliott bill, which was more favorable to labor than had been the Senate bill. Nevertheless, the AFL–CIO spokesmen refused to buy it. This turned out to be a very bad mistake for them.

The House Democratic leadership put its full support behind the moderate committee bill, but the AFL–CIO's objection to this bill divided the prolabor forces within the House. At first, supporters of the labor position had no bill at all which they favored. This gave the impression that labor would just as soon not have any legislation at all. Finally, in the eleventh hour, Congressman Shelley (former president of the California Federation of Labor and an opponent of Hoffa in the 1957 Teamsters' election) introduced a labor-sponsored bill which also won Teamsters' support. At the other extreme, a coalition of southern Democrats and Republicans favored the Landrum-Griffin bill, which won President Eisenhower's acclaim.

Spokesmen for the AFL–CIO continued to press for the Shelley bill, though it was generally conceded that the bill did not have the slightest chance of passage. It was actually defeated by a two-to-one vote; only 30 percent of the House membership voted for the bill. On the real test vote, the Landrum-Griffin bill received 229 of a total of 430 votes cast, or a majority of 28 votes. A switch by 15 members would have defeated the bill.

Only a handful of southern Democrats voted against the Landrum-Griffin bill, despite Rayburn's opposition to the measure. For example, four of the 21 Texas Democrats voted to reject the Landrum-Griffin bill. On the other hand, the Republicans succeeded in closing their ranks for the bill favored by the Administration. Only 17 of the 153 Republicans in the House voted against the bill to which labor objected.

Parenthetically, the vote shows the terrific interest that the controversy engendered. The total vote represents a record in the history of the House. On the issue of labor reform legislation, no lawmaker could afford to remain on the fence. Only four members failed to vote on that bill, and all of them were unable to reach the floor of the House because of illness. Included among the absentees was Congressman Elliott, who was the sponsor of the committee bill. Floor leadership by the able Alabama congressman might have swung some of his southern colleagues in favor of his bill.

But labor's actions in connection with the reform legislation appear to have been crucial. Until the last week prior to the House approval of the Landrum-Griffin bill, lobbying by AFL–CIO representatives lacked any coordination. In some cases they even worked at cross purposes. It was alleged that some railway union spokesmen concentrated their efforts to secure exemption for unions subject to the Railway Labor Act. Similarly, building trade representatives devoted their attention to securing pet provisions of special interest to their unions. These crosscurrents among labor lobbyists certainly failed to make friends for labor's cause. On the other hand, the Teamsters presented a coordinated force for the mildest labor legislation, but their over-zealous efforts contributed a negative influence.

It is reasonable to speculate that if the AFL–CIO had thrown its full united support behind the Elliott bill, this might have swung enough votes in favor of the middle-of-the-road bill to defeat the Landrum-Griffin bill. Some top union presidents advocated the more reasonable and realistic approach. However, Mr. Meany remained adamant, and the council of moderation did not prevail. The federation's lobbyists on the Hill continued to attack the bill sponsored by the coalition of southern Democrats and Republicans, as well as the Elliott bill. Labor's opposition to the latter bill apparently drove enough southern Democrats, who might have gone along with Speaker Rayburn and liberal Republicans, to support a bill which had undivided and well-coordinated conservative support. One may as well be hanged for a sheep as a lamb.

Possibly, the experience of Representative Erwin Mitchell, the only Georgian who voted against the Landrum-Griffin bill, best illustrates the pressures to which Congressmen were subjected in connection with this legislation. When it became known in his district that he was opposed to the Landrum-Griffin bill, the calls started to pour in. According to the Congressman, as reported in the Atlanta *Journal Constitution:*

> The tempo began to pick up day by day and night by night. All day Tuesday, Wednesday, Thursday and Friday, I was taking call after call and was doing nothing else.

The ironic thing about all this, according to the Congressman, was that not one of his callers or correspondents asked him to support the Elliott bill, which he was backing. He is reported to have stated:

> The business interests all wanted the Landrum bill. The few telegrams I got from labor wanted the Shelley bill.
> Not a soul wanted the [Elliott] bill except me.

It may be wrong to interpret the vote on labor reform legislation as a sign of erosion of labor's political strength in the present Congress. Labor succeeded in keeping the support of those members whom the various state labor organizations supported in the 1958 election. According to a COPE calculation, only 16 out of 181 members to whose campaigns labor made contributions in 1958 voted for the Landrum-Griffin bill. The rigid tactics of labor in connection with labor reform legislation had apparently alienated enough votes, among southern Democrats and Republicans, to assure victory for the bill opposed by the labor lobbyists. It is quite apparent that labor has miscalculated its strength. The vote on the labor reform legislation makes it evident that labor does not have sufficient influence to carry Congress on an issue in which it stands alone and at odds with the more moderate elements in Congress.

Lobbyists and Legislators

Alan K. McAdams

Cornell University

IT HAS BEEN INTIMATED that the [House] Committee on Education and Labor was expected by the AFL–CIO to be a rubber-stamp committee. When some members, the five mentioned earlier [Democrats Elliott

---

Excerpted by permission of the publisher from *Power and Politics in Labor Legislation,* New York: Columbia University Press, copyright 1964.

(Ala.), Green (Ore.), Thompson (N.J.), Udall (Ariz.) and O'Hara (Mich.)] plus Representatives Daniels, Brademas, and Giaimo, showed a mind of their own, they were immediately subjected to considerable pressure. Representative Udall (COPE score 13–0), a Mormon, and an athletic and fiery young Congressman, is given credit for an effective explosion in the face of Teamster Zagri's statement that "I am going to get you in line." Udall, making reference to his state's lack of strong unions, the fact that it had a right-to-work law, and its increasingly conservative climate of opinion, said: "Barry Goldwater sets the tone in my state." His intent was to demonstrate that threats of Teamster opposition were relatively ineffective on him. Zagri translated Udall's statement into "Goldwater calls the tune in my state" and used it to rally other unionists against the congressman. In the propaganda campaign which followed, this was carried another step to: "Udall's afraid of Goldwater, so he's voting antilabor."

On June 18 Udall issued a statement to the press emphasizing that the committee could report out a bill "despite the Hoffas and the Lewises." This statement included reference to hot cargo prohibitions and the outlawing of extortion picketing as necessary provisions for a committee bill. It gained him the animosity of the AFL–CIO, which had come to oppose such measures. The AFL–CIO joined the Teamsters in a campaign to change the congressman's mind.

Representative Thompson (COPE score 13–0), who was a tall, handsome, slightly graying man, was accused by the Teamsters of "buckling under to the Chamber of Commerce" and voting "wrong" on the committee. This was because of alleged ambitions to run for governor of New Jersey in order to bring the state's delegation to Kennedy at the Democratic convention. Thompson received threatening phone calls and eventually asked the FBI to have his wife and three daughters put under guard. At some point direct AFL–CIO pressure was also brought to bear on Thompson. In the final week of consideration of the committee bill Thompson expressed his reaction to the pressure from the federation directly to Andy Biemiller in very colorful language. . . .

Edith Green, a very pleasant woman of middle age, had had, like the others just mentioned, a virtually spotless voting record from the point of view of the labor movement up to this time (COPE score 12–1). Her district in Oregon is a strong labor district representing large numbers of Teamsters Union members and building tradesmen. The latter are now dominant politically, but this was not always the case. Teamster Zagri contacted local unionists in Mrs. Green's district and intimated that she was trying to repudiate her old relationships with the Teamsters by her actions on the bill. On behalf of the AFL–CIO, legislative representative Walter Mason personally called on Mrs. Green on several occasions. He was attempting to enlist her support for the lead of Representative Teller within the committee. One of his calls happened to come on June 25.

During the committee session on that day, Teller had done something that had confused the other Democratic Representatives. He had introduced Chairman Barden's proposals on employer reporting instead of the similar sections of his own bill. Just the evening before, in discussion with other Democrats, Teller had scoffed when he read the proposals circulated by Barden, and commented: "Well, look at what [he] is trying to do!"

With the aid of Ken Meikeljohn of the Industrial Union Department and his own administrative assistant, Donald Baker, freshman Representative O'Hara had spent a good part of the evening preparing modifications to the language of the Teller bill. Teller's actions came as a complete surprise to him the next day. He exclaimed in a whisper in the committee room: "No, introduce your own language!" Teller replied: "This is what our friends (the AFL–CIO) want. We'll humor [Barden]. We can come back to it and change it later." O'Hara voted against Barden's language, but it was carried by the committee. O'Hara then introduced language from the Teller bill as an amendment to Barden's amendment. Teller voted with a majority against it.

Mason's urging of Mrs. Green to "follow Ludwig Teller" was more than the ladylike Mrs. Green could stand on this afternoon. She exploded with "You can go to hell!"[1] Mason dutifully reported his reception by the lady from Oregon at the next meeting of legislative representatives.

The AFL–CIO flew members of Mrs. Green's campaign committee down to Washington to "camp on her doorstep" and convince her that she was doing the wrong thing. A Mr. Roberts, the chairman of her labor committee during the campaign, was one of these people.

The federation also contacted Michigan's politically powerful Gus Scholle to inform him that O'Hara was "going wrong." Rather than call O'Hara directly, Scholle called some people he knew in Washington, told them of the calls from the AFL–CIO, and asked what was wrong with O'Hara. He was told that there was nothing wrong with O'Hara except that he was working night and day with a group of other congressmen to try to determine just what the labor movement

---

[1] It is interesting to note that both *Time* and *Life* report Mrs. Green's words, but refer them to Teamster Zagri instead of Mason.

wanted and had to have in the way of legislation. And he wasn't getting any help from labor's representatives in the Capitol.

The Teamsters did contact O'Hara directly. They notified him that they had one million dollars that they could use in a campaign against him and that "they would put a Teamster on every corner" of his district, if necessary, to defeat him at the polls if he persisted in his activities.

Representative Carl Elliott of Alabama (COPE score 11–2) was the fifth to bear the brunt of labor's wrath. As a Southerner, with relatively weak union representation in his district, Elliott was not very susceptible to direct union pressure, but he was open to pressure from his conservative colleagues for being "too liberal" in his thinking. Yet, he appears to have been able to maintain the respect of both groups.

When Sidney Zagri visited the offices of various congressmen, he was usually accompanied by a group of union people from AFL–CIO locals in the man's district. Zagri did most of the talking in such interviews, usually demonstrating a great deal of information about the bills under consideration and misinformation about the degree of support among Democrats and labor groups for his own thinking about them. An example of this was his visit to the office of Representative Brademas. Zagri entered with his troupe and began a discussion with the congressman. In the course of his conversation he stated, among other things, that the Speaker backed his position on a clean bill and other matters. Brademas lifted the phone and called the Speaker to question this. The reply came back unmistakably: "That's a damn lie!" This cleared the air of misunderstanding for the union representatives who had come along with Zagri, but it did not relieve the pressure on Brademas.

The group which held the balance of power in the committee consisted of the five members mentioned above—Elliott, Thompson, Udall, Green, and freshman O'Hara—plus three other freshmen, Daniels, Brademas, and Giaimo. The role of the last three was not as well publicized as that of the first group, who gained fame under the title given them by William Whyte, the "faithful five" (translated by the Teamsters into the "faithless five"). This is because the three freshmen were especially susceptible to pressure from their districts. The violence of the reaction of union representatives to the 20 to 10 vote showed that the path to a House labor bill would not be an easy one. The three were advised by the House leadership to "lay low" and go along with the AFL–CIO as far as they could. "There is no need in your continuing to lacerate yourselves," they were told. . . .

Headquarters at the Congressional Hotel

After it was abundantly clear that the committee would go ahead with consideration of the bill in spite of the wishes of the AFL–CIO, the federation decided to use its influence to make the bill as good as possible.

It was generally agreed that the efforts of the federation in the Senate had not been well coordinated. The same senator was often given conflicting information by different representatives of the AFL–CIO. This resulted in confusion, exasperation, and inefficiency. Then, too, there was the problem of the lack of technical advice for the numerical majority of the congressmen on the House committee. The majority staff was controlled by, and loyal to, Chairman Barden. Thus, the two Southern Democrats had ample technical support. The minority staff, augmented with a legal consultant, was under the control of Representative Kearns. The eighteen liberal Democratic members— the majority of the committee—had no staff support at all.

To rectify the situation, the AFL–CIO set up lobbying headquarters in the Congressional Hotel, a short distance from the Capitol. Its staff would coordinate the lobbying effort and make the services of competent lawyers available to the liberal committee members. A "drafting group," consisting of lawyers for the various interested unions, was organized to prepare amendments to S.1555. Lawyers from the union most directly affected were given overall responsibility for the section of the bill most important to them.

The drafting group operated from the downtown headquarters of the federation, had a shifting membership over time, and numbered from five to seven in all. Under the initial working arrangements, proposed amendments were prepared, mimeographed, and distributed to friendly members of the committee. The suggestions would be discussed (in caucus) and a decision on the general Democratic position would be made.

Time magazine indicated that the Teamsters were also submitting proposed amendments to the committee through certain Democratic Representatives and were receiving regular reports on the progress made at each of the meetings.[2] The men named by *Time* are Representatives Roosevelt and Pucinski. It should be noted that roll-call votes of committee members were known to representatives of all interest groups, as reported by members sympathetic to the groups. They also appeared regularly in Drew Pearson's column and in the reports of the

---

[2] *Time*, Vol. LXXIV, No. 4 (July 27, 1959), 36.

Labor Relations Reporter of the Bureau of National Affairs. Press reports imply that there is something sinister about the transmittal of such information. Perhaps the practice is sinister, but it was almost universal. . . .

Labor Lobbying Strategy

The Congressional Hotel headquarters of the AFL–CIO was more active after the committee bill had been reported than before. Professor Cox arrived in town to work as a member of the operations group, serving as advisor to Representative Elliott and as working head of the drafting group. A large-scale organization was set in motion to coordinate the importation of labor people from all parts of the country. Regular union representatives served as "directors" for specified regions. They advised and briefed the local delegations called into town to influence their congressmen. The delegations were informed of the federation policy on the bills before Congress and conducted on visits to congressmen from their areas whom they knew, many on a first-name basis. Reports of conversations were closely followed, and a running record of the probable voting tendency of each congressman was kept. The "amateur status" of many of these local men sometimes made their estimates less than reliable. The union people, however, apparently believed strongly in the personal approach in lobbying.

At the same time the Teamsters also brought in a large number of people from various districts. They conducted daily tours to the offices of congressmen, but they had nowhere near the "professional" support for their importees that the federation had. The New York *Times* quotes President Hoffa as stating at a dinner meeting on August 4 that he had two hundred local Teamsters in Washington to call on their congressmen.[3] All reports, both public and private, indicate that these men caused a good deal of damage to labor's cause by their lack of appreciation for the finer points of lobbying techniques. They often antagonized staff people in the outer offices of congressmen as well as the congressmen themselves. The Teamster representatives had a single purpose: to prevent legislation. They were well organized (if not well schooled), and they made their presence known. They had a real impact, but apparently produced reverse "English."

It is interesting to note Representative Frank Thompson's statements made at Princeton University several weeks after the Congress recessed. He said that, in addition to threats from both management and labor groups in his district, there were also promises of reward

---

[3] *New York Times,* Aug. 6, 1959, p. 17.

from both groups. He indicated that it was made clear to him that large sums of money would become available if a congressman voted "properly."[4] There is little question that both sides were playing this one for keeps.

A House Divided

The official policy of the AFL–CIO was not receiving wholehearted support from its affiliated unions. Although the official position of the Building Trades Council had been reversed and the building trades were again opposing the Elliott bill, they could hardly be expected to oppose it enthusiastically. The switch in position imposed on them by federation pressure greatly impaired their effectiveness. Some unions from the Industrial Union Department, the UAW and Steelworkers for instance, were both lukewarm to the official policy, but for opposite reasons. The UAW wanted to stress its opposition to corruption and make its stand against the Teamsters Union emphatic and clear. They felt that the public should be aware of the difference between the level of conduct required of officers of the Auto Workers as opposed to the Teamsters. The Steelworkers, through Nordy Hoffman, their legislative representative, were more in sympathy with the Teamsters than with the AFL–CIO itself.

In dealing with congressmen most union legislative representatives were confronted with a very difficult and perplexing question. "All right," the congressman would say, "so I'll back the Shelley bill, but you know as well as I do that it isn't going to pass. What do I do then? You fellows say that both the Elliott and Landrum-Griffin bills are anti-labor, but with all the feeling in my district I have to vote for something."

As was pointed out earlier, the AFL–CIO was in the position of being against all available alternatives from the time that the Landrum-Griffin bill was introduced on July 27 until the Shelley bill was put forth on August 3. The Shelley bill was an apologia, but there was so little chance of its passage that its congressional advocates would still be essentially in the position of supporting no bill. In answer to the question "What do I do then?" the official policy of the federation was silent. The operational result was hemming and hawing and double talk on the part of many legislative representatives.

Local AFL–CIO unions were equally hamstrung. An example was the Texas AFL–CIO. Tremendous pressure was being put on all

---

[4] The *Daily Princetonian*, reported in the *Courier-Post*, Camden, N. J., Oct. 29, 1959, p. 24. Thompson's statements about threats from both sides appear in the New York *Times*, July 28, 1959, p. 16.

the state's Representatives by management groups. What union pressure did exist was directed to backing the Shelley bill. The Speaker's assistant, D. B. Hardiman, asked the Texas AFL–CIO president to round up some support for the Elliott bill, but he was told that such action would violate official policy. Support would first have to come from the parent body.

One state AFL–CIO group was first told to oppose the Elliott bill as antilabor, then told not to oppose it but to stand by for further instructions. Periodically they wired AFL–CIO headquarters in Washington for instructions. They were still standing by two weeks after a bill had passed the House. . . .

Lobbying Intensity

The AFL–CIO lobbying effort was continuing in a manner unchanged from before. Unity was found only in opposition to the "killer" Landrum-Griffin bill (so characterized by the Teamsters). The Elliott bill was more or less ignored both by management and the unions, except for some building trades representatives and legislative representatives from certain other unions. It was still officially opposed by the AFL–CIO. The United Auto Workers, among others, continued to try to create a more positive stand within the AFL–CIO but grudgingly accepted the official position. One legislative representative expressed his feeling toward the official stand in this way: "It's awfully hard to line up support behind an idiotic strategy."

The federation made no change in its effort except to increase its intensity. Union people from various districts were shepherded to the offices of their congressmen with increasing frequency. This led one member of Congress, who had been under almost constant pressure for many weeks, to remark: "The thing these people seem to forget is that I don't have to be a Congressman!" This is quite a departure from the stereotype of congressional behavior. Apparently, there are some things which a politician will not do, no matter how much pressure is put on him.

The Teamsters Union continued its organized visitations to congressional offices. The visitors continued to antagonize the legislators and to threaten them with certain election defeat for voting "wrong." Teamster tactics caused a heightened antagonism and an impact the opposite of the intention. As the bill headed for a vote, congressmen spent more and more time on the floor of the House as the only refuge from the visitors of one side and the phone calls and telegrams of the other. The relative calm of the debate was a soothing balm to these weary men.

Chapter 9

Organized Labor in the Electoral Process

IN MID-TWENTIETH CENTURY AMERICA, the organized labor movement's political activity has one characteristic shared only with the political parties themselves. Labor is the only significant group in our society which has built a basic grass-roots organization for political purposes. Particularly in states where workers are numerically strong and where unions are well organized and active, the labor movement and its political arms operate at times much like a political party, mobilizing dollars and votes to achieve election victories.

Unions, of course, are active in the electoral process at many different levels of government and for differing reasons. Even in states where labor can do little on a statewide basis it still may be deeply involved in local politics in the major cities. With their membership of well-paid workers who compete primarily in local labor markets, craft unions today, as traditionally, are concerned most about activities of city and county governments. They desire sympathetic treatment from building and fire inspectors, local police, and many other kinds of locally-appointed and elected officials. Even today, they fear national political alliances that would disturb their established relationships with whatever party is in power in their city.

Industrial unions, on the other hand, are far more likely to be concerned about state-wide and national problems. They are primarily interested in state workmen's compensation legislation and unemployment insurance, and in federal legislation affecting welfare and tax policies.

Moreover, differences in the way that unions are organized, the labor markets in which their members compete, and the kinds of industries in which they have contracts will affect their political behavior. In labor organizations where collective bargaining is primarily the responsibility of local union leaders, such leadership is apt to be primarily concerned with municipal and state elections. The national officers of such unions may be concerned with national issues, but ordinarily this concern is not reflected in a matching interest or commensurate response by the membership or the local union leadership. In contrast, unions that bargain industry-wide contracts, or which have collective bargaining relationships with companies that sell in national markets, often have more centralized control within their organizational structure. This affects their political as well as their economic activities. In such unions, the local leadership ordinarily shares to a greater extent the broad political interests of the national officers, and engages more systematically in state and national electoral activities.

These differences are well-documented in the first reading in this chapter, by Edward C. Banfield and James Q. Wilson. The authors analyze the way in which labor market orientation affects a union's political behavior and detail the dissimilar relationships that exists between the major unions and local political parties in cities such as Detroit, New York, Chicago, and Los Angeles.

The second selection, "Reaching the Voter," is a detailed report on how a well-organized local union successfully set out to reelect a state senator. It documents an important fact known to all politicians. Successful political activity requires intensive and continuing day-to-day political participation: attendance at frequent meetings, posting placards and handing out automobile bumper-strips, standing on street-corners collecting contributions and passing out campaign buttons and literature. "Getting out the vote" involves climbing endless flights of stairs, driving voters to the polls, and pounding the pavements from one block to the next performing the multitude of unglamorous tasks which are the lifeblood of American politics.

Those who have written about labor and politics frequently fail to note, or at least to document, the fact that the relationship between politicians and labor leaders is often based on immediate mutual gain. In "The Politics of the West Coast Teamsters and Truckers," Irving Bernstein digs deeply into a number of such relationships, politics of reward and fear, opportunistic at best and corrupting at worst. In commenting on Bernstein's paper, Paul Jacobs asks whether a union should be expected to behave otherwise in the context of contemporary American society.

The last two selections in this chapter are case histories of two Ohio elections. In 1950, Senator Taft was reelected despite the intense opposition of labor which campaigned vigorously for his opponent. Yet, only eight years later, in the same state organized labor overwhelmingly defeated right-to-work legislation supported by business and farm organizations as well as by most of the public opinion media in the state. The reasons for labor's failure in the one campaign and success in the other cast fascinating light upon the circumstances under which labor may fail or succeed in building permanent and successful political organizations for general election purposes.

As noted in Chapter 7, labor's national political participation is heavily oriented towards registration drives, "get-out-the-vote" campaigns and encouraging local and state labor bodies to develop permanent political organizations. In many parts of the United States, labor's political participation transcends the special interests of the trade union movement itself and attracts the political support of many working-class and minority-group people who are not themselves union members. Labor's national goals such as expansion of job opportunities, more extended distribution of social and welfare services, and equal employment opportunity, make the labor movement's political participation particularly effective in urban and industrialized areas.

In summary, the role of labor in the American electoral process today is that of a pressure group which has taken on some of the vote-mobilizing functions of a political party. It is still a pressure group, but one which has in some areas and some ways transcended its traditional role to become a quasi-party adjunct to the Democratic party.

Organized Labor in City Politics

Edward C. Banfield, *Harvard University*
James Q. Wilson, *Harvard–M.I.T. Joint Center for Urban Studies*

Perhaps the most striking thing about the part played by organized labor in city politics is its variety. Some unions want nothing more from city government than assurance that the police will not interfere with pickets during strikes. Others aspire to take possession of the city government and to run it as an adjunct of the union. Between these extreme positions there are many intermediate ones. Which position a union takes depends upon many factors, including its organizational structure, the ideological bent of its leaders, the nature of the industry and of the local economy, and the structure of party competition within the city.

The Interest of the Union in Local Affairs

The range of interests that unions have in local affairs is suggested by the findings of Joel Seidman and his associates in their study of six

Excerpted by permission of the publishers from *City Politics*, Cambridge, Mass.: Harvard University Press, copyright 1963, by the President and Fellows of Harvard College.

locals in and near Chicago.[1] All six of the locals wanted friendly treatment from police, courts, and city officials, especially in the event of a strike. Beyond that, their goals differed considerably. For example, one local of the United Mine Workers paid practically no attention to local politics; it was in a community consisting entirely of miners who could be depended upon to elect fellow miners to office. Although the leaders of this local were very much interested in politics in the state capital and in Washington—where crucial safety and work regulations were framed—they ignored city and county politics.

At the opposite extreme, locals of the United Steelworkers of America and the United Auto Workers (UAW) felt keenly the need for organized political action at the local level. The Steelworkers were engaged in collective bargaining with a powerful firm under conditions of mutual hostility and suspicion, and were therefore particularly anxious to retain political support from the local Democratic machine in order to ensure its sympathy or at least neutrality. Many local Steelworkers leaders disliked the machine politicians but felt they could not defeat them or dare to risk alienating them. The UAW, on the other hand, did not need political reinforcement of its collective bargaining position because contracts were not negotiated locally, but nationally. At the same time, however, the UAW leaders desired broader political involvement for what were essentially reasons of ideology rather than union security. Since the motivation was ideological, the choice of party tended to be made on ideological grounds, without reference to what party or what party faction controlled local government.

A local of the plumbers' union, one of the nineteen craft unions associated with the building and construction trades department of the AFL–CIO, was vitally concerned with city political matters. Entry into, and the rewards of, the plumbing profession were crucially dependent upon the licensing regulations which control the apprenticeship program and upon building and housing codes. Plumbers, like other building trade unions, must work with whatever party or faction happens to be in power locally in order to get favorable codes and the appointment of sympathetic building and plumbing inspectors. Not infrequently the union approves city inspectors or even nominates them from its own ranks. Furthermore, the city and county government is a prime source of construction contracts. The building trades unions have in common with contractors an interest in seeing that these con-

---

[1] Joel Seidman et al., *The Worker Views His Union* (Chicago: University of Chicago Press, 1958), pp. 227–36. [The full text of the Seidman findings on this subject is contained in Chapter 11.—Eds.]

tracts are large and frequent and that the work is done by private industry rather than by municipal or county employees.

These studies and others lend general support to the familiar observation that with respect to political involvement there is a sharp difference between industrial and craft unions. Industrial unions, with a large membership of unskilled or semiskilled workers in nationwide industries, are concerned about industry-wide or national wage contracts and with the state and federal welfare measures which redistribute income in favor of lower-income groups. Craft unions, with a membership of well-paid skilled workers in competitive local markets, are concerned about access to the local bureaucracy, sympathetic treatment from local police, and local wages and hours.[2] The industrial union finds itself drawn into national political alliances, in particular with that party which seems most favorable to certain welfare measures; craft unions can and must resist such alignments, for they must not allow ideology to prevent them from working with whatever party or faction is in power locally.

Differences in markets create other differences among union leaders. The heads of the state and national federations of unions involved in local markets (e.g., building trades unions) have few direct links with rank-and-file members. The local leaders negotiate contracts and service the members; the state and national leaders can maintain their position only by persuading union members that they have common interests which only state or national leaders can serve. Legislative campaigns waged in Washington, D.C., are thus often dictated not so much by the felt needs of the rank-and-file worker as by the maintenance needs of higher-echelon officials who lack any other relationship with the members.

Unions dealing with national markets, by contrast, are apt to vest a much higher degree of influence in state and national leaders. Industry-wide and nation-wide contract negotiations give national union officials considerable authority over the locals. This bargaining pattern, together with the importance of federal legislation for nationwide and industry-wide markets, imbues the entire organization with a more "political" or even "ideological" tone. As a result, even the local officials of, for example, the United Auto Workers may have more comprehensive political goals than the national leaders of a building trades union.

Given these differences, however, it is nonetheless true that local

---

[2] See Richard Baisden, "Labor Unions in Los Angeles Politics," Unpublished thesis, Department of Political Science, University of Chicago, 1958.

union leaders are generally less ideological than national ones. Where the leader's contact with the members is direct, ideology is typically of minor importance. If the industry is still unorganized, the leaders will be absorbed in establishing themselves as the bargaining agents of the workers and in arranging for the security of the union. Once the industry and the city are organized, however, other activities must be found for local unions. In the case of many craft unions, these other activities consist largely in enforcing agreements and supervising work conditions and job assignments—particularly when, as with the building trades, work is done on widely scattered sites by small groups of workers hired on a contract basis by small, highly competitive contractors. In the case of industrial unions,[3] the leaders must devise other services.

These other services, while something more than a concern for wages and hours, are usually a good deal less than an active involvement in local politics. Where industry-wide contracts have eliminated local wage negotiations, the development of local welfare services becomes even more important.[4] These day-to-day services—often of crucial importance in ensuring the reelection of local officers—include handling individual grievances, providing free legal advice, filling out workmen's compensation applications, dealing with eviction notices or medical needs, helping to get loans, interceding with the police, and arranging social events and beer supplies. Many of these activities, not unexpectedly, are of precisely the same kind as a political ward leader spends his time on. . . .

Even among the union activists who share a belief in political action of some sort, the precise strategy to employ is often in dispute because of the conflicting roles of the union *lobbyist* and the union *campaign director.*

The lobbyist sees political action in terms of getting concessions from elected officials, particularly legislators. He works alone in attempting to influence a fairly small group of men whose primary concern is with getting reelected. Often he needs the votes of men from

[3] Seidman et al., *Worker Views His Union*, pp. 42–47.

[4] See the account of the UAW in Windsor, Ontario, in C. W. M. Hart, "Industrial Relations Research and Social Theory," *Canadian Journal of Economics and Political Science*, February 1949, esp. pp. 60–63. Community involvement also emerged as a substitute for collective bargaining among the unions in Lorain, Ohio; see James B. McKee, "Status and Power in the Industrial Community: A Comment on Drucker's Thesis," *American Journal of Sociology*, January 1953, p. 367.

both political parties; thus, he dare not risk aligning himself entirely with one party or faction. Ideally, he would like to be free to commit his union to whoever has helped him the most; this sometimes means supporting—or at least not opposing—a conservative politician not normally friendly to labor. He avoids making allies if by so doing he must take on his ally's causes—"don't get stuck with the other fellow's fights." He chooses his issues carefully and concentrates on specific goals.

The union's campaign director, on the other hand, sees the requirements of political action in entirely different terms. He desires to elect a slate of local candidates. To do so he must create an organization of volunteers. Because of their political convictions, these volunteers often insist on working entirely within one party—usually the Democratic. The campaign director must, therefore, reject "deals" with Republicans and he must avoid endorsing conservative candidates who are not likely to arouse volunteer enthusiasm. He is inevitably restless with prior union commitments for they deprive the volunteers of a sense of participating in making decisions about endorsements. He must seek out allies from other liberal groups; this means he must make their causes his.

This tension means that the unions with the most to gain from local lobbying (like the building trades unions) will tend to reject political campaigns, while those with the least to gain by local lobbying (such as the UAW) will emphasize such campaigning. Between these extremes there are unions which are not infrequently split between the two strategies. Even within the normally "political" industrial unions formerly of the CIO, campaigning has often been undertaken half-heartedly.[5]

The Union as an Agency of Civic Leadership

Leaders of organized labor do not appear as frequently as businessmen among the ranks of reputed civic leaders or on the rosters of important civic or government organizations.[6] It is customary to find in most large cities one or two "labor representatives" appointed to the board of education, the board of the Community Chest, and various public commissions. However, when the members of, say, the board of edu-

---

[5] For an account of the difficulties experienced in political campaigning in Chicago by certain CIO unions, see James Q. Wilson, *Negro Politics* (Glencoe, Ill.: Free Press, 1960), pp. 125–27, and Fay Calkins, *The CIO and the Democratic Party* (Chicago: University of Chicago Press, 1952), pp. 70, 77, 81–84.

[6] See the tables in William H. Form and Delbert C. Miller, *Industry, Labor, and Community* (New York: Harper, 1960), p. 43.

cation are elected rather than appointed, and when—as in most non-partisan cities—there is no powerful political organization which can draw up and elect a "balanced ticket" to such boards, labor is likely to be unrepresented. This seems to be the case in Detroit and Los Angeles, for example.

Furthermore, there appears to be a crucial difference between business and union membership on such bodies. Organized labor—even if it includes in its ranks the majority of all the adult citizens in the community—is generally regarded as a "special interest" which must be "represented"; businessmen, on the other hand, are often regarded, not as "representing business" as a "special interest," but as serving the community as a whole. Businessmen, in Peter Clark's term, often are viewed as "symbols of civic legitimacy." Labor leaders rarely have this symbolic quality, but must contend with whatever stigma attaches to being from a lower-class background and associated with a special-interest group. . . .[7]

Labor's preoccupation with strictly labor goals and its concern for general civic legitimacy have combined to produce in many cities an antipathy between union leaders and municipal reformers. Although there are cases such as Detroit where the UAW and liberal and re-form Democrats have joined forces, the more common pattern is that of New York, Chicago, Los Angeles, and other cities where reform efforts have had to deal with the indifference or active hostility of most unions.[8] To the extent labor is concerned with strictly union objectives —wages and hours, workmen's compensation, unemployment benefits, union security guarantees—it finds the programs of civic reformers largely irrelevant. To the extent labor is concerned with acquiring influence in the local political parties and legislature, it regards the reformers as a rival. And to the extent labor is anxious about its civic reputation, it often sees the liberal reformers as the source of extreme and politically damaging ideology.

Thus, the Los Angeles County Federation of Labor passed a resolution in 1961 opposing the right of the liberal California Democratic Council to make pre-primary endorsements in state and local

---

[7] One measure of this difference in civic roles is found in the underrepresentation of labor leaders among those given certain kinds of public honors, including citation in *Who's Who*. See Orme W. Phelps, "Community Recognition of Union Leaders," *Industrial and Labor Relations Review*, April 1954, pp. 417–33.

[8] The discussion of unions and reform follows Wilson, *The Amateur Democrat: Club Politics in Three Cities* (Chicago: University of Chicago Press, 1962), pp. 273–77.

contests. The New York Central Labor Council in 1961 was largely indifferent to the anti-Tammany campaign then being waged by the reformers in the New York Committee for Democratic Voters, although it joined with the reformers in backing Robert Wagner, the anti-Tammany candidate. In Chicago, with some minor exceptions, union leaders have publicly supported the candidates of the Democratic machine, not those of the reform-minded Independent Voters of Illinois. The Liberal Party in New York, largely backed by unions in the garment industry, has remained independent of the various reform movements in the city.

In those few cases in which there has been a labor-reform alliance (as in Chicago's Fifth Senatorial District in 1950[9]), the union involved has typically been the United Auto Workers. But even the UAW cannot always act independently, for it must consider the costs of political isolation from other unions in the city and from state federations as well as from the local Democratic party. The desirability of playing politics in city affairs must be measured against the necessity of playing politics within labor affairs. It probably takes an energetic and persuasive labor leader to make the advantages of independent civic action more attractive than it costs.

Unions in Urban Political Parties

The common view that "labor is tied to the Democratic party" requires much modification before it is accurate, particularly with regard to local politics. Unions have many different relations with local parties. In a very few cases unions (mostly the UAW) have attempted to take over the leadership of the Democratic party; with the help of allies, they succeeded in this in Detroit, in Gary, Indiana, and in Rockford, Illinois.[10] Or they may act in coalition with party leaders, as in the Democratic Farmer-Labor party in Minneapolis and St. Paul. They may stay aloof from local politics, as in Houston. They may confine themselves to seeking favors from local party organizations, as in Chicago. They may form independent parties to win votes and thereby bargaining power, as in New York City. They may, as do most CIO unions, carry over into city politics their national attachment to the Democrats; or they may, as do many AFL unions, support local politicians with little reference to national party labels. Where the city is nonpartisan, unions may—as they have in the past in St. Paul—endorse

---

[9] See Calkins, *CIO and Democratic Party*, pp. 59–85.
[10] *Ibid.*, chaps. V and VI.

and elect a slate of candidates. Or they may—as in Los Angeles—instinctively oppose, with meager resources, whatever candidate the *Los Angeles Times* supports. (Labor-*Times* agreement in backing Mayor Norris Poulson in 1961 was an exception. And he lost anyway.)

Some representative cases of labor involvement in party politics follow.

1. The Unions Capture a Party: The Case of Detroit

Beginning in 1948, the Wayne County CIO Political Action Committee (PAC), then made up almost entirely of UAW members, began, in alliance with certain liberal Democrats, an effort to take control of the state leadership of the Michigan Democratic party. State law required that precinct captains be elected directly by the voters. The PAC-liberal coalition elected 720 captains in Wayne County in 1948, about one third of the total. This was enough to give them control of the Democratic conventions in five of the six Wayne County Congressional districts; control of these, in turn, was enough to give the liberal coalition control of the state Democratic convention. After a bitter struggle with the party's Old Guard, this victory was repeated in 1950, and since then the liberals—dominated by the UAW—have controlled the state party.[11]

In the city of Detroit, however, elections are nonpartisan. Here labor's Committee on Political Education (the successor to the PAC since the AFL–CIO merger) functions directly as a political party.[12] The AFL–CIO Council, acting on COPE recommendations, endorses candidates and operates the strongest precinct organization in the city. Although the UAW has only slightly more than half of all union members in the city, it provides almost all the key COPE officials. In some cases, COPE is open to nonlabor Democrats, and some liberals from business and professional backgrounds participate. Most nonlabor liberals, however, work directly through the Democratic party rather than through COPE. About 40 percent of all precinct captains are COPE members; alliances with non-COPE but liberal captains give COPE clear control of the county and thus of the state party. In city elections, these same captains work on behalf of nonpartisan labor endorsees.

The Detroit COPE has had imparted to it by the UAW a militant

---

[11] *Ibid.*, pp. 112–46.

[12] This account follows Kenneth E. Gray and David Greenstone, "Organized Labor in City Politics," in Banfield, ed., *Urban Government* (New York: Free Press of Glencoe, 1961), pp. 368–73.

attitude toward political action. Kenneth Gray and David Greenstone offer several reasons to explain this militancy:

> First, the union was organized and led for some time by radicals . . . who fought violently among themselves but who agreed on the crucial importance of programmatic political action. Second, a bitter and violent struggle for recognition left the UAW with a deep hostility toward management. This hostility was manifested in political action. . . . Third, the union sought to ease a serious problem of ethnic and racial hostilities among its own members by emphasizing class solidarity of workers against management. This emphasis on the members' interest as a class strongly implied broad political goals rather than an exclusive concern with collective bargaining. . . . Fourth, the automobile workers have a tradition of rank-and-file participation, which contributes to the intensity of their activity in COPE.[13]

Militancy may have contributed to the state-wide successes of the Democrats, but it has not produced comparable successes in Detroit. Between 1946 and 1955, CIO-PAC endorsees won 67.5 percent of all primary and 91.2 percent of all general elections for partisan offices at the state, Congressional, and county level, but less than 38 percent of all contests for nonpartisan municipal offices.[14] As observed in an earlier chapter, union members have not hesitated to desert labor nominees in nonpartisan local elections—if, indeed, these members have even known who the labor candidates were. The CIO failed three times (1943, 1945, and 1949) to elect a mayor of Detroit after bitter contests in which labor's political arm emphasized "liberal issues"— Negro rights, public housing, urban redevelopment, and the right of public employees to strike. In 1953, labor regarded opposition to the incumbent as hopeless and made no endorsement. By 1957 a new strategy was emerging: play down ideological issues, back a sure winner, and hope for favors if he is elected. That year COPE joined with business and newspaper groups in supporting the man who won. Pleased with their success, labor leaders tried again in 1961, only to have the noncontroversial incumbent, despite almost unanimous business, labor, newspaper, and civic support, lose to an unknown who had strong support from Negroes.

Despite the 1961 setback, it is unlikely that COPE will revert to the militancy of the 1940's. First, Detroit city government has begun

---

[13] *Ibid.*, p. 370.

[14] Nicholas A. Masters, "The Politics of Union Endorsement of Candidates in the Detroit Area," *Midwest Journal of Political Science*, August 1957, p. 149.

to be responsive to the demands of lower-class and Negro voters even without labor control of the city government. Second, labor has learned "to conform to the peculiar rules of the nonpartisan game" which require that it refrain from overly aggressive political behavior, that it stress the most widely shared community sentiments, and that it avoid the appearance of seeking to "take over" city government.[15]

Not all cases of labor dominance in local affairs are confined to industrial unions, however. For many years, the AFL unions associated with the "Labor Temple" in St. Paul (now the St. Paul AFL–CIO Trades and Labor Assembly) were continually successful in electing their candidates to office in that nonpartisan city. These labor leaders were conservative in temper, but eventually their influence was undermined by the rise of an aggressive coalition of CIO leaders and intellectuals which made up the Democratic Farmer-Labor Party (DFL) that emerged in 1948. After much controversy, an uneasy alliance between the DFL and the Labor Temple developed.[16]

In Minneapolis too the AFL craft unions were powerful. Between 1941 and 1957, they made the Central Labor Union (CLU) the most important political force in that nonpartisan city.[17] With the advent of the DFL, the CLU remained the dominant partner; no liberal candidate felt he could win without labor support. The terms of the DFL-CLU alliance allowed the DFL to nominate candidates for state and national office (where the liberal ideologies of the DFL intellectuals were engaged anyway) while the CLU elected candidates for city posts. After the defeat of labor candidates in 1957 (owing to scandals, indiscretions, and poor tactics), CLU strength began to decline.

2. Unions Defer to the Party: The Case of New York and Chicago

In large, industrially diversified cities such as New York and Chicago, where political parties have (or have had) power independent of the support of other organized groups, labor has had to be content either with bargaining with elective officials (usually after, rather than before, the election) from a position of relative weakness, or with forming third parties to strengthen that bargaining position. In contrast with Detroit, unions have not attempted to take over party posts, and in contrast with Minneapolis they have not been able to make them-

---

[15] Gray and Greenstone, "Organized Labor in City Politics," p. 373.

[16] Alan Altshuler, A Report on Politics in St. Paul (Cambridge, Mass.: Joint Center for Urban Studies, 1959, mimeo) pp. II–3 to II–10.

[17] Alan Altshuler, A Report on Politics in Minneapolis (Cambridge, Mass.: Joint Center for Urban Studies, 1959, mimeo), pp. II–8 to II–9 and V–5 to V–7.

selves senior partners in a labor-liberal coalition. Only very rarely
have a few unions challenged the regular party leadership (the Democrats, of course) in primary contests.

In Chicago, labor needs the politicians more than the politicians
need labor. Both sides know this, and a kind of half-hearted good
fellowship results. The craft unions typically remain close to the party
and attempt to share in the patronage, particularly in the licensing and
building-inspection departments. The industrial unions—notably the
steel, auto, and meat-packing workers—usually support regular party
candidates. But occasionally they assert their independence in what
they know in advance is a lost cause; for example, certain unions
backed an insurgent candidate for the Democratic nomination for governor in 1960. He lost, but the result of the challenge was to increase
somewhat the vigor with which the regular candidate attempted to
meet union demands in order to arouse their enthusiasm for the general election contest with the Republican. Indeed, labor leaders can
probably wield greatest influence by endeavoring to control rather precisely the ardor with which they help Democrats mobilize voters in
the closely contested county and state elections. The few union leaders who have been successful at this and at the same time have stayed
clear of charges of "left wing" leanings have become important forces
in local politics. In case of a showdown with the party, however, there
is not much doubt as to who would win.

New York's Democratic party has in recent years been much
weaker than its counterpart in Chicago, and therefore labor has probably been more influential. First with the American Labor party and
then (after 1944) with the Liberal party, certain New York unions—
mostly those Jewish-led unions in the garment industry—have endeavored to act as a third force in city and state politics. The ALP was in
1937 and 1941 a crucial source of votes for Fiorello H. La Guardia.
After it was destroyed by the struggle between Communist and anti-
Communist factions, the Liberal party continued the strategy of always
endorsing Democrats nationally but of playing one side against the
other locally. It has always polled a substantial vote, and in 1951 it
managed to elect, on its own, a city council president.

Most New York unions, however, have never had any association
with either the ALP or the Liberal party. The AFL unions, organized
into the Central Trades and Labor Council, followed an almost un-
varying policy of supporting regular Democrats in city elections and
expecting in return to be given certain assurances about police attitudes toward strikers and certain concessions on local codes, licenses,
inspections, and prevailing wage rates on city construction work. The

very size of the New York labor movement—the Council had over three quarters of a million members—made it exceptionally difficult for it to speak with one voice on even crucial matters, much less on the secondary issues of political participation. The building trades unions and the Teamsters had their own councils which were part of the larger Council, and union autonomy was jealously guarded.[18]

In 1959, the CIO and AFL unions in New York merged into a Central Labor Council with a total membership of a million and a half workers. Such an organization, even if it did nothing in politics, would be a force to be reckoned with because of the vast audience it could provide politicians fortunate enough to enjoy access to it. Union meetings are one way politicians have of dealing with the perennial and insoluble problem of how to reach the people.

But the new organization set out to be something more than just an audience. Its first president, Harry Van Arsdale, was a vigorous exponent of union education and political action. In 1961, he persuaded the Central Labor Council to support Mayor Robert Wagner for reelection even though the mayor had broken with the regular party leaders, and to organize a new political force, the "Brotherhood party," which would do for unions generally what the Liberal party had done for the needle trades. At the time this new party was created, it was widely believed that Wagner would not win the Democratic primary and thus he would need such third parties as the Brotherhood to enable him to run as an independent in the general election. Instead, Wagner won easily in the primary and the immediate need for the Brotherhood party vanished. Though the party had a strong start, organizing political units in most assembly districts in the city, its future became uncertain.

3. The Dormant Unions: The Case of the Southwest

In the large cities of the Southwest, where strong political parties do not exist and where population and industry are rapidly expanding, labor has been a recent and still minor civic actor. An aggressive union may be able to convert a one-industry town into a one-party town, as in Detroit. And unions may extract concessions from professional politicians in the old, stable cities of the Northeast and Midwest, such as New York and Chicago. But in such booming cities as Houston, Dallas, San Diego, and Los Angeles, where rapid growth is occurring, business (and, more generally, middle-class) influence is often such that organ-

---

[18] This account follows Wallace S. Sayre and Herbert Kaufman, *Governing New York City* (New York: Russell Sage Foundation, 1960), pp. 508–10.

ized labor (which, in most of these communities, is only a recent arrival) is lacking in either legitimacy or power.

Businessmen often dominate the politics of these cities (sometimes by default) so long as they can agree among themselves. Furthermore, business and conservative values are widely shared. Business leadership is not an imposition; it is generally accepted. In Houston and Los Angeles, strong anti-union feelings are still widespread among citizens. The absence of a mass production heavy industry (such as an auto plant) means the absence of a large pool of easily organized unskilled workers. The largest CIO unions are often found in the aircraft plants where there is a high proportion of skilled workers. In San Diego, for example, the largest local industrial union is the International Association of Machinists. As Table 15 shows, these are the cities with the largest percentages of white-collar workers in the labor force, and such workers are extremely difficult—often impossible—to organize.

TABLE 15. Cities over 500,000 population ranked by the percentage of employed persons in white-collar occupations, 1960

Rank	City	Percent white-collar	Rank	City	Percent white-collar
1	Seattle	47.8	12	Boston	35.5
2	Dallas	45.9	13	Pittsburgh	35.2
3	Los Angeles	45.0	14	Philadelphia	35.1
4	San Diego	44.8	15	Baltimore	34.2
5	San Francisco	43.0	16	Chicago	33.4
6	New York City	42.8	17	Detroit	32.1
7	Washington	42.7	18	Milwaukee	31.5
8	Houston	41.6	19	Buffalo	30.4
9	New Orleans	39.0	20	St. Louis	30.2
10	San Antonio	38.1	21	Cleveland	24.8
11	Cincinnati	36.8			

Note: "White-collar" refers to professional, technical, official, managerial, sales, and clerical occupations.

Source: 1960 Census of Population.

Despite such constraints, labor in these cities may be a major participant in at least state and national politics. In Houston and San Diego, for example, some labor unions are principal partners in a liberal-labor coalition which contests Democratic primaries. The very absence of a strong party organization, the result in part of nonpartisan, business-dominated city politics, often gives rise to intraparty factional warfare at the county and state level in which labor, albeit weak, is strong enough to play an important role.

Reaching the Voter

Report to the 14th Annual City-Wide Shop Conference,
Teamsters Local 688, St. Louis, Missouri

In 1956, running for his third term in the Missouri Senate, Robert
Pentland was faced with the stiffest contest of his political career.

1) His area had been redistricted. The heavily-Democratic 10th
Ward was taken from his district, and the predominantly Republican
13th Ward was substituted.

The 10th Ward had provided the winning margin in both 1948
and 1952:

Year	10th Ward Margin	Total Winning Margin
1948	1,377	1,306
1952	2,133	1,541

Loss of the 10th Ward, on the face of it, therefore, made 1956
a losing battle.

2) Pentland's opponent was a popular and respected ex-Senator,
Milton Napier, whose home ward was Pentland's newest—the 13th.

3) Faced with the national popularity of President Eisenhower,
and a strong-running and popular Republican candidate for Governor,
the outcome in this predominantly Republican Senatorial district was
distinctly in doubt.

Faced with this challenge, more than 350 rank-and-file members
of Pentland's union—Teamsters Local 688—turned out to work in his
campaign.

When the votes were counted, Pentland's victory margin was
the largest ever. Not counting absentee ballots, he had carried the
district by 1,927 votes. He had not only won the Democratic 11th
Ward, but had carried the Republican 23rd Ward (which he lost by
1,000 votes in 1952), and the 13th Ward as well. He had lost the Republican 12th Ward by only 278 votes, compared with 1,239 in 1952.

(Absentee ballots reduced his margin by 245 votes, but gave
him an overall majority of 1,682—still his largest victory margin. They
also carried the 23rd Ward into the Republican column by 66 votes,
and raised the 12th Ward margin to 358.)

The District

The First Senatorial District in Missouri, following the changes, is
composed of the 11th, 12th, 13th, and 23rd Wards.

Reprinted by permission of the President of Teamsters Local 688, St. Louis,
Missouri.

The City of St. Louis has four Republican Aldermen out of 28—and three of them are from this district—the 12th, 13th, and 23rd Wards.

In 1948 and 1952, Pentland had run as follows:

Ward	1948	1952
10th	Won by 1,377	Won by 2,133
11th	Won by 1,612	Won by 2,027
12th	Lost by 962	Lost by 1,239
13th (2 precincts)	——	Lost by 419
23rd	Lost by 721	Lost by 1,000

Thus the 10th Ward was a vital element in Pentland's previous victories. Further, a study showed that the 13th Ward, of which Pentland previously had two heavily Republican precincts, was in the Republican column by 89 votes, taking the entire ward in the last State Senatorial election.

This redistricting, therefore, posed serious problems.

Yet, when the election was over, this was the comparative picture:

Ward	1948	1952	1956
11th	Won by 1,612	Won by 2,027	Won by 1,990
12th	Lost by 962	Lost by 1,239	Lost by 358
13th	Not in district	Lost by 89	Won by 116
23rd	Lost by 721	Lost by 1,000	Lost by 66

The Campaign

The approach used in the 1956 Pentland campaign represented a departure from usual practices. Political organizations ordinarily "play from strength"—that is, they concentrate on bringing out the votes in their best precincts.

In the Pentland campaign, it was felt that it was necessary to reach Republican and Independent voters, rather than Democratic voters, in order to overcome the deficit he faced on paper.

Accordingly, two principal means of approach were decided upon:

1) Of the 127 precincts in the district, Pentland had lost 72 of these, either in 1948 or 1952, or had won by a very narrow margin. It was decided to cover every home in each of these 72 precincts on a door-to-door basis.

2) In an effort to reach every home in the district with something other than a routine mailing, it was decided to publish a four-page, tabloid newspaper, called the "Pentland Record." This paper detailed the candidate's record, platform, qualifications, endorsements, etc. Two issues of this paper were mailed to each of the 42,000 homes in the area.

Numerous other campaign devices were also used—a card party, a parade, a Citizens' Committee, balloon distribution in the schools, etc.

While concentrating largely on the Republican and borderline precincts in the 12th and 23rd Wards in the pre-election campaigning, Pentland and his co-workers on election day worked closely with the regular Democratic ward organizations, with the majority of the Pentland workers engaged in the 11th and 13th Wards.

The overall strategy seems to have paid dividends, resulting as it did in his largest victory.

Evaluation

As with any statistics, a number of interpretations could be given to the results in the First Senatorial District.

The picture is complicated by the fact that in 1952, in the Eisenhower landslide, most Democratic candidates dropped considerably in the percentage of votes they received. Pentland, due to a strong campaign in that year, held his own or improved.

In 1956, due to the intensive door-to-door campaign and the "Pentland Record," Pentland's percentage of votes increased substantially in the 12th and 23rd Wards, where the bulk of the effort was made. By contrast, the Governorship race showed a continued decline, and the Presidential race remained virtually the same.

In such other races as U. S. Congress and Missouri Secretary of State, their percentage increased substantially over 1952, but still did not reach their level of 1948.

Pentland not only had to reach his level of 1948 or 1952 to win. He had to increase it substantially in the 12th and 23rd Wards. This he did, and without a concentrated campaign, it could never have been done.

Here is the Pentland picture, by percentage (omitting the 13th Ward, for which there were no comparisons):

Percentage of Votes

Ward	1948	1952	1956
11th	56.2%	57.2%	57.9%
12th	46.3%	46.7%	49.2%
23rd	47.8%	47.8%	50.0%

It is significant, in this table, that the minimum door-to-door effort was made in the 11th Ward, the maximum in the 12th and 23rd Wards.

Also of interest is the composite picture for the 11th, 12th, and 23rd Wards, comparing Pentland with the Democratic candidate for President (Truman and Stevenson), and for Governor (Forrest Smith, Phil M. Donnelly, James T. Blair, Jr., all victorious state-wide):

Percentage of Votes

11th Ward

Democratic Candidate	1948	1952	1956
President	62.3%	56.1%	54.9%
Governor	60.2%	61.8%	54.3%
Robert Pentland	56.2%	57.2%	57.9%

12th Ward

Democratic Candidate	1948	1952	1956
President	50.9%	45.1%	45.1%
Governor	49.9%	45.5%	43.5%
Robert Pentland	46.3%	46.7%	49.2%

23rd Ward

Democratic Candidate	1948	1952	1956
President	50.0%	46.0%	46.4%
Governor	47.4%	48.6%	44.5%
Robert Pentland	47.8%	47.8%	50.0%

Doubtless, many factors enter into an election campaign. But it seems evident that 135 volunteer workers engaged in door-to-door campaigning in 72 doubtful precincts, plus the "Pentland Record," were able to increase the percentage of votes for Pentland substantially and thus achieve a victory which at first seemed beyond grasp.

The Candidate

Effective as the work of the campaign proved to be, it must be emphasized that Local 688 was backing a candidate whose record and abilities gave the union something to boast about.

Robert Pentland was a rank-and-file shop steward at J. C. Penney Co. warehouse in St. Louis when he was first elected in 1948. The first victory was a surprise to political veterans. Even at that time, his district was considered safely in the Republican column.

Following his 1948 victory, two heavily Republican precincts in the 13th Ward were added to his district. Again in 1952, Pentland won.

In 1956, it appeared that an even stronger effort was being made to unseat Pentland, when the 10th Ward was taken away from him and the 13th Ward was substituted.

This redistricting, combined with Pentland's noteworthy legislative record in such areas as unemployment compensation, workmen's compensation, labor legislation, and other matters of concern to working people, provided strong incentive to rank-and-file union members to work for his reelection.

In addition, such things as Pentland's tireless efforts in behalf of honest elections (voting machine bills, modernization of voting

procedures), his support of good social welfare legislation, his perfect
attendance record, and numerous testimony about his conscientious and
able performance in the State Legislature, were matters upon which he
could capitalize in reaching the voters of his district, the majority of
whom have no particular affinity for organized labor.

Recruiting Workers

To pursue the type of campaign envisioned, a large number of volunteer workers would be required. Beginning with the union's 500-mem-
ber Stewards Council in July, and later in the union's regular shop
meetings, members of the campaign committee began to emphasize the
importance of the Pentland campaign to Local 688 and its members.

Most important, of course, was Pentland's record in behalf of
legislation affecting working men and women, and social welfare laws
which involved the whole community.

Continual redistricting made it appear that some interests were
concerned about Pentland's consistent success. If they could beat Pentland, it was reasoned, they would be encouraged to seek victories over
other progressive candidates.

Another important consideration was the fact that Local 688,
itself, was a target. Known, respected, and in certain quarters feared
as a militant and progressive union, Local 688's defeat in the political arena, after considerable success, would gladden the hearts of some
people.

Even more, with the effort to restrict labor's freedom and growth
having moved from the bargaining table and picket line, and into the
legislative halls, many people hoped that a defeat for labor in this key
contest would signal a mounting campaign against labor's proportionate
representation in law-making assemblies.

Among a membership which has been schooled through the
years in its stake in political and community affairs, this appeal was
realistic. Shop stewards took special volunteer cards and endeavored
to enroll their fellow employees as campaign workers.

The fact that Pentland himself was a former rank-and-filer and
a close personal friend of many of the members, added to the appeal.

All volunteer work during the campaign was unpaid, except for
election day, when workers were paid the equivalent of the wages they
lost by taking off work.

Yet a grand total of 324 rank-and-file workers took part in various phases of the campaign, including the 135 who worked door-to-door.

Some of the larger Local 688 shops produced numerous volunteers. At Crown Cork, chief steward Dorothy DeBlaze was successful

in recruiting 51 volunteers. At Cupples-Hesse, steward Norma Eller-brock produced 36 workers. Brown Shoe, long a stalwart of union activity and interest, had 31. But the rank-and-file volunteers also came from far and wide, from small shops as well as large, and represented a wide cross-section of the union.

The Door-to-Door Campaign

To cover 72 precincts door-to-door, especially when each worker was to take only one-half precinct, would require many workers. Ultimately, 135 people were working at this project, with some taking several assignments, and union staff members completing the remainder.

The purpose of the campaign was to swing normally Republican and Independent votes into Pentland's column, on the basis of his record. Door-to-door workers were cautioned, therefore, not to engage in political controversy or to inquire about political affiliations.

A special brochure was prepared, which proclaimed: "South St. Louis Has the Best—Let's Keep Him." This folder outlined Pentland's voting record, quoted from laudatory newspaper editorials, and set forth his platform for the coming session.

Workers were instructed to do simply the following: to greet the resident, state his interest in Pentland's reelection, present the folder and ask that it be read, and encourage a vote for Pentland.

Kits were prepared in advance for each half-precinct, containing: a half-precinct list, instruction sheet, supply of folders, and special cards which offered election day information, services such as baby-sitting and transportation, and an invitation to call upon the candidate for help.

On the basis of those volunteers who had indicated a willingness to work door-to-door, assignments were made in advance and were ready for the first general volunteers' meeting on October 8. More than 100 workers turned out for this meeting and accepted kits. For those who would work but could not be at the meeting, kits were delivered to their shops.

A number of follow-up procedures were established. Meetings in each of the four Pentland ward headquarters were set up for the following week. The turnout for those meetings was very small. In retrospect, they were needless meetings, taking out a valuable night that could otherwise be used for canvassing.

An effective technique, however, was the appointment of a telephone committee composed of volunteers from the truck line offices. They divided the list of volunteers and followed up by telephone. This seemed to be helpful in encouraging workers to complete their assignments.

On Oct. 29, the Political Education Committee of Local 688 (P.E.C.), most of whose members were active in the door-to-door campaign, was called together and asked to help in completing the precinct assignments. Several additional kits were distributed in this way.

In the final week of the campaign, union staff members took on the responsibility of completing the list of 72 precincts.

The "Pentland Record"

The second principal approach used in the campaign was publication of a special, four-page tabloid newspaper called the "Pentland Record," co-edited by Carl Leathwood and Jake McCarthy.

Dealing with issues, qualifications, and platform, and sprinkled liberally with photographs, the "Record" was felt to be a particularly effective medium, certainly more than a normal political mailing would have been.

Two issues of the paper were mailed—to a total of 42,472 homes each, or every home in the district.

The economy of such a campaign device was interesting. Not only was a saving made in postage, compared with an ordinary first-class mailing. Printing of the "Pentland Record" actually represented less an expenditure than an effective advertisement in the daily press would have cost.

Members of the P. E. C. Committee and other volunteers took care of the large task of addressing an original and carbon copy of the names and addresses of all registered voters in the district, a project which began in August.

The Results

The fact that Republican or borderline precincts had been selected for intensive work, and that so-called "safe" precincts were not covered, resulted in some interesting figures.

Not only was there a substantial swing to Pentland in the apparently Republican precincts. In the 12th Ward, for example, there was a heavy swing *away* from Pentland, and other Democratic candidates, in those precincts which were *not* worked.

Another interesting occurrence developed. Apart from ticket-leading races such as President and Governor, where there were declines, a number of other Democratic candidates also experienced similar upswings.

One conclusion is obvious: there is a shifting pattern of voting habits in the district, particularly in the 12th and 23rd Wards.

How much of this was due to Pentland's campaigning, and how much was due to other factors, is hard to determine.

But it was certainly true that the results of the Pentland campaign were gratifying. And, remembering the pessimistic picture in the First Senatorial District before the campaign got under way, it would be difficult to say that the Pentland victory was due to anything but hard and effective work.

Certainly, there were other factors. The tremendous popularity of U. S. Senator Thomas C. Hennings, Jr., who led the Democratic ticket, no doubt helped. But the continued decline of Democratic vote percentages in the races for President and Governor indicated a heavy pattern of "ticket-splitting," and Pentland, with a popular opponent, probably could not have won in a traditionally Republican district without a concentrated effort.

Here was the Pentland picture, ward-by-ward:

12th Ward

23 of the 38 precincts were worked door-to-door.

Average Gain Per Precinct—	10.9 votes
Average Gain Per Precinct Worked—	38.5 votes
Average *Loss* Per Precinct Not Worked—	59.4 votes

Pentland gained in 18 of the 23 precincts worked, lost in 5. Of those not worked, he gained in only 2 of 9, lost in 7. The remaining six precincts were newly established and no comparisons were available.

23rd Ward

23 of the 39 precincts were worked door-to-door.

Average Gain Per Precinct—	19.6 votes
Average Gain Per Precinct Worked—	27.9 votes
Average Gain Per Precinct Not Worked—	7.6 votes

Of the precincts worked, Pentland gained in 17 of 23, lost in 6. Of those not worked, he gained in 11 of 16, lost in 5.

13th Ward

(Comparisons were made with the 1954 State Senatorial race, involving different candidates.)

12 of the 28 precincts were worked door-to-door

Average Gain Per Precinct—	10.6 votes
Average Gain Per Precinct Worked—	14.2 votes
Average Gain Per Precinct Not Worked—	7.9 votes

Of the precincts worked, Pentland gained in 8 of 12, lost in 4. Of those not worked, he gained in 10 of 16, lost in 6.

11th Ward

In this Democratic ward, where the minimum effort was made (only 10 of the 28 precincts were covered door-to-door), Pentland lost 37 votes from his 1952 total, but nevertheless gained a larger percentage of the votes than previously.

Another factor that may be significant in the total picture was that absentee ballots were cast against Pentland, 708 to 463, throughout the whole district. Such voters were probably not reached by any of the campaigning.

The Citizens Committee

In addition to the "Pentland Record," a principal mailing piece used was the "Citizens-for-Pentland" committee letter, which also went to the more than 42,000 homes in the district.

With Circuit Attorney Edward L. Dowd as chairman, the letterhead also included the names of other prominent South Side Democrats.

This letter, mailed in a plain envelope to minimize its chances of being ignored as "another campaign piece," was sent the last week of the campaign as a final reminder.

Other Unions

A number of other labor unions also gave generous cooperation to the campaign. The following unions, through their officers, sent letters to each of their members in Pentland's district, calling attention to his labor record:

International Brotherhood of Electrical Workers, Local No. 1, Paul Nolte; Amalgamated Meat Cutters and Butcher Workmen, Local No. 88, Nick Blassie; United Hat, Cap, and Millinery Workers, Isadore Drucker; and Street Car and Bus Operators, Local No. 788, John Rowland. The Meat Cutters also invited Pentland to address their regular monthly meeting just prior to the election.

The great majority of local unions in Teamsters Joint Council No. 13 also provided lists of their members residing in that area. One mailing went to these Teamster members, inviting them to the kick-off meeting on Oct. 1; the second was a last-minute reminder just prior to the election.

Mailing

In a comprehensive campaign such as this, the task of addressing envelopes and labels is monumental. Large numbers of volunteers undertook this job, which was one of the most important in the campaign.

A special meeting was also called, late in October, to stuff the Citizens Committee mailing. Some 60 volunteers attended.

Pentland Parade

On Saturday, Nov. 3, the campaign committee organized a colorful parade through Pentland's district. With a special motorcycle escort of young ladies who belong to the St. Louis Cyclettes, about 15 highly-decorated automobiles attracted a good deal of attention along the parade route. The Cyclettes' president, Lois Schroeder, is employed by the union's Labor Health Institute.

Card Party

On Sunday, Nov. 4, the campaign was brought to a peak with a free card party at Kolping House. This was advertised throughout the district in the final issue of the "Pentland Record."

Some 400 persons attended this afternoon event, which was supervised by a group of union volunteers from Rice-Stix, with Martha Fannen as chairman.

A number of employers generously donated prizes for the free event. Some 300 attendance prizes were given away, and the card party was considered to be another effective device in the campaign.

Ward Headquarters

As in previous campaigns, Pentland headquarters in each ward were rented in late August. During September, openings were held in each of the headquarters.

Members living in those wards were invited to the openings. There was not a large turnout at any of these, however, and the principal value of the headquarters was advertising in the district.

As the campaign progressed, a few volunteers manned these headquarters in the evenings to distribute campaign literature. . . .

Balloon Distribution

In the last two weeks before election, some 20,000 Pentland balloons were distributed to children of the public and parochial schools of the district.

While it is difficult to assess the value of this project, particularly compared with the man-hours required to distribute them, an excellent suggestion was made that would bear consideration in future campaigns.

This was the suggestion that the balloons might more effectively be used if they were distributed as favors by those campaigning door-to-door.

Kick-Off Meeting

The Pentland kick-off meeting, held Oct. 1 at Alhambra Grotto, was attended by Local 688 members living in the district, in lieu of their regular union "community meetings" held during October.

U. S. Senators Stuart Symington and Thomas C. Hennings, Jr., and the successful candidate for Governor, James T. Blair, Jr., headlined the speaking program.

The event gained useful newspaper publicity, and the laudatory comments of the speakers were successfully used in the final issue of the "Pentland Record."

Other Projects

On Saturday, Oct. 13, a group of volunteers, chiefly from the union staff, put up Pentland placards on telephone poles along the main streets of his district.

Those placards, along with some 2,000 bumper strips, were also distributed to members living in that area, via their regular shop meetings during September.

Pentland matchbooks were distributed in stores and taverns in the area by A-1 Cigarette and American Cigarette vending companies, whose employees are members of Local 688.

Publicity

During the campaign, the committee was successful in gaining publicity in the daily press. Coverage was given to the kick-off meeting. In addition, the press gave good coverage to such Pentland campaign proposals as: annual sessions for the State Legislature, abolition of the household "nuisance" tax, and the establishment of a Missouri State Youth Authority.

While not giving a strong editorial endorsement, the Post-Dispatch commended Pentland's record in the closing days of the campaign, and this was helpful in his district, which is comprised of so-called "newspaper wards."

In addition, Pentland appeared on a League of Women Voters TV panel on Channel 9, and on the Teamsters' TV panel, "Labor Views the News," on Channel 36, discussing his proposal for a Youth Authority.

Election Day

Whereas the bulk of the pre-election campaigning had been done in 72 Republican and borderline precincts, it was deemed important to do the bulk of election-day work in the Democratic precincts.

Accordingly, although most of the pre-election efforts had been in the 12th and 23rd Wards, on election day the emphasis shifted to the 11th and 13th Wards.

Working closely with the ward organizations, the Pentland committee assigned its volunteer workers as follows: 33 in the 11th Ward; 36 in the 13th; 15 in the 12th; and 14 in the 23rd.

Pentland workers wore the candidate's lapel ribbons, and handed out "last minute reminder" Pentland cards, in addition to the regular ward literature.

On election day, staff members manned the ward headquarters in the hope of providing baby-sitting services and transportation, as promised on cards handed out door-to-door.

Election day was a day of excellent weather, however, and there were few calls for transportation. Nor were there more than one or two calls for baby-sitters. The offer of such services, however, had been another gesture of good will during the campaign.

Summary of Materials

85,000 Copies, the "Pentland Record" (Two issues)
42,000 Citizens Committee letters
30,000 Pentland Folders (door-to-door distribution)
30,000 Election Day information cards (door-to-door)
 2,000 Pentland personal cards (for ward mailings, etc.)
20,000 Pentland balloons
25,000 Pentland match books
 2,000 Pentland posters
 2,000 Bumper strips
 5,000 "Last minute reminder" cards (election day)
   200 Lapel ribbons.

The Politics of the West Coast
Teamsters and Truckers

Irving Bernstein
University of California, Los Angeles

IN THE FALL OF 1954 there was a political race for sheriff in a city of
the Pacific Northwest. The Republican candidate was Callahan, and
the Democratic, McCullough. The International Brotherhood of Teamsters endorsed Callahan. The union made this decision without consultation with the remainder of the labor movement. McCullough won.
On December 1, 1954, Frank Brewster, president of the Western Conference of Teamsters, presented McCullough with a check for $2,500
to help clear up his campaign deficit. When Senator Karl E. Mundt,
a member of the McClellan rackets committee, expressed wonderment
that the Teamsters should back an unsuccessful Republican and then
contribute to his victorious Democratic opponent, Brewster explained:
"Well, they are in office, you know, for 4 years, so we have to get
friendly with them. . . . Senator, we always try to pick winners."
Brewster, whose well-advertised love for horseflesh goes back to the
days when he drove a team, also put it this way: "We ride a couple
of horses in the race once in a while." [1]

At the 1957 session of the California Legislature the Teamsters'
legislative representative was exceedingly active and worked in close
harmony with the California Federation of Labor. His organization
supported an increase in the maximum unemployment compensation
benefit from $33 to $40 per week and in the disability benefit from
$40 to $50, in both cases successfully. The Teamsters backed a comprehensive bill regulating health and welfare plans, which was enacted.
This union also threw its weight behind bills to establish state-supported
child care centers, state aid for local mental health clinics, a $225 mil-
lion bond issue for school construction, and an emergency appropriation
of $37 million for higher pay for teachers. Finally, the Teamsters unsuc-
cessfully worked for a fair employment practices law for California. [2]

Reprinted from *Tenth Annual Proceedings* [1957], Industrial Relations
Research Association, by permission of the Association and the author.
[1] *Investigation of Improper Activities in the Labor or Management Field,*
Hearings on S. Res. 74, Sen. Select Committee on Improper Activities . . . ,
85th Cong., 1st sess. (1957), pp. 1142, 1294–97. Hereafter cited as McClellan
Committee Hearings.
[2] Vern Cannon, *Legislative Report to the California Teamsters Legislative
Council on the 1957 Session of the California State Legislature,* June 24, 1957.

Here in these two illustrations is the dilemma of the Teamsters Union in the era of [former Teamster President] Dave Beck. This rich and powerful organization does not know whether it possesses the sovereign right to act with independence or whether it is constrained by the rules and mores of the labor movement. Nor does it know whether its political policy should be to elect the winners and defeat the losers or to serve the welfare of labor regardless of short-term Teamster interests.

1.

The political policies of the Teamsters are a function of their collective bargaining objectives. They practice business unionism pure and simple. Hence it is necessary to understand the industries in which they operate.

These industries are predominantly local-market oriented. The Western Conference, for example, is composed of the following thirteen trade divisions: automotive (car dealers, service stations, parking lots, etc.); bakery; beverage (breweries, wineries, distilleries, soft drinks); cannery; building and construction; chauffeurs (taxis, for-hire drivers, etc.); dairy (wholesale and retail drivers, plant and office personnel, milkers); general hauling (fuel, heavy machinery, railway express, sanitation drivers); highway drivers (intra- and interstate over-the-road haulage); laundry; log hauling; miscellaneous sales drivers (messenger, parcel delivery, motion picture, food distribution, armored car, newspaper, and many other drivers); and warehouse, produce, and cold storage. These divisions by no means encompass the total membership of the Conference.[3]

In virtually all these industries the market is the community or, at most, the state. Even the over-the-road group is far from a national force. Only one company operates coast-to-coast. Further, in Teamsters Joint Council 42 in Southern California, which has 103,000 members, fewer than 10 percent are over-the-road people, and two other groups, local haulage and dairy, are approximately as large. Even in industries with some national firms, like baking and dairy, local market forces tend to be decisive.

Hence the typical employer with whom the Teamsters deal is small and often tiny, as in the case of the owner-operator, or "gypsy." He is conventionally grouped for bargaining purposes in an employers' association based upon his product or service. These associations are

---

[3] J. B. Gillingham, *The Teamsters Union on the West Coast* (Berkeley: Institute of Industrial Relations, University of California, 1956), pp. 3–5.

notoriously difficult to organize and have a propensity to disintegrate. "While I'm negotiating with the union," an official of such an association complained, "the truckers I represent are out stealing my own accounts."[4] In many of these industries competition is intense and constitutes a continuing threat to price-wage stability.

The Teamsters Union is the product of these market forces. Historically organizational strength had clustered in the local, the international constituting a loose confederacy with essentially non-bargaining functions. Even locals in the same town had few interests to share. "Teaming in one industry," John R. Commons observed a half-century ago, "is distinct from teaming in another. The laundry driver has little in common with the coal teamster, except horses and streets."[5]

Some things have changed. The over-the-road drivers serve as a cohesive force in drawing communities together, and their settlements have an influence upon other industries. The Trotskyite Dunne brothers with Local 574 in Minneapolis in the thirties demonstrated the strategic importance of trucking in organizing a region.[6] Beck, first in the West and later nationally, has imposed so fantastic a superstructure of committees, conferences, and divisions upon the union as to leave even a university president gasping in admiration. The Western Conference, one of whose major purposes is organization, influences the negotiations of the new locals it creates. Further, by imposing regional pension as well as health and welfare plans, the Conference has tended to take major issues away from the locals.

The Teamsters Union, structurally considered, is caught in a state of tension between centripetal and centrifugal forces. The Becks, Hoffas, and Brewsters centralize; the inertia of the old-line locals and the nature of the market pull the organization apart. As this paper will demonstrate, the union Commons described is not dead. Milk drivers in Los Angeles care little about coin machine service men in Portland, and the neglect is mutual.

The market has also made the Teamsters unusually sensitive to the economic well-being of the employers with whom they deal. Commons tells us that the nineteenth-century predecessor of the interna-

---

[4] Cited by Paul Jacobs, "The World of Jimmy Hoffa—I," *The Reporter* (Jan. 24, 1957), p. 14. See also Martin A. Cohen and Martin Lieberman, "Collective Bargaining in the Motor Freight Industry," *Industrial and Labor Relations Review*, III (Oct. 1949), 29.

[5] John R. Commons, "Types of American Labor Organization, The Teamsters of Chicago," *Quarterly Journal of Economics*, XIX (May 1905), 401.

[6] For the development of this point see Jacobs, *op. cit.*, pp. 15–16.

tional admitted an owner to membership provided that he operated no more than five teams and that the organization was more preoccupied with prices than with wages. The present union has numerous owner members and is profoundly concerned with keeping its employers solvent so as to protect its members' jobs. In the dead of winter in 1902 the Chicago coal drivers in "a spectacular demonstration" of power stopped fuel deliveries to the Marshall Field store and compelled Field to agree to use coal rather than natural gas during the summer, thereby creating a market for their employers. Nowadays the Teamsters join with the truckers on all fronts in battle royal with the common enemy, the railroads, for the same purpose. A result of the Field strike was to put employers in the coal dealers' association. Today the Teamsters devote great energy to the establishment and maintenance of such associations because individual employers are too weak, too selfish, or too short-sighted to do so themselves. Finally, the Field stoppage provided an imaginative shakedown artist, one J. C. Driscoll, with the opportunity to set up a number of associations whose main object was the lining of his pockets. Corruption between friendly business agents and trucking employers, the McClellan Committee has reminded us, has not entirely disappeared.

The Teamsters' preoccupation with the welfare of the employer is a rather statesmanlike response to an imbalance in bargaining power. In many industries the union is not only much stronger than the individual employer but is much stronger than the concert of employers. Most firms simply cannot afford an interruption of their deliveries. Further, there is an unwritten law of the Teamsters that its leaders must create the impression of power. In his salad days, ironically enough, Beck posed as a tough guy. The public's view of Jimmy Hoffa is that of a bantam rooster spoiling for a fight. In Los Angeles the Teamsters sponsor promising young prize fighters. However, real though it is, one should not exaggerate the union's strength. The Teamsters have many nontrucking units with only limited loyalty to the organization and a marginal strategic position in the employers' operations. A dramatic illustration of the union's weakness is the defeat George Harrison administered to Beck over Railway Express jurisdiction in 1954. A wise old Teamster, "Bloody Mike" Casey of San Francisco, used to admonish, "Don't tist yer strength!" [7]

A final characteristic of the Teamsters is that it is in actuality what its name says it is—a brotherhood. Teamsters look after each

---

[7] Cited by Gillingham, *op. cit.*, p. 35.

other in fair weather and foul. Although there is probably no union today with as high a level of internal distrust and even detestation, no one is talking for publication. When I asked a prominent West Coast official what he could tell about a fellow officer, knowing full well that he had no use for him, he replied, "I cannot talk against a brother." "My friends in the labor business," Hoffa told Jacobs, "are mostly all Teamsters. The rest you gotta watch with both eyes."[8] To my knowledge this is the only organization that refers to itself as "the movement," using the term as other unionists do when they talk about the whole of organized labor.

2.

This insularity reflects itself in politics. The Teamsters are enthusiastic do-it-yourselfers. In 1956, AFL–CIO endorsed the Stevenson-Kefauver ticket; on the White House steps Beck announced his support for Eisenhower and Nixon. . . . In Portland in the now notorious race for District Attorney of Multnomah County in 1954 the Central Labor Council endorsed the Republican incumbent, John McCourt, and the Teamsters came out for his Democratic opponent, William ("Old Honest Abe") Langley.[9]

Perhaps the most dramatic exhibition of do-it-yourselfism occurred in the state of Washington in 1956. Proponents of right-to-work, whose enthusiasm for principle outran their political sagacity, put forth Initiative 198. In February, Brewster engaged a Seattle public relations man named Howard Sylvester to run the campaign against 198, and Sylvester was told that the Teamsters would put up $600,000, a figure close to the amount actually spent. He established The Citizens Committee for the Preservation of Payrolls and began a vigorous campaign. When other unions sought to participate, Sylvester was ordered to have nothing to do with them. He was told, for example, to return a check for $750 to the Yakima Central Labor Council. As he saw it, the Teamsters expected to defeat 198 and wanted to share the credit with no one else. In November, 198 was rejected by the voters of Washington 685,000 to 218,000.[10]

The fact that a labor union should spend upwards of half a million dollars on a single state issue is startling and deserves explanation. In the West, at least, right-to-work is much the most important political

---

[8] Paul Jacobs, "The World of Jimmy Hoffa—II," *The Reporter* (Feb. 7, 1957), p. 10.

[9] Gillingham, *op. cit.*, pp. 84–85; McClellan Committee Hearings, p. 315.

[10] McClellan Committee Hearings, pp. 1326–35; *Northern California Teamster*, Nov. 1956, p. 1.

issue the Teamsters face. The Western Conference has had a considerable experience upon which to base this conclusion. Arizona, Nevada, and Utah have right-to-work laws, while Colorado requires that three-fourth of the employees must approve before an "all-union" agreement may be signed. Even in California, where the Teamsters and organized labor as a whole have unusual political strength, right-to-work forces are gaining ground. The town of Palm Springs and the counties of Tehama and San Benito have recently enacted ordinances that make union security provisions unlawful.[11] The love affair between the Teamsters and Republican Governor Goodwin J. Knight, to be developed below, rests largely upon this issue.

If the Teamsters were as strong as some would have us believe, they would have no reason to fear right-to-work. In fact, as I have pointed out, they are not so powerful and are deeply concerned. Many members are recruited and kept in the organization by the union shop alone. Automobile salesmen, female office employees, and cannery workers—to cite only a few examples—feel a lesser identification with the Teamsters than the truck drivers who are its core. A survey made by this writer in the summer of 1956 of the members of two Los Angeles dairy locals, one of plant and office people and the other of drivers, revealed that 31 percent did not even know what "right-to-work" meant. Further, almost 13 percent actually favored such a law in California and 28 percent were undecided as to its desirability, leaving little more than half clearly opposed. The drivers, of course, were better informed, and more heavily opposed than the plant and office employees.[12]

Brewster, therefore, had good reason to spend so lavishly to defeat Initiative 198. He has followed up by naming a committee to fight right-to-work in the eleven western states under the chairmanship of Jack Annand, the president of Joint Council 42.[13]

3.

A fundamental reason why the Teamsters and the employers with whom they deal are driven into political activity is that an unusually large proportion of their industries is subject to governmental regulation. In a few cases, notably interstate trucking and the Railway

---

[11] These ordinances have been held unconstitutional in the lower courts of California. Stephenson v. City of Palm Springs, 31 CCH Labor Cases 70,490 (Calif. Super. Ct., 1957); Hobson v. Five Counties Central Labor Council, 33 CCH Labor Cases, 70,888 (Calif. Super. Ct., 1957); Chavez v. Sargent, 33 CCH Labor Cases 70,887 (Calif. Super. Ct., 1957).

[12] Irving Bernstein, *Survey of Teamsters Locals 93 and 306*, Aug. 10, 1956, p. 12.

[13] *Northern California Teamster*, Dec. 1956, p. 3.

Express Agency, they fall within federal jurisdiction, namely, the Interstate Commerce Commission and the National Mediation Board.

More typical, however, is regulation at the state and local levels. Intrastate over-the-road haulage, to take California as an illustration, where 83 percent of the freight moved as measured by revenue is by truck, is subject to a wide variety of controls: the size and weight of vehicles, the loads they may carry, the roads they may travel, the tariffs that can be charged, the taxes that must be paid, the qualifications for chauffeurs' licenses, and so on. In addition, both the truckers and the union have a more than passing interest in highway development.

The industry provides a dramatic illustration of union-management political cooperation. In 1955, the Teamsters struck the long-lines firms in the state of California and were out for twenty-three days. While the strike was in progress, the legislative representatives of the California Motor Transport Associations, Bert Trask, and of the Teamsters, Vern Cannon, cooperated in getting nineteen bills through the legislature in Sacramento. They dealt with such matters as vehicle braking distances and truck speed limits. "This is certainly a good example," Trask wrote a high Teamster official, "of how management and labor can work together for a common cause." [14]

A number of other industries in which the Teamsters are prominent—notably milk (of which more later), horse racing, and liquor—are also subject to state regulation. In Oregon, for example, Manton J. Spear of the K. & L. Beverage Co. told the McClellan Committee, "control of the liquor commission poses many advantages. . . . The commission would be in a position to buy merchandise from sources that were friendly. . . ." [15]

Finally, there are several industries which are regulated by municipalities. Many cities, for example, fix the number of taxicabs that may operate by licensing, thereby influencing the incomes of drivers. Some communities either prohibit or regulate coin machines used for gambling. In Los Angeles private rubbish collectors and dumps are licensed.

The milk industry in California is an interesting illustration of the political problems of union and employers at the state level in an industry which has been characterized as "subject to more governmental regulation than is any other . . . engaged in the production

---

[14] *Northern California Teamster*, Aug. 1955, p. 8.
[15] McClellan Committee Hearings, p. 338.

and distribution of agricultural products."[16] The key to the California milk problem is price.

In the twenties the industry was prosperous. The price per quart was identical for home and store delivery, averaging 15¢ in 1929; a result was that store sales were of little consequence. The Great Depression turned the industry upside down. By 1933, the average store price had fallen to 7¢ and there were numerous price wars in which milk served as loss leader and sold for a penny a quart. Home delivery virtually collapsed and everyone connected with milk from the dairy farmer onward suffered. As a consequence, the legislature in 1935 passed the Young Act, providing for the fixing of minimum producer prices by the California Department of Agriculture, and in 1937 enacted the Desmond Act, establishing minimum prices at the wholesale and retail levels. With minor exceptions, a policy of uniform pricing as between home and store delivery has been followed by the Department.

This policy has expressed the wishes of the majority of the dairies and distribution firms, seeking to maximize home delivery, and of the Teamsters Union, trying to protect the jobs of its members. The fact is, however, that uniform pricing has failed to take account of significant cost differentials in delivery. A study of the city of Fresno in 1954, for example, showed that the cost of retail delivery labor and trucking ranged from 10¢ per quart for one quart to only 2¢ for ten quarts of wholesale delivery from 4¢ per quart for ten quarts to less than 1¢ for over 300 quarts.[17]

These differentials have given rise to an important political controversy. The largest retail food chain in California is Safeway Stores; for many years Safeway has operated its own milk producing and distributing subsidiary, Lucerne, whose products are sold only in Safeway's supermarkets. Its delivery costs are only a fraction of home delivery. Another captive milk operation is run by Ralphs, an important Southern California retail chain. Under uniform pricing Safeway and Ralphs have enjoyed unusually high profits in their low-cost, high-volume operations. They have, nevertheless, vigorously sought differential pricing, presumably on the theory that they would thereby draw off a larger share of the home delivery market. The constitutionality

---

[16] D. A. Clarke, Jr., Special Report to the Joint Legislative Committee on Agriculture and Livestock Problems, *Fluid Milk Price Control in California*, California Senate, 1955, p. 27.

[17] *Ibid.*, pp. 156–57.

of the legislation and the procedures of the Department of Agriculture have both been challenged in the courts. Periodically Safeway and Ralphs have petitioned at hearings before the Bureau of Milk Control for permission to lower their prices, proposals which they have suitably advertised to their customers. The political combination of farmers, other dairies, delivery firms, and the union has thus far frustrated this endeavor. These forces, whatever other differences they may have, have worked closely together in Sacramento and in the courts.

Milk in California is an illustration of an industry in which control of the critical economic mechanism, price, is vested in the state rather than in private parties. As a result, the bulk of the employers and the Teamsters have joined forces against a common enemy in the interest of price parity and consequent employment stability. They have had a common stake in a friendly governor, legislature, director of agriculture, and Bureau of Milk Control.

4.

There are several industries in which the Teamsters operate which, though usually legal, either have a propensity to run afoul of the law or need political influence to maintain their lawful status. Prominent among them are coin machines (particularly juke boxes, pinballs, and slots), private rubbish disposal, horse racing, and liquor. Two such situations, coin machines in Portland and combustible rubbish in Los Angeles, have been the subjects of recent investigations and are instructive.

In 1954 in the city of Portland the pinball industry consisted of some twenty distributors servicing between 1,200 and 2,000 machines in taverns, drugstores, and other locations. The operators were associated in an organization called the Coin Machine Men of Oregon, Inc., one of whose major functions was the legalization of pinballs. The distributors employed about 150 men, some of whom were Teamster members. John Sweeney, the international organizer for Oregon, had made desultory efforts to unionize all the operators without success. On October 1, 1954, Sweeney became secretary of the Western Conference and was succeeded by Clyde Crosby, who decided to invigorate the pinball organizational drive.

This intention was complicated by uncertainty over the law. In 1951, the City Council had outlawed "coin in the slot operated devices." The distributors challenged this ordinance in the Circuit Court of Multnomah County, which held that the Council lacked authority to write the prohibition into the police code. The city appealed to the Oregon Supreme Court which some time later reversed. The distributors then appealed to the Supreme Court of the United States. In 1954, therefore, the status of pinballs was in doubt and the Portland police took this into account by permitting the machines to operate.

The distributors and the Teamsters, obviously, shared an economic interest in legalizing pinballs and they were politically active to this end. The issue appears to have played some and perhaps a major role in the unsavory contest for district attorney of Multnomah County in 1954.

According to pinball distributor "Big Jim" Elkins, the acknowledged overlord of Portland vice and the celebrated nightingale whose "singing" made him a star witness before the McClellan Committee, the candidacy of William M. Langley was the key. During the primary campaign in the spring, Sweeney, Elkins declared, proposed a joining of forces. When asked "why he was romancing a man in my business," Sweeney, in Elkins' words, is alleged to have said: "The Teamsters was a powerful organization, politically, and he understood I had put up quite a bit of money politically now and then and there wasn't any use to wasting it, that we could reach some kind of an agreement on it." [18] Elkins and Langley were pals, having run together a restaurant, bar, and gambling place, the China Lantern. After Langley won the Democratic nomination by default, Sweeney introduced Elkins to Crosby. The Teamsters, who had supported Republican McCourt in the primary, then broke with the rest of the labor movement and threw their support to Langley.

Langley's campaign, in fact, was run by Tom Maloney, an interloper from Spokane, who is the most shadowy figure in the affair. Maloney himself took the Fifth Amendment. He was allegedly a racketeer who wanted to move in on Portland gambling and other vice. His stock in trade was to pass himself off as an official of the Teamsters, which he was not, and as an influential friend of Brewster and Sweeney, which he may have been. It is certainly a fact that the Western Conference picked up his hotel and telephone bills. In any case, Maloney ran an effective campaign and elected Langley, which was what the Teamsters wanted.

Sweeney's story has never been told because he died before the hearings opened. As for Crosby, when asked, "What has your relationship been with Mr. Tom Maloney?" Crosby replied, "Unfortunate." [19] He admitted that the switch between the primary and the election was made without consultation with the membership. He explained it lamely

---

[18] McClellan Committee Hearings, pp. 81–82.
[19] *Ibid.*, p. 792.

as having been based upon the discovery that Elkins was behind McCourt, which was probably not true.

The events that followed Langley's election are clear enough. Elkins wanted protection for his gambling operations and that is precisely what he got from Langley. "Old Honest Abe" has since been convicted of neglect of duty.[20] Langley obviously owed a great debt to the Teamsters which was in no way diminished by the fact that after the election he took a family vacation in San Francisco at the expense of the Western Conference.

This was followed in March by Crosby's success in organizing the Portland pinball industry. The master contract between the Coin Machine Men and Local 223 provided, in addition to the labor clauses, that "Service to equipment on location shall be limited to installations . . . owned by recognized Union operators under contract to Local No. 223. . . . Employees shall service only equipment owned by their employer and shall not service location owned equipment."[21] The purpose was to use the union's power to prevent entry into the Portland pinball industry.

A test case arose almost immediately. One Clyde DeGraw, owner of Dekum Tavern, had a device known as a shuffleboard which was supplied by W. M. Goble, a member of the Portland association. In August 1955, DeGraw asked Goble to remove this machine from his premises. DeGraw had purchased a similar device from the American Shuffleboard Sales Co. of Seattle. The latter was installed by a Teamster from that city. Goble and an official of Local 223 then informed DeGraw that his device was "nonunion" and told him to get rid of it. DeGraw refused. Local 223 then set up a picket with the result that no beer was delivered to his tavern. DeGraw, however, filed suit in the federal district court, which held the picketing in violation of the Sherman Act and enjoinable.[22]

Much the same pattern emerges in the case of combustible rubbish in Los Angeles. For the outlander it is necessary to explain that this problem involves a now virtually departed landmark as distinctive to the City of the Angels as the Golden Gate Bridge is to San Francisco and the Statue of Liberty is to New York, namely, the backyard incinerator. Until recently the city has followed a policy of burn-your-own for combustible rubbish. Many citizens have done so in their

---

[20] *Portland Oregonian,* July 17, 1957, p. 1.

[21] The contract is reprinted in McClellan Committee Hearings, pp. 1074–76.

[22] The text of Judge East's decision is in McClellan Committee Hearings, pp. 843–46.

incinerators, and others out of laziness or obstinacy have preferred to engage the services of a private rubbish collector. Within the past few years the rubbish issue has become politically charged because of the view, by no means universally accepted, that incineration is a major cause of smog.

From an economic standpoint the rubbish industry has been a study in chaos. Anyone with a truck and a strong back could start a business and all too many did. Since rubbish collection is a natural monopoly, intense competition led to gross inefficiency and price wars. The industry cried out for an organizational genius of the order of John D. Rockefeller, and not one but two emerged: Louis Visco—rubbish collector, dump owner, and mogul of the San Fernando Valley Disposal Association as well as of the City Coordinating Council of six such associations—and Frank Matula, Jr., secretary of Local 396 of the International Brotherhood of Teamsters.[23]

The Visco-Matula syndicate was of classic simplicity. The city was zoned, with a collectors' association having jurisdiction over each district. The association then allocated exclusive control over local territory to its members within its zone. The cardinal sin was for a collector, member or not, to take a stop assigned to someone else. The bylaws of the State Rubbish Association, for example, declared that a member "shall not in any manner whatsoever encroach upon the territory of any member." A collector who lost a stop was required to notify the secretary, and the board of directors had power to impose a fine upon the one who took the stop. This particular association had an added means of enforcement: John Andikian. His title was "inspector" and he worked for the "State" Association, leaving the impression had he officially represented California. Further, Andikian traveled armed, or, as Moody Nesesoff, a recalcitrant collector, stated, "I think he goes to bed with that gun."[24] Local 396 organized both owner-operators and employees of collectors and dumps. Thereby Matula could enforce the rules of Visco's associations. By refusing to accept a collector as a member, he could deny him the dumps. A rubbish collector without a dump is in a bad way, or as Mayor Poulson put it, ". . . the dumps is the key to this situation."[25]

---

[23] The source of this material is the unpublished hearings conducted by Mayor Norris Poulson: Office of the Mayor, *Preliminary Investigation into the Matter of Rubbish Collection in Los Angeles*, June 20–28, 1955. Charles A. Cooney, public relations officer in the mayor's office, generously made the transcript available to me.

[24] *Ibid.*, p. 123.

[25] *Ibid.*, p. 131.

Let us take the case of W. C. Crowder, an independent collector who developed a route with 1,250 stops in the San Fernando Valley. Told to join Local 396, he saw Matula and paid a $25 initiation fee. Matula sent him to Visco to "get squared away with the association." Visco said he would have to pay a large fee to join and would have to give up half his stops. When Crowder refused, his truck was stopped at the dump. The union then tried him in effect for failure to obey Visco, dropped him from its rolls, and returned his $25. He then was barred from the dumps because he was not a union member.

The Visco-Matula syndicate needed political protection. Visco boasted that he controlled the California Legislature and could prevent any municipality from running its own rubbish disposal system. He also claimed that he could make or break the mayor of Los Angeles and had defeated a hostile supervisor. Visco employed a full-time public relations man, one Gellison, who was seen frequently around City Hall. Joe Fallon, an official in the city's Street Maintenance Department, which licensed trucks and dumps, was cooperative. Collectors who refused to fall in line had their trucks cited for failure to comply with regulations and were fined. When J. E. O'Connor, a waste paper converter, asked for a list of licensed collectors, Fallon told him that it was confidential. The following day an underling of Matula's appeared with the list and sold it to him. W. R. Ward, also a processor, was told by Fallon that the latter wanted a piece of his Admiral Mills. Fallon has since been discharged by the Board of Public Works.

As a consequence of the exposure of these conditions and the political pressure to do something about smog, the backyard incinerator has been banned. At the election of April 2, 1957, the voters of Los Angeles by referendum authorized a system of municipal collection of combustible rubbish and it is presently taking effect. Matula, who denied under oath that he formed a syndicate with Visco to control prices, eliminate competition, and police the combination, has been convicted of perjury and has been sentenced to six months in jail and fined $2,500.[26] No charges have been brought against Visco.

5.

In view of the growing national impact of California politics it is necessary to deal with the strange alliance that Republican Governor Knight has made with organized labor and especially with the Teamsters. California is a Republican state. Within the memory of

---

[26] *People v. Matula*, Superior Court of Los Angeles County, No. 181844.

man it has had only one Democratic governor and he lasted but one term. It is also a state with a powerful labor movement, whose biggest union by far is the Teamsters with 225,000 members. The membership is overwhelmingly Democratic. Brewster, for example, estimated that only one Teamster in five is a Republican. In the study referred to earlier of the two Los Angeles dairy locals I found that 76 percent of those who had made up their minds intended to vote Democratic in the 1956 president election.[27] The reasons for this preference are the obvious ones: Teamster members are drawn primarily from the ethnic strains that have identified themselves with the Democratic Party, are mainly manual workers, are largely at the lower end of the income scale, and are trade unionists.

The Republican Party in California has maintained its control at the state and local levels by espousing progressive programs. The party, while conservative in national politics, has been liberal within California. Norris Poulson, for example, voted as a right-wing Republican when he served in the House of Representatives. As the mayor of Los Angeles he has acted like a Socialist, vigorously supporting public ownership of both rubbish collection and urban transit. Former Governor Earl Warren, of course, had a deserved reputation as a liberal. His lieutenant governor, Knight, was known as a conservative because he played up to elements within the party for whom Warren did not speak. Knight's consuming ambition was to become governor. Eisenhower paved the way for him in 1953 by naming Warren Chief Justice. A major political task that Knight faced upon becoming governor was to clear the conservative stigma from his name in anticipation of the 1954 elections. The California State Federation of Labor and the Teamsters in particular were prepared to help him do so— for a price.[28]

The first public display of mutual admiration occurred at a huge labor-management Valentine Day banquet in February 1954, at the Ambassador Hotel in Los Angeles, celebrating the governor's twenty years of public service. This affair was staged largely by Raymond F.

---

[27] McClellan Committee Hearings, p. 1165; Bernstein, *op. cit.*, p. 6.

[28] In California, unlike the state of Washington, there is a close relationship between the State Federation and the Teamsters. A Teamster has been president of the Federation since 1946, the incumbent being Thomas L. Pitts of Los Angeles Wholesale Delivery Drivers No. 848. Among the vice-presidents are John T. Gardner of Los Angeles Municipal Truck Drivers No. 403, Jack Goldberger of San Francisco Newspaper Drivers No. 921, Howard Reed of Martinez Teamsters No. 315, and Harry Finks of Sacramento Cannery Workers No. 857.

Leheney. Leheney, now dead, was the public relations director of Teamsters Joint Council 42 and by some accounts Dave Beck's best friend.[29] Leheney gave Knight a fulsome introduction at the banquet, the theme of which was "A Sweetheart of a Guy." No one could accuse Leheney of being niggardly. Bob Hope was toastmaster, and the floor show included Dan Dailey, Peggy Lee, and Gordon MacRae. The climax was reached when a brigade of waiters carried in a mass of ice two feet high spelling out, "OUR GOVERNOR GOODY KNIGHT."[30]

Knight was not slow in responding. In March 1954, he called a special session of the California Legislature which enacted his proposal to raise unemployment compensation benefits by $5 a week. He easily won the Republican nomination for governor in the June primaries and, for whatever it was worth, had Teamster support.[31]

The question facing labor then was whether to endorse Knight or his Democratic rival, Richard Graves. The matter came to a head at the meeting of the AFL Labor League for Political Education in late August in Santa Barbara, held coincidentally with the convention of the California Federation of Labor. For the AFL unions and especially the Teamsters there were two key issues: right-to-work and hot cargo. In his address to the convention Knight gave them the specific assurances they wanted:

> As long as I am your Governor, I shall never approve a law designed to punish labor, or to discriminate against labor. . . . I mean among others, such legislation as the so-called "Right-to-Work Bill" and the so-called "Hot Cargo" or "Secondary-Boycott Bill." I have said this before and I repeat it here and now, I will oppose such legislation, and if either one of them is approved by the legislature, I will veto it.[32]

This statement won the governor the endorsement of LLPE and the Teamsters as well as a denunciatory front page editorial in the *Los Angeles Times*, whose darling he had previously been. With this coup

---

[29] So distressed, in fact, was Beck with Leheney's demise in 1956 that he established in behalf of the widow the Raymond F. Leheney Memorial Fund. "I personally will act as the director," Beck declared. He certainly did. According to a Seattle mortgage broker named Hedlung, he and Beck cleared a neat profit of $11,585 by using the fund in a mortgage deal. *Southern California Teamster*, March 28, 1956, p. 1; *New York Times*, May 11, 1957, p. 1.

[30] *Southern California Teamster*, Feb. 17, 1954, p. 1.

[31] *Southern California Teamster*, May 12, 1954, p. 3; *Northern California Teamster*, July 1954, p. 7.

[32] California State Federation of Labor, *Proceedings and Officers Reports*, 52d Convention, Santa Barbara, Aug. 23–27, 1954, p. 139.

Knight established himself as a "liberal" and his election became a fore-gone conclusion. . . .

6.

What, one may inquire, is the significance of this series of incidents that I have chosen to describe? Are they merely disparate events with no interrelationship or do they suggest generalizations about the political behavior of the union and the truckers? It seems to me that they do have a significant connection.

The Teamsters and the employers with whom they deal engage in a politics of fear. With this language I do not wish to be histrionic. Much if not most of political activity stems from fear. It was, for example, the cement that bound together that loose political movement whose spokesman was the late Senator Joseph R. McCarthy. But here the anxiety was of a public rather than a private nature. Except for a tiny neurotic minority, McCarthy's followers were not apprehensive that secret agents with long beards and sinister eyes would plant bombs in their cellars. Their concern, rather, was with a real or imagined challenge to the social structure and political system to which they were devoted.

For the Teamsters and the truckers, on the other hand, the fear is wholly private. Neither this *business* union nor these *business*men are concerned with public issues in the larger sense. As Neil Curry, chairman of the board of the American Trucking Associations told the Western Conference in 1956: "We should apply one test to every candidate for public office regardless of party. How does he stand on trucking?"[33] The union is apprehensive that anti-union employers and farmers will jam right-to-work laws down its throat, thereby illegalizing the machinery for preserving much of its membership. The Teamsters and the over-the-road truckers are fearful that the railroads will gain a competitive advantage in freight haulage. Taxi drivers are anxious that municipalities may cut the available traffic too many ways by licensing an excessive number of cabs. Milk distributors and drivers in California are worried that supermarkets with low unit costs will take their customers away. Coin machine operators and service men in Portland were afraid that the City Council would outlaw their industry and that outside competition would take away their business. Rubbish collectors and their employees in Los Angeles were disturbed about rival owner-operators and were fearful of the catastrophe of municipal operation.

---

[33] Cited in *Southern California Teamster*, July 4, 1956, p. 1.

A private politics of fear, such as I have been describing, arises mainly from the threat of competition. In many of these industries the levels of employment, wages, and profits depend upon a managed market. Interindustry or intraindustry competition upsets its stability. Where a market may be controlled by economic action alone, the union and the cooperating employers join to do so. But, as I have pointed out, a disproportionate share of Teamster industries is subject to regulation. Hence the parties are forced into politics in order to exert influence over the mechanism of the state in lessening competition.

With the exception of interstate haulage, the arenas of union and trucker political activity are the state and the locality. Employers and union alike are more concerned with who becomes governor, assemblyman, or director of agriculture or who becomes mayor, city councilman, or chief of police than with who becomes president or senator. "I tried to build up a friendly relationship with those people [the police]," Clyde Crosby told the McClellan Committee, "because we represent drivers, and they occasionally have problems. If we can get one of them out of jail and get him back to work, we certainly wouldn't be above trying to do it."[34] Private fears are more comfortably expressed at the state and local levels than at the national level.

This makes it less difficult for the Teamsters to justify an opportunistic political policy to its membership. A milk wagon driver, for example, may be a loyal Democrat who would resent the union's endorsement of a Republican for president. But this driver would certainly understand and might even vote for a Teamster-endorsed Republican for governor who was for uniform milk pricing.

The union, at least in the West, makes little or no effort to deliver the vote of its members. This is because the line of communication between leadership and membership on political issues is tenuous and because the hierarchy realistically recognizes that it could not do so even if it tried. What the union does deliver is money, a commodity of which the Teamsters suffer no visible shortage. When Brewster was asked whether it was right for a few leaders to spend large sums on politics without an accounting to the membership, he replied: "Well, I believe that those things are done in other businesses."[35] To a candidate Teamsters' backing means that his campaign bills will be paid; it may or may not mean that the members will vote for him.

But political behavior expressed in monetary form is self-corrupting. I am old-fashioned enough to believe that voting is in large part

---

[34] McClellan Committee Hearings, p. 827.
[35] Ibid., p. 1147.

a moral act, that the citizen in a democracy should cast his ballot for the person and the principle he believes is right. Hence I return to the unresolved political dilemma of the Teamsters posed at the outset of this paper: to elect the winners or to serve the welfare of labor. These purposes, though they sometimes coincide, are frequently in conflict. A labor union, I believe, is more than a business; it must have some conception of the good society and the part workers take within it. A politics based upon private fears and expressed in dollars is a politics of cynical opportunism. It may pay a short-term dividend, but it can hardly serve even a rich and powerful union as a long-run policy.

Comments on Bernstein's Paper on the Teamsters Union

Paul Jacobs
University of California, Berkeley

ALTHOUGH ON THE WHOLE, I agree with the emphasis in Bernstein's paper, I do have a few minor disagreements with him and one major question I should like to raise concerning his conclusions.

Bernstein is correct in making his assessment of the Teamsters as a product of "local-market oriented" forces, but I think the future look of the union may be something quite different. The shift from highly autonomous locals operating under well-defined area duchies, ruled by vice-presidents, to the present more centralized conferences is associated by a much greater degree of international control.

This shift will take place both because the hitherto fragmented trucking industry is beginning to coalesce and because the union itself represents a powerful force towards driving the smaller and weaker employers out of business, both in trucking and in some of the other jurisdictions encompassed by the Teamsters. In this sense, the union is an important element in establishing the future economic nature of the industries with which it deals.

I think Bernstein omitted one key element in his discussion of the political role played by the Teamsters in assisting marginal industries like pinballs, slot machines, and juke boxes to achieve legality

Reprinted from *Tenth Annual Proceedings* [1957], Industrial Relations Research Association, by permission of the Association and the author.

and respectability. The interest of the union in these industries is not
limited to only getting their employees organized and then keeping
them working. Indeed, this may be a minor aspect of the union's
interest.

In Portland, Oregon, where the union, in cooperation with the
operators' association, had a large stake in the political campaign to
legalize pinballs, there were less than a hundred union members employed by the association. Similarly, in other cities, like Detroit, where
dues in the local covering these workers are $30.00 monthly, the union's
interest in these industries seems to have in it strong elements of underworld connections. Juke boxes, pinball machines, and coin-operated
amusement devices have always been prizes over whose control bitter
underworld battles have been fought. In fact, one explanation advanced
for Hoffa's obviously successful relationship to underworld elements
is that he once successfully played the role of arbitrator in the struggle
being waged between the Italian and Jewish underworlds over control
of juke boxes and pinballs in the midwest.

It may very well also be true that some Teamster leaders have
had a personal, financial interest in these marginal industries. At one
point in the Portland fight over pinballs, a City Councilman was reportedly offered a "piece" of a pinball operation by a Teamster representative in exchange for a favorable vote. It is entirely possible that
such considerations are a factor in some of the political decisions made
by the Teamster union leaders.

On the general problem of Teamster political action, Bernstein
states that the Teamster union "does not know whether it possesses the
sovereign right to act with independence or whether it is constrained
by the rules and mores of the labor movement. Nor does it know
whether its political policy should be to elect the winners and defeat
the losers or to serve the welfare of labor regardless of short-term Teamster interests."

I think that the dilemma posed by Bernstein is more fancied
than real and is by no means restricted to the Teamsters. The self-
conscious political policies of the Teamsters, like that of most unions,
are almost always directed towards protection of their own economic
interests. If those interests, either short or long term, conflict with those
of the remainder of the labor movement, the Teamsters will resolve
the conflict in their own favor, as do most unions. Cooperation with
the rest of the labor movement, as in the cases cited by Bernstein, is
always possible but usually only takes place when the issues are those
in which either the Teamsters have the same economic stake and where
there is no conflict with the Teamsters' own interest, or where the

union's relations with the community or the labor movement demand a purely formal demonstration of support, never intended to be carried out, in fact.

One of the instances cited by Bernstein as representative of the dilemma is an excellent example of formal statements without real meaning. Bernstein states that according to the Teamster legislative representative's report on his activities the union supported, unsuccessfully, an FEPC bill in California. Nothing could be further from the truth. One or two union officials lent their names to the committee sponsoring the bill, but the union itself did not even formally endorse it nor did the legislative representative really work for its passage.

Bernstein himself resolves this only apparent dilemma when he states that "the political policies of the Teamsters are a function of their collective bargaining objectives." If this is true, and I would agree, then there is no dilemma for the Teamsters. There may be a public relations problem not shared by other unions whose economic position makes it possible for them to take *pro forma* principled positions on policy questions, but there is no dilemma. If the collective bargaining objectives of the Teamsters require political action, that action is carried out, perhaps regretfully, if there is a conflict with other unions, but, nevertheless, firmly.

But how else should the Teamsters be expected to behave in the context of modern American society? Do we not demand of a union that it carry out its "collective bargaining objectives" and isn't the efficiency with which it does this one of the standards by which the union is assessed? Bernstein believes that "politics based upon private fears and expressed in dollars is a politics of cynical opportunism" and that a labor union "is more than a business." But Bernstein's concept of the labor movement is not shared, realistically, by many elements in either the unions themselves, the business community, or the society as a whole, no matter what facade to the contrary is erected.

When Bernstein asks for a labor movement with "some conception of the good society and the part workers take within it," he is asking for a labor movement with a social ideology embodying such a set of beliefs. In the United States, the only operative ideology of the labor movement is its commitment to the business enterprise system; a system in which interest groups almost always represent their own policy exclusively, sometimes in conflict with other groups and sometimes by accommodation. The labor movement, too, has been constructed in this model and its politics, like that of the system itself, are normally those reflecting immediate economic necessity.

Bernstein's dream of a political labor movement might represent a nightmare to those groups in industrial society who value labor-management peace far more than principled political conflict, bringing with it industrial strife and disruption of the productive establishment. If we are to have an ideological movement in the United States, we must be prepared to accept the possible consequences—industrial conflict. The present labor movement, as embodied in an extreme form by the Teamsters, may be something of a monster, but, if so, the society as a whole has been a well-satisfied Dr. Frankenstein.

The Reelection of Senator Taft
Samuel Lubell

ELECTION DAY OF 1950 brought Gregory Stebbins a warm, satisfied feeling. An organizer for the steelworkers, Stebbins led the anti-Taft offensive in the Seventeenth Ward of Columbus. With seventy helpers he canvassed every house in the word, stuffing mailboxes with leaflets and exhorting people not to miss voting in "the political battle of the century." When crowded polling booths indicated a record turnout, Stebbins glowed. Going to bed before the ward returns were available, he felt serenely confident that the Seventeenth had turned in its usual heavy Democratic majority.

Because Stebbins left town early the next morning, it was several days before he could check the ward results. He was astounded. Probably three fourths of Ward Seventeen's families are union members, mainly railroaders and steelworkers. Not many of their frame houses would bring more than $10,000 even in today's inflated markets. Yet, a sizable majority voted for "labor's worst enemy," as Taft had been tarred.

Bewildered, Stebbins called in his union stewards, but none could explain what had happened. Three weeks later when I saw him in the course of doing a postelection analysis of the Taft vote, Stebbins confessed, "I still can't understand it. We thought we needed only to get out the vote. Well, the vote came out but it went against us."

A good part of Taft's 430,000 majority can rightly be credited to his opponent, Joseph Ferguson, the state auditor. Shortly after "Jumping Joe" won the Democratic primary a canny Ohioan observed,

Excerpted by permission of the publisher from *The Future of American Politics* by Samuel Lubell, copyright Harper and Row, 1951, 1952.

"If the Democrats want to win, they should send Ferguson on a mission abroad." Ferguson's habit of slipping on grammatical banana peels repelled many voters. Others whom I interviewed couldn't recall his name. Even those kindly disposed felt that "Joe is a nice guy and okay for state auditor, but I wouldn't want him in Washington with war threatening."

But if Ferguson's dismal showing confirms the adage, "You can't beat somebody with nobody," the real significance of the election was that it proved to be a dramatic referendum on what Ohio voters thought of labor unions. Taft had been singled out as the prime target for what was intended as a mighty demonstration of labor's political power. It turned out to be a shattering demonstration of labor's political weaknesses.

Those weaknesses might be summed up:

1. On overly militant labor campaign provokes so much fear and opposition that it promotes an antilabor coalition.
2. Labor and the Democratic party are still uneasy, mutually suspicious allies.
3. Labor is unable to deliver its membership except in the direction toward which that membership is inclined—as for example, in voting for Roosevelt.
4. Even among union members there is a deep distrust of labor's becoming too big politically.

"We didn't want labor to go too far" and "we didn't want labor running the country" were the most frequent reasons given me by voters in explaining their support of Taft. This feeling was expressed both by farmers, never overly sympathetic to labor, and by persons who believed in unions. "I used to work in a department store for $3.50 a week," a barber's wife told me. "When I think what stores pay now how I wish we had had unions when I was working. But labor shouldn't have too much power. We have only a little shop here. The union made us raise the price of haircuts to a dollar and a quarter and business fell off. We have to close at six on Saturday nights. We're poor people. It would mean so much if we could open an hour longer."

In three counties I visited it was commonly bruited about that the local Democratic chairman had voted for Taft—which, even if untrue, shows how intense was the friction between labor and the regular Democratic organizations. Many old-line Democrats took their cue from Governor Frank Lausche. With an eye to 1952, Lausche refused to endorse Ferguson and almost openly supported Taft. In some localities there were bitter quarrels between labor leaders and the regular party heads. In many places labor virtually took over the campaign. Whether this was because the unions had the campaign funds, or because the regular Democratic politicians were laying down on the job, the effect was the same. The more labor pushed to the forefront the more resentful became other Democratic elements.

A farmer in Holmes County explained how his neighbors felt, "If Ferguson won, labor would have taken all the credit and farmers wouldn't be represented."

The operator of a supermarket in Columbus Grove, a registered Democrat, observed, "I felt we had to vote for Taft to keep the Socialists from taking over the Democratic party."

At no time was there a real meeting of minds between labor leaders and the Democratic regulars. Unable to agree on a mutually acceptable candidate, they left the choice to a wide-open primary in which Ferguson won over five other contestants. Both the unions and the regular Democratic organizations felt let down. Thereafter no unified strategy guided the anti-Taft forces.

Not only was much of the normal Democratic vote alienated, along with the bulk of farmers and nearly all of the urban middle class; the unions could not deliver their own membership. An Akron beer-trucker, who voted for Ferguson, startled me by remarking: "Don't get the idea I'm too disappointed that Taft won." This trucker had been denouncing Taft as a "rich man." He said, "I've never had any use for rich men since the depression when I drove a big car for a millionaire at fifty cents an hour." He went on to explain, "Ferguson would have been a yes man for the labor party. I don't want a labor government here, like in England."

Many workers seized upon Taft's candidacy to voice a protest against their own union chiefs. In Toledo the rank-and-file hatred—the word is used advisedly—of Richard Gosser, the local auto-union boss, spilled over so violently that Thomas H. Burke, a CIO member of Congress, was defeated for reelection. An auto worker, a Navy veteran, explained, "He was Gosser's Congressman, not ours."

In a Youngstown dairy an employee was laid off. A delegation of fellow workers asked the union for help in reinstating the man. They were told, "Forget it. Our first job is to beat Bob Taft."

"Right there," two dairy workers told me, "we decided to vote for Taft."

In Cincinnati a cutter—he belonged to the Amalgamated Clothing Workers, the home union of PAC-head Jack Kroll—complained, "Sure we elect our union officers by secret ballot, but there's only one slate to vote on. That's like Russia." In 1948 this cutter opposed the

Taft-Hartley Law. "I'm for it now," he said. "There have been fewer strikes. When other workers strike, business drops and we get laid off."

A machinist who belonged to a company union liked the Taft-Hartley ban on the closed shop. "It means if I quit my job I can go to work elsewhere," he said. A drop-forger in Toledo, remarked, "Under the Wagner Act the union bosses had the upper hand. If you said something they didn't like, they could kick you out. Now you are protected."

One union head confessed, "We couldn't convince the workers Taft-Hartley is a 'slave labor law.' They've been living with it for three years and nothing bad has happened to them."

Part way through the campaign, the labor chieftains tried to soft-pedal Taft-Hartley as an issue. But Taft kept hammering at it. Carrying the fight directly to the workers, he visited more than 300 plants. Efforts to turn these visits into anti-Taft demonstrations backfired repeatedly. In one factory, on the day Taft was scheduled to speak, a union official appeared and stuck a Ferguson button on every worker's overalls. I found that probably half of that plant's workers voted for Taft. When Taft came to Campbell Sheet and Tube in Youngstown, the local CIO chief ordered a walkout of the power unit. Before operations were resumed several thousand men had lost almost a full day's pay.

Their anger was written, hot and loud, into the vote of four precincts adjoining the mill, whose residents are mainly millworkers. Truman got 56 percent of their vote in 1948. Taft got 63 percent in 1950.

It wasn't difficult to find workers in these precincts who had voted for Truman two years ago and had swung to Taft. Their reasoning was summed up fairly well by one white-haired mill hand. "I didn't like the CIO shutting the mill," he told me as he stood by his open door. "And I don't like the war. We oughtn't to be fighting in a place like Korea, so far from home, losing all those boys and not on the real enemy. I've been a Democrat, but I'm ready to vote Republican. We need to clean house in Washington. There must be some Communists in the Government or the newspapers wouldn't be printing all those charges."

Until recently, this millworker had been planning to retire. "With all this inflation," he complained, "I don't know what my pension will be worth a few years from now."

Down the street, Richard Bates, Jr., a gunner in the last war, got out the orders calling up his reserve unit. Quite philosophic about going back into the service—"by getting in now, I figure I'll get out earlier"—Bates did not blame Truman for the Korean War. A Truman voter in 1948 he voted for Taft because "I didn't like that kid stuff the union pulled, like shutting the mill. Then they beat up Skinny Green-wood next door for campaigning for Taft."

President Truman, along with some labor leaders, has tried to attribute Taft's victory to the enormous sums spent in his behalf. The impression left with me was that each side had all the money it needed and that if labor had had more money it might have suffered a worse defeat. The plain fact was that the campaign put on by labor divided its own membership while solidifying the opposition.

In Cleveland, the CIO alone marshaled a force of 800 election workers, the largest number it ever has had in a single city. Taft got more votes in Cleveland than in either his 1944 or 1948 campaigns, and came fairly close to carrying the city.

The essence of Taft's whole strategy was to gamble on being reelected by labor. The Taft forces drummed insistently on the theme of "outside political carpet-baggers" coming into Ohio with "unlimited funds" to "tell Ohioans how to vote." They reprinted and circulated the more abusive attacks on Taft made by labor leaders. One, which became a virtual Republican battle slogan, was the boast of James Petrillo, the head of the musicians union, "There will be nothing we won't do to knock your [Taft's] silly head out of the U.S. Senate and keep it out."

The political weaknesses of labor which were demonstrated in the Taft campaign have cropped up in other elections in which labor has been the prime issue. Akron, for example, once an open-shop citadel, became strongly prolabor during the depression. When the rubber workers struck in 1936 the newspapers were benevolently neutral; local merchants donated $25,000 of foodstuffs. That November, seven of every ten Akronites voted for Roosevelt. The next year, though, when the CIO tried to elect its man mayor, he got only 44 percent of the vote. The Republicans bettered their vote over 1936 in every ward, indicating that the whole city, including many union members, shared the fear of labor going too far politically.

Organized Labor in the Political Process: A Case Study of the Right-to-Work Campaign in Ohio

Glenn W. Miller, *Ohio State University*
Stephen B. Ware, *Ohio Wesleyan University*

Introduction

OHIO IN 1958 furnished an excellent opportunity to study labor in the political process. At that time an effort was made to put an anti-union-security, or right-to-work, provision into the State Constitution by an initiative vote in the general election. The issue was a clear-cut one on which there was only one position for the great bulk of organized labor in the State,[1] and it received the primary attention of organized labor and many other groups. Before long, it became the major political issue on the state-wide ballot.

The attempt to prohibit the union shop by initiative was encouraged by conditions both within and outside the State. Spurred to a considerable extent by Section 14-B of the Taft-Hartley Act, eighteen states had already adopted such measures by 1958. A wide-scale effort was made in that year to extend the coverage of these laws by placing the issue on the ballot in six other states.[2] This activity heartened proponents in Ohio who had failed in six previous attempts to have the Ohio Legislature pass a right-to-work law. (Right-to-work bills had been introduced in every regular session of the legislature since World War II, but never had been reported out of committee.) However, a right-to-work law was enacted in Indiana in 1957,[3] marking the first extension of the laws into a northern industrial state. This, plus

---

Reprinted from *Labor History*, Vol. 4, No. 1 (Winter 1963) by permission of the authors and the publisher. Additional analysis of voting behavior in the Ohio right-to-work election may be found in the selection by Donald Stokes in Chapter 11.

[1] No union officially favored the proposal. Some individual union members, largely from the railroad brotherhoods supported the proposal openly. However, the number was infinitesimal when compared to the total labor movement in Ohio. The organization through which this support was expressed was "The Ohio Labor Committee for Right To Work, Inc.," chartered September 12, 1957.

[2] Ohio, California, Colorado, Kansas, Washington, and Idaho.

[3] For a discussion of the events related to enactment of the Indiana Law see: Fred Witney, "The Indiana Right-to-Work Law," *Industrial and Labor Relations Review*, Vol. 11, No. 4, July 1958. [The Indiana right-to-work law was repealed in 1965, after labor helped elect a Democratic Governor and Democratic majorities in both Houses of the Indiana legislature.—Eds.]

the tendency of Indiana and Ohio to move along similar political paths, suggested that Ohio might be ripe for such an effort.

Proponents of right-to-work in Ohio were encouraged by still another fact. Although the position of unions on candidates or issues might prove significant in the northern part of the State, organized labor in Ohio never had shown itself to be a powerful political force on a state-wide level. For example, Senator Robert Taft, whose name was attached to legislation which in the eyes of organized labor was the most objectionable federal measure in many years, won reelection handily in 1950. Union efforts to develop any significant opposition proved insufficient. This failure, among others, caused many to question the strength of organized labor in Ohio politics.

More recent and probably much more significant, was Ohio's experience in 1955. In that year organized labor, primarily the state CIO, sought to use the initiative process to obtain a major increase in unemployment compensation benefits, as well as to allow concurrent payment of supplemental unemployment benefits and unemployment compensation. Its effort was made after the state legislators had failed to enact such a law. The proposal was opposed by the state Chamber of Commerce and, in addition, was given less than wholehearted support by organized labor outside the CIO. The result was a nearly two-to-one defeat for labor. This convinced officers of the Ohio Chamber of Commerce that union labor in Ohio was not to be feared greatly at the polls. The executive vice-president of the state Chamber spoke at the 44th annual meeting of the Chamber of Commerce of the United States, outlining the program which he felt accounted for the easy victory in 1955.[4] In essence, the report asserted that a wedge could be driven between the members and the leaders of unions and between various groups of unions, as was the case in 1955 with the AFL and CIO. It was further reported that farmers and other "conservative" groups could be mobilized in opposition to the unions' political aims.

The deep-seated difference between the attitudes of business and of organized labor toward union security clauses is commonplace, and the Ohio situation ran true to form. This conflict, along with the defeat of organized labor's bid for a new unemployment compensation measure in 1955, fostered the 1958 struggle. Before the right-to-work effort, the Ohio Chamber of Commerce, in 1957, conducted a survey of its members' attitudes toward "compulsory unionism," expenditure of union funds for political purposes, and the probable result of a vote

---

[4] Reported in *U.S. News and World Report*, May 11, 1956.

in Ohio if a right-to-work proposal were placed on the ballot. Chamber members were asked: "Should Ohio law prohibit compulsory union membership resulting from union security provisions in collective bargaining contracts?" Ninety-six percent of the respondents answered in the affirmative. They were also asked: "If a state-wide referendum were to be held, do you believe that a majority of the Ohio electorate would cast their votes to forbid compulsory union membership?" Here again the opinion was clear cut; more than 76 percent thought that Ohio voters would support a right-to-work measure. Our analysis suggests that the Ohio Chamber made significant errors in its evaluation. For the fact was that, in 1958, the Ohio union movement was more unified and politically knowledgeable than in 1955.

Groups in the Campaign

In the latter part of November 1957—slightly more than a month after the Ohio Chamber of Commerce had decided to support a right-to-work proposal at its annual membership meeting—the "Ohioans for Right-to-Work" filed incorporation papers with the Secretary of State. It was, to say the least, an ill-kept secret that there was close contact between Ohioans for Right-to-Work and the officers of the Ohio Chamber of Commerce.

After incorporation, in early January 1958, a committee representing Ohioans for Right-to-Work filed with the Secretary of State a proposed amendment to the Ohio Constitution in the form of a section to be added to Article I. The proposed amendment read as follows:

> No employer or labor organization shall deny or abridge the right-to-work by requiring membership or non-membership in, or payment or non-payment of money to, a labor organization as a condition of employment or continued employment in this state. All agreements in conflict with this section are to the extent of such conflict, unlawful and of no effect in this state.[5]

If the proposed amendment were adopted, the schedule provided that agreements in existence at the time the amendment took effect would escape its prohibitions for a period not to exceed two years.

Having filed the proposed amendment, it was necessary for the advocates to secure the signatures of some 355,000 qualified voters in order to have the proposal placed on the ballot for November's general

---

[5] Taken from the official publicity pamphlet mailed to electors by the Secretary of State in September 1958.

election. The Ohioans for Right-to-Work began the task of obtaining the signatures, and in early February opened an office in Columbus.

Organized labor in Ohio responded by forming the United Organized Labor of Ohio (UOLO). Its steering committee included representatives of the AFL, CIO, Railroad Brotherhoods, and United Mine Workers; and in late March it, too, opened an office in Columbus. (The separate terms "AFL" and "CIO" are used advisedly, since the merger convention in Ohio was not held until the late spring of 1958.) In the initial days of the campaign, the leaders of the AFL and CIO could not give their undivided attention to the right-to-work fight, so the steering committee of UOLO selected a dedicated unionist and professional journalist as its director. Moreover, organized labor in Ohio took an unusual step: it retained public relations and advertising firms to plan and prepare materials to be used in the campaign. All in all, policy-making in UOLO appeared strongly centralized and relatively untouched by dissension. And, in addition to UOLO, many counties and large metropolitan areas formed similar joint committees to work at the local level. Even where joint committees were not formed, individual locals often contributed heavily to the campaign, both in money and in man-hours.

The work of these groups was directed primarily toward solidifying labor against the right-to-work issue. But it was also necessary to gain the support of groups outside labor's ranks. The votes of farmers, professional people, and housewives, along with religious and racial groups, were considered important by organized labor, as they were by the proponents of the amendment. Both sides sought the support of organizations that had some hold on the allegiance of these blocs of voters. As it turned out, organized labor fared much better in this venture than did proponents of the amendment.

The farmers remained basically uncommitted. The Ohio Farm Bureau Federation, for example, took no official stand; but this in itself was a victory for organized labor, considering the relatively conservative political tendencies of the farm block. (One Farm Bureau vice-president even came out in opposition to right-to-work late in the campaign.) Several fraternal and veterans groups also expressed hostility. The housewives' attitude necessarily remained an unknown quantity, but the Women's Activities Division of the AFL–CIO expended great energies. Almost without exception, organized religious groups officially opposed right-to-work. The six Catholic bishops of Ohio issued a joint statement to this effect, and many Protestant church councils and conferences did the same. Some religious leaders did in fact support the amendment, though they were comparatively few. And to the already long list of opponents of right-to-work, the nation's most active racial organization, the NAACP, officially added its name.

Against this imposing list was arrayed the Ohio Chamber of Commerce, a few city Chambers of Commerce (none of the State's major city Chambers of Commerce contributed funds to the proponents' State Committee), the Ohio Manufacturers' Association and a small number of individual industrial associations. With only a few exceptions, the large companies in Ohio refrained from taking a public stand. (Although the Timken Roller Bearing Company was outspoken in its support of the amendment, the few other large companies which evidently "participated" avoided as much as possible the glare of publicity.)

The preceding comments apply to particular "interest" groups, but there was also an attempt made to enlist "general" opposition to the proposed amendment by means of a broadly based nonlabor organization. Such an organization, "Citizens to Defeat State Issue No. 2," was formed at the state level late in the campaign, and a few local groups were initiated even later, primarily by the state labor movement. Organized labor had hoped that a group of this kind would be formed earlier in the campaign, but had not been successful in getting suitable nonlabor people to implement the idea. . . .

The Campaign

Taken as a whole, the campaign was bitter and vindictive with charges and counter-charges being the order of the day.[6] Both opponents and proponents of the amendment frequently resorted to highly emotional appeals; and dispassionate, factual presentations were exceptional. . . .

As mentioned earlier, in order to place the issue before the voters, supporters of the proposal had to file petitions with the Ohio Secretary of State signed by some 355,000 voters asking that the suggested amendment be placed on the ballot.[7] Formation of Ohioans for Right-to-Work already has been noted. It became the task of this organization and its successor to direct the drive for signatures and the subsequent campaign for favorable votes.

The campaign for signatures was in fact successful. At first there were instances of boycotts or other forms of reprisals (attributed

---

[6] Much of the material on which this summary of the campaign is based comes from the daily papers in Ohio, notably those in Columbus. In most instances individual issues of the newspapers are not cited.

[7] The requirement is signatures equal to 10 percent of the votes for governor in the last preceding election for that office. Signers had to be drawn from at least one-half the counties in the State.

to organized labor) against persons whose names appeared on the petitions. These actions were well publicized and drew considerable criticism; perhaps as a result such retaliatory tactics were "played down" and largely discontinued. In any event, by early August the Ohioans for Right-to-Work was able to file petitions with roughly 465,000 signatures. The organization's executive director estimated that roughly a quarter of a million dollars was expended on this phase of the campaign.

Meanwhile, organized labor had not been marking time. The UOLO was formed and specialists in public relations were employed; also, the merger of the state central labor bodies had taken place in May. The frictions that came into the open and were publicized at the time of the merger probably were resolved sufficiently by the time that the campaign reached peak intensity to allow organized labor to function more effectively than would have been the case had the merger not occurred. In the meantime, a search was being made for help from influential organizations and individuals, and considerable support was brought into the open.

City councils in some two dozen industrial areas, including such populous ones as Akron, Cleveland, and Youngstown, made their opposition known; so, too, did such people as former President Truman and Mrs. Eleanor Roosevelt. Thus an imposing array of well-known institutions and individuals came out in opposition to right-to-work in Ohio, but it was not clear then—nor is it clear now—just how much this opposition influenced the votes cast.

The major candidates for political office and the political organizations in the state became involved in the issue. Positions taken in the party platforms differed sharply. The Democratic platform favored "permitting labor and management to retain the freedom of providing . . . union security provisions according to contracts arrived at by collective bargaining. We urge the people to vote no on Constitutional Amendment Issue No. Two. . . ."[8] The Republican Party, on the other hand, said of the amendment: "It is not an issue to be decided on partisan political grounds. Support of this issue as well as opposition to it exists among the members of both political parties. We urge all citizens to inform themselves of the provision of this proposed amendment and to vote in accordance with their conviction."[9]

At the outset of the campaign most of the major candidates of both parties sought to avoid the right-to-work issue as much as possi-

[8] Article No. 15 of the 1958 Platform of the Ohio Democratic Party.
[9] "Ohio Republican Platform, 1958," p. 9.

ble. However, sufficient pressure was applied by some Ohio business interests to influence incumbent Governor C. William O'Neill, firmly to endorse right-to-work, making it one of the major issues of his campaign. O'Neill's move was made over the strong objection of then Senator John Bricker, also a candidate for reelection as well as the State Republican Party Chairman.[10]

After the Governor's action, some candidates either took a position for the first time or stated a stronger one than they held before he made right-to-work a central issue. Those Republican candidates who took a stand usually backed the proposal; Democrats, on the other hand, opposed it. But many candidates in both parties were reluctant to make right-to-work a major point of debate. And in the end it is not likely that the position of the parties significantly affected the final vote on this issue.

The organization, "Citizens to Defeat State Issue No. 2," which has been briefly noted, evolved from conversations between university teaching personnel and officials of the state AFL–CIO. Essentially, the thought behind this organization was that a group carrying the name "citizen," rather than "union," would be more acceptable to those voters who were not favorably disposed toward organized labor. Yet the president and executive secretary of the "Citizens" evidently arranged a close tie with labor without the knowledge of other members, and contrary to the stated intentions of many of them. Thus the greatest part of the radio, television, and newspaper advertising, arranged by the two top officers of the executive committee, was essentially a "labor front" effort. Many committee members, on the other hand, filled speaking engagements, circulated letters to professional people and participated in local citizens' groups, generally unaware of the "Citizens" connection with organized labor.

Ohioans for Right-to-Work, after petitions were filed and the issue was on the ballot, was involved in much the same activities as UOLO and its supporters. Many brochures aimed at various economic groups were printed, speakers were provided for all manner of meetings and debates, and materials for newspaper, radio and television appeals were prepared. One major asset of the proponents of right-to-work was the support they received from the majority of Ohio's newspapers. This, of course, constituted sizeable backing that does not show in any of the reports of expenditures. . . .

----

[10] Reported by Joseph Alsop in the Cincinnati *Enquirer*, November 10, 1958. The general accuracy of Mr. Alsop's report has been confirmed in private conversations.

The obvious campaign strategy of both supporters and opponents of the amendment was to ensure the registration and voting of those endorsing their viewpoint, and the "education" of undecided voters. While neither faction admitted it, presumably each accepted the fact that a quarter to a third of the voters were beyond the reach of their efforts.

Organized labor in Ohio probably did the best job it ever had done of registering its members and their families. Strictly comparable figures are not available for pre-1958 elections, but it seems clear that the effort made resulted in a larger number and proportion of workers registered to vote than in any previous state election. This result was the product of much volunteer work by trade unionists and their wives, fearful lest unions be severely damaged or destroyed if the proposed amendment were adopted. Volunteer work by women, directed through the Women's Activities Division of the state AFL–CIO, was reported in excess of 120,000 hours; over 300 women each gave more than 100 hours to the campaign.[11] This work centered on checking registrations, addressing and stuffing envelopes, telephoning prospective voters, distributing literature at homes, shopping centers, fairs, and elsewhere. Many union men did volunteer work of a similar nature. In addition, the great bulk of the work of paid union officials in Ohio centered on defeat of right-to-work for several months before the election. In the last analysis, the success of the opponents of the proposed amendment seems to be best explained in terms of greater expenditure of manpower.

Finances [12]

Organized labor made money an issue in the right-to-work campaign from the very start. It claimed that interests represented by the Ohio Chamber of Commerce were about to drown the State's organized labor in a flood of dollar bills. Union leaders exhorted the membership to greater and greater contributions of time and energy, and to more effective campaigning to counteract the huge amounts of money being spent by proponents of the amendment; organized labor responded with greater efforts, and in the end outspent the opposition nearly two to one. . . .

---

[11] These figures represent efforts in 32 areas in which records were kept and reports were made, and include activities primarily in the early parts of the campaign. The total effort by women in opposition to right-to-work is considerably understated by these figures.

[12] All figures reported are corrected for interorganizational payments and represent final expenditures as stated.

The expenditures of the participants in the campaign presents a rather standardized picture. The main groups retained professional advertising agencies and relied heavily on advertising techniques and media. The next largest category of expenditures in each case was for printing—primarily for the numerous pamphlets and circulars produced by each side. It is perhaps significant that organized labor relied so heavily on professionals to implement its presentation of the campaign, for this represents a major shift in policy as compared to previous campaigns.

While these were the major groups involved in the right-to-work fight at the state level, numerous labor organizations at the local and district levels poured considerable money into the campaign. The total spent by these local-county-district groups, and including the minor-spending state groups—such as Ohio AFL–CIO, $48,180, and Teamsters Anti-Right-to-Work Committee, $51,409—amounted to $579,869. Adding to this sum the $437,854 spent by UOLO and the $365,100 spent by the Citizens to Defeat State Issue No. 2, results in a grand total of $1,378,824 spent in behalf of organized labor, compared to the $776,923 spent by the supporters of the amendment. Hence, on this matter of finances, the frequent suggestion that business will always outspend labor in a political campaign is not clearly established in Ohio's right-to-work struggle.

Election Statistics

The total registration of votes in Ohio in 1958 set a new record, topping not only the previous "off year" high, but even exceeding the presidential election year record set in 1956. While some of this increase in registration over 1956 may be attributed to population growth, or campaign issues other than right-to-work, it seems reasonable to assign major importance to the right-to-work fight—because of its generally controversial nature, and more specifically because of organized labor's all-out registration efforts. A look at the 1952 and 1954 registration figures supports this contention: in 1954, an "off year" (with no issue comparable to right-to-work), registration decreased from the presidential election year of 1952.

When the count was complete, most political observers were surprised by the results. The total gubernatorial vote *did* set a new "off year" record. But it did not meet expectations, failing to match the gubernatorial vote in either of the presidential election years of '52 or '56. Michael DiSalle did indeed defeat incumbent Republican O'Neill by an unexpectedly large plurality, reversing the 1956 decision when O'Neill had defeated him. Senator Bricker, a man who previously had immense political stature in Ohio, was defeated by Democrat Stephen Young, a perennial but frequently unsuccessful candidate. Equally surprising, the right-to-work proposal was defeated by a margin of almost 2 to 1.

Analysis of these results is difficult. It was an election year in which most of the major forces were mutually reinforcing—the recession under a Republican Administration, a weak Republican gubernatorial candidate, right-to-work identified with the Republicans (particularly O'Neill), and a uniquely strong and unified campaign by organized labor.

Some analysts suggested that the GOP had failed to "get out" the rural vote. And this vote did make some difference, for of the sixteen counties that voted majorities in favor of the right-to-work amendment, ten were among the twenty-three "most rural" counties in the state and only one of the sixteen could be called even relatively industrial-commercial. On the other hand, none of the twenty-five "most industrial-commercial" counties gave the right-to-work amendment a majority; and only one, Franklin County, in which Columbus is located, came even close to doing so.

Evaluation of the Campaign

Despite front organizations and catchy names, the right-to-work campaign was actually a political struggle between organized labor and the state Chamber of Commerce. The Chamber, or at least those directing its activities, was probably over-confident of its ability to "take the measure" of organized labor in a political campaign as a result of the 1955 vote on liberalized unemployment compensation. However, the issue and conditions in 1958 were different—and significantly so—from those of 1955.[13]

Essentially, the outcome was a result of the work done by individuals in furthering registration and voting, and converting undecided voters to a firm position on the issue. This was probably much more important than the funds spent or the arguments made during the campaign. On this point the union forces had a considerable advantage once it was clear that the issue would be on the ballot. For they had a large reservoir of volunteers who did much of the campaign work;

---

[13] In 1955 the Ohio Chamber of Commerce and its supporters were waging a defensive campaign—opposing basic *changes* in the Unemployment Compensation Law. In 1958 the Chamber's campaign was offensive, designed to secure a major addition to Ohio labor regulations. It has been suggested that Ohio business interests have been most effective when opposing, rather than urging change—in defensive, rather than offensive, political maneuvers.

and here the work of women directed through the Women's Activities Division of the state labor organization is considered especially important. Not only was union volunteer work a vital source of help, but the unions were able to get much influential support from nonunion groups in the State, particularly church officials (of the Catholic diocese) and the Citizens Committee.

Another factor that was of considerable importance was apathy on the part of the proponents of the amendment. Once it became clear that the right-to-work issue would be on the ballot, it seems that they became over-confident and rested on their oars, while there was no letdown in labor's efforts right up to election day. In fact, many union members said privately that they feared the amendment would be adopted or at least thought the vote would be very close. Thus the effort that they expended in the latter weeks of the campaign was considerable, and quite effectively directed.

Not only did the proponents of the amendment lose their initiative late in the campaign, in the sense that contributions came in slowly and volunteer work became inadequate, but they also lost it in the method in which they presented their program. For one thing, they were told not to answer the allegations of the opposition, and instead to make a positive approach by urging the points that they thought should be made. However, opposition arguments—among them the loss of social security protection, lowered wages, and the complete destruction of the union movement in Ohio—seem to have been reasonably effective.

Opponents of the amendment also received considerable help from the economic recession. There can be little doubt that the recession of 1957–58 made the outcome of the right-to-work vote in Ohio quite different from what it might have been at another time. While the economic downturn was not expected by organized labor, nor effectively exploited, it was nevertheless a windfall. Moreover, the support of organized labor by rural residents was surprisingly strong. Perhaps this was a result of the work over a number of years by certain Ohio labor leaders who had sought friendly relations with farm organizations, notably the Farm Bureau and the Grange. It was, however, more likely a result of the fact that each year nearly a third of the State's farm operators work 100 days or more off the farm.[14]

---

[14] Andrews, Wade H. and Snow, Lorenzo H., "Comparative Population, Agricultural, and Industrial Data for Ohio Counties, 1940–1950," Ohio Agricultural Experiment Station, Wooster, Ohio.

Conclusion

The question arising from the defeat of the right-to-work amendment in Ohio is whether the outcome indicates a new level of competence by unions in the political process. Much should have been learned by labor leadership about the importance of registration and voting campaigns, the volunteer work of "union women," and the use of specialists in communications and public relations; and probably key personnel in the Ohio union movement did gain new insights and political acumen as a result of the election of 1958. Moreover, union mistrust of professional and specialized workers was no doubt markedly weakened, and it seems likely that communications and public relations personnel will be used more readily in future campaigns. Knowledge was gained, too, on how to approach and to communicate with nonunion groups. Indeed, the lesson in communicating with the public may well be the most important learned by labor in the Ohio campaign. Almost as important, unionists were made aware of the necessity of political action, and of what can be done given proper incentive and organization. . . .

It seems likely that, in Ohio, organized labor can be a more influential political force in the future. However, so much of the organization and data of the 1958 campaign disappeared so rapidly after the election that confidence should be tempered by an awareness that a major rebuilding job will be needed if unions are to be a significant political "power bloc." Whether labor uses its political strength consistently and continuously may not be the vital factor; more important perhaps is the recognition that a powerful, though often inert, force can be brought into action when labor feels itself seriously threatened.

Chapter 10

Labor's Money and Politics

IN THE NEXT PRESIDENTIAL ELECTION YEAR in the United States, nearly $200,000,000 will be spent on politics. Of this total outlay, approximately $3,000,000 in voluntary cash contributions will come from trade union members. In addition, an indeterminate amount of goods and services in kind, provided and paid for by local and national unions, will also be expended on political and citizenship activities and will probably equal or exceed the cash contributions from union members. On balance, however, it is unlikely that the total union expenditure and union member contribution will exceed 5 percent—certainly not 10 percent—of the total amount spent on American politics in any contemporary campaign year. Yet organized workers and their families make up a quarter of the American electorate.

Assuming the reasonable reliability of the above figures (data on political money are notoriously imprecise) the many years of controversy, legislation, and litigation over labor money in politics are somewhat difficult to understand. In part, the animosity toward labor's political spending results from the obvious hostility of labor's political opponents. Moreover, this hostility is reinforced by a general public attitude that political contributions are made for selfish purposes and antisocial ends. Such views have been reinforced by statements like that of John L. Lewis,

> Everybody says I want my pound of flesh, that I gave Mr. Roosevelt $500,000 for his 1936 campaign, and I want my quid pro quo. The United Mine Workers and the CIO have paid cash on the barrel for every piece of legislation that we have gotten. . . . I say that labor's champion has to a large extent here been a bought and paid-for proposition.[1]

Yet the fact remains that statements of this kind both exaggerate the influence of political contributions and unduly simplify the motives of political givers. From the politician's point of view, much as he values campaign money, there is one commodity he values more —votes. A political contribution that threatens his voter appeal is, there-

---

[1] Quoted in Saul Alinsky, *John L. Lewis*, New York: Cornwall Press, 1949, pp. 177–78.

fore, unacceptable. From the contributor's point of view, much as he may desire to influence governmental policy, the higher the level of government he seeks to influence the less likely he is to achieve his ends. Where broad national policy issues are concerned, many organized groups compete, and no one group is likely to be able to call the turn no matter how large its contribution.

In the main, labor's political expenditures have two general objectives:

1. A concern for general governmental policy. This concern is reflected in support of policies and candidates commonly called "liberal" and generally identified with the Democratic party.
2. A desire for entree or easy access to government officials in both legislative and executive branches.

The first is primarily a society-oriented rather than selfish motive, although, to a lesser extent, it may also involve the achievement of certain group preferments. The second of these motives, access, is the concept most frequently used by practical politicians to describe the objective desired, and benefit received, by large contributors. Although it cannot be equated with decisive influence, access means the ready opportunity to voice one's case at crucial times and places. Thus, it directly affects the advantage or disadvantage that labor enjoys vis-à-vis competing interest groups in our society.

Despite the seeming reasonableness of these motives and objectives, repeated legislative attempts have been made to limit the amounts and ways in which trade unions can contribute to political campaigns and spend money for political purposes. The history of the various enactments to limit labor's campaign contributions is recounted in the first article in this chapter, Joseph Tanenhaus' "Organized Labor's Political Spending."

Complex legislation often requires judicial interpretation. The two readings that follow are excerpts from U.S. Supreme Court decisions, illustrating the Court's attempts to find a viable and Constitutional balance between two competing and legitimate goals of American society. On the one hand, the Congress is entitled to maintain the purity of the election process. On the other hand, labor like any other group is entitled to the Constitutional guarantee of the right of free speech. The numerous concurring and dissenting opinions to the majority holdings of the Court illustrate that the Justices find the middle way between these sometimes conflicting rights no easy one to delineate.

In the selection that follows the Court decisions, Harry M. Scoble deals with the complex problem of trying to follow the ways and means by which labor's money goes into politics. His conclusion is striking: although the amount of labor's financial involvement in politics is relatively small, labor's dollars are rather efficiently distributed in terms of the achievement of its political objectives.

Although the controversy concerning labor's political expenditures has abated somewhat in recent years, it is unlikely that it will ever die out completely. The subject is too involved with hotly debated and defended issues—freedom of speech, monopoly power, majority and minority rights, and the whole controversy surrounding compulsory union membership.

The heart of the problem lies in the question of whether democratic doctrine can be reconciled to using the dues of dissenting members for political purposes—purposes that may run contrary to their political beliefs—in an organization to which they must belong in order to continue working. This question of personal freedom will persist even though the use of funds for politics may be approved by an overwhelming majority of the union's members.

Alternatively, however, to allow a disapproving minority to prevent political expenditures would mean limiting the right of the democratic majority to be free to act. In the economic realm, it is generally conceded that unions can properly decide by majority vote whether to accept or reject an employer's offer, or to strike or not to strike. Practically no one would now contend that the dissenters from such decisions should be entitled to refuse the use of their dues money to implement the will of the majority. Thus the dilemma. Can or should a line be drawn between normal union economic activities on the one hand, and, on the other, union political activities which the majority may approve as being in the best interests of the organization and its members?

Organized Labor's Political Spending

Joseph Tanenhaus
New York University

IN 1936 ORGANIZED LABOR dramatically leaped into the political arena by investing some three-quarters of a million dollars in Franklin Roosevelt's first reelection campaign. John L. Lewis' United Mine Workers

Reprinted by permission of the publisher from *The Journal of Politics*, Vol. 16, 1954.

contributed or lent $469,000 to the Democratic cause, and two other CIO affiliates added $141,000 more. The Mine Workers' expenditure alone was five times greater than the total amount the AFL reported raising for political purposes in the preceding thirty years. One-third of labor's total expenditure in 1936 went directly into the coffers of the Democratic National Committee, and more than one-half went to Labor's Non-Partisan League (a special organization set up by those AFL and CIO unions benefiting most from the New Deal) and to the League's New York state offspring, the American Labor Party.[1]

Labor's political contributions in 1936 were impressive—so much so that the excitement generated by the Landon-Roosevelt battle had barely subsided before suggestions for restricting labor's political spending echoed through Congressional chambers. In the turbulent years that succeeded, three pieces of legislation affecting labor's political spending were written onto the statute books: the second Hatch Act in 1940,[2] the War Labor Disputes Act (Smith-Connally) in 1943,[3] and the Labor Management Relations Act (Taft-Hartley) in 1947.[4] It is purpose of this article to examine the development of the law and to assess the impact it has had on the political activities of organized labor.

I. Hatch Act of 1940

The desirability of controlling the strings to labor's political purse received scattered attention in Congress during the years immediately following the 1936 elections.[5] However, no restrictions on labor's political spending actually became law until shortly before the Presidential election of 1940. Early in that year Congressional energies were turned toward consideration of S.3046,[6] a bill destined to become the second Hatch Act. Originally designed to limit the political roles of those state

---

[1] Louise Overacker, *Presidential Campaign Funds* (Boston: University Press, 1946), pp. 50–51; Lewis L. Lorwin, *The American Federation of Labor: History, Policies, and Prospects* (Washington: The Brookings Institution, 1933), pp. 90, 422; *Senate Report No. 151*, 75th Cong., 1st sess. (1937), pp. 127–33; Louise Overacker, "Campaign Funds in the Presidential Election of 1936," *The American Political Science Review*, XXXI, No. 3 (June 1937), 489; Louise Overacker, "Labor's Political Contributions," *Political Science Quarterly*, LIV, No. 1 (March 1939), 56.

[2] 54 *Stat.* 767 (1940).

[3] 57 *Stat.* 163 (1943).

[4] 61 *Stat.* 136 (1947).

[5] Joseph E. Kallenbach, "The Taft-Hartley Act and Union Political Contributions and Expenditures," *Minnesota Law Review*, 33, No. 1 (December 1948), 1–26.

[6] 76th Cong. 3d sess. (1940).

employees whose salaries were paid at least in part from federal funds, S.3046 as it passed the Senate in no way affected labor organizations. A $5,000 per year ceiling on political contributions (proposed by Senator Bankhead in an effort to kill the bill by making it unpalatable to Republicans) did slip into the Senate version by an extremely narrow margin.[7] This restriction applied only to natural persons and not to associations, committees, or groups. The House Judiciary Committee, to which the bill had been referred upon reaching the lower chamber, extended the $5,000 limitation to organizations by defining "person" as "an individual, partnership, committee, association, corporation, and any other organization or group of persons."[8]

If this addition were the only revision of the Senate bill, labor's freedom to engage in politics might have been seriously cramped. The Judiciary Committee, however, made two further alterations partially nullifying the impact of its definition of "person."[9] According to the Bankhead proposal, no one could contribute more than $5,000 during any campaign; the Judiciary Committee revised this restriction to make it possible to give $5,000 to each of any number of different candidates and political committees. In the second place, a completely new section was added to S.3046 permitting any political committee to spend up to $3,000,000. Organizations such as Labor's Non-Partisan League could, as a result, qualify as "political committees" in the $3,000,000 category, rather than be forced to operate as "persons" under the $5,000 rule.

A loophole more substantial than either of those opened by the House Judiciary Committee was provided when the Committee of the Whole, without reflection and without debate, accepted Representative Vreeland's suggestion that "contributions made to or by a State or local committee, or other State or local organization" be exempt from the $5,000 proviso.[10] Associations as well as individuals could as a result legally contribute without limit to any candidate of their choice if only state or local organizations were set up to receive and spend these funds. This series of emendations survived subsequent legislative pitfalls and ultimately became law.

The upshot of Hatch Act II, insofar as organized labor was concerned, seems to be as follows:

---

[7] 86 *Congressional Record* 2852 (1940). A $1,000 per year limitation on contributions proposed by Bankhead had been defeated a day earlier.

[8] *Ibid.*, p. 9447.

[9] *Ibid.*, p. 9447.

[10] *Ibid.*, p. 9452.

1. A union could contribute no more than $5,000 to any *one* candidate for federal office or to committees engaged in supporting him.

2. Any union could contribute as much as it liked to the various state and local committees even though they were primarily concerned with supporting candidates for federal office.

3. Each political committee set up by organized labor could spend a total of $3,000,000. There was no limit to the portion of the $3,000,000 that might be given to or expended on behalf of any one candidate or national committee.

The Second Hatch Act, in short, was so full of loopholes as to place no effective restriction on labor's political contributions—or anyone else's for that matter.

II. War Labor Disputes Act of 1943: Legislative History

The 1942 elections produced the Seventy-eighth Congress, the most hostile legislature the Roosevelt administration had faced since it had swept into power ten years before. From the moment the new Congress convened, John L. Lewis and his United Mine Workers had been front page news. The miners, who finally struck in early May of 1943, had been threatening to leave the pits since the first of the year. By spring Congressional tempers were fast approaching their boiling points. On May 5, the Connally bill (S.796), a measure providing for the seizure of struck war plants, passed the Senate after heated debate. Referred to the House Committee on Military Affairs, S.796 emerged a few days later with a number of new and irrelevant provisions hostile to labor, but still no restriction on political spending.[11]

No sooner had the House resolved itself into the Committee of the Whole to consider amendments to S.796 under the five-minute rule than Representative Harness of Indiana offered a complex amendment largely rewriting the bill.[12] His amendment, in reality a substitute measure, proposed deletion of crucial sections of S.796 and the inclusion of an entirely new one amending the Corrupt Practices Act of 1925 so as to prohibit labor organizations from making any

> contribution in connection with any election at which Presidential and Vice Presidential electors or a Senator or Representative . . . are to be voted for, or for any candidate, political committee, or other person to accept or receive any contribution prohibited by this section.[13]

---

[11] *House Report No. 440*, 78th Cong., 1st sess. (1943).
[12] 89 *Congressional Record* 5328 (1943).
[13] *Loc. cit.*

Harness, who admitted that he had prepared his amendment only hours before, alleged that the individual sections had been previously discussed in committee.

Neither Washington's temperature nor the House's state of mind, as many Representatives attested, was conducive to thoughtful legislation, and the debate deteriorated rapidly.[14] But whether "hysteria" or "acrimony" better describes the sense of the House on that June 3, "appalling confusion" accurately characterizes its action. The parliamentary situation soon grew so intricate that Andrew Jackson May, the Representative in charge of guiding S.796 through the House, became entangled in the procedural meshes and had to request on point of order an explanation of the business before the House. An amazing scene followed in which member after member arose to confess that he was at sea without a compass.

On the next day a somewhat more self-possessed House passed Smith-Connally, as S.796 had come to be known, by a wide margin. The House version included Harness' proposal for restricting union political spending, which had been written into the bill by the Committee of the Whole after less than ten minutes of debate. Perhaps the lack of serious effort on the part of labor's friends to resist inclusion of this section is explained by a statement of administration stalwart John Sparkman. Congressman Sparkman thought that the failure to delete the limitation on political contributions of little significance "because we have pretty much the same law already in the Hatch Act." [15] The War Labor Disputes Act, S.796's official title, emerged from conference committee with the political contributions provision (section 9) intact. The House conferees, explained Senator Connally, insisted upon retaining the provision. The Senate had "to give in" on something, and this was one of the "bargains." Despite strong objections to section 9 as irrelevant, discriminatory, and a politically-motivated attempt to weaken labor, the Senate accepted the conference report by a comfortable vote. President Roosevelt remanded the War Labor Disputes bill to Congress without his signature on June 25, 1943.[16] On that same day both Houses turned the bill into law by the requisite two-thirds majority.

III. War Labor Disputes Act: Its Consequences

Representative Sparkman was certainly ill-advised in thinking section 313 of the Corrupt Practices Act, as amended by section 9 of the War

---

[14] See *e.g., Ibid.,* pp. 5228, 5243, 5310, 5337, 5339, 5344, 5348 (1943).

[15] *Ibid.,* p. 5401.

[16] The President's message was reprinted as *Senate Document No. 75,* 78th Cong., 1st sess. (1943).

Labor Disputes Act, "pretty much the same law already in the Hatch Act." According to the revised section 313, no labor organization could make any "contribution whatsoever in connection with any election at which presidential and vice-presidential electors, or a Senator or Representative . . . are to be voted for. . . ." ("Labor organization," it should be pointed out parenthetically, was defined exactly as in the National Labor Relations Act, and, therefore, included unions but not the political committees set up by organized labor.) Under Hatch Act II a union could use its general funds to make donations of up to $5,000 to each of any number of candidates for federal office, or to national committees engaged in supporting them, and unlimited gifts to state and local committees established for the same purpose. Between these two provisions there was obviously a very considerable difference. Two less important distinctions are also worth mentioning. The Corrupt Practices Act did not (either before or as amended by the War Labor Disputes Act) apply to primaries in which candidates for federal office were selected; the Hatch Act presumably did.[17] A union could, therefore, even after 1943, contribute $5,000 to the primary campaign fund of each federal office candidate it wishes to support. Neither the Corrupt Practices Act nor the Hatch Act could, of course, restrict donations for exclusive use in state and local elections. Secondly, the War Labor Disputes Act would by its own terms expire six months after the termination of the war. The status of the law after the passage of the War Labor Disputes Act may then be characterized as follows: for the duration of World War II a labor union as such could not legally make "contributions" to the actual election campaign of any candidate for federal office; a union could donate a maximum of $5,000 to the primary campaign fund of each candidate for federal office and unlimited amounts for use in state and local elections—state law permitting.

Less than two weeks after the War Labor Disputes Act became law the Executive Board of the CIO set up the Political Action Committee under the chairmanship of Sidney Hillman, able head of the Amalgamated Clothing Workers. In October 1943, several CIO unions transferred substantial funds from their treasuries to a special PAC bank account. Four gave $100,000 each and others supplied lesser sums. The CIO itself added another $100,000 from its own funds to bring the

---

[17] It might be argued, on the other hand, that the Hatch Act does not apply to primaries, because at the time the Act was passed many persons believed that Congress had no authority to regulate primary elections.

total to approximately $650,000.[18] On July 23, 1944, the day after the Democratic Convention made its nominations, Hillman ordered the unexpended portion of the $650,000, about $170,000, "frozen." . . .

Some AFL and independent unions did find it expedient to back candidates by direct expenditures of union funds. But the CIO unions had from the outset elected to channel their major political activities through a special organization, the Political Action Committee. Since the Corrupt Practices Act as amended prevented political committees from receiving contributions from labor unions, elaborate steps were taken to separate the operations of PAC and the unions. Once their initial pledges to PAC made in October of 1943 had been paid, the unions gave no further monies to the Committee until after the 1944 elections. And after the trade union contributions fund had been frozen in July 1944, the PAC paid its bills with its share in the proceeds of the CIO campaign to have every member volunteer "A Buck for Roosevelt." One-half of the $750,000 thus raised went into a separate PAC bank account, the rest remaining with local unions or their political committees.[19] Once the 1944 elections were over the PAC defrosted its trade union contributions account. From then until September 3, 1946, the "arbitrary date" set by the PAC as the beginning of the 1946 election campaign, the unfrozen balance, augmented by additional union donations, paid PAC bills.[20] In 1946, as in 1944, a voluntary drive for individual contributions financed the post-primary operating budget. This drive supplied the national PAC with some $130,000 for its activities during September and October.[21] Roughly two-thirds of the Committee's expenditures were made before September 3 and so were covered with general union funds. . . .

---

[18] *Senate Report No. 101,* 79th Cong., 1st sess. (1945), p. 25; *Hearings Before the Committee to Investigate Campaign Expenditures, House of Representatives,* 78th Cong., 2d sess. on H. Res. 551, Part 1 (1944), p. 12; Louise Overacker, "Presidential Campaign Funds, 1944," *The American Political Science Review,* XXXIX, No. 5 (October 1945), 920.

[19] A parallel organization, also chaired by Mr. Hillman, the National Citizens' Political Action Committee, raised another $350,000 from sympathizers outside CIO ranks.

[20] *Hearings Before the Committee to Investigate Campaign Expenditures, House of Representatives,* 79th Cong., 2d sess. (1946), on H. Res. 645, Part 2, p. 144.

[21] *The New York Times,* Jan. 18, 1947. For a complete reporting on PAC contributions and expenditures through Oct. 31, 1946, see *Hearings, supra,* fn. 25, pp. 104–44.

IV. Labor Management Relations Act of 1947: Legislative History

Thorough revision of existing labor legislation stood high on the calendar of the Eightieth Congress. The House Committee on Education and Labor, although it had in six weeks of hearings paid little more than cursory attention to labor's political activities, reported out a bill, H.R. 3020, with a section (304) limiting political spending. Section 304, according to the Committee majority, was designed to do three things: (1) place the restrictions on union "contributions" contained in the temporary War Labor Disputes Act on a permanent basis; (2) extend the prohibition on both union and corporate spending to include "expenditures" as well as "contributions"; (3) make the restrictions applicable to primaries as well as to regular elections.[22]

House debate on H.R. 3020 lasted for three days and was for the most part more bitter than enlightening. Only one member, Miller of California, addressed himself squarely to section 304.[23] He attacked it as irrelevant, unnecessary, undesirable, and discriminatory. Representative Charles Halleck, in briefly defending section 304, reminded the House that it had subscribed to a similar proposal when it passed the War Labor Disputes Act.[24] Opponents of H.R. 3020 did not try to have section 304 deleted or modified when amendments were in order. Apparently their strategy called for defeat of the bill in its entirety, or if this proved impossible (as was almost certain to be the case), the enactment of a law so severe that it would have to be vetoed. The House defeated a motion to recommit H.R. 3020 on April 17, 1947, and immediately thereafter passed the bill by a very substantial margin. The labor bill which was subsequently passed by the upper chamber contained no reference to political spending, nor for that matter did the subject even arise during Senate debate.

On May 15 the House and Senate version of H.R. 3020 went to conference. Taft, Ball, Ives, Murray, and Ellender acted as managers for the Senate, with Hartley, Hoffman, Landis, Lesinski, and Barden representing the House. Three of the conferees, Ellender, Hoffman, and Landis, had been outspoken advocates of limiting labor's political role. Section 304 of the compromise bill finally worked out by the conference committee constituted an almost verbatim adoption of the lim-

---

[22] *House Report No. 245,* 80th Cong., 1st sess. (1947), p. 46. Apparently the source of the section was a draft bill then pending before the Senate Judiciary Committee. See *House Report No. 317,* 81st Cong., 1st sess. (1947), Part 2, p. 12.

[23] 93 *Congressional Record,* pp. 3522–23 (1947).

[24] *Ibid.,* p. 3666.

itations on political contributions and expenditures contained in the House version of H.R. 3020.[25] The lower chamber, after one hour of debate, which included only fleeting references to section 304, accepted the compromise measure.

Discussion of the conference report in the Senate took place on June 5 and 6. About two-fifths of the time spent in debate was devoted to section 304, which was for the first time subjected to searching public examination. Senator Taft, in presenting the conference report, pointed to section 304 as one of two major additions to the Senate bill.[26] The War Labor Disputes Act, which the Senate had approved by more than two to one, Taft reminded his colleagues, would expire on June 30. He stated that in his opinion, section 304 raised no really new question. Congress, thought the Senator, had intended its definitions of "contribution" in the Corrupt Practices and Hatch Acts to cover expenditures. A loophole had developed, and section 304 sought to close it.

Senators Pepper, Barkley, Taylor, Magnuson, Kilgore, and Murray questioned Taft sharply about the implications of extending the Corrupt Practices Act to cover union and corporate expenditures. They wanted to know precisely how the addition of the phrase "or expenditure" would affect newspapers, particularly the labor press. Each case, Taft replied, would depend on the facts involved. In every instance the first matter to be determined was the source of the funds. According to section 304, the Ohioan maintained, newspapers and radio programs subsidized by union or corporate funds could not endorse, or in any way support, candidates. On the other hand, publications whose production and distribution costs were paid for entirely by subscription could take political sides if they wished to do so. Senator Barkley, in observing that editorials take up space, and that space costs money, asked Taft whether newspapers published by corporations (as almost all are) would not violate the law by endorsing candidates for federal office. Taft replied in the negative. A political editorial, he asserted, is not "an expenditure of the sort prohibited, because it seems to me it is simply the ordinary operation of the particular corporation's business."[27] Barkley's exposure of this reply as patently circular prompted Taft to agree that the real reason regular commercial newspapers would not be affected was that the Federal Corrupt Practices Act had never been intended to apply to them. He refused to consider the labor press exempt on similar grounds.

[25] *House Report No. 510*, 80th Cong., 1st sess. (1947).
[26] *93 Congressional Record*, p. 6436 (1947).
[27] *Ibid.*, p. 6437.

Taft's dogged determination to defend the distinction he drew between newspapers financed from union or corporate funds and those supported by subscriptions and advertising had an impelling logic behind it. "If the newspaper is prepared and distributed and circulated by means of the expenditure of union funds, then how could a line be drawn between that and political literature or pamphlets or publications of that nature?"[28]

Some uncertainty existed as to the status of newspapers financed by money collected as part of regular union membership dues. Ball and Ellender maintained that if a portion of the dues were earmarked for support of the publication and never became part of the union's general fund—as they thought the usual procedure—section 304 would not be applicable. Taft's stand was not entirely clear. Senator Pepper received the impression that Taft believed voluntary yearly subscriptions necessary to exempt a paper from the reaches of the law. Senate debate, in fine, reveals that the three Senate conference managers who took part in the discussion of section 304 (Taft, Ellender, and Ball) were all convinced that the section forbade the use of unsegregated and unearmarked union funds in printing newspapers which took sides in federal primaries and elections.

Two other problems concerning the meaning of section 304 received lesser attention. The first was a question of timing. At what point can an election campaign be said to have begun?[29] And the second related to content. How can one tell whether a statement publicized during an election campaign at union or corporate expense is political (and therefore illegal) rather than informational, educational, or cultural in nature?[30] A number of hypothetical cases illustrating both problems were presented to Senator Taft. He ventured his opinion as to how the law would be applied in most. But each case, he repeatedly told his interrogators, would have to be decided on the basis of the exact facts. When a roll call on the conference report was finally ordered, the Senate approved it by a more than three to one majority.

President Truman returned H.R. 3020 without his signature on June 20, 1947.[31] The bill, wrote the Chief Executive, "raises serious issues of public policy which transcend labor-management difficulties," among them being the section restricting political contributions and expenditures. His objections to section 304 were two in number. In

---

[28] Loc. cit.

[29] Ibid., p. 6447.

[30] Ibid., pp. 6438 ff., 6447, 6533.

[31] House Document No. 334, 80th Cong., 1st sess. (1947).

the first place, the "ordinary" union ("ordinary" went undefined) would be prevented from taking a stand on any candidate or issue in a national election. "I regard this as a dangerous intrusion on free speech, unwarranted by any demonstration of need, and quite foreign to the stated purpose of this bill."[32] . . .

The House overrode the veto without discussion. As soon as the result of the voting was announced, Representative Robsion rose to attack the President's criticism of the Taft-Hartley bill, the name by which H.R. 3020 had come to be most widely known. While defending section 304, Congressman Robsion said: "[304] *will not prevent the publishers of labor papers and editors of such papers from expressing themselves freely whether they are a journal of business or labor.*"[33] At no time during the entire legislative history of Taft-Hartley had section 304 been given such a narrow gloss. The Senate, held in overnight session by the famous week-end filibuster of Morse, Taylor, Murray, Kilgore, Pepper, and Johnston, suffered additional hours of wearisome commentary on the alleged evils of Taft-Hartley before voting whether to upset the President's veto. The filibusterers, who had little new to say about section 304, failed to turn the sentiments of the Senate; and on June 23, 1947, the Labor Management Relations Act became law. . . .

All hope for repeal of the Labor Management Relations Act rested upon the election of a Congress friendly toward organized labor. With prospects for the return of a Congress so disposed darkened by the restrictions on labor's political spending in section 304, the unions turned to the courts.

V. Labor Management Relations Act: Judicial Construction

The Labor Management Relations Act of 1947 had been law for less than a week when the CIO executive board resolved, for the purpose of testing its constitutionality, deliberately to violate the ban on political expenditures.[34] Anxious to force a Supreme Court ruling on section 304 before the 1948 campaign got under way, the CIO publicly disclosed its intention of violating section 304 by intervening in two special elections to fill vacancies in the House of Representatives.[35] The first was scheduled for July 15 in the Third Congressional District of Maryland (Baltimore), and the second for September 9 in Pennsylvania's

---

[32] *Ibid.*, p. 9.
[33] *Ibid.*, p. 7492 (emphasis added).
[34] *The New York Times*, June 28, 1947.
[35] *Ibid.*, July 4, 1947.

Eighth (Allentown area). The July 14 issue of the CIO *News* carried a statement by Philip Murray, entitled "Test of Political Freedom," which urged the election of Judge Garmatz to the Maryland seat. To remove all doubt, that an expenditure of general union funds was involved, 1,000 extra copies of the paper were printed and distributed in Maryland's Third District.

Arraigned on February 20, 1948, Murray and the CIO pleaded not guilty and filed a motion for dismissal, alleging that section 304 was unconstitutional. The defendants openly admitted their intention of breaking the law but attacked the ban on expenditures as an invalid interference with freedom of speech, press, and assembly. The prohibition on expenditures, government counsel agreed, did seem to run counter to the First Amendment. Nevertheless, they insisted, Congress' desire to preserve free elections justifies these restrictions on free speech.

Judge Moore sustained the motion for dismissal on March 15.[36] Deference to the will of the legislature, he said, dictates a construction "free from imputation of unconstitutionality" if one can "logically" be made. But if "the words of the statute are plain and can have only one meaning," a judge must rule on its validity. In this case the legislative history "copiously related" in the government's brief "shows that the legislation was aimed at the very type of political activity which is charged as an offense in this indictment, namely, the publication and distribution of newspapers containing editorials favoring or opposing candidates for federal office." Statutes abridging speech, continued the judge, are valid only if directed at a clear and present danger of substantive evils. No such danger "can be found in the circumstances surrounding the enactment of this legislation."[37]

Government counsel, as permitted under the Criminal Appeals Act, appealed directly to the Supreme Court. Reacting with uncharacteristic rapidity, the Court scheduled argument for late April. The major point at which the parties locked horns was this: the CIO argued that section 304 must be struck down because it could not satisfy the clear and present danger test; the government believed the "reasonable" or "rational" basis test rather than the clear and present danger test applicable, even though it felt that Congress had fulfilled the requirements of both. During oral argument Justice Frankfurter stingingly rebuked government counsel for their handling of the case. The

---

[36] *United States v. Congress of Industrial Organizations*, 77 F. Supp. 355 (1948).

[37] *Ibid.*, pp. 356, 357, 358.

government, Mr. Justice Frankfurter stated, should have questioned the application of the statute to the facts of the instant case and not confined its argument to merely abstract issues. Because the government did not properly contest the case, the Court is being asked to give what is in effect an "advisory opinion."[38] Justice Jackson concurred.

The Supreme Court handed down its decision in *United States v. Congress of Industrial Organizations* on June 21, 1948.[39] The Court's opinion, representing the views of Justices Reed, Jackson, Burton, and Vinson, affirmed the district court's dismissal of the indictment, though on vastly different grounds. Mr. Justice Reed, speaking for the Court, ruled that the indictment did not charge any violation of section 313 of the Federal Corrupt Practices Act as amended by section 304 of the Labor Management Relations Act of 1947. By so holding, the Court avoided the necessity of determining the constitutionality of the ban on political expenditures. Announcing this conclusion was one matter; providing convincing documentation in support of its validity quite another.

Exactly what Congress expected section 304 to do, the Justice stated, is far from clear; nonetheless, "We find . . . in the Senate debates definite indication that Congress did not intend to include within the coverage of the section as an expenditure the costs of the publication described in the indictment."[40] Excerpts from the Senate debate on the conference report were then quoted in purported demonstration of this "definite indication." The "we" Justice Reed was embarrassingly obliged to reveal did not include all those who joined in his opinion. "Some members of the Court, joining in this opinion, do not place the reliance upon legislative history that this opinion evidences, but reach the same conclusion without consideration of that history."[41] Whether by intuition, logic, natural principles of justice, common sense, political weathervane watching, or other canon of judicial review, those who joined in Reed's opinion agreed on the following: (1) Congress "was keenly aware" that the Court tends to invalidate legislation contravening the First Amendment; (2) Congress did not want to pass any unconstitutional legislation; (3) the Court would entertain the "gravest doubt" about the constitutionality of a law construed "to prohibit the publication, by corporations and unions in the regular course of conducting their affairs, of periodicals advising their members, stock-

---

[38] *United States Law Week,* 16 (1948), 3329.
[39] 335 U.S. 106 (1948).
[40] *Ibid.,* 116.
[41] *Ibid.,* 120.

holders, or customers of danger or advantage to their interests from the adoption of measures, or the election to office of men espousing these measures;" (4) Congress, therefore, could not have intended section 304 to apply to the acts specified in the indictment. The indictment as construed by the Court, it should be emphasized, did not clearly allege that the 1,000 extra copies had been circulated free of charge to nonsubscribers, nonmembers, or others "not regularly entitled" to receive them. . . .

Justice Rutledge in a trenchant concurring opinion (joined in by Black, Douglas, and Murphy) accused the Court of abdicating "its function in the guise of applying the policy against deciding questions of of constitutionality unnecessarily." The Court, he argued, is not justified in its efforts to avoid invalidating legislation in invading "the legislative function by rewriting or emasculating the statute." [42] Justice Reed's interpretation of section 304 finds support in neither the phraseology of the statute nor its legislative history.

Justice Frankfurter, in a separate concurring opinion, expressed his conviction that the case as presented to the Court ought not to be adjudicated. He restated in embellished form (and in a more conciliatory tone) his feeling disclosed during oral argument that the issue had been "formulated so broadly as to bring gratuitously before the Court that for which there is no necessity for decision. . . ." [43]

Several weeks after the Supreme Court Justices read their opinions in *United States v. Congress of Industrial Organizations,* Judge Hincks of the United States District Court handed down his decision in a second test case, *United States v. Painters Local Union No. 481.* [44] The Connecticut Federation of Labor (AFL) sought to induce prosecution in January 1948, by running political advertisements in a Hartford newspaper and over the radio. These facts, felt the Judge, unlike those in the CIO case, are "of that very kind which Congress intended to forbid." [45] Judge Hincks was then, faced, as Judge Moore had been before him, with the necessity for assessing the constitutionality of Section 304. He decided in favor of the statute because he believed it narrowly drawn to meet a substantive evil, the danger of concentrated wealth to free elections. Subsequently, the union and its former president were tried, found guilty, and heavily fined. [46]

---

[42] 335 U.S. 106 at p. 130.
[43] *Ibid.,* p. 126.
[44] 79 F. Supp. 516 (1948).
[45] *Ibid.,* p. 519.
[46] *The New York Times,* Sept. 24, 1948.

The United States Circuit Court of Appeals, second circuit, in a brief opinion, unanimously reversed the convictions by holding the statute inapplicable to the facts of the case.[47] The circuit court offered four reasons for reaching this conclusion. The expenditure was small ($111.14 for the newspaper space, and $32.50 for the radio time). The advertisements did not affect more persons than Murray's front page editorial in the CIO *News*. The union utilized a "natural" way of communicating with its membership. It is reasonable to assume that no minority opposition to the political expenditures existed. None of the four reasons finds support in the wording of the statute or in its legislative history, and only the fourth received sanction in the CIO decision. Two criteria used by the Supreme Court in holding the law inapplicable to union periodicals—regularity of publication and restriction of the audience to union members—could not possibly have been met and were ignored. All told it would seem that the four reasons set forth by the circuit court can without gross injustice be refined into one: minor violations of the expenditures ban will be tolerated.

One may indeed doubt whether the able judges who heard this case (Augustus Hand, Clark, and Frank) took much stock in the *ratio decidendi* they presented. Rather, they seem to ask, if the Supreme Court has gone to such extraordinary lengths to avoid invalidating a law which had been quite properly challenged, what business has an inferior court to force the high tribunal to consider a second attack on the law in essential elements quite similar to the first?

The third and most recent case arising under Taft-Hartley's restrictions on labor's political spending was decided in a federal district court in December of 1951. Unlike its predecessors, *United States v. Construction & General Laborers Local Union*, not a test case, had apparently been induced by a disgruntled former official of the union.[48] A twelve-count indictment alleged that the union's automobiles, employees, and funds had been used illegally in support of its president, Theodore Irving, in his campaign for election to Congress in the fall of 1948. Defendants, who offered no testimony, attached the adequacy of the indictment and the constitutionality of the law. The court dismissed nine counts as based on insufficient and unsatisfactory evidence. The three remaining counts, charging that union checks for $60.20, $59.00, and $20.00 had been paid to its employees as compensation for services rendered in connection with Irving's campaign, were ultimately dismissed as failing to state a violation of the law. The statute,

---

[47] 172 F. 2d 854 (1948).
[48] 101 F. Supp. 868 (1951).

if strictly construed, the court openly asserted, would proscribe this activity, but the judge could not believe that Congress intended section 304 to be interpreted literally. "If a strict construction is to be given to the statute, then it is not the degree of the activity, but the type of activity which would determine whether or not an expenditure had been made."[49] The district court in the Construction and General Labor Union case reached the same conclusion as had the circuit court in *United States v. Painters Local* (a case which it did not cite), albeit in a less circuitous fashion: minor violations of the expenditures ban will be tolerated. . . .

VII. Concluding Observations

Section 9 of the War Labor Disputes Act and section 304 of the Labor Management Relations Act were, this writer believes, motivated primarily by the desire to weaken materially labor's ability to influence public policy to its advantage. With rare exception, the most vocal sponsors of prohibitions on union spending were Congressmen with records conspicuous for hostility toward organized labor. Still, it does not follow that the three major arguments advanced in justification of restricting labor's political activities ought not to be examined for intrinsic merit.

First, spending general union funds for political purposes, it is commonly asserted, constitutes an improper use of union assets. This proposition rests on the following logic: a union's general funds are collected for a specific purpose—to finance the organization's efforts to obtain better wages, shorter hours, and improved working conditions for its members; union officers, since they hold these funds in fiduciary capacity, cannot use them in ways unrelated to the attainment of the stated purpose; political spending constitutes an extraneous use of funds, and, therefore, ought not to be tolerated. This train of reasoning is simply an application, *mutatis mutandi,* of a justification long given for banning corporate political spending.

Those who attack this position almost invariably begin by asserting that while admirably applicable to corporations, it does not suit unions at all. A corporation, they continue, is a fictitious entity created by law for facilitating the production or distribution of commodities, or the rendition of services—all for the sake of making a profit; a union, on the other hand, is a voluntary nonprofit-seeking association of natural persons which ought to be permitted to use its funds as it sees fit. This distinction (apart from its untenable implication that the

---

[49] *Ibid.,* p. 876.

officers of unincorporated associations have no responsibility for the proper use of organizational funds) entirely misses the point. The crux of the matter is not whether an organization is incorporated but whether political spending can help fulfill its purposes. If spending union funds in connection with elections is unrelated to the purpose for which they were collected, then the funds are being misused just as completely as corporate funds similarly expended.

But is political spending by any organization unrelated to attaining its goals? A moment's reflection on the pervasive role of government in American society lays to rest any possibility of a negative response. Associations representing ballroom operatives, outdoor advertisers, symphony orchestras, women, racial and religious groups, the professions, veterans, highway users, realtors, colleges, "educational" foundations, consumers, farmers, fisheries, the national guard, conservation interests, nut growers, and a host of others have registered under the lobbying law as engaged in attempting to influence the Congress.[50] As Senator Barkley pointed out during Senate debate on the Taft-Hartley conference report, there is no "fundamental difference in principle" between electioneering and lobbying.[51] Both are among the several methods useful in affecting the course of public policy. The history of the American labor movement demonstrated irrefutably that labor's economic objectives cannot be entirely divorced from politics. Indeed, consciousness of the interconnection of politics and economics has advanced to the point where many union constitutions specifically authorize expenditures for political action.

In the second place, those favoring restrictions on labor's political spending almost invariably contend that no union should be permitted to use its funds in support of political causes that some of its members might find objectionable. Union membership, it is pointed out, cannot be considered voluntary when union security provisions exist. If a union is permitted to use its funds on behalf of political candidates, those members opposed to the slate endorsed would in effect be forced to act contrary to their political convictions. This constitutes an interference with freedom of speech and thought.

Any sizeable organization, it has been submitted in rebuttal, if it is to function at all, must operate on the assumption that decisions may be made by less than the unanimous membership. Majority rule has long been a fundamental operating procedure in democratic asso-

---

[50] See *House Report No. 3197*, 81st Cong., 2d sess. (1950); House Report No. 3234, 81st Cong., 2d sess. (1950).

[51] 93 *Congressional Record*, p. 6533 (1947).

ciations. Every union member has at some stage or other the opportunity of participating in the formulation of union policy. To require
more would result in hamstringing the majority for the sake of a
minority.

Each side clearly is backing a different half of the age-old controversy of majority rule versus minority rights. The dispute in this
case, however, is of a special character. If the majority has its way,
the minority is forced to lend support to a program or candidates
against its will. If the minority triumphs, then the majority is deprived
of the privilege of throwing its collective strength behind the causes
of its choice. In each instance essentially the same principle is at stake
—the right to participate freely in the political process. Should a choice
between identical liberties of a majority and a minority be necessary,
surely the American Civil Liberties Union is right in giving the nod
to the former.[52] Such a choice, however, is unnecessary, for a Scylla or
Charybdis dilemma does not exist. The freedom of political action for
both majority and dissenters can be largely protected by what the
British call "contracting out." Political spending under this procedure
would have to be financed by special assessments which could be made
noncompulsory. Anyone objecting to the programs, parties, or candidates backed by his organization would by properly registering his
disapproval of the assessment be exempt from paying it.

Third, proponents of banning union electoral contributions and
expenditures emphasize the desirability of preventing labor from gaining undue influence in the formulation and administration of public
policy. Protection against corruption per se has seldom been offered
as a principal reason for restricting union spending, since a bevy of
Congressional investigations destroyed most honest suspicion that labor
electoral spending had bred corruption. However, allegations that
union contributions and expenditures have brought labor tremendous
influence after 1936 dance across the pages of the *Congressional Record*.
Political spending does beyond any shadow of doubt have an effect on
public policy. That is precisely why money is so expended. Labor's
staunchest supporters never seek to deny this. The center of disagreement lies not in the proposition that political spending garners influence
but rather in the question, "Is the influence undue?"

"Undue influence" is a term so subjective as to be wholly meaningless. Claire Hoffman and Walter Reuther do not speak a common
language when discussing the desirable role of organized labor in policy

---

[52] See the *amicus curiae* brief submitted by the American Civil Liberties
Union in *United States v. CIO*, p. 8.

determination. Since the average person tends to consider that policy desirable which squares best with his own interests, whether one thinks organized labor's political influence "undue" is likely to depend on the weight he would prefer to see unions carry in policy determination. In any case the future of restrictions on labor's political spending will most probably be decided by the balance of power existing in Congress. Only if it swings much more nearly in labor's favor can repeal of the law be expected.

The law restricting labor's political spending, the writer further believes, has thus far failed to hamper labor seriously. The sums organized labor is capable of raising through drives for voluntary contributions are, though far from negligible, certainly limited. If voluntary funds had to pay all of labor's political bills, then union electoral activities would have to be considerably diminished. But this is not the case. The Supreme Court's decision delivered in *United States v. Congress of Industrial Organizations* withdrew regular union publications from the coverage of the law. *United States v. Painters Local* and *United States v. Construction and General Labor Union* made convictions for minor campaign expenditures by local unions unlikely. Much more important than the loopholes opened by judicial construction is the widely accepted practice of listing many expenditures as educational rather than political. Prospects that the courts might be persuaded to reject the validity of the distinction between educational and political expenditures are, because of the thorny free speech questions involved, extremely remote.[53]

As long as educational activities during election campaigns can be financed from general organizational resources, the job of insuring sufficient funds for electioneering is, in substantial part, reduced to a task of bookkeeping. Some varieties of campaign spending, such as direct contributions to candidates, payments to precinct workers and poll-watchers, and printing literature specifically endorsing particular candidates, cannot conceivably be debited in educational account books. Direct monetary contributions to candidates, by all odds the most significant of these unquestionably political expenditures, did not at first interest labor very much. In 1946 the PAC reported no direct contributions at all. Explained Mr. Kroll, union people feel "that if they have a few hundred dollars they can spend it to better advantage than the candidate himself can spend it. They feel that they know what it is that will appeal to the particular voters with whom they work, eat, and

---

[53] In this connection cf. the conclusion of the Green Committee, *Senate Report No. 101, supra,* fn. 22, p. 83.

sleep."[54] But in recent years labor has reconsidered the wisdom of its earlier stand, and direct contributions to candidates have jumped spectacularly. According to *Congressional Quarterly News Features* researchers, labor's political committees made outright campaign contributions to Congressional candidates which totaled more than $140,000 in 1950[55] and $160,000 in 1952.[56] The reason for the change in tactics is implied in a statement by James McDevitt. "All our friends in Congress and in the Senate who have stood up so loyally and fought for our cause [are] asking us now for help, because we are the only people to whom they can appeal. Surely the National Association of Manufacturers won't help them."[57] The legal necessity for raising by voluntary appeals all funds contributed directly to candidates for federal office, and to the committee supporting them, may, if the cost of campaigning continues to rise, prove to be the most serious limitation on labor's political spending contained in the present law.

United States v. United Automobile Workers

SUPREME COURT OF THE UNITED STATES, 1957

MR. JUSTICE FRANKFURTER delivered the opinion of the Court.

The issues tendered in this case are the construction and, ultimately, the constitutionality of 18 USC § 610, FCA 18 § 610, and Act of Congress that prohibits corporations and labor organizations from making "a contribution or expenditure in connection with any election for federal office." This is a direct appeal by the Government from a judgment of the District Court for the Eastern District of Michigan dismissing a four-count indictment that charged appellee, a labor organization, with having made expenditures in violation of that law. Appellee had moved to dismiss the indictment on the grounds (1) that it failed to state an offense under the statute and (2) that the provisions of the statute "on their face and as construed and applied" are

---

[54] *Hearings, supra,* fn. 25, p. 147.

[55] Based on data in *Congressional Quarterly Almanac,* 7 (1951), 44 ff.

[56] Based on data in *Congressional Quarterly Weekly Report,* 11 (1953), 915 ff.

[57] American Federation of Labor, *Proceedings, Seventy-First Annual Convention* (1952), p. 504.

---

352 U.S. 507 (1957). Footnotes and portions of the original text have been deleted.

unconstitutional. The district judge held that the indictment did not allege a statutory offense and that he was therefore not required to rule upon the constitutional questions presented. . . .

As the historical background of this statute indicates, its aim was not merely to prevent the subversion of the integrity of the electoral process. Its underlying philosophy was to sustain the active, alert responsibility of the individual citizen in a democracy for the wise conduct of government. . . .

Shortly thereafter, Congress again acted to protect the political process from what it deemed to be the corroding effect of money employed in elections by aggregated power. Section 304 of the labor bill introduced into the House by Representative Hartley in 1947, like the Ellender bill, embodied the changes recommended in the reports of the Senate and House Committees on Campaign Expenditures. It sought to amend Section 313 of the Corrupt Practices Act to proscribe any "expenditure" as well as "any contribution," to make permanent Section 313's application to labor organizations, and to extend its coverage to federal primaries and nominating conventions. The Report of the House Committee on Education and Labor, which considered and approved the Hartley bill, merely summarized Section 304, H. R. Rep. No. 245, 80th Cong., 1st Sess., p. 46, and this section gave rise to little debate in the House. See 93 Cong. Rec. 3428, 3522. Because no similar measure was in the labor bill introduced by Senator Taft, the Senate as a whole did not consider the provisions of Section 304 until they had been adopted by the Conference Committee. In explaining Section 304 to his colleagues, Senator Taft, who was one of the conferees, said:

> I may say that the amendment is in exactly the same words which were recommended by the Ellender committee, which investigated expenditures by Senators in the last election. . . . In this instance the words of the Smith-Connally Act have been somewhat changed in effect so as to plug up a loophole which obviously developed, and which, if the courts had permitted advantage to be taken of it, as a matter of fact, would absolutely have destroyed the prohibition against political advertising by corporations. If 'contribution' does not mean 'expenditure,' then a candidate for office could have his corporation friends publish an advertisement for him in the newspapers every day for a month before election. I do not think the law contemplated such a thing, but it was claimed that it did, at least when it applied to labor organizations. So, all we are doing here is plugging up the hole which developed, following the recommendation by our own Elections Committee, in the Ellender bill.—93 Cong. Rec. 6439.

After considerable debate, the conference version was approved by the Senate, and the bill subsequently became law despite the President's veto. It is this section of the statute that the District Court held did not reach the activities alleged in the indictment. . . .

Thus, for our purposes, the indictment charged appellee with having used union dues to sponsor commercial television broadcasts designed to influence the electorate to select certain candidates for Congress in connection with the 1954 elections.

To deny that such activity, either on the part of a corporation or a labor organization, constituted an "expenditure in connection with any [federal] election" is to deny the long series of congressional efforts calculated to avoid the deleterious influences on federal elections resulting from the use of money by those who exercise control over large aggregations of capital. More particularly, this Court would have to ignore the history of the statute from the time it was first made applicable to labor organizations. As indicated by the reports of the Congressional Committees that investigated campaign expenditures, it was to embrace precisely the kind of indirect contribution alleged in the indictment that Congress amended Section 313 to proscribe "expenditures." It is open to the Government to prove under this indictment activity by appellee that, except for an irrelevant difference in the medium of communication employed, is virtually indistinguishable from the Brotherhood of Railway Trainmen's purchase of radio time to sponsor candidates or the Ohio CIO's general distribution of pamphlets to oppose Senator Taft. Because such conduct was claimed to be merely "an expenditure [by the union] of its own funds to state its position to the world," the Senate and House Committees recommended and Congress enacted, as we have seen, the prohibition of "expenditures" as well as "contributions" to "plug the existing loophole."

Although not entitled to the same weight as these carefully considered committee reports, the Senate debate preceding the passage of the Taft-Hartley Act confirms what these reports demonstrate. A colloquy between Senator Taft and Senator Pepper dealt with the problem confronting us:

> Mr. Pepper: Does what the Senator has said in the past also apply to a radio speech? If a national labor union, for example, should believe that it was in the public interest to elect the Democratic Party instead of the Republican Party, or vice versa, would it be forbidden by this proposed act to pay for any radio time, for anybody to make a speech that would express to the people the point of view of that organization?

MR. TAFT: If it contributed its own funds to get somebody to make the speech, I would say they would violate the law.

MR. PEPPER: If they paid for the radio time?

MR. TAFT: If they are simply giving the time, I would say not; I would say that is in the course of their regular business.

MR. PEPPER: What I mean is this: I was not assuming that the radio station was owned by the labor organization. Suppose that in the 1948 campaign, Mr. William Green, as president of the American Federation of Labor, should believe it to be in the interest of his membership to go on the radio and support one party or the other in the national election, and should use American Federation of Labor funds to pay for the radio time. Would that be an expenditure which is forbidden to a labor organization under the statute?

MR. TAFT: Yes.—93 Cong. Rec. 6439.

The discussion that followed, while suggesting that difficult questions might arise as to whether or not a particular broadcast fell within the statute, buttresses the conclusion that Section 304 was understood to proscribe the expenditure of union dues to pay for commercial broadcasts that are designed to urge the public to elect a certain candidate or party. . . .

Our holding that the District Court committed error when it dismissed the indictment for having failed to state an offense under the statute implies no disrespect for "the cardinal rule of construction, that where the language of an act will bear two interpretations, equally obvious, that one which is clearly in accordance with the provisions of the constitution is to be preferred." *Knights Templars' Indemnity Co. v. Jarman*, 187 US 197, 205, 47 LEd 139, 23 SupCt 108 (1902). The case before us does not call for its application. Here only one interpretation may be fairly derived from the relevant materials. The rule of construction to be invoked when constitutional problems lurk in an ambiguous statute does not permit disregard of what Congress commands.

Appellee urges that if, as we hold, 18 USC § 610, FCA 18 § 610, embraces the activity alleged in the indictment, it offends several rights guaranteed by the Constitution. The Government replies that the actual restraint upon union political activity imposed by the statute is so narrowly limited that Congress did not exceed its powers to protect the political progress from undue influence of large aggregations of capital and to promote individual responsibility for democratic government. Once more we are confronted with the duty of being mindful of the conditions under which we may enter upon the delicate process of constitutional adjudication. . . .

Counsel are prone to shape litigation, so far as it is within their control, in order to secure comprehensive rulings. This is true both of counsel for defendants and for the Government. Such desire on their part is not difficult to appreciate. But the court has its responsibility. Matter now buried under abstract constitutional issues may, by the elucidation of a trial, be brought to the surface, and in the outcome constitutional questions may disappear. Allegations of the indictment hypothetically framed to elicit a ruling from this Court or based upon misunderstanding of the facts may not survive the test of proof. For example, was the broadcast paid for out of the general dues of the union membership or may the funds be fairly said to have been obtained on a voluntary basis? Did the broadcast reach the public at large or only those affiliated with appellee? Did it constitute active electioneering or simply state the record of particular candidates on economic issues? Did the union sponsor the broadcast with the intent to affect the results of the election? As Senator Taft repeatedly recognized in the debate on Section 304, prosecutions under the Act may present difficult questions of fact. See *supra,* pp. 585–87, n. 1. We suggest the possibility of such questions, not to imply answers to problems of statutory construction, but merely to indicate the covert issues that may be involved in this case.

Enough has been said to justify withholding determination of the more or less abstract issues of constitutional law. Because the District Court's erroneous interpretation of the statute led it to stop the prosecution prematurely, its judgment must be reversed and the case must be remanded to it for further proceedings not inconsistent with this opinion.

[Editors' note. Mr. Justice Douglas, with whom the Chief Justice and Mr. Justice Black joined, dissented on the grounds that (1) Section 304 should be construed to limit the word "expenditure" to activity that does not involve First Amendment rights and (2) if construed more broadly, it is unconstitutional.

The dissent concluded:

> The Act, as construed and applied, is a broadside assault on the freedom of political expression guaranteed by the First Amendment. It cannot possibly be saved by any of the facts conjured up by the Court. The answers to the questions reserved are quite irrelevant to the constitutional questions tendered under the First Amendment.

On remand to the District Court for trial, the jury returned a verdict of not guilty.]

International Association of Machinists v. Street

SUPREME COURT OF THE UNITED STATES, 1961

MR. JUSTICE BRENNAN delivered the opinion of the Court.

A group of labor organizations, appellants here, and the carriers comprising the Southern Railway System, entered into a union-shop agreement pursuant to the authority of § 2, Eleventh of the Railway Labor Act. The agreement requires each of the appellees, employees of the carriers, as a condition of continued employment, to pay the appellant union representing his particular class or craft the dues, initiation fees, and assessments uniformly required as a condition of acquiring or retaining union membership. The appellees, in behalf of themselves and of employees similarly situated, brought this action in the Superior Court of Bibb County, Georgia, alleging that the money each was thus compelled to pay to hold his job was in substantial part used to finance the campaigns of candidates for federal and state offices whom he opposed, and to promote the propagation of political and economic doctrines, concepts, and ideologies with which he disagreed. The Superior Court found that the allegations were fully proved and entered a judgment and decree enjoining the enforcement of the union-shop agreement on the ground that § 2, Eleventh violates the Federal Constitution to the extent that it permits such use by the appellants of the funds exacted from employees. The Supreme Court of Georgia affirmed, 215 Ga. 27, 108 S. E. 2d 796. . . .

Each named appellee in this action has made known to the union representing his craft or class his dissent from the use of his money for political causes which he opposes. We have therefore examined the legislative history of § 2, Eleventh in the context of the development of unionism in the railroad industry under the regulatory scheme created by the Railway Labor Act to determine whether a construction is "fairly possible" which denies the authority to a union, over the employee's objection, to spend his money for political causes which he opposes. We conclude that such a construction is not only "fairly possible" but entirely reasonable. . . .

The conclusion to which this history [of the Railway Labor Act Amendments of 1951] clearly points is that § 2, Eleventh contemplated compulsory unionism to force employees to share the costs of negotiating and administering collective agreements, and the costs of the adjustment and settlement of disputes. One looks in vain for any suggestion

367 U.S. 740 (1961). Footnotes and portions of the original text have been deleted.

that Congress also meant in § 2, Eleventh to provide the unions with a means for forcing employees, over their objection, to support political causes which they oppose. . . .

A congressional concern over possible impingements on the interests of individual dissenters from union policies is . . . discernible. It is true that opponents of the union shop urged that Congress should not allow it without explicitly regulating the amount of dues which might be exacted or prescribing the uses for which the dues might be expended. We may assume that Congress was also fully conversant with the long history of intensive involvement of the railroad unions in political activities. But it does not follow that § 2, Eleventh places no restriction on the use of an employee's money, over his objection, to support political causes he opposes merely because Congress did not enact a comprehensive regulatory scheme governing expenditures. For it is abundantly clear that Congress did not completely abandon the policy of full freedom of choice embodied in the 1934 Act, but rather made inroads on it for the limited purpose of eliminating the problems created by the "free rider." That policy survives in § 2, Eleventh in the safeguards intended to protect freedom of dissent. Congress was aware of the conflicting interests involved in the question of the union shop and sought to achieve their accommodation. As was said by the Presidential Emergency Board which recommended the making of the union-shop agreement involved in this case:

> It is not as though Congress had believed it was merely removing some abstract legal barrier and not passing on the merits. It was made fully aware that it was deciding these critical issues of individual right versus collective interests which have been stressed in this proceeding.
>
> Indeed, Congress gave very concrete evidence that it carefully considered the claims of the individual to be free of arbitrary or unreasonable restrictions resulting from compulsory unionism. It did not give a blanket approval to union-shop agreements. Instead it enacted a precise and carefully drawn limitation on the kind of union-shop agreements which might be made. The obvious purpose of this careful prescription was to strike a balance between the interests pressed by the unions and the considerations which the Carriers have urged. By providing that a worker should not be discharged if he was denied or if he lost his union membership for any reason other than non-payment of dues, initiation fees, or assessments, Congress definitely indicated that it had weighed carefully and given effect to the policy of the arguments against the union shop.—Report of Presidential Emergency Board No. 98, appointed pursuant to Exec. Order No. 10306, Nov. 15, 1951, p. 6.

We respect this congressional purpose when we construe § 2, Eleventh as not vesting the unions with unlimited power to spend exacted money. We are not called upon to delineate the precise limits of that power in this case. We have before us only the question whether the power is restricted to the extent of denying the unions the right, over the employee's objection, to use his money to support political causes which he opposes. Its use to support candidates for public office, and advance political programs, is not a use which helps defray the expenses of the negotiation or administration of collective agreements, or the expenses entailed in the adjustment of grievances and disputes. In other words, it is a use which falls clearly outside the reasons advanced by the unions and accepted by Congress why authority to make union-shop agreements was justified. On the other hand, it is equally clear that it is a use to support activities within the area of dissenters' interests which Congress enacted the proviso to protect. We give § 2, Eleventh the construction which achieves both congressional purposes when we hold, as we do, that § 2, Eleventh is to be construed to deny the unions, over an employee's objection, the power to use his exacted funds to support political causes which he opposes. . . .

Under our view of the statute, however, the decision of the court below was erroneous and cannot stand. The appellees who have participated in this action have in the course of it made known to their respective unions their objection to the use of their money for the support of political causes. In that circumstance, the respective unions were without power to use payments thereafter tendered by them for such political causes. However, the union-shop agreement itself is not unlawful. *Railway Employes' Dept. v. Hanson, supra.* The appellees therefore remain obliged, as a condition of continued employment, to make the payments to their respective unions called for by the agreement. Their right of action stems not from constitutional limitations on Congress' power to authorize the union shop, but from § 2, Eleventh itself. In other words, appellees' grievance stems from the spending of their funds for purposes not authorized by the Act in the face of their objection, not from the enforcement of the union-shop agreement by the mere collection of funds. If their money were used for purposes contemplated by § 2, Eleventh, the appellees would have no grievance at all. We think that an injunction restraining enforcement of the union-shop agreement is therefore plainly not a remedy appropriate to the violation of the Act's restriction on expenditures. . . .

Since the case must therefore be remanded to the court below for consideration of a proper remedy, we think that it is appropriate to suggest the limits within which remedial discretion may be exercised consistently with the Railway Labor Act and other relevant public policies. As indicated, an injunction against enforcement of the union shop itself through the collection of funds is unwarranted. We also think that a blanket injunction against all expenditures of funds for the disputed purposes, even one conditioned on cessation of improper expenditures, would not be a proper exercise of equitable discretion. . . . Moreover, the fact that these expenditures are made for political activities is an additional reason for reluctance to impose such an injunctive remedy. Whatever may be the powers of Congress or the States to forbid unions altogether to make various types of political expenditures, as to which we express no opinion here, many of the expenditures involved in the present case are made for the purpose of disseminating information as to candidates and programs and publicizing the positions of the unions on them. As to such expenditures an injunction would work a restraint on the expression of political ideas which might be offensive to the First Amendment. For the majority also has an interest in stating its views without being silenced by the dissenters. To attain the appropriate reconciliation between majority and dissenting interests in the area of political expression, we think the courts in administering the Act should select remedies which protect both interests to the maximum extent possible without undue impingement of one on the other.

Among possible remedies which would appear appropriate to the injury complained of, two may be enforced with a minimum of administrative difficulty and with little danger of encroachment on the legitimate activities or necessary functions of the unions. Any remedies, however, would properly be granted only to employees who have made known to the union officials that they do not desire their funds to be used for political causes to which they object. The safeguards of § 2, Eleventh were added for the protection of dissenters' interest, but dissent is not to be presumed—it must affirmatively be made known to the union by the dissenting employee. The union receiving money exacted from an employee under a union-shop agreement should not in fairness be subjected to sanctions in favor of an employee who makes no complaint of the use of his money for such activities. . . .

One remedy would be an injunction against expenditure for political causes opposed by each complaining employee of a sum, from those moneys to be spent by the union for political purposes, which is so much of the moneys exacted from him as is the proportion of the union's total expenditures made for such political activities to the union's total budget. The union should not be in a position to make up such sum from money paid by a nondissenter, for this would shift a disproportionate share of the costs of collective bargaining to the dissenter and have the same effect of applying his money to support such political activities. A second remedy would be restitution to each individual employee of that portion of his money which the union expended, despite his notification, for the political causes to which he had advised the union he was opposed. There should be no necessity, however, for the employee to trace his money up to and including its expenditure; if the money goes into general funds and no separate accounts of receipts and expenditures of the funds of individual employees are maintained, the portion of his money the employee would be entitled to recover would be in the same proportion that the expenditures for political purposes which he had advised the union he disapproved bore to the total union budget.

The judgment is reversed and the case is remanded to the court below for proceedings not inconsistent with this opinion.

Mr. Justice Douglas concurred.

Mr. Justice Whittaker concurred in part and dissented in part.

Mr. Justice Black, dissenting. . . .

Unions composed of a voluntary membership, like all other voluntary groups, should be free in this country to fight in the public forum to advance their own causes, to promote their choice of candidates and parties and to work for the doctrines or the laws they favor. But to the extent that Government steps in to force people to help espouse the particular causes of a group, that group—whether composed of railroad workers or lawyers—loses its status as a voluntary group. The reason our Constitution endowed individuals with freedom to think and speak and advocate was to free people from the blighting effect of either a partial or a complete governmental monopoly of ideas. Labor unions have been peculiar beneficiaries of that salutary constitutional principle, and lawyers, I think, are charged with a peculiar responsibility to preserve and protect this principle of constitutional freedom, even for themselves. A violation of it, however small, is, in my judgment, prohibited by the First Amendment and should be stopped dead in its tracks on its first appearance. With so vital a principle at stake, I cannot agree to the imposition of parsimonious limitations on the kind of decree the courts below can fashion in their efforts to afford effective protection to these priceless constitutional rights.

I would affirm the judgment of the Georgia Supreme Court. . . .

Mr. Justice Frankfurter, whom Mr. Justice Harlan joins, dissenting.

. . . [T]he question before us is whether § 2, Eleventh of the Railway Labor Act can untorturingly be read to bar activities of railway unions, which have bargained in accordance with federal law for a union shop, whereby they are forbidden to spend union dues for purposes that have uniformly and extensively been so long pursued as to have become commonplace, settled, conventional trade-union practices. No consideration relevant to construction sustains such a restrictive reading.

The statutory provision cannot be meaningfully construed except against the background and presupposition of what is loosely called political activity of American trade unions in general and railroad unions in particular—activity indissolubly relating to the immediate economic and social concerns that are the raison d'être of unions. It would be pedantic heavily to document this familiar truth of industrial history and commonplace of trade-union life. To write the history of the Brotherhoods, the United Mine Workers, the Steel Workers, the Amalgamated Clothing Workers, the International Ladies Garment Workers, the United Auto Workers, and leave out their so-called political activities and expenditures for them, would be sheer mutilation. Suffice it to recall a few illustrative manifestations. The AFL, surely the conservative labor group, sponsored as early as 1893 an extensive program of political demands calling for compulsory education, an eight-hour day, employer tort liability, and other social reforms. The fiercely contested Adamson Act of 1916, see *Wilson v. New*, 243 U. S. 332, was a direct result of railway union pressures exerted upon both the Congress and the President. More specifically, the weekly publication "Labor"—an expenditure under attack in this case—has since 1919 been the organ of the railroad brotherhoods which finance it. Its files through the years show its preoccupation with legislative measures that touch the vitals of labor's interests and with the men and parties who effectuate them. This aspect—call it the political side—is as organic, as inured a part of the philosophy and practice of railway unions as their immediate bread-and-butter concerns.

Viewed in this light, there is a total absence in the text, the context, the history, and the purpose of the legislation under review of any indication that Congress, in authorizing union-shop agreements, attributed to unions and restricted them to an artificial, nonprevalent scope of activities in the expenditure of their funds. An inference that Congress legislated regarding expenditure control in contradiction to prevailing practices ought to be better founded than on complete silence. The aim of the 1951 legislation, clearly stated in the congressional reports, was to eliminate "free riders" in the industry—to make possible "the sharing of the burden of maintenance by all of the beneficiaries of union activity." To suggest that this language covertly meant to encompass any less than the maintenance of those activities normally engaged in by unions is to withdraw life from law and to say that Congress dealt with artificialities and not with railway unions as they were and as they functioned. . . .

Nothing was further from congressional purpose than to be concerned with restrictions upon the right to speak. Its purpose was to eliminate "free riders" in the bargaining unit. Inroads on free speech were not remotely involved in the legislative process. They were in nobody's mind. Congress legislated to correct what it found to be abuses in the domain of promoting industrial peace. This Court would stray beyond its powers were it to erect a far-fetched claim, derived from some ultimate relation between an obviously valid aim of legislation and an abstract conception of freedom, into a constitutional right. . . .

If higher wages and shorter hours are prime ends of a union in bargaining collectively, these goals may often be more effectively achieved by lobbying and the support of sympathetic candidates. In 1960 there were at least eighteen railway labor organizations registered as congressional lobby groups.

When one runs down the detailed list of national and international problems on which the AFL–CIO speaks, it seems rather naive for a court to conclude—as did the trial court—that the union expenditures were "not reasonably necessary to collective bargaining or to maintaining the existence and position of said union defendants as effective bargaining agents." The notion that economic and political concerns are separable is pre-Victorian. Presidents of the United States and Committees of Congress invite views of labor on matters not immediately concerned with wages, hours, and conditions of employment. And this Court accept briefs as *amici* from the AFL–CIO on issues that cannot be called industrial, in any circumscribed sense. It is not true in life that political protection is irrelevant to, and insulated from, economic interests. It is not true for industry or finance. Neither is it true for labor. It disrespects the wise, hardheaded men who were the authors of our Constitution and our Bill of Rights to conclude that their scheme of government requires what the facts of life reject. As Mr. Justice Rutledge stated: "To say that labor unions as such have nothing of value to contribute to that process [the electoral process] and no vital or legitimate interest in it is to ignore the obvious facts of political and economic life and of their increasing interrelationship in modern society." *United States v. CIO*, 335 U. S. 106, 129, 144 (concurring opinion joined in by Black, Douglas, and Murphy, JJ). Fifty years ago this Court held that there was no connection between outlawry of "yellow dog contracts" on interstate railroads and interstate commerce, and therefore found unconstitutional legislation directed against the evils of these agreements. Is it any more consonant with the facts of life today, than was this holding in *Adair v. United States*, 208 U. S. 161, to say that the tax policies of the National Government—the scheme of rates and exemptions—have no close relation to the wages of workers; that legislative developments like the Tennessee Valley Authority do not intimately touch the lives of workers within their respective regions; that national measures furthering health and education do not directly bear on the lives of industrial workers; that candidates who support these movements do not stand in different relation to labor's narrowest economic interests than avowed opponents of these measures? Is it respectful of the modes of thought of Madison and Jefferson projected into our day to attribute to them the view that the First Amendment must be construed to bar unions from concluding, by due procedural steps, that civil-rights legislation conduces to their interest, thereby prohibiting union funds to be expended to promote passage of such measures? . . .

In conclusion, then, we are asked by union members who oppose these expenditures to protect their right to free speech—although they are as free to speak as ever—against governmental action which has permitted a union elected by democratic process to bargain for a union shop and to expend the funds thereby collected for purposes which are controlled by internal union choice. To do so would be to mutilate a scheme designed by Congress for the purpose of equitably sharing the cost of securing the benefits of union exertions; it would greatly embarrass if not frustrate conventional labor activities which have become institutionalized through time. To do so is to give constitutional sanction to doctrinaire views and to grant a miniscule claim constitutional recognition. . . .

I would reverse and remand the case for dismissal in the Georgia courts.

The Magnitude and Method of Labor's Financial Involvement in Politics

Harry M. Scoble

University of California, Los Angeles

[V]OTER-MOBILIZATION is the end-purpose of the flow of money into elections; therefore it is appropriate to examine what is known concerning the extent, methods, and impact of labor money in politics.

To begin with, it is extremely difficult to obtain any reliable and comparable data that span more than two elections—as Alexander Heard, the author of the most exhaustive treatment of money in politics, has carefully noted.[1] However, it is possible to examine a variety of alternative data presented by Heard in an attempt to establish the upper limit of the extent of spending in elections by labor unions. A first, and perhaps the best, measure is that of direct expenditure (for goods and services consumed during a campaign) by national-level campaign groups. For 1952, labor money constituted 15 percent of all direct expenditures in behalf of Democrats, and in 1956 this proportion was 11 percent.[2] At a second and quite different level, Heard estimates that the *voluntary* political giving by some 17,000,000 unionists in 1956 constituted about $2,000,000 which in turn just about balanced the voluntary contributions in amounts of $500 or more recorded by 742 officials of the 225 largest business concerns in the nation.[3] Approximately one union member in eight contributed voluntarily during this period, with the average contribution something less than $1.00 and with considerable variation: in highly politicized unions such as the UAW or the ILGWU, both the rate and the average amount of contribution were considerably higher (e.g., one in two members and an average of $2.57 in the latter union). But voluntary contribution is

---

Excerpted by permission of the publisher from "Organized Labor in Electoral Politics: Some Questions for the Discipline," *Western Political Quarterly*, XVI, No. 3, September 1963.

[1] Alexander Heard, *The Costs of Democracy* (Chapel Hill: University of North Carolina Press, 1960).

[2] *Ibid.*, pp. 20.

[3] *Ibid.*, pp. 195–96. Heard estimates this to be 0.3 percent of annual union dues; the significance of such money does not, however, lie solely in its magnitude but in its legal status as well; i.e., opponents of organized labor have sought to restrict the use of union-dues by a variety of legal controls; for example, the Taft-Hartley Act of 1947 sought to prohibit unions from *expenditures* as well as contributions in *nominations* as well as general elections for federal offices.

only part of the process, as Heard notes; for dues-money may flow into election campaigns through one or more of a wide variety of activities: donations (e.g., the ILGWU donated an average of $15,500 annually to the ADA in 1953–56); the maintenance of political departments, such as the "political shop-steward" program of the ILGWU; the creation of special "Citizenship Funds" (in the UAW, 5 percent of the member's dues goes into such a fund maintained by the international and another 5 percent into a local fund); the development of "education and information" programs, such as the IAM training classes on the relation between legislation and political activity; or undertaking communications and public service activities (e.g., the AFL–CIO sponsors Edward P. Morgan on ABC nationally, while the UAW sponsors the radio-television newscasts of Guy Nunn in the Detroit metropolitan area). In addition, it should be obvious that electoral purposes may be served through union expenditures on: public relations and research; union legal departments; union-executive expense accounts; general administrative costs; and, of course, salaries. All of these account for some hard-to-measure but nonetheless real methods for organized investment in the electoral process by unions. In an effort to provide some estimate of the dollar magnitude of such investment, Heard has taken organized labor's numerical membership as a proportion of the potential electorate—roughly 17 percent—and concludes that "labor money in politics from all sources pays *a much smaller share* of the nation's campaign-connected costs than union members constitute of the population of voting age."[4] However, such an estimate may unintentionally conceal the significance of such labor money to the Democratic party. For example, one might arbitrarily take 10 percent as labor's actual share of the roughly $165,000,000 in cash-and-kind costs for financing all the electoral activities entailed in a presidential election year; but that 10 percent of the *total* would be highly significant in Democratic party finance for two reasons: very close to 100 percent of all labor money goes to the Democratic side *and*, for the period under review, the two-party division of resources and expenditures was roughly 60–40 in favor of the Republicans; therefore the 10 percent overall share of labor actually would constitute close to 25 percent of

---

[4] *Ibid.*, pp. 196–208, at p. 208; my emphasis. The estimate of others occasionally runs higher than this. See for example Ivan Hinderaker, *Party Politics* (New York: Holt, 1956), p. 585. The evidence is sketchy; but to judge from data assembled from the *Congressional Quarterly* and Heard, it seems likely that longer-term analyses will show that organized labor—unlike most party and nonparty groups—is able to sustain its level of operation from one election to the next, i.e., it does not suffer post-presidential atrophy.

all Democratic funds. Whether the empirical basis for testing this tentative conclusion will ever be unearthed seems highly problematical; such a project would require even more time, money, and effort than were put forth in the heroic labors of the University of North Carolina (Heard) project. Meanwhile one may infer that the apparent autonomy, decentralization, and disarray of the organizational structure of unions provide national labor leaders with a convenient excuse for saying that they simply do not and cannot know all the facts;[5] and one might equally suppose that some, perhaps many, Democratic (and Republican) candidates also prefer not to know too much about the entire process of money in elections.

When one turns from the *magnitude* of labor's financial involvement in elections to the *method* of its involvement, three additional aspects of Heard's analysis of labor money become relevant. Heard's available evidence on the geography of labor support in 1956 indicated that such support was concentrated within the ten states whose populations include two-thirds of all organized labor.[6] His next analysis, focused on the partisan recipients of funds transferred by labor committees, showed the almost exclusive support of Democrats. In 1952, for example, $833,000 could be traced, and $5,450 had been transmitted to one senatorial and five House Republican candidates (an average of $908 each); the analysis for 1956 of $1,616,000 of national-level and of $430,000 of state-local-level labor committee transfers showed a total of $3,925 going to eight House Republican candidates (about $491 each).[7] A final aspect of the method of labor's financial involvement is depicted by Heard. . . . The major point of interest . . . is the clear indication that labor union leaders desire to, and primarily do, deal directly with Democratic *candidates* (or their personal committees); they deliberately bypass the established Democratic party committees at both national and state-local levels. Heard also indicates the obverse of this, in that there is evidence that union leaders have frequently sought to prevent Democratic party solicitation within and among their local memberships.[8] In the broader context of my analysis, these data on voter-mobilization are further indications of the tendency of interest

---

[5] See Heard, *op. cit.*, pp. 183–84, on the Gore Committee experience in 1956. Furthermore, as seems true in almost all aspects of the study of American politics, information is most full and accurate at the national level and least at the local level—yet six-sevenths of all electoral expenditures are incurred at the state, district, and local levels.

[6] *Ibid.*, pp. 173–75 and 187–88.

[7] *Ibid.*, recomputed from footnotes to Table 23, p. 185, and text at p. 187.

[8] *Ibid.*, p. 193, n. 58.

groups to expend such potential resources as exist within the electoral process and to expend them at such a rate and with such efficiency that the group takes over *all* of the *relevant* functions of the political party.

This last broad generalization unfortunately creates more intellectual problems than it solves, for it begs three additional questions: How much in fact has organized labor committed its potential resources to electoral politics? How efficiently in fact has it exploited these committed resources? And what in fact have political scientists done by way of systematic analysis to answer these first two questions?

At several points I have pointed out the lack of both data and analysis; consequently I recommend the following specific questions for focusing disciplined inquiry into the increasing electoral action of organized labor. Does a strongly held and economically based ideology —for business or for labor—lead to efficiency in electoral action? Does a left-oriented *labor* ideology incorporate, ignore, or conflict with the central cultural concept and value of "efficiency" in the first place? Furthermore, to what extent is organized labor activity confined to *general* elections? Are the electoral practices of organized labor similar in disbursement and endorsement to those of the party groups and of other nonparty political groups? Does organized labor in its electoral action normally aid established incumbents, or do its major efforts go into support of nonincumbent challengers? Lastly, to what extent has political science analysis provided intelligible answers to these questions?

Before surveying the substantive material available for answering such questions, several explanatory comments are required. To begin with, as one committed to group theory I am acutely aware of gross inaccuracies in the monolithic assumption implied by speaking of "organized labor" or, conversely, "the business community." In my usage of "organized labor," therefore, let it be understood that I believe that sufficient evidence already exists to justify working upon the assumption that in political behavior a unimodal (rather than a bi- or multimodal) tendency exists and that political science can advance only by working out from this initial primitive—yet empirically based—assumption. After that, the necessary refinements can be made. Secondly, it should be clear from the particular phraseology of the questions posed in the last two paragraphs that I believe that the scheme of analysis framed by these questions is appropriate to the study of *all* interest groups that engage in electoral action. Finally, I am knowingly taking on the unpopular but necessary task of bringing to the threshold of consciousness the very perplexing question of just how much we political scientists really know.

What precisely have political scientists stated about the electoral impact of organized labor? One text[9] notes that organized labor spoke of Election Day 1946 as "Black Tuesday" because only 73 of 318 House candidates and only 5 of 21 Senate candidates endorsed by labor won—but it is impossible to learn whether these were Democrats or Republicans, incumbents or nonincumbents, or how well labor did relative to, say, the Democratic party itself in that Republican year. One author has taken the analysis of 1946 somewhat further, however, in noting that California Republicans uniformly centered their campaign attack on CIO-supported Democratic congressional candidates; that this attack on "CIO-PAC package" candidates became a campaign theme for Republicans almost everywhere in the nation; and that CIO-PAC endorsement of some congressional candidates proved to be a "kiss of death" under certain circumstances.[10] That is, in a number of constituencies the PAC leaders made only a public announcement of endorsement of the candidate and either did not think it important to, or in fact could not, commit labor to any other campaign activity; as a consequence, the labor endorsement in those constituencies provided an issue to opponents of the candidate and permitted them to activate their members and sympathizers with no offsetting gains for the labor-endorsee. As for 1948, which was critical in many ways, slightly more information and analysis are available. Hugh A. Bone pointed out that after the 1948 election the new Labor's League for Political Education (AFL) claimed 172 "friends" of labor elected and 106 "enemies" retired (i.e., now ex-incumbent). Interestingly the most sophisticated analysis of 1948 is to be found in Truman's book—published eleven years ago.[11] Noting generally that the CIO-PAC had endorsed 215 House candidates in 1948 and that 144 of these were elected, the author breaks down the 144 victories in several ways: first, 64 were of incumbents, 74 involved defeating incumbents, while the remaining 6 were in non-incumbency situations; next, 57 of the labor-endorsed incumbents reelected had voted against the Taft-Hartley Act of 1947 while all 74 of the incumbents defeated had voted for it; and finally, a partial analysis of such factors as the two-party division of the popular vote at the

---

[9] John P. Roche and Murray S. Stedman, Jr., *The Dynamics of Democratic Government* (New York: McGraw-Hill, 1954), p. 71.

[10] Hugh A. Bone, "Political Parties and Pressure Group Politics," in *Annals*, 319 (1958), 73–83; also Bone, *American Politics and the Party System* (New York: McGraw-Hill, 1949), pp. 146–49.

[11] David B. Truman, *The Governmental Process* (New York: Knopf, 1951), pp. 315–16, citing his earlier data and analysis in Frederick Mosteller *et al.*, *The Pre-Election Polls of 1948* (New York: Social Science Research Council, 1949).

last election and the partisan control of the constituencies leads to the conclusion that "the changes in 1948 were of major importance. Presumably the CIO-PAC efforts had something to do with them."

Despite the fact that a tentative scheme for analysis has been in existence for at least a decade,[12] neither textbook writers nor the researchers they cite have done anything further on this subject. To be sure, one can find conclusions that, for example, in 1950 "the labor-endorsed candidates took a fearful drubbing,"[13] or that "in California, following the 1958 elections, labor's power emerged as a great part of the substance behind the Democratic Party's victory."[14] What one finds is unrelieved anecdotalism, and not very good anecdotes at that. This may be partly a result of the combined tendency of politicians (including labor politicians), news media, and the political scientist audience alike to personify the issue of labor's electoral activity in one key race at a time, *viz.*, Taft and Ohio in 1950 or Goldwater and Arizona in 1958. And there is some evidence that labor, especially in its allocation of funds, may be inefficient in such races. For example, organized labor *reported* expenditures of $180,880, Senator Taft *reported* expenditures of $243,740, and probably more than $2,000,000 was spent in that one 1950 contest.[15] As for 1958, the close reader of the *New York Times* found that "Rumor has it that the national COPE organization has been pouring money—as much as $400,000—and political workers into Arizona to defeat Senator Goldwater. . . ."[16] COPE officials and Arizona labor leaders immediately denied this, of course, indicating that labor's financial involvement would be about the same

------

[12] In some ways, for almost twenty years. See V. O. Key, Jr., "The Veterans and the House of Representatives: A Study of a Pressure Group and Electoral Mortality," *Journal of Politics*, 5 (1943), 27–40.

[13] Roche and Stedman, *op. cit.* It is only fair to point out that their book was published in 1954; on the other hand, the sole reference they make is to the reelection of Republican Senator Robert Taft of Ohio.

[14] William Goodman, *The Two-Party System in the United States* (2d ed.; New York: Van Nostrand, 1960), p. 355.

[15] The labor figure is given in the *New York Times*, November 25, 1950, p. 8, and includes $74,470 reported by the secretary-treasurer for the Ohio CIO-PAC; the Taft figure may be found in *ibid.*, November 17, 1950, p. 30. The overall estimate is that of the Senate Committee on Rules and Administration, Subcommittee on Privileges and Elections, 82nd Cong., 1st and 2d sess., *Hearings on Investigation into the 1950 Ohio Senatorial Campaign* (1951 and 1952). The *New York Times*, November 8, 1950, p. 1, characterized Taft's reelection as "the worst labor defeat since 1932" and most readers, political scientists included, probably agreed.

[16] October 15, 1958, p. 1, article by Gladwin Hill.

as the $33,000 expended in Arizona in 1956; but when the battle had ended, labor's reported contributions to McFarland (Goldwater's opponent) interestingly totaled only $3,500.[17] Meanwhile, Goldwater's reelection effectively obscured the fact that two other COPE-endorsed Arizona candidates had been elected with impressive vote-margins.[18] The focus upon one great personalized contest at a time may also result from the facts that organized labor, even the AFL–CIO, has no centralized endorsement machinery and that it is therefore difficult, though hardly impossible, as indicated below, to learn what the state, district, and local political units of labor are doing; and as a general rule in this country, that which it is difficult to learn normally goes unreported and necessarily unanalyzed.

But at least one political scientist has provided interesting clues concerning the behavior of organized labor in endorsements. In a tentative survey of CIO–PAC activity in the Detroit area, Nicholas Masters has generalized that "the PAC attempts to endorse the candidate who most nearly meets the claims of the group and who commands the greatest prestige, but it will endorse the mediocre or weak candidate if he is opposed by a candidate who is closely identified with business groups."[19] Thus there is evidence of the push and pull of ideological stereotypes in electoral behavior. Furthermore, Masters has noted that the Democratic partisanship of the candidate is the primary criterion for PAC endorsement in Wayne County, with liberal position coming next in importance; and—

> The term "liberal" does not puzzle PAC leaders as it does academicians. A candidate may prove his liberalism by allowing the PAC to evaluate his stand on ten or twelve key and current issues with which the CIO is concerned. *The usual method for evaluation of a candidate, however, is to tabulate his recorded votes on such issues. Thus the incumbent has the inside track for endorsement. . . .*[20]

This in turn is evidence—if tentative and subject to further testing— that the influence of organized labor, even in a labor-dominated area, may be inoperative or ineffectual until *after* the candidate has established himself; it may also mean that organized labor operates as a conservative force in the limited sense of freezing out challengers and

---

[17] *Congressional Quarterly Almanac*, 15 (1959), p. 809.

[18] *New York Times*, November 6, 1958, p. 22.

[19] Nicholas A. Masters, "The Politics of Union Endorsement of Candidates in the Detroit Area," *Midwest Journal of Political Science*, 1 (1957), 136–50.

[20] *Ibid.*, p. 149; emphasis added.

preventing intraparty conflict; at the minimum Masters' evidence suggests that repeated endorsements of incumbents is the major factor in explaining the high rate of success of the CIO-PAC in the 1946-55 period.[21]

More information is available concerning the national level of politics and especially concerning the 1960 election. For example, that election is the first in which data both on the Senate campaign committees and on labor endorsements and disbursements are readily available to the political analyst. Using such data, then, Table III [Tables I and II in the original were not included in this excerpt] compares the Democratic Senate Campaign Committee and the AFL–CIO. Labor made only approximately half as many major-support decisions (de-

Table III

Rank-Order Comparisons of Major-Support Decisions (of $5,000 or More) Made by the DSCC and by the AFL–CIO Respectively in 1960 Senate Elections

DSCC			AFL–CIO		
Rank	Name	State	Rank	Name	State
1	Frear (Delaware)		1	Kefauver (Tennessee)	
2	Anderson (New Mexico)		2	Humphrey (Minnesota)	
3	Bartlett (Alaska)		3	Douglas (Illinois)	
4	Humphrey (Minnesota)		4	McNamara (Michigan)	
5	Whitaker (Wyoming)		5	Neuberger (Oregon)	
6	Neuberger (Oregon)		6	O'Connor (Massachusetts)	
7	Pell (Rhode Island)		7	Pell (Rhode Island)	
8	Metcalf (Montana)		8	Knous (Colorado)	
9	McLaughlin (Idaho)		9	Metcalf (Montana)	
10	McNamara (Michigan)				
11	Burdick (North Dakota)				
12.5	Knous (Colorado)				
12.5	Kerr (Oklahoma)				
14	Randolph (West Virginia)				
15.5	Long (Missouri)				
15.5	McGovern (South Dakota)				
17	Douglas (Illinois)				

Source: *Congressional Quarterly Almanac*, 17 (1961).

---

[21] *Ibid.*, p. 149, ". . . the PAC endorsement average was 67.5 percent in the primary elections and 91.2 percent in the general elections for Congressional, state, and county offices."

fined as allocations of $5,000 or more)[22] as did the DSCC in 1960; sight inspection of this figure also shows that the order of preference varied considerably between the two groups; and a rank-order correlation co-efficient (Kendall's *tau*) of the candidates appearing commonly in both the DSCC and the AFL–CIO lists was only .143–quite close to full independence–for the particular election.

We may also compare the disbursement practices of the AFL–CIO with those of the political party Senate campaign committees (in Table IV). These data for 1960 show several interesting behavioral

Table IV

Major-Support Decisions (of $5,000 or More) of Senate-Oriented Party and Labor Political Groups in 1960 Elections–Analyzed by Incumbency and Non-Incumbency Situations

Political Group	All Major Support Mean Amount	No. of Races	Incumbent Support Mean Amount	No. of Races	Non-Incumbent Support Mean Amount	No. of Races
DSCC	$ 9,880	17	$10,876	10	$8,457	7
AFL–CIO	14,511	9	20,980	5	6,425	4
RNCC	8,327	22	8,119	10	8,500	12

Source: *Congressional Quarterly Almanac*, 17 (1961).

differences. First, as many political scientists have long suspected, the DSCC in 1960–at least–operated to the distinct advantage of incumbent members of The Club–by a mean difference in excess of $2,400. The Republican National Campaign Committee, secondly, contested the greatest number of races at the level of major-support and, also presumably reflecting the mathematical decline of Republicans in the Senate since 1952, the party allocation policy actually worked to

----

[22] The assumption is that a contribution of less than $5,000 is considered to be relatively insignificant by most senatorial candidates. This cut-off is unrealistically low for states like New York and probably too high for states like Vermont or New Hampshire; presumably electoral costs bear some observable relation to numbers of constituents. Thus when political scientists get about their proper business, the analyst will finally be able to make class discriminations of senatorial constituencies similar to those the Senate itself makes with regard to allocation of office expenses.

See George B. Galloway, *The Legislative Process in Congress* (New York: Crowell, 1953), pp. 391–94.

the slight advantage of their nonincumbent candidates. In between these two, the AFL–CIO concentrated its activity—disbursing a much higher mean contribution to a much reduced total number of candidates. Furthermore, for an established electoral interest group such as organized labor, 1960 must be regarded as a year of consolidationist effort. That is, the AFL–CIO devoted its major efforts to helping reelect five preferred incumbents,[23] disbursing to them almost three times the mean amount contributed to nonincumbent Democratic candidates.

The question of electoral efficiency (and power) can be dealt with least satisfactorily here. At best, until comparable data for a sequence of elections become available, I can only illustrate the types of assumptions that seem immediately relevant to this question. The crudest measure of efficiency, of course, is whether the endorsed-supported candidates of the electoral interest group in fact win their elections. By one form of this measure—examining the proportion of all disbursements (not just major-support allocations) according to the final division of the two-party total vote in the constituency—Table V indicates that the AFL–CIO was more efficient than either party campaign committee, for it allocated 81 percent of all 1960 disbursements to winning candidates whereas its closer competitor (the DSCC) could claim only 61 percent here. But the data previously given, regarding incumbencies, suggest that this very primitive assumption on which Table V is based is appropriate only where one has a very limited num-

Table V

Relative Efficiency of Senate-Oriented Party and Labor Groups in 1960
Elections—Measured in Terms of Proportions of Disbursements
to "Close" and "Not Close" Races

Senate Races: Division of Two-Party Total Vote	Party and Labor Political Groups		
	DSCC	AFL–CIO	RNCC
"Not close"—more than 55 percent	39	52	23
"Close"—50 through 54 percent	22	29	27
"Close"—46 through 50 percent	23	8	25
"Not Close"—less than 46 percent	16	11	25
Total	100	100	100

Source: *Congressional Quarterly Almanac*, 17 (1961).

---

[23] Because of the recent history of the Oregon constituency and the Neuberger-Lusk-Neuberger sequence during 1960, I have classified the 1960 Oregon contest as the reelection of a Democratic incumbent.

ber of cases with which to deal. When the number of cases has increased significantly, the analyst would do well to invoke a second assumption here, already implied by the construction of Table V, that devoting group efforts to "close" contests is more efficient—in terms of the psychology of indebtedness—than either winning too easily (presumably by backing only incumbents) or losing too badly. As the number of cases becomes truly adequate, a third and more important assumption is necessary: that it is more efficient to help a non-incumbent challenger defeat an incumbent than it is merely to aid an already-incumbent candidate win re-election. Furthermore, in this context, efficiency is a function of *net* impact on the distribution of legislative seats (i.e., victories minus losses) rather than of *gross* (victorious) behavior alone. But such more sophisticated and, it is believed, realistic analysis clearly requires detailed information on individual constituencies not now available in any numbers.[24]

To conclude this section, then, one must presently fall back upon fragmentary and discontinuous *aggregate* data such as have been brought together in Table IV. This table provides a framework for summary analysis of four aspects of the electoral activity of organized labor. A first cluster is indicated in Table VI: for example, the magnitude of organized labor's electoral involvement in House races has

Table VI

Type, Number, and Frequency of Victory of Organized Labor Endorsements
in Selected Congressional General Elections

Year	House of Representatives			Senate		
	Contests	Victories	Percent	Contests	Victories	Percent
1946 (CIO–PAC)	318	73	23	21	5	24
1948 (CIO–PAC)	215	144	67	----	----	----
1954 (CIO–PAC)	256	126	49	26	16	61
(AFL–LLPE)	------	154	----	30	18	60
1956 (AFL–CIO)	288	159	55	29	12	41
1958 (AFL–CIO)	199	------	----	34	24	71
1960 (AFL–CIO)	193	106	55	21	12	57

Note: This table has been pieced together from the sources previously cited in this section plus *Congressional Quarterly Almanac*, 15 (1959), and 17 (1901).

---

[24] I have been able to obtain sufficient data to permit invoking these assumptions in the case of the National Committee for an Effective Congress. The analysis of the efficiency of that electoral interest group is presented in my *Ideology and Electoral Action*, Chandler, San Francisco, 1966.

significantly diminished in the past fifteen years; and I infer from this that labor strategists have acquired experience in limiting labor money to the lesser number of constituencies in which it can make a difference. (When the post-1960 Census redistricting is completed, probably by the 1964 election, the number of House seats that labor can hope to contest should increase.) As for the Senate, analysis of the geography of endorsements indicates that labor now participates in virtually the full 100 percent of contested general elections, reflecting the greater advantage of statewide constituencies for labor's electoral resources. And, lastly, labor's electoral efficiency—measured solely by percentage of victories—has closely paralleled the ebb and flow of Democratic party fortunes in the past fifteen years.

A related aspect, not revealed by Table VI, is the fact that labor money is almost wholly concentrated within the Democratic party, probably more so recently than Heard's earlier figures indicated. For example, of 199 money-endorsements for House seats in 1958, only 6 were of Republican candidates. In 1958 senatorial races, only 2 of 34 candidates supported by labor were Republicans; one of these (Knight of California) received less than one-twenty-fourth the sum contributed to his Democratic opponent, while the other (North Dakota's Langer) was noted as a domestic Democrat. In 1960's Senate races, 3 of 21 labor-endorsed candidates were Republicans; 2 of these received relatively token contributions of $500 each (incumbent Cooper of Kentucky and successful challenger Boggs of Maryland) while in the third contest, in New Jersey, incumbent Case received $2,500 to the $1,000 given to his Democratic opponent.

The influence of incumbency may be treated as a third aspect of analysis, in that endorsements of incumbents seem to account for a greater proportion of labor victories in the House than in the Senate. The data are not extensive, but they indicate the following: 10 of the 24 Senate victories in 1958 and 7 of the 12 in 1960 involved support of a successful incumbent, while in the case of the House, 95 of the 106 victories claimed in 1960 were of reelected incumbents.

A final point may be gleaned from the available data, namely the fact that labor-money activity is *not* confined, as the limited data that Heard had available seemed to indicate, to those seventeen states in which three-quarters of all unionists reside. In 1960, for example, a full half of labor's major financial efforts for the Senate fell outside those seventeen states; despite the artificialities of federalism, money is a highly mobile political resource, and the recent extension of this activity by both business and labor would seem both a cause and a reflection of the nationalization of electoral politics in America. . . .

Chapter 11

The Response of the Members

BEGINNING WITH THE PROMISES of the "full dinner pail" in turn-of-the-century America, the vote of the Northern wage earner was predominantly Republican. Not until 1928, in response to the candidacy of Al Smith for the presidency, did significant numbers of workers shift allegiance to the Democratic party. This shift, apparent in the 1928 and 1930 elections, became a landslide during the Great Depression of the 1930's. Since then, except in unusual circumstances, a majority of industrial workers vote for Democratic party candidates.

These developments are reasonably familiar to all Americans who follow political events. They say little, however, as to what has been the *union* impact upon the members' voting behavior. Certainly workers were responding to the New Deal with an avalanche of support long before their unions gave up "voluntarism." Yet the change in labor's political role, and the political activity of unions that has increased steadily since the mid-1930's, must have had some impact upon the voting behavior of union members and their families. But what impact, and how much, remains controversial.

Actually, the response of the members to union political activity involves consideration of two questions:

1. What do trade union members think of the political activities of their unions?

2. To what extent does a "labor vote" exist in the United States?

These two issues are often treated as one in the existing literature on labor and politics. Although they are related, they require separate analysis and treatment.

So far as the members' attitude toward union political activity is concerned, it appears that their reaction will vary depending upon their personal political leanings, the labor market orientation of their union, the degree of political activism of their local and national union leadership, and the leadership's success in convincing those to whom it speaks that workers have an immediate personal interest in the outcome of elections.

The selection by Joel Seidman, *et al.*, in this chapter illustrates the diversity of membership reaction to political activities that can be found among different local unions. In general, it would appear that the membership of the local unions they studied was, at best, luke-warm toward union political activity. Much stronger support for politi-cal activity was found among United Automobile Worker members in the study "When Labor Votes," by Arthur Kornhauser, Harold L. Shep-pard, and Albert J. Mayer. Their surveys showed that a majority of UAW members thought their union should publicly endorse candidates and make voting recommendations to the membership. Only 15 percent of the UAW membership appeared to be opposed to union participation in politics.

The second question, the extent to which union members and their families vote the way the leadership recommends, has been far more hotly controverted. In the 1940 Presidential elections, John L. Lewis attempted to swing the CIO membership to the Republican candidate. That he had almost no success is well-known, and is care-fully documented and analyzed in the article by Irving Bernstein. Again, in 1950, as was described in Chapter 9, labor in Ohio was equally unsuccessful in convincing its membership that it should vote against Robert A. Taft. The failure of labor's political effort to make a sig-nificant change in the voting behavior of its membership in these two elections, along with the favorable union member family response to the Eisenhower candidacies, led most American political commentators to conclude that a "labor vote" is nonexistent in America.

If by "labor vote," one means that unions control a large bloc of votes that can be swung to one party or another, it is quite true that such a vote does not exist. American labor unions have never had this kind of influence over the voting behavior of their members. Like Americans generally, workers when questioned will reply, "No one tells me how to vote." This response, however, ignores the real point. Every-one who votes must make up his mind in some manner how to vote. Thus, the fundamental question is—what are the sources and influences that bear upon the individual's decision? In immediate terms, how important is the union in influencing the voting decisions of members and their families?

In certain circumstances the union has a very significant influ-ence on this decision. Studies like those summarized in "Voting Re-search and the Labor Vote" and "Labor Unions and Political Affiliation" show that more than four-fifths of workers who feel close identification with a militantly pro-Democratic union will vote for Democratic party candidates. But if workers do not feel closely identified with their union, or if their union does not take a strong stand in favor of the Democratic party, the union member is almost as likely to vote Repub-lican as Democratic.

Thus, the labor vote is a limited tool. Through political action, unions can encourage more workers to vote, and encourage a higher percentage of them to vote Democratic. As things now stand, unions cannot effectively swing this same bloc of votes to the Republican party or to a third party. Labor's political influence is, therefore, almost wholly within the Democratic party, in that the actions taken by labor can fundamentally affect the size of urban pluralities for Democratic candidates. Labor's political activity or inactivity is therefore an important factor in determining who wins many statewide elections.

How many votes are involved cannot be clearly ascertained on the basis of presently available data. E. E. Schattschneider calculated that 960,000 is the net gain in votes for Democratic party Presidential candidates that can be attributed to union political efforts.[1] Harry M. Scoble, using a more complex approach and slightly more recent data, concluded that the net gain to Democratic Presidential candidates is actually almost 3,000,000.[2]

Whatever the real figure, there can be little doubt that union members often do respond to labor's political effort, and that this response is a significant factor in contemporary American politics.

Radio Address by John L. Lewis, October 25, 1940

. . . THE PRESENT CONCENTRATION OF POWER in the office of the President of the United States has never before been equaled in the history of our country. His powers and influence in this republic are so far-reaching that they intimately and vitally affect the lives and fortunes of every citizen. In like measure, they may affect the lives and fortunes of other nations and their populations.

How startling, therefore, is the spectacle of a President who is disinclined to surrender that power, in keeping with the traditions of the republic. The suggestion of a third term under these conditions is

---

[1] *The Semi-Sovereign People*, New York: Holt, Rinehart and Winston, 1960, p. 51.

[2] "Organized Labor in Electoral Politics: Some Questions for the Discipline," *Western Political Quarterly*, Vol. XVI, September 1963, p. 674.

New York Times, October 26, 1940, p. 1. This address was carried by the three major broadcasting chains and 322 radio stations. The *New York Times* estimated that it was heard by 25,000,000 to 30,000,000 Americans.

less than wholesome or healthy. Personal craving for power, the overweening abnormal and selfish craving for increased power, is a thing to alarm and dismay. . . .

Power for what? Personal and official power to what end? In all history, the unwarranted exercise of continuously vested authority has brought its train of political and social convulsions for which humanity has paid an appalling price in loss of liberty, in disorder, tragedy, and death.

America needs no superman. It denies the philosophy that runs to the deification of the state. America wants no royal family. Our forebears paid the price in blood, agony, privation, and sorrow, requisite for the building of this republic. Are we now to cast away that priceless liberty, which is our heritage? Are we to yield to the appetite for power and the vaunting ambitions of a man who plays with the lives of human beings for a pastime?

I say 'No,' and whether I stand alone, or whether I am sustained, as I think I will be, by the overwhelming number of American citizens, I should retain these convictions. It is time for the manhood and the womanhood of America to assert themselves. Tomorrow may be too late. . . .

President Roosevelt is asking the American people to contribute to him at least four more years out of their individual lives. What will be done with those lives and this nation in the next four years, and how does he propose to do it? He has not said, and he asks from the people a grant of discretionary power that would bind him to no course of action, except the unpredictable policies and adventures which he may later devise.

After all, Americans are not a nation of guinea pigs, constantly subject to the vicissitudes of the economic and political experiments of an amateur, ill-equipped practitioner in the realm of political science. . . .

If not Roosevelt, whom do I recommend to do the job of making secure our nation and its people? Why, of course, I recommend the election of Wendell L. Willkie as the next President of the United States.

He is a gallant American. He has opened his heart to the American people. He is not an aristocrat. He has the common touch. He was born to the briar and not to the purple. He has worked with his hands, and has known the pangs of hunger. . . . He has had experience in various fields of American enterprise, and is an administrator and an executive. . . .

He is strong enough to enlist the services of other strong men to do the job of saving our nation, whether from attack by external foes, or disintegration from disunity within. . . .

It is obvious that President Roosevelt will not be reelected for the third term, unless he has the overwhelming support of the men and women of labor. If he is, therefore, reelected, it will mean that the members of the Congress of Industrial Organizations have rejected my advice and recommendation. I will accept the result as being the equivalent of a vote of no confidence and will retire as President of the Congress of Industrial Organizations, at its convention in November. This action will save our great movement, composed of millions of men and women, from the embarrassment and handicap of my leadership during the ensuing reign of President Roosevelt.

To the leaders of the CIO, its executives, staff officers, and field representatives—I know and have worked with each of you. Upon some of you, I have bestowed the honors which you now wear. Through the years of struggle, you have been content that I should be in the forefront of your battles. I am still the same man. Sustain me now, or repudiate me. I will not chide you and will even hope that you will not regret your action.

To the mine workers of the nation who know me best, and who have always been the shock troops in the forward march of labor, I say it is best for you, and for those you love to help oppose the creation of a political dictatorship in free America.

To the steel workers, the automobile workers, the shipbuilders, the maritime workers, the lumber workers in the far northwest, the textile workers, the white-collar workers, and the men and women of labor in the miscellaneous industries, I say I have worked for you and have fought for you. Believe me now, when I say that your interest, and the interests of the families you support, lie in the acceptance of the truth of the words I speak tonight.

John L. Lewis and the Voting Behavior of the CIO

Irving Bernstein

University of California, Los Angeles

As THE 1940 POLITICAL CAMPAIGN went into its penultimate week, the result of the presidential election became increasingly doubtful. The reelection of President Roosevelt, which a month before had seemed certain, now hung in the balance. The political experts and the polls were virtually unanimous in proclaiming that this would be the closest election since 1916. The Republican Party, hungering for the power it had not known for so long and convinced that it now had a chance of attaining it under the vigorous leadership of Willkie, cast about for some dramatic event to clinch the victory.

Into this setting came the voice of John L. Lewis on the night of October 25. Speaking to an enormous radio audience, he expressed a view which had been a subject of debate for weeks among his followers, politicians, and millions of the voting public. The shaggy leonine labor leader, the most dramatic and powerful individual in the labor movement, threw in his lot with Wendell Willkie. . . .

The labor press in late October and early November 1940 revealed that the official reaction to Lewis' speech fell into three divisions. One group endorsed Willkie and said that Lewis, regardless of the outcome of the election, should remain as head of the CIO. A second group very forcefully endorsed Lewis and said nothing about the presidential candidates. Affiliated with it was a small group which maintained complete silence. The third group repudiated Willkie, endorsed Roosevelt, and some repudiated Lewis as well. . . .

Analysis of CIO Vote

Though the official reaction of the union leaders was important, the basic test of Lewis' influence came at the polls on the fifth of November. If Lewis could have carried 20 or 25 percent of the rank and file of the CIO for Willkie, the Republicans would have won. Since this block of votes was so strategically distributed in the Eastern and Midwestern states with large electoral votes, every one of which was doubtful, the control of the block determined the outcome of the election.

There are difficulties in discovering how CIO workers vote because they vote with the rest of the population in communities which

Excerpted by permission of the publisher from *Public Opinion Quarterly*, Vol. V, June 1941.

include all classes of voters. To meet this problem, a careful selection of 63 counties and fourteen towns in twelve states was made. In each locality at least 20 percent, and in many cases more than 50 percent, of the voters were members of CIO unions. The assumption is that these 77 cases, which best reflect CIO voting behavior, will also reflect it in those communities where the CIO vote is so diluted in the general vote as to be unmeasurable. The localities selected represent the states of Colorado, Illinois, Indiana, Kentucky, Massachusetts, Michigan, New Jersey, New York, Ohio, Pennsylvania, Utah, and West Virginia, and virtually every union of the CIO.

The only objective was to determine whether John L. Lewis was able to swing the industrial workers of the CIO to Willkie and no attempt was made to segregate motives in voting. The essential factor in measuring Lewis' influence is not the candidate who won (which is important in another connection) but the decline in the Roosevelt percentage of the two-party vote[1] in 1940 from the percentage of 1936. A decline from the Roosevelt majority of 1936 took place in every social segment of the population and in virtually all regions and there were many reasons for it, most of them having nothing to do with Lewis. If the decline in the selected localities is greater than the decline over the whole state where all classes of voters are counted, it is frequently possible to attribute the decline to Lewis. If the decline is not greater than that over the whole state, it may be assumed that Lewis exerted little or no influence.

Of the 63 counties selected, 61 were carried by Roosevelt in 1936 and 55 were retained by him in 1940; Landon carried two and Willkie eight. But in 61, Roosevelt's proportion of the total vote dropped in 1940 from 1936 and in only two did it rise. The towns present the same pattern. All fourteen were carried by Roosevelt in 1940 as they had been in 1936. But in twelve his percentage of the total vote declined and it rose in only two. Roosevelt, in other words, was able consistently to maintain a margin of victory from his enormous majorities of 1936.

The breakdown into figures shows that, in the 63 industrial counties, of the 3,847,594 votes cast in 1936 Roosevelt received 64.3 percent, and of the 4,265,622 cast in 1940 he received 58.2 percent. This marks a decline of 6.1 percent but it is still a handsome margin of victory. In the fourteen industrial towns, of the 709,852 votes cast in 1936 Roose-

---

[1] Whenever the term "total vote" is employed it applies only to the combined Democratic–Republican vote. Third parties are a confusing factor and in no case significant enough to change any of the conclusions and they have, therefore, been omitted.

velt received 68.1 percent, and of the 834,982 cast in 1940 he received 61.2 percent. This is a decline of 6.9 percent and once again a substantial victory. The combined figures for all 77 counties and towns show Roosevelt receiving 64.9 percent of the 4,557,446 votes cast in 1936 and 58.7 percent of the 5,100,604 cast in 1940, a decline of 6.2 percent.

Since the figures for the national vote reveal that Roosevelt's percentage dropped from 62.5 to 55.0 percent, or 7.5 percent, from 1936 to 1940, it is possible to say that Roosevelt ran well ahead of his national position in the CIO regions, for in the former he polled only 55.0 percent as compared with 58.7 percent in the latter. And his decline from 1936 was sharper over the nation, 7.5 percent, than it was in these industrial areas, 6.2 percent.

The consistency of the results for these localities is their most impressive feature and this consistency is reinforced by the results of a Gallup poll taken shortly after the election. The poll revealed that Roosevelt suffered losses in every labor group from 1936 to 1940 as follows: CIO declined from 85 to 79 percent; AF of L from 80 to 71 percent; other union groups from 74 to 57 percent; and nonunion labor from 72 to 64 percent. In every group he maintained a large margin of victory. As in 1936, the CIO group provided him with the largest percentage of votes and, in addition, it showed the smallest decline, revealing his enormous hold on its rank and file. . . .

Extent of Lewis' Influence

In the election returns there is little evidence that John L. Lewis' action moved any appreciable number of CIO workers, their families, or their sympathizers to vote for Willkie. If the Gallup poll figure of a 6 percent decline in the CIO vote from 1936 to 1940 is accurate, then Lewis may have provided 2 or 3 percent over the nation, a pathetically small figure. There is evidence, however, that he exerted an influence in a few individual localities. He undoubtedly convinced a minority of miners in Pennsylvania and perhaps in West Virginia and Ohio, though nowhere else, to follow his plea, at least negatively, in abstention from voting. In Akron, Ohio, one of the most highly organized cities in the country, the substantial decline in the Democratic vote from 71.4 to 59.6 percent, 3.2 percent greater than the statewide decline, must be partly attributed to Lewis, though the confusion in the local political situation was a factor. Roosevelt, however, won by a substantial majority which indicated that the Rubber Workers were loyal to him in the main.

Over the country the Roosevelt vote showed no more than a normal decline from 1936 and in some instances it rose. It was only where the election was extraordinarily close that Lewis' slight influence was decisive in terms of electoral votes. It is quite likely that Willkie carried Michigan because of Lewis, for the election was won by 6,926 votes in a total of 2,072,908, and the decline in Flint, which was substantially over the statewide decline, probably provided the margin of victory. There is also the very slight possibility that Lewis carried Indiana for Willkie. . . .

By his endorsement of Willkie, Lewis created a problem in divided loyalties among his followers. He asked the common man to choose between his loyalty to the labor leader, who asked him to vote contrary to his economic interests, and the political leader, who asked him to vote for his economic interests. The issue of personalities was exciting, but the decision was grounded on something far more important, the commonsense attitude of the workingman that the New Deal had given him a stake in society. That stake was too important to expose it to any danger.

It was not a choice between two leaders but a choice between the New Deal and that vague something called Republicanism. To the man on the bench the New Deal was something specific to him personally. It meant more money in his pocket, a sense of security in his job, and the knowledge that people in positions of responsibility were looking after his interests. He did not know what the Republican Party meant to him and, if he had a long memory, he was not inclined to trust it. In that simple line of reasoning lies the crux of John L. Lewis' failure.

That failure revealed the innate stability of electoral habits in the majority of the people. No last minute effort, even one so dramatic as Lewis', can basically alter these habits. Changes come slowly and cumulatively, resting upon economic foundations. The bustle and excitement in the last moments of a campaign serve little purpose beyond sharpening nerve-ends already too sharp and increasing bitterness already too embittered. A party cannot win a general election by having the endorsement of this individual or that one or by spending a large sum in a certain locality during a campaign; it can win an election only by the loyalty it produces in the interests and minds of a majority of the people built up cumulatively over the years. . . .

Voting Research and the Labor Vote

Donald E. Stokes
University of Michigan

DESPITE THE VARIETY of our politics, there are impressive constants in the life of the citizen. One of these is the level of his interest and involvement in political affairs over time. Some people are habitually alert to politics. They are informed about current issues and personalities and are imbued with a keen sense of what depends on an election outcome. Other people are much less interested; knowing little of the political wars, they care little about who emerges the victor. To be sure, the degree of individual interest is not wholly unchanging. Our most critical presidential elections catch the eye of all but the most politically withdrawn, while other campaigns can fail to arouse the interest even of the confirmed political buff. But variation of this sort is overlaid on modes of individual response that are stable enough to be regarded as political life-styles.

Basic Partisan Orientations

An important element of the individual's political life-style is the degree and direction of his basic partisan loyalties. Despite the stress on political independence in American civic education, loyalty to party is very general in the electorate. Studies by the Survey Research Center show that three Americans out of four freely classify themselves as Democrats or Republicans, and most of those who call themselves Independents grant that they are closer to one party than they are to the other. These attachments do not express a tie to a party apparatus. A number of states do have partisan registration or partisan primaries. But these evidences of party membership are nominal indeed. Except for a very thin layer of activists, the party identifications formed by Americans are psychological in nature.

In view of the slight involvement of most Americans in politics, why is it that party loyalties are so widespread? Part of the answer is that they serve important psychological needs. To the common citizen the affairs of government are remote and complex. Yet this same citizen is obliged to make judgments about political affairs. At the very least, he will have to decide periodically how he will vote, what choice

---

Excerpted by permission of the publisher from *Voting Research and the Businessman in Politics*, Copyright 1960, Ann Arbor, Mich.: Foundation for Research on Human Behavior.

he will make between candidates offering different programs and different interpretations of contemporary political events. In this dilemma, the political party serves as a convenient guide. If the party's name is stamped on a candidate or program or issue position, the individual has a simple cue as to how he should respond. As a result, when a party nominates a presidential candidate, millions of people identified with his party respond favorably to his personal qualities, his experience, and his probable performance in office. Millions of other people, identified with the opposite party, reach a less favorable estimate of these things. So, too, with issues. Faced with the endorsement of a policy or program by one of the parties, many citizens will react to the issue in terms of their enduring partisan commitments.

The partisan element of the individual's political life-style expresses a variety of influences in his prior experience. Party identifications usually take root in the years of adolescence or early adulthood—in the language of social psychology, the years of "political socialization." Many young people are inducted into a party identification much as they are inducted into a religious identification, and the socializing agencies are much the same. The family is of greatest importance; the evidence as to the stability of party loyalties from generation to generation is plentiful enough. But other associations—in the neighborhood, at school, or on the job—may reinforce or attenuate the influence of family. And the location of these primary groups within larger secondary groupings plays an important role in forming political attitudes. From his face-to-face contacts the child may learn that he is Negro and working class and Democratic. But he may also learn a connection between these things: that being Negro and working class, he *ought* to be Democratic—or that being a middle class Connecticut Yankee, he ought to be a Republican.

Although proof of the stability of party loyalty in the adult must come from panel studies that follow the same individuals over a number of years, two indications of its constancy are furnished by existing research. The first of these is the stability of the division of party loyalties as it is observed over time in independent samples of the electorate. Repeated measurement of this division by the Survey Research Center from 1952 to 1958 showed not a single difference that could not be laid to sampling error alone. The stability of the distribution of party identification in these years is shown in Table I.

And far from what we would expect if party loyalty were easily moved by the political currents of the day, the Democrats enjoyed a three-to-two advantage throughout this period. The other evidence of the stability of party identification is the constancy attributed to it by

Table I

Party Identification of the American Electorate

	Oct. 1952	Sept. 1953	Oct. 1954	Apr. 1956	Oct. 1956	Nov. 1957	Oct. 1958
Strong Republicans	13%	15%	13%	14%	15%	10%	13%
Weak Republicans	14	15	14	18	14	16	16
Independent Republicans	7	6	6	6	8	6	4
Independents	5	4	7	3	9	8	8
Independent Democrats	10	8	9	6	7	7	7
Weak Democrats	25	23	25	24	23	26	24
Strong Democrats	22	22	22	19	21	21	23
Apolitical, don't know	4	7	4	10	3	6	5
Total	100%	100%	100%	100%	100%	100%	100%
Number of cases	1614	1023	1139	1731	1772	1488	1269

Source: *The American Voter*, p. 124.

people recalling their prior partisan commitments. Most people who now have a sense of allegiance to one of the parties say that they have always had the same allegiance. If party loyalty varies through adult life, this fact has been missed by the American voter.

Yet party identification is not entirely proof against change in the adult years. Some changes occur in response to strong personal influence. Marrying someone of the opposite political faith changes the politics of many women, and of some men as well. And shifts of partisanship can follow changes of occupation or residence or other conditions of life that define our face-to-face associations. However, the resistance of party identification, once formed, to influences of this kind is impressive. Many mature voters weave an unbroken thread of partisan allegiance through repeated, drastic changes in their life situation. And some very popular notions about partisan change, such as the hypothesis that Republican conversion follows a move to the suburbs, dissolve fairly quickly when they are confronted by careful evidence.

Changes in the party loyalties of adults also can result from powerful issues or personalities in the world of politics, particularly as these impinge on the life of the individual voter. Indeed, at rare moments of our political history great national events have pried loose the party loyalties of very large numbers of citizens who were beyond the years of early political awareness. In the past hundred years both the Civil War and the Great Depression caused the allegiances of millions of

Americans to come unstuck, producing a fundamental realignment of party strength. Yet even at these critical points of political history, the impact of men and issues was probably greatest on those who were still forming a partisan orientation. Almost certainly the personalities and issues of the New Deal-Fair Deal era produced a long-term shift in the party balance more by making Democrats out of new voters than by making Democrats out of Republicans.

Party identification may color the citizen's view of the things he sees in the world of politics, but it will not completely govern his view of these things. However much the partisan voter is inclined to see issues and candidates in a partisan light, these changing elements of politics have some independent effect on the vote. In fact, to predict the outcome of a particular election, knowing the division of party loyalties in the population may be less useful than knowing the electorate's response to current personalities and issues. The voter who thinks of himself as belonging to one party but who plans to vote for the candidate of the *other* party is the man to watch, and count, in predicting what will happen at the polls. . . .

Group Influences on Voting

In forming its basic partisan commitments and its choice between candidates the American electorate is not a great collection of discrete, disassociated individuals. Tens of millions of voters who make up this electorate are bound together by common group memberships and life experiences. Expressions about the farm vote, the labor vote, the Catholic vote, and so forth are the coin of many discussions of politics, and they reflect an important aspect of voting behavior. Although group influence is not a master key to what happens at the polls, it is a significant force on the acts of the American voter.

Group differences can easily be found in official election statistics by examining the vote in areas of different social composition. For example, the reactions of Americans of German descent to the Second World War has been studied by inspecting the vote within counties having the highest concentration of people of German background. However, the rise of survey techniques has permitted still more sensitive measurement of group voting. By obtaining information directly from individual voters, surveys have obviated the need for inferences from election totals to the behavior of the several groups that make up those totals. . . .

As it has evolved in survey research, the theory of group influence has focused on the triangular relationship of the individual, the group, and the world of politics. Of primary importance in the relation of individual to group is the emotional feeling a person has toward the group—is this feeling favorable or unfavorable and what is its strength? There is no doubt that the direction and intensity of individual feeling toward a group varies widely between people. For example, some labor union members have strong positive attitudes toward unions, whereas others are much more indifferent. In fact, because of the automatic way many people enter unions, some individuals become members who actually have *negative* feeling toward the labor organizations to which they belong.

Several aspects of the relation of the group to politics are important for understanding group influence. The likelihood of influence depends a good deal on whether the group sets a clear political standard for its members. And it depends, too, on whether the group has a natural tie to politics and on the degree to which members accept political action by the group as legitimate. For some groupings in American society political standards are clearly defined and the stake of the group in politics clear enough that political action is approved by most members. But for other groupings political standards are less well defined and the forces drawing the group into politics less strong.

The use of these factors to probe the nature of group influence may be illustrated by the example of labor unions. It is widely known that union members are more Democratic than the country at large, although there is a great deal of uncertainty as to the realities lying behind the "labor vote." In the election of 1956 labor union members voted 21 percent more Democratic than the rest of the country. What's more, union members were 20 percent more Democratic than were people of the same social characteristics—the same occupational status, race, region of the country, religion, and so forth—who were *not* union members. But this Democratic margin was drawn disproportionately from among workers who had strong positive feelings toward a union that took a strong pro-Democratic stand. In fact, more than four-fifths of the workers who were closely identified with a militantly pro-Democratic union, voted Democratic in 1956 as is shown by Table III. [Table II, in the original, was deleted from this excerpt.] But if either of these predisposing factors was absent, that is, if the worker did not have strong positive feeling toward the union *or* if his union did not have a clear pro-Democratic stand, the union member was *more likely to vote Republican* than Democratic.

This mode of analysis can be applied to any group to which the citizen may belong psychologically—whether the basis of the group is race or occupation or religion or ethnicity or any other social characteristic. Even the political party may be regarded as a group. Indeed,

Table III

Proportion of Union Members Voting Democratic According to Strength of Identification with Union and Clarity of Union Political Position, 1956 Presidential Election

Identification of Member with Union	Clarity of Union Position			
	High	High Medium	Low Medium	Low
Strong	81%	66%	59%	43%
Weak	50%	42%	41%	45%

Source: *The American Voter*, p. 316.

the party is an interesting case because it falls at the extreme limit in terms of the clarity of its political standards and the willingness of its members to accept political action by the group. As a result, the parties can influence the opinions and behavior of millions of people who are, psychologically speaking, members of these mass political groups.

In some cases a group not only exerts *positive* influence on persons favorable to it; it also exerts *negative* influence on persons whose attitude is unfavorable. It is well known that labor's endorsement can be the kiss of death in a deeply conservative area, that a portion of the electorate, hostile to labor unions, uses the labor stand as a guide to how it ought *not* to vote. In a case of this sort, labor has indeed influenced the vote, but in a direction opposite to that intended. Again, the example of the political party is instructive. By nominating a candidate for high office, a party causes its own adherents to form a more favorable image of the candidate's personal qualities. But it also causes the adherents of the other party to form a *less* favorable image of these personal qualities.

The influence a group has on the attitudes and acts of its members depends on the dimensions we have discussed, and there are in fact wide differences in the influence exerted by prominent groups in American society. Group effects have made *union members* considerably more Democratic than nonunion blue collar workers, although this influence is greater in the more militant CIO unions than it is in the old-line AFL unions. . . .

Right-to-Work in Ohio: A Case Study of Economics and Politics

A dramatic example of an electoral decision between competing economic interests that reflected the movement of the business cycle is provided by the right-to-work referendum in Ohio in the election of 1958. Two interview studies by Louis Harris and his Associates in Ohio in August of 1958 and February of 1959 permit a comparison of public opinion at the beginning and the end of the battle over the right-to-work proposal to outlaw the union shop. Taken with the official vote on the referendum issue and on statewide candidates for office, these studies give a remarkable account of a political issue whose content and determining forces were economic.

The background of the right-to-work issue in Ohio was the recession of 1957–58. Like any downturn in the economy, this recession hurt some areas more than others. It cut particularly deeply into the economic welfare of a band of states stretching from New Jersey on the east through Pennsylvania and West Virginia and out into the midwestern states of Ohio, Indiana, and Michigan. The sense of economic distress in these states was at a high in the early months of 1958. By late spring it had fallen off somewhat, but the recession left in its wake feelings that were easily projected into politics. In particular, it had reinforced the public's latent fear that the Republican Party would not prevent severe distress.

Moved partly by the assumption that the resistance of workers to the adoption of right-to-work would be weaker in a period of high unemployment, a group of Ohio industrialists decided in early summer to place the issue on the November ballot. Their decision was strenuously opposed by the Republican state leadership, which saw all too clearly the possible danger to the party's ticket of a strong negative reaction to the right-to-work referendum issue. The counsel of the party leaders went unheeded. The issue was placed on the ballot, and its friends and foes prepared an intensive campaign.

At the beginning of the campaign the Louis Harris organization found that little more than half the Ohio electorate was familiar with the right-to-work issue. Of those who were aware of it, about half favored adoption of a right-to-work law. The initial support for the law was strongest among businessmen and professional people, with opposition strongest among union workers. White collar employees were fairly evenly divided, as were the nonunion workers who were aware of the issue. Farmers were somewhat less favorable. Of the few Negroes who responded to the issue, many apparently mistook right-to-work for some sort of fair employment practices bill, giving the issue an initial majority among Negroes.

The campaign for and against right-to-work, fought with growing bitterness through the fall months, greatly increased the public's awareness of the issue. The follow-up survey in February 1959 by Louis Harris and associates showed more than three-quarters of the electorate familiar with the issue. As Table IV makes clear (compare

Table IV

Change in Public Response to the Right-to-Work Issue in Ohio,
August 1958 to February 1959

	Percent aware of issue		Percent favoring right-to-work (of those aware)	
	(1) Aug.	(2) Feb.	(3) Aug.	(4) Feb.
Total electorate	58	76	52	36[1]
Businessmen	67	92	61	62
Professionals	72	94	57	47
White collar employees	61	71	48	40
All workers	47	78	42	24
Union workers	61	87	38	18
Nonunion workers	32	63	48	38
Farmers	38	52	44	40
Negroes	21	65	53	32

[1] Percent voting "yes" on referendum issue in November election, as reported on official election statistics.

Source: Louis Harris and Associates.

columns 1 and 2), this increase extended to every major element of the Ohio population, and was in several cases of dramatic magnitude. The right-to-work referendum, linked, as it was, with statewide races both for Governor and for United States Senator, made the 1958 campaign one of the most visible in the recent history of the state. As an indicator of the extent of public interest and awareness, the balloting for congressional candidates in 1958 was up 600,000 votes—more than twenty-five percent—over the previous mid-term election of 1954.

If the campaign substantially increased the public's awareness of right-to-work, it also set in motion important changes in popular feeling toward the issue (compare columns 3 and 4 in Table IV). Among businessmen, the overall majority favoring enactment held firm. However, right-to-work lost ground in every other element of the population until, at the end, businessmen alone gave the law majority support. Although the growth of opposition appeared everywhere, it was most marked among workers, particularly those belonging to unions, and Negroes, among whom a vigorous effort had been made to correct the widespread misunderstanding of the law.

What explains the tide of opposition to right-to-work that rose steadily through the campaign? As we might expect, special reasons could be found for the attitudes of particular elements of the electorate.

For example, the chief explanation for the opposition of farm people was apparently the highly individualistic feeling among farmers that if somebody wanted to work no law was needed to let him do so. And there is evidence that a minority of the business community was kept in opposition to right-to-work by the pressure that labor brought to bear on small businessmen, particularly retailers.

However, the primary source of the rising tide against right-to-work was the connection the public drew between the issue and the recession. Responsibility for the economic distress of 1957–58 was not at first charged to the business community. The recession *had* reinforced the public's belief that the Republicans, as the party of business, would not prevent unemployment. But it was not until right-to-work was brought before the public that the economic distress was given a forceful political translation. To many people in Ohio, placing right-to-work on the ballot looked like an effort by business to kick the working man when he was down. With this idea planted in the public's mind, labor was able to rally the opposition to the issue successfully, leaving business isolated in its support for the law.

Labor Unions and Political Affiliation

Samuel J. Eldersveld, *University of Michigan*
with the assistance of Ronald Freedman,
Richard W. Dodge, and Sidney Belanoff

APART FROM CHURCH GROUPS, unions are numerically the most important formal organizations in the Detroit area. More than twice as many people belong to labor unions as to any other type of nonchurch organization in the Detroit area. Before considering our survey data on labor unions and political affiliation, we will review briefly the role of labor unions in Detroit politics in order to provide a context for our analysis.

Detroit is one of the most heavily unionized industrial areas in the United States. Not only are labor unions large numerically in Detroit, but the labor leadership has exhibited an acute awareness of the relationship between labor and the political process. Labor in Detroit

Excerpted from *Political Affiliation in Metropolitan Detroit,* by permission of the Bureau of Government, Institute of Public Administration, Copyright © by The University of Michigan, 1957.

has long been involved in practical politics on all levels of government. This has been particularly true of the UAW–CIO (by far the largest union in Detroit), under the leadership of Walter Reuther. Official political activity by labor unions has been exerted generally on behalf of the Democratic party, with the CIO having backed Democratic candidates almost exclusively. Union political activity has taken the form of registration drives among union members, participation in get-out-the-vote campaigns, endorsement of candidates for office, publication of campaign literature exhorting the laboring man to throw his support to the Democratic party, and so on. In some parts of Wayne County, this effort has been so extensive as to exceed that of the regular Democratic organization. In fact, in a few of the Detroit Congressional Districts the regular organization has been largely supplanted by the CIO–PAC. Labor's entry into politics has met more success in Michigan than it has in most places. Besides helping to produce large Democratic majorities in Wayne County, labor is an important element, although not necessarily the controlling one, in the state Democratic organization in Michigan, which has succeeded in holding on to the governorship since 1948, even in the face of the Eisenhower landslide of 1952.

Detroit municipal elections, nonpartisan in form, are a special case. Despite the absence of party labels, the affiliation of the candidates is frequently recognized. Labor has sought, in vain, over the past decade and more to elect "its" candidate for mayor. Invariably, the nonlabor candidate has won without too much difficulty, which suggests that he has been the recipient of widespread support from labor union members. However, it should be mentioned that organized labor has often been divided in Detroit municipal elections with the AFL and the CIO supporting different candidates.

From this brief résumé, it is apparent that organized labor in Detroit is deeply involved in politics. What is not so clear is whether the official policy of the leadership of organized labor reflects accurately the views of the mass of union workers in Detroit. The results of the mayoralty elections indicate that at least on the local level there are important defections within labor's own house from officially announced policy. In the following pages an attempt will be made to investigate the political affiliation of union members to discover the degree of adherence to the Democratic party, and the relationship between affiliation and such factors as activity in unions, union attendance, and attitudes toward unions.

Turning to the survey data on union membership, we shall divide the sample into the following three groups:

1. Union members: respondents in the survey who are themselves members of labor unions
2. Union-member relatives: respondents who are not themselves
   members of a labor union but who have a union member in
   their immediate family
3. Nonunion families: the remainder of the sample, not included
   in the first two categories, i.e., respondents who are not themselves members of labor unions and who do not have a labor
   union member in their immediate family.

We shall use the term union families to include both the first
and second categories, that is, persons with either a personal or family
connection with labor unions.

Table XXXVIII

Political Affiliation by Union Affiliation

	Total Sample			Voters		
Union Affiliation	Percent Democrat	Percent Republican	N	Percent Democrat	Percent Republican	N
Union families						
Union members	80.5	19.5	169	81.8	18.2	121
Union-member relatives	80.8	19.2	151	85.4	14.6	89
All union families	80.6	19.4	320	83.3	16.7	210
Nonunion families	57.4	42.6	209	57.0	43.0	149
All families	71.5	28.5	534	72.3	21.7	361

Table XXXVIII [Tables I–XXXVII, and Table XLV, in the original, have been deleted from this excerpt] presents the major party
affiliation of the three groups of respondents, classified by union connections. While Democrats are in the majority in all three groups, the
nonunion members are clearly more frequently Republican than either
union members or union-member relatives. For the total sample, 43
percent of the nonunion members are Republicans as compared with
less than 20 percent among each of the two union family categories.
There is essentially no difference between union members and union-
member relatives in major party affiliation. This is not surprising, since
most of those classified as union-member relatives are the wives of
union members. However, there is concrete empirical evidence here
that the connection between party affiliation and union membership
applies equally to union members and to members of their immediate
families.

The findings in the previous paragraph for the entire sample are valid also when only voters are considered. This is also indicated by the data in Table XXXVIII. The results are not significantly different from those for all Democrats and Republicans, although the Democratic proportion of the two-party vote is slightly larger for both union members and union-member relatives.

If we subdivide the party-vote categories into two components on the basis of strength of partisan conviction, we have the pattern shown in Table XXXIX. For both union groups, the majority are consistent Democrats, 52.9 percent and 50.6 percent for union members and union-member relatives, respectively. Almost two out of three Democratic voters among union members are consistent party adherents, with the proportion somewhat less for union-member relatives. On the other hand, while a majority of nonunion voters (57 percent) prefer the Democratic party, this group is almost equally divided between strong and weak supporters. Thus, it would appear from these data that not only are persons in Detroit with some degree of union affiliation likely to be overwhelmingly Democratic as compared with only a slight Democratic majority among the nonunion element, but there seems to be a greater degree of consistent Democratic support within these union groups than for the nonunion portion of the voting population. Admittedly, this conclusion is based on only two elections and the proportion of consistent union support for the Democratic party may have decreased in 1952. Further study of this particular phenomenon is needed before we are entitled to make confident assertions. The data seem to indicate a rather even division of consistent and irregular Republicans in each category, although analysis of the two union groups is hampered by the small numbers involved.

Table XXXIX

Strength of Political Affiliation by Union Affiliation
(Voters Only)

	Percent Consistent Democrats	Percent Consistent Republicans	Percent Irregular Democrats	Percent Irregular Republicans	Number of Cases
Union families					
Union members	52.9	9.1	28.9	9.1	121
Union-member relatives	50.6	10.1	34.8	4.5	89
All-union families	51.9	9.5	31.4	7.1	210
Nonunion families	28.2	23.5	28.9	19.5	149
All families	42.1	15.3	30.4	12.3	359

Table XL

Composition of Party Affiliation Groups by Union Affiliation
(Percent)

	Consistent		Irregular			
	Demo-crats	Repub-licans	Demo-crats	Repub-licans	Independ-ents	Total
Union Families	(N=151)	(N=55)	(N=109)	(N=44)	(N=68)	(N=427)
CIO members	31.8	7.3	23.9	4.6	20.6	22.0
AFL and other members	9.9	10.9	7.3	18.2	11.8	10.5
Total union members	42.4	20.0	32.1	25.0	32.4	33.5
Union-member relatives	29.8	16.4	28.4	9.1	33.8	26.2
Total union families	72.2	36.4	60.5	34.1	66.2	59.7
Nonunion Families	27.8	63.6	39.5	65.9	33.8	40.3
Total	100.0	100.0	100.0	100.0	100.0	100.0

The composition of the hard core of Democrats and Republicans reveals the sharpness of the division between the party regulars along union lines. (See Table XL.) Thus, union families constitute more than 72 percent of the consistent Democrats in the Detroit area but only slightly more than one-third of the consistent Republicans. Union members alone, although amounting to less than 30 percent of the adult population, provide over 42 percent of all regular Democrats. Conversely, the nonunion group is correspondingly strong among the Republican regulars and weak among the Democrats. Some kind of union affiliation, therefore, whether it be formal bond of membership or informal family association, seems to be dominant among consistent Democratic voters. Consistent Republican voters, on the other hand, are largely drawn from persons outside of similar contact with unions. There are, of course, exceptions on both sides. A significant minority of consistent Democrats comes from families without union membership, while a not inconsiderable number of regular Republican voters can be found in union families. Despite this, however, there is strong evidence that in the Detroit area the preponderance of hard-core partisans in each political party is recruited from sharply different milieus and that a union connection is a significant distinguishing factor in determining with which party an individual will affiliate. A comparison of the same kind between irregular partisans shows that although the contrast is not quite as sharp as it was for consistent voters, it is sufficiently great to apply the same conclusion that was made for regular party adherents.

The CIO and Other Unions

In the Detroit area the CIO is generally considered to be more strongly oriented to the Democratic party than other labor unions. Therefore, we have provided in Table XLI a comparison of the political affiliation of union families, classified as CIO and non-CIO. The non-CIO category consists mainly (83.1 percent) of AFL union families.

Table XLI

Political Affiliation of Union Members and
Union-Member Relatives by Union of Affiliation

	Total Sample			Voters Only		
Union of Affiliation	Percent Demo- crat	Percent Repub- lican	N	Percent Demo- crat	Percent Repub- lican	N
	Union Families					
CIO	85.1	14.9	201	89.6	10.4	134
AFL and other	74.0	26.0	100	71.9	28.1	64
All union families	80.6	19.4	320	83.3	16.7	210
	Union Members					
CIO	87.9	12.1	116	92.5	7.5	80
AFL and other	66.7	33.3	48	62.2	37.8	37
All union members*	80.5	19.5	169	81.8	18.2	121
	Union-Member Relatives					
CIO	81.2	18.8	85	85.2	14.8	54
AFL and other	80.8	19.2	52	85.2	14.8	27
All union-member relatives*	80.8	19.2	151	85.2	14.8	89

*Includes union members for whom the particular union membership is unknown.

While both CIO and non-CIO union families are heavily Democratic, the CIO group has a significantly larger proportion of Democrats. Among union families our classification shows 85 percent of the CIO group are Democrats as compared with 74 percent of the non-

CIO group, a difference of 11 percent. This difference is increased to 18 percent when only voters are considered. In our sample this CIO-non-CIO divergence is entirely a result of the difference in political affiliation among union members. Union-member relatives, whether in CIO or non-CIO families, show a nearly identical division in party affiliation. The difference in political affiliation between members of the CIO and other union members is considerable. Among voters the difference between Democratic CIO members and other Democratic union members is most marked, 30 percent. It is striking that more than 92 percent of the CIO union members in our sample of voters were classified as Democrats. The generality of the comparisons made in this paragraph is limited by the fact that the size of subgroups is quite small when the CIO and non-CIO groups are further subdivided into union members and union-member relatives. Nevertheless, the completely one-sided affiliation of CIO members is very striking.

Table XLII

Strength of Political Affiliation by Union Affiliation
(Voters Only)

Union Members	Percent Consistent Democrats	Percent Consistent Republicans	Percent Irregular Democrats	Percent Irregular Republicans	N
CIO	60.0	5.0	32.5	2.5	80
AFL and other	40.5	16.2	21.6	21.6	37
All-union	52.9	9.1	28.9	9.1	121

The next step is to examine our two union groups on the basis of their degree of adherence to the major political parties. The results, as portrayed in Table XLII, are based on a small number of cases, particularly with regard to non-CIO unions. Sixty percent of all CIO party voters are consistent Democrats as compared with slightly more than 40 percent for the AFL and independent unions. For both union groups, consistent Democrats outnumber irregular Democrats by nearly two to one. Thus, although CIO members are considerably more Democratic than other union members, both union groups evidence a similar preference for party regularity over varying degrees of independence. There is an insufficient number of union voters in our sample who are Republicans to permit a comparable analysis for adherents.

Turning briefly to a consideration of the CIO-non-CIO contributions to bedrock party strength, we can observe, by referring to Table XL, that CIO members alone comprise nearly one-third of all consistent Democrats, more than three times the proportion supplied by the non-CIO unions. Non-CIO unions provide a greater proportion of regular Republican strength than does the CIO, although in both cases the percentage is small. However, it should be recalled that in spite of the greater Republican proclivities indicated by persons belonging to non-CIO unions, their preference lies with the Democratic party by a two to one margin.

Amount of Union Activity

Is extent of activity in the union related to political affiliation? This is the question we turn to next. We have seen that union membership is associated with Democratic political affiliation. Does greater activity in the union involve even more likelihood of such affiliation? How much difference does active membership make as compared with passive membership?

Some answers to these questions are provided in relation to two indexes of union participation for union members:

   a. *Attendance at union meetings*—members are divided into those who have and those who have not attended a union meeting in the preceding three months.

   b. *Activity in unions*—the classification of "active in union" is based on activity apart from attendance at regular meetings. Such activity includes at least one of the following:
   1) Being an officer at the present time
   2) Having been an officer in the past
   3) Any other activity such as committee membership or distributing union literature, which involves more than attendance at regular meetings.

Table XLIII

Political Affiliation of Union Members by Attendance at Union Meetings

Attendance at Union Meetings	Total Sample			Voters Only		
	Percent Demo- crat	Percent Repub- lican	N	Percent Demo- crat	Percent Repub- lican	N
Attends*	90.0	10.0	50	94.6	5.4	37
Does not attend	79.3	20.7	82	77.2	22.8	57
Attendance not ascertained	70.3	29.7	37	74.1	25.9	27
Total	80.5	19.5	169	81.8	18.2	121

*Attended at least one meeting in previous three months.

Table XLIII [1] shows that there is a higher percentage of Democrats among union members who reported attending union meetings than among those who did not attend. Similarly, Table XLIV discloses that those union members who are active in the union are more likely to be Democratic than those who are not. The results are similar whether the whole sample or only voters are considered. Among voters, approximately 95 percent of those who attend meetings or who are active in other ways are classified as Democrats. This is a striking result, even if we recognize the small size of the sample and the possibility of some error in classification.

Table XLIV

Political Affiliation of Union Members by Activity in Unions

| | Total Sample | | | Voters Only | | |
| | Percent Demo-crat | Percent Repub-lican | N | Percent Demo-crat | Percent Repub-lican | N |
Activity in Unions						
Active	95.8	4.2	24	95.5	4.2	22
Inactive	78.8	21.2	132	78.0	22.0	91
Not ascertained	69.2	30.8	13	87.5	12.5	8
Total	80.5	19.5	169	81.8	18.2	121

Our data do not permit us to judge whether the high percentage of Democrats among active union members results from the impact of the union on those who are active or from the self-selection of Democrats for union activities. It is certainly understandable that a selective process may lead those who do not subscribe to the political orientation of the union to remain inactive and isolate themselves from contact with the union. A more intensive type of study would be required to investigate such a question. However, it is clear that there is a very high degree of political homogeneity among those who are active in the union in any way, even when that activity only consists of attending an occasional union meeting.

Again, it is clear that all of the union groups have a high percentage of Democratic affiliation. The differences we have discussed are relative. Inactive union members are still predominantly Democratic.

---

[1] The differences reported on the basis of Table XLIII are not based on large enough samples to be statistically significant, but they fit in every case the general pattern described.

Political Affiliation and Attitudes Toward Unions

Another way of assessing the relationship of union membership to political affiliation is to take into consideration attitudes toward the union. We have only a crude measure of such attitudes, but the results seem to be sufficiently clear-cut to justify presenting them with proper reservations. . . .

[F]or *both* union families and nonunion families there is a very strong association between pro-union attitudes and Democratic political affiliation. For both of these groups a majority of those rated as having attitudes unfavorable to unions are classified as Republicans. The relationship is somewhat greater among nonunion families than among the union families. This results from a stronger Republican affiliation in the nonunion group among those neutral or unfavorable to labor unions.

It is not possible to state any direct line of causation between union attitudes and political affiliation, but it is clear that an important connection exists here that transcends any direct connection with a union. "Pro-union" and "pro-Democratic" are very strongly associated in the Detroit area both inside and outside of unions.

Income and Political Affiliation of Union Members

Income has already been shown to be strongly associated with political affiliation in the Detroit area. Therefore, the question may be raised as to whether the relationship observed in this chapter between union affiliation and political affiliation may be a function of income. Does the difference in political affiliation between union and nonunion groups persist within income groups? For example, are low-income union families more frequently Democratic than low-income nonunion families?

Table XLVI contains data bearing on these questions. The sample is divided into two family-income groups: Below $5,000 ("low income") and above $5,000 ("high income"). Roughly, this divides the families into those below and those above the median income figure for the whole sample. The relationship between union affiliation and political affiliation may therefore be observed within these two income groups. The difference in political affiliation between union families and nonunion members which we observed previously persists within the two income groups. Persons in union families are more likely to be Democratic than nonunion members regardless of income category.

Income does have an effect on political affiliation independent of union membership. For both nonunion members and the members of union families, the percentage of Republicanism rises for the higher income group. However, with the income classification used, the effect of income is less marked than that of union affiliation.

Table XLVI

Political Affiliation by Union Affiliation and by Family Income

Union Affiliation	Total Sample			Voters Only		
	Percent Demo-crat	Percent Repub-lican	N	Percent Demo-crat	Percent Repub-lican	N
Family Income Under $5,000						
Union families	82.2	17.8	197	85.0	15.0	120
Nonunion families	61.8	38.2	102	65.3	34.7	69
All families	75.3	24.7	299	77.8	22.2	189
Family Income Over $5,000						
Union families	78.4	21.6	111	80.5	19.5	82
Nonunion families	53.8	46.2	93	47.9	52.1	71
All families	67.2	32.8	204	65.4	34.6	153

Since income and union affiliation both have some independent relation to political affiliation, the differences under study are maximized when both of these variables are taken into account. Thus, 18 percent of the members of "low-income" union families are Republicans as compared with 46 percent of "high-income" nonunion members. When voters only are considered, the corresponding figures become 15 percent and 52 percent, respectively.

Summary of Findings on Labor Unions

Our data indicated that labor-union membership is strongly related to Democratic political affiliation. Moreover, this relationship is also valid for persons in the families of labor-union members. Further, this relationship does not appear to be explained by income differences. Being a union member or having one in the family did not seem to result in a considerably greater degree of party regularity among Democrats than was observed among individuals with nonunion backgrounds. There was a sharp contrast in the composition of the regular party voters on the basis of the existence of a union connection, the Democrats being predominantly from union families, while the Republicans came from nonunion backgrounds. Among those who showed some activity in labor unions, there was a greater tendency to be Democratic than was the case with nominal members. Members of CIO unions are more likely to be Democrats than members of other unions. Finally, both inside and outside labor unions, persons whose attitudes are favorable to unions are more likely to be Democrats than those whose attitudes to labor unions are unfavorable.

At least in 1952, it would appear that the strong position adopted by labor unions in the Detroit area in favor of the Democratic party was consistent with the views of their membership.

Membership Reaction to Political Action in Six Local Unions

Joel Seidman, *University of Chicago*
Jack London, *University of California, Berkeley*
Bernard Karsh, *University of Illinois*
Daisy Tagliacozzo, *Illinois Institute of Technology*

IF UNION COMMUNITY ACTIVITIES fail to obtain complete support from workers, it is not surprising that excursions into the political arena should arouse far greater opposition. Political activity is almost always controversial, concerned as it is with the structure of power in the community and in the nation.

The six locals, it should be noted, were in rather different situations with regard to political action. Two of them were peculiarly in need of political influence, the miners at the state and national levels for the passage and enforcement of safety legislation and the plumbers at the city level for the adoption of favorable provisions in the building code and the appointment of friendly inspectors. All the others, as industrial-type locals including workers with various skills and incomes, needed some favorable legislation concerning the right to organize, social security, and the like, though none was in a depressed industry and therefore dependent on legislative action rather than collective bargaining. Friendly behavior by police, city officials, and judges in time of a strike was important to some extent to all the locals, though the solidarity of the miners and the lack of skilled replacements for the plumbers put these two unions in the most independent positions.

So far as the opportunity to influence local elections was concerned, the miners and the steel workers were in the strongest positions. The miners, indeed, had little need to organize for political purposes through their union, since there were relatively few other sources of

---

Excerpted by permission of the publisher from *The Worker Views His Union*, Chicago: University of Chicago Press, copyright 1958.

livelihood in their towns or in the county where the mine was located. Coal miners, usually active members if not officers of their locals, were officials of the mining towns and of the county because they were among the natural leaders of the dominant occupational group, which was almost solidly organized into the United Mine Workers. Under these circumstances there was perhaps little more that the UMW could do with regard to local elections in many municipalities, though there were doubtless other municipalities—and larger political units, such as Congressional districts—where vigorous political leadership by the union might have had a greater impact.

The steel workers' union, as the largest labor organization in a strongly unionized town, was potentially an important political influence in the community.[1] Union influence was weakened, however, by the tendency of the local to make independent indorsements during political campaigns, with little coordination with other locals of the same union or with other CIO unions in town. The fact that most union leaders and perhaps half the members lived outside the city weakened the interest and effectiveness of the local in community political affairs.

In recent years the Democratic party has been in almost unchallenged control of the city where the steel plant is located. The Democratic machine is viewed as undesirable and corrupt by many of the local's leaders; they doubt, however, that they could defeat the machine's candidates and in any event have never tried to organize their members with that end in view. Members of the local who have been active in Democratic politics, it is believed, would probably support the machine, not the local, in the event of a clash. Under these conditions the local has generally supported the Democratic organization's candidates for city office in return for their benevolent neutrality in time of union-management strife. Except in the area of collective bargaining, however, the company has been able to exert influence within the community to get whatever it desired.

The steel workers overwhelmingly agreed that the police treated the union well. Only 3 union members out of 108 said that the police were neutral, and not one said that the police favored the company. An important union leader asserted that favorable police treatment was due to a "deal" made with city officials. "We don't have any trouble with the cops," he added. "They help us on the dues inspection lines.

---

[1] For a fuller discussion of the steel local's political behavior and influence see the authors' article, "Political Consciousness in a Local Union," *Public Opinion Quarterly*, XV (Winter, 1951–52), 692–702.

I remember the last picket line we put around the mill. I was arguing with some guy that didn't want to join the union and a cop came up and asked what the matter was and said to the guy: 'What do you want to do, cause trouble here? Join the union.' "

The police have not always been so friendly to the union, however. During the 1937 strike the influence of the police and of the entire city administration, headed by a Republican mayor, had been exerted against the union's strike efforts.

An overwhelming majority of management officials shared the belief of union members that the police were sympathetic to the union. When no labor dispute was involved, management officials had no criticism of police conduct, and those whose duties brought them into contact with the police found them friendly and cooperative. "But when there is a strike," said a general foreman, "they're on the union side." Asked how the police treated the union, a member of the top management group replied: "With kid gloves. The police have never interfered with the union . . . regardless of how illegal their activities are. . . . Whenever there was trouble [in the last strike] you couldn't find the police within miles. . . . Evidently they have an arrangement —whenever the police are there all is quiet; the baseball bats are all put away."

The national heads of the six unions responded very differently to the question of political action. The strongest lead by far in the direction of union activity was taken by the officers of the UAW, one of the national unions most interested in active participation in political life at all levels. The national leaders of the ILGWU and the Steelworkers likewise engaged in sustained efforts to increase the political awareness and effectiveness of their members. Leaders of the telephone workers and the plumbers were rather less active in this field—the telephone workers perhaps because the primary job of building a strong collective bargaining organization was still in process, the plumbers perhaps because the political influence most valuable to their members had to be exerted locally within whichever party was dominant.

Despite these differences in their needs for political influence, the opportunities open to them, and the attitudes of their national union leaders, the rank-and-file members of the six locals showed a high degree of uniformity in their attitudes to union political action. In four of the cases a clear majority rejected union action; in a fifth case—that of the metal workers—half did so, and in only one local, the steel workers, did slightly more than half favor political action and then usually with reservations. Since the CIO has had a strong interest in political action from the time of its formation and since the AFL has similarly been quite active politically since the passage of the Taft-Hartley law in 1947, it is evident that either a failure of communication or deep-seated resistance on the part of rank-and-file unionists or both have played a part.

In each of the four locals of coal miners, plumbers, knitting mill workers, and telephone workers a clear majority of the rank-and-file members interviewed answered in the negative some form of the question, "Should unions be active in politics?" The question did not specify what was meant by "politics," leaving the respondent to make his own interpretation. This led to some ambiguity in the answers, since a number of those who said they opposed union political activity nevertheless approved of lobbying for favorable legislation or indorsing pro-labor political candidates. It was a greater degree of political involvement that met with such widespread opposition.

The grounds advanced for opposing union political action were quite similar in these locals. The reasons most frequently assigned were that politics constituted a private matter, that unions should restrict themselves to in-plant problems, and that politics was a corrupt business that unions would do well to avoid. Less frequently it was also argued that union heads would become too powerful, that dissension would arise within the organization, and that retaliation might occur if candidates opposed by the union were nevertheless elected. As one of the plumbers put it, "It never helps at any time to bet on the wrong horse, whether it is for two bucks or for a local." There was opposition to being told how to vote—as against being given information and allowed to make up one's own mind—and fear that somehow this would occur if the union engaged in political action. The plumbers, incidentally, were familiar with a limited amount of political activity, since candidates for city office were invited to membership meetings to present their views. Despite the importance of the licensing system and the building code, however, most of the plumbers rejected union political activity at the municipal as strongly as at other levels.

The great majority of the rank-and-file unionists were completely uninformed about the CIO's Political Action Committee and the AFL's Labor's League for Political Education, and most of them opposed the idea of having such organizations after it was explained to them. Some CIO members who did not favor political action nevertheless contributed a dollar to PAC "to be sociable with the fellows" or because the union urged them to. Fully half of the inactive members of the steel local, when asked for their views on PAC, responded with variations of "What's PAC?" or even "Who's he?" Such political activity as the local carried on was largely undertaken by the leaders and active members, leaving the vast majority of inactive members uninvolved and almost completely untouched. If this situation was at all typical—at least of large locals of mass production workers—it helps explain the weakness of union political efforts.

In each of these locals there was a substantial minority of rank-and-file unionists who favored political action, the number rising to just above half in the case of the steel local. The activity consistently favored by these workers was the support of friendly candidates and favorable legislation. Many of those who expressed opposition to political action favored these two types of activity, however, so that majority support or something close to it was achieved in several of the other locals. Those who supported union political action saw a meaningful connection between politics and the collective bargaining problems faced by the union. Several pointed out that all other large organizations were in politics and asserted that unions had to engage in similar activity for their own protection. Some of the members of the UMW wanted to send coal miners to the legislatures so that their point of view on safety legislation and other matters could be presented properly.

Some of the metal workers, perhaps influenced by the political pronouncements of Walter Reuther or other UAW leaders, supported union political activity because they saw possible benefits to workers in general or to the people as a whole. The overwhelming tendency, however, was to define occupational interests and problems rather narrowly and to support only those political activities directly related to collective bargaining or occupational problems. Often those who favored political action expressed reservations as to the types of action that should be engaged in or the issues in which the union should interest itself. Some of these made it clear that they wished to operate within the traditional two-party system, avoiding anything "pink," and others insisted that the rights of the individual be respected.

In each of the six locals there was a substantial number either undecided about union political action or with no opinion on the subject. The number of such workers was understandably high among the knitting mill workers, who were so new to unionism, and among the telephone workers, whose relationship to the labor movement was most tenuous. Even in the case of the steel local, however, one worker out of six could express no opinion.

Though some surveys of members' political attitudes have yielded results similar to ours, two recent studies have shown somewhat greater support for union political action. In their study of the attitudes of the members of District 9 of the International Association of Machinists in an Illinois area, the Rosens found that 55 percent of the rank and file thought the union should always or usually take an active part in politics, 24 percent wanted it to do so sometimes, and the remaining 21 percent seldom or never. There was overwhelming sentiment (81 percent) for the support of candidates who backed legislation good for labor, but divided opinion as to whether the union should discuss politics at local lodge meetings (31 percent favored doing so usually or always, 35 percent sometimes, with the remaining 34 percent opposed). There was overwhelming opposition to having unions tell members whom to vote for or ask members for donations for union political action.[2]

A study of the UAW membership in Detroit showed 78 percent approving of the union's working for Stevenson in the 1952 campaign, and approximately half of them trusting the voting recommendations of labor groups in particular. Newspapers and business groups, by way of contrast, were trusted by only 9 and 7 percent, respectively.[3] Some of the differences between these results and ours might be due to the phraseology of the questions; in the case of the auto workers, part of the difference is probably the result of the active political education and campaigning carried on by the UAW staff in the Detroit area. . . .

A Labor Party?

In four of the cases—those of the coal miners, the plumbers, the metal workers, and the knitting mill workers—union members were asked whether they thought labor should have its own political party instead of supporting the existing parties. Considering their widespread reluctance to support labor political action in general, it is not surprising that the workers overwhelmingly rejected the idea of a labor party. The strongest support for one came from the metal workers, where one out of five favored the idea,[4] only a tenth of the miners and of the plumbers reacted favorably, and among the knitting mill workers the

---

[2] Hjalmar Rosen and R. A. Hudson Rosen, *The Union Member Speaks* (New York: Prentice-Hall, Inc., 1955), p. 37.

[3] Arthur Kornhauser, Harold L. Sheppard, and Albert J. Mayer, *When Labor Votes: A Study of Auto Workers* (New York: University Books, 1956), pp. 100, 105.

[4] Part of this support may have been due to the influence of Walter Reuther, whose statements in support of a labor party under certain circumstances were referred to by some of the workers. In his study of Local 688 of the Teamsters in St. Louis, Arnold Rose found that 45 percent of the members, an unusually high proportion, wanted their union to help start a labor party sometime in the future (*Union Solidarity: The Internal Cohesion of a Labor Union* [Minneapolis: University of Minnesota Press, 1952], p. 84). This high degree of support probably reflected the unusual background of the able leaders of the local, as well as the political education carried on by them over a long period of time.

percentage was only moderately higher. Half of the knitting workers, new to the labor movement, did not know how to answer the question.

Much the same reasons for opposing a labor party were offered by the three experienced groups of unionists—the metal workers, the miners, and the plumbers. Most workers felt that the existing parties were doing their jobs satisfactorily, that too much power would lead to corruption or other evils in the labor movement, or that a labor party would somehow become too radical. Images of communism, socialism, dictatorship, Soviet Russia, Nazi Germany, or labor-influenced Britain were associated by various workers—and negatively—with the idea of a labor party. In addition, there were some feelings that other elements in society were entitled to representation in a political party and in government, that too few qualified persons were available within labor's ranks, and that a labor party could not win elections. Among the knitting mill workers the ideas were less well crystallized; there was a widespread fear, however, of separating labor from the other groups in society, of losing the sympathy and help of other people.

The relatively small numbers who favored the formation of a labor party argued that more could be done for workers through a party of their own that was not dependent upon the good will of other parties, and that one could be sure that its candidates would favor labor. . . .

When Labor Votes

Arthur Kornhauser, *Wayne State University*
Harold L. Sheppard, *Upjohn Institute for Employment Research*
Albert J. Mayer, *Wayne State University*

UNION MEMBERS AND THEIR FAMILIES comprise one-third of all eligible voters in the United States. If they were to go to the polls and vote overwhelmingly in one direction, they could carry almost any national election. In an urban industrial center like Detroit, well over half of the potential voters are union members or persons in the immediate families of union members. Assuming that unions continue to work predominantly with and through the Democratic party, the fortunes of that party will rise or fall to the extent that union members and their families support labor political programs and leadership.

This confronts organized labor with a twofold challenge: On the

Excerpted by permission of the authors from *When Labor Votes*, New Hyde Park, New York: University Books, Inc., 1956.

one hand it must win and hold the political allegiance of its own members in ever-larger proportions; on the other hand, it must formulate programs and carry on activities in a manner that does not alienate many nonlabor sections of the Democratic combination or cause a polarization of sentiment against the threat of "big labor." The future of a New Deal-Fair Deal type of Democratic party depends upon the ability of unions to make common cause with other groups devoted to similar objectives.

The UAW holds a key position among the forces that are shaping this political future. It is one of the largest and most vigorous unions, with heavy stress on political action and a history of successful cooperation with the Democratic party in Michigan and elsewhere. It appears likely to continue in the forefront, with some probability that it will exercise increased influence as a leading member-union within the AFL–CIO merger. Especially significant for present purposes, its members represent a major sector of mass production workers—and they will presumably behave on the political front not too differently from other millions in other unions. As a result of years of union educational effort and constant emphasis by the organization's leaders, however, they are probably a jump ahead in political understanding and readiness for political action. Consequently, what is found to be true of them, we believe, may be indicative of potential political behavior and attitudes in much wider labor circles. . . .

In Regard to Auto Workers

1. On the whole, auto workers in the Detroit area were found to vote in agreement with union recommendations, to express trust in these recommendations, and generally to approve labor's political activities. There is no support here for a picture of top-level political maneuvering that lacks membership backing. To be sure, a small minority of the members stand opposed (15 to 20 percent); slightly more (about 25 percent) lack clear convictions and remain uncommitted, ready to sway with whatever pressures play most tellingly upon them in a particular campaign. The active majority sets the tone of prevailing sentiment in the union, however, and most of the wavering middle group goes along. Nevertheless, defections may occur when the opposing candidate or party has special appeal as in the case of Eisenhower.

2. Not only are UAW members predominantly loyal to the union's political endeavors; at the same time, many more of them oppose than approve the political influence of business. They not only trust the voting recommendations of labor organizations much more than those of any other groups; they correspondingly *distrust* the recommendations of *business groups* and *newspapers* much more than

those from other sources. Similarly, while a clear majority of auto workers declare that they would like to see unions have more to say in government, only one in five wants business to have more say; and more important, twice this number explicitly want business to have *less* say. The reasons auto workers gave for voting as they did in '52 and their statements about campaign issues further reinforce the conclusion that large numbers of them see the political world in terms of opposed goals and group interests as between organized labor and business. The unionism of these UAW members extends a long distance beyond simple and direct job-centered concerns; their predominant spirit fails to accord with the currently popular philosophy of emerging unity between labor and management, a doctrine of basic harmony and "dual allegiance."

3. In view of the union's active political campaigning the auto workers' degree of political interest and personal involvement in political action can be considered only moderate. Active forms of participation in the '52 campaign were infrequent and information regarding candidates and issues was distinctly limited. While workers gave a good deal of attention to newspaper, radio, and television during the campaign (TV was outstanding as a trusted source), while most workers reported that they talked with others about the election, and while almost all of them felt before the election that they cared "very much" which party would win, the extensive acceptance of defeat without negative feelings or words of regret would scarcely indicate any deep arousal or abiding political concern. Scores on an index of political interest based on replies to 14 questions suggest that most auto workers fall in the middle range rather than manifesting either very strong interest or notable lack of interest.[1]

---

[1] Statements similar to those in this paragraph could doubtless be made about most other sections of the population. Our findings do not mean that auto workers are *less* interested or concerned than are other citizens. On the contrary, to take an example, it was found in a nationwide sample of voters in 1952 that 25 percent said they did not "care very much which party wins the election" (A. Campbell *et al, The American Voter*, p. 36) while among Detroit auto workers only 17 percent answered in this negative way. On this matter of political interest and many other points in our study, it is most important to recognize that we are discussing what is true of auto workers—whether the implications are favorable or unfavorable—without reference to whether other groups are better or worse. Thus, the fact that auto workers manifest a moderate amount of political interest, though with relatively few members actively involved in the campaign or intensely aroused, does not signify any negative evaluation in comparison with other groups. It nevertheless, does point up a challenge, both for those wishing to see more grass roots political activity in labor and likewise for those who may prefer that working people remain indifferent and inert.

4. Union efforts to "get out the vote" appear to have met with some degree of success. This we infer from the finding that registration among union members was no less than that for the Detroit area population as a whole. This contrasts with typical election figures which show smaller proportions voting among low income people including industrial workers. According to our figures, approximately one-fifth of the UAW members eligible to register did not vote in the presidential election. Nonvoters (among those eligible) were especially numerous among auto workers of lowest economic status and most limited education and among the younger workers of middle or relatively high economic status. Somewhat paradoxically, most nonvoters are about as interested in politics and as high in pro-labor political loyalties as are voters. Presumably, since their failure to vote is not traceable in most instances to special apathy or "off-sideness," it should not be too difficult for the union to get them to the polls with only slight additional stimulation.

The campaign on reapportionment of state voting districts—vigorously pushed by the union—highlights both the shortcomings and the achievements of the union's political communication with its members. The issue remained relatively unfamiliar and poorly understood: only 57 percent of registered UAW members could clearly recall if and how they voted; but of those who *could* remember, 90 percent voted in accord with the union's recommendation.

5. A substantial section of the UAW membership consists of those workers who are both politically interested and strongly pro-labor in orientation. These are the people whose full and effective support the political action program has gained within the union. They are found to differ in significant ways both from the pro-labor group having little political interest and from the workers who are not pro-labor in regard to political matters.

First of all, this actively interested and on-side group—members who represent the best type of political participants from the union standpoint—tends also to display high interest and involvement in the union organization and activities apart from its political activities. They are also better educated than the average; they include more skilled workers; they have above average incomes; and they tend to be relatively young. The proportion of Negroes among them is greater than average; they have the largest percentage of fathers who were semi-skilled workers and the lowest percentage who were farmers; their parents were more frequently American-born than were those of other members and the foreign-born fathers came disproportionately from the British Isles and Canada. Among the smaller group of *extremely* pro-labor and politically interested, similar characteristics are present in even more pronounced degree. However, one important difference occurs in that a very high proportion of these members *most* active politically are Catholics, and few are Negroes.

These data carry a strong suggestion that existing trends toward increasing skill levels, higher income, greater education, and diminishing numbers coming from farm and foreign backgrounds do not pull workers away from union political interests and affiliations as is often alleged; on the contrary, these are the very characteristics that we find most associated with the combination of strong pro-labor orientation and lively political interest. These facts carry important implications regarding the future of labor in American politics. . . .

Union Members and Political Action

[T]here are additional important changes taking place among working people that could conceivably lead to far-reaching effects on the way they relate themselves to politics and to organized labor's role in politics.

Most challenging in this connection is the question whether industrial workers are becoming "middle class" in outlook as well as status and hence undependable as supporters of union political purposes.[2] The thesis that this is the case can be argued with considerable cogency. Certainly the tangible bases for distinctions between middle class and working class have been fast disappearing. They give promise of continuing to vanish. Working people have experienced spectacular improvements of employment relations and life conditions—to a point, indeed, that has caused one sociologist seriously to speak of the "professionalization" of labor in Detroit.[3] Surely the conception of an exploited, submerged, and underprivileged industrial working class imbued with an "underdog" mentality, corresponds to no substantial reality in today's American society. Whether this rise toward "middle class-ness" means the decline of organized labor as a countervailing

---

[2] "Middle class" is a questionable category for our purposes but no better term is available. It is used here and through the following pages to refer to the more traditional and conservative parts of the heterogeneous middle-income population. Although large numbers of people at middle socio-economic levels are liberals, New Deal type Democrats, pro-labor in sympathies, we are not speaking of them when we refer to a middle class outlook. The reference is to the more individualistic (and Republican) sections of the middle class—the medium and upper range of white collar employees, small businessmen, professionals employed in business or self-employed, etc.

[3] Nelson Foote, "The Professionalization of Labor in Detroit," *American Journal of Sociology*, January 1953, 371–80.

force against the power of business and wealth is quite another matter.

The general question here might be rephrased in this way: Can working people attain comfortable and respectable middle-class planes of living and yet persist in their loyalty to organized labor and labor's political aims? More provocatively perhaps, the question could ask: Is there any ideological stopping place on the road upward from underdog to middle-class status?

The essential fact with which to begin here is that decade after decade, almost year by year, wage earners are moving to higher levels, not only of real earnings, but also of education, leisure, health, economic security, status on the job and conditions of work. The present acceleration of technological change points to even greater alterations of the occupational structure, particularly the further elimination of the most routine and lowest level jobs in factory and office. Distinctions between skill levels and between manual and white collar jobs are growing dim and blurred.

There is little question that all these changes have vital implications for the social perspectives and political participation of the people involved. As working people rise to new levels of income and education; as they enjoy greater security and more leisure; as ever greater numbers occupy technical, skilled, and responsible positions; as they increasingly become home owners, suburbanites, stock holders; as the number of first and second generation immigrants continue to decline, and as all assume a more respected place in society, important shifts are bound to occur in their political orientation.

It is worth speculating a little about these impending shifts. It would be most unwise to *assume* that they spell a conservative trend. Research like that of our study can furnish useful bits of information on these matters, but only as straws in the wind—perhaps we should say as benchmarks by means of which continuing inquiries may be able to establish trends. Clearly current evidence is dated. General interpretations must stretch beyond the time-bound descriptions of single studies. Yet, even research fragments have value in the absence of more adequate knowledge. In that spirit we shall refer to certain of our results as we now raise questions and venture possible answers as to where the political attitudes of working people may be going.

In our study, and in many others, it has been found that political inertia and indifference are associated with low socioeconomic position. The auto workers who showed greatest political interest were better educated on the average and had higher level jobs and incomes than those with less political interest. The apathy and feeling of impotence among people of low status is based on a more fundamental attitude of incompetence and inadequacy in the political sphere. It is probable that as income and education improve, such a feeling of incompetence—a feeling of a lack of qualification for making judgments and for participating in politics—will decrease. Our data support this expectation, for example, in the findings on political interest. If we take those workers who, for the purposes of this discussion, can be considered the "underdogs" in our sample, namely, those with a family income of $4000 or less and a low education (less than nine years of schooling), we find that only 13 percent have a relatively high degree of political interest (above the middle range of interest), in sharp contrast to 52 percent of the UAW members with $6000 or more family income and a better education.

As another example, consider the responses of these same two groups to the statement, "People like me don't have any say about what the government does." Three-fifths of our "underdogs" (61 percent) agree with such a sentiment, while one-fifth (21 percent) of the opposite group feel the same way. These wide contrasts between the high and the low income-education workers show up in the many other measures we used in the study that bear on the point under discussion, such measures as their appraisal of chances for upward mobility, their social alienation, and their social participation.

On the basis of such data and reasoning, we can rather confidently anticipate that working people's interest and participation in politics will continue to increase. This will occur both because of greater feelings of political adequacy, more information, more appreciation of the rights and responsibilities of citizenship, and also because workers will increasingly perceive their own stake in political decisons. Unions, as well as political parties and other organizations, can be counted on to hammer home the idea that many of the worker's problems demand political solutions—and that their social and economic gains are jeopardized by unfavorable governmental actions at the hands of political "enemies." In short, industrial workers are developing greater political interest and involvement for precisely the same reasons that the upper classes have done so.

The directions that this growing participation will take can be analyzed with far less assurance. The moot question is: Will working people participate *as members of unions* or as members of the broad "middle class"? On the one hand we see factors that would push them toward conservative and nonlabor oriented political objectives; on the other, there are influences that may prove supportive of pro-labor aims and continuing New Deal-Fair Deal types of social change. Which way the political winds of the future will blow depends on emergent forces only partly foreseeable, including prominently the still-to-be-decided behavior of political leaders—those in the labor movement and those outside labor circles. . . .

Toward Contentment and Conservatism?

Assuredly, working people are becoming better off—as to income, security, occupational conditions, and status. Therefore, they will be more satisfied with things as they are. Being satisfied, they will grow conservative. So runs the argument. Or, with a variation in key: The New Deal was sustained by adversity. Republicans returned to power as years of prosperity gradually covered over the bitter memories of the 30's. A resurgence of political liberalism or radicalism would require a period of "hard times." Assuming that the economy is kept on an even keel, labor political programs and liberal Democrats will hold no strong appeal for the contented middle-class worker. All this may indeed prove to be the case. Or it may not.

It is true that election statistics and opinion surveys uniformly reveal a positive relationship between higher economic levels and political conservatism—for example, as represented in proportions voting Republican versus Democratic.[4] To cite a few illustrative figures, a careful nationwide survey[5] in 1952 found that income groups above $5000 voted 68 percent Republican; those below $5000 were 53 percent Republican. By occupational categories, managerial, professional, and white collar people voted 68 percent Republican in contrast to 43 percent among manual workers. Corresponding figures for 1948 show larger differences: by occupational level, 68 percent versus only 24 percent. Similarly, a cross-section sample of the Detroit area population in 1951 yielded the following figures: upper socioeconomic class, 67 percent Republican, middle group, 27 percent; lower group, 17 percent.[6]

It is noteworthy that the 1952 national sample reveals strikingly little variation among the different income groups *below* the $5000 level (constituting three-fourths of the total sample). The percentage of Eisenhower votes in the $4000 to $5000 bracket was, in fact,

---

[4] The facts on this point are incontrovertible. Confirmatory findings have been obtained in scores of studies, local and national. Results of studies in other countries are fully in accord with those of the United States.

[5] The survey was conducted by the University of Michigan Survey Research Center and is reported in Angus Campbell *et al., op. cit.* The percentages used here are derived from their tabulations, pp. 72 and 73.

[6] Arthur Kornhauser, *Detroit as the People See It*, Wayne University Press, 1952, p. 206.

less than among those lower than $4000. This fact itself places a large question-mark beside any simple interpretations along the lines of the argument quoted at the beginning of this section. The thesis stated there would hold that the better-off "middle class" should have voted more Republican than the lower groups, say those under $3000 income. But in 1952 they did not.

Results from our study of UAW members partially fit into the pattern of higher socioeconomic groups voting more Republican and partially run counter to it. Eisenhower votes were most frequent among the white collar and skilled auto workers living in upper income neighborhoods. However, among the much greater numbers of semi-skilled workers there is no such tendency; those living in higher income districts actually voted more strongly for Stevenson than did their fellows at lower levels (considering only white workers since no Negro workers lived in the better income districts). Moreover, as previously noted, the most pro-labor politically active group in the union includes a disproportionate number of better educated and skilled workers.

This leaves us with the puzzling question: Which of the contrasting patterns, a *pro*-labor or a *non*labor political orientation, are wage workers more likely to follow as their economic lot improves? Available data, including our own, fail to answer the question. Our results do add a warning signal, cautioning against too ready acceptance of the more-money-more-contentment-more-conservatism formula. . . .

Chapter 12

What of the Future?

DURING THE 1930's, '40's AND '50's, labor's participation in the American electoral process was an important source of national controversy. It was widely feared that organized labor might somehow be able to manipulate vast blocs of votes to serve its "special" interests. Labor was continually accused of using dues money coerced from unwilling members for political ends. Federal and state legislative enactments were undertaken to limit labor's political spending and resulted in many years of litigation. Representatives of the business community and other opponents of labor repeatedly decried the totality of labor's increasing political participation.

By the 1960's, however, it appeared that labor's political participation had acquired a substantial degree of legitimacy, at least if judged by the decline in the controversy surrounding it. This was particularly apparent in the 1964 presidential election year, a year of intense liberal-conservative conflict. Yet labor's considerable political participation, although undiminished from preceding presidential campaigns, was hardly mentioned as a campaign issue. One might almost conclude that labor's political activity as a public issue has become equated with that of the business community, no better and no worse than attempts by any of the other pressure groups in our society to strengthen their position and achieve their objectives.

So far as the future is concerned, labor's political effectiveness will be related, in part at least, to the public's image of the labor movement. The disclosures of the McClellan Committee during the late 1950's, for example, undoubtedly served to weaken labor's political effectiveness in those years. To a substantial extent, organized labor has cleaned its own house and has improved its smudged image. It has thus become a more successful proponent of the political objectives that it seeks.

In 1964, labor was united behind the candidacy of Lyndon B. Johnson for the presidency to a greater extent than it had been toward any candidate in our history. No labor leader of prominence supported the Republican candidate. Generalizing solely from historical precedents, it is not likely that labor will be as single-voiced in approval of any particular candidate in the future or as monolithic in his support.

By 1966, in fact, the labor movement had become somewhat disenchanted with the Johnson Administration. The U. S. Senate failed to approve removal of the controversial 14(b) clause from the Taft-Hartley Act. The minimum wage was increased, but not as rapidly or as much as labor wished. Conflict over these and similar issues presaged a possible search by labor for a more diversified political role.

Nonetheless, in the near future at least, organized labor's political activities and objectives will continue largely to be bound up with the success or failure of the Democratic party. This alliance has its drawbacks. Many candidates supported by labor were defeated in the 1966 congressional elections, in part because of public disfavor of administration policies. Yet labor's political influence is almost wholly within the Democratic party, in that labor can by its electoral actions increase or decrease the likelihood that Democrats will be elected. Thus, to be effective, its political efforts must, in the main, continue to be directed toward the support of those programs and candidates which labor votes can influence and help elect.

The readings in this chapter discuss various aspects of some of these comments. Nicholas A. Masters develops in detail the reasons why organized labor's political efforts are almost entirely concerned with the Democratic party and Democratic candidates and why, at the same time, labor cannot successfully take over the Democratic party machinery.

In "Labor Should Get Out of Politics," Dick Bruner expresses concern regarding the limited extent of grass roots participation in politics on the part of union members. He also suggests that perhaps the only way organized labor can increase its influence within the Democratic party is to withdraw temporarily from the political wars. By this means it could demonstrate clearly the importance of labor's support to those who sometimes take it for granted.

In the reading that follows, Walter Reuther discusses his attitude toward political action and some of his hopes for the future.

Finally, in "Unions and Politics," Jack Barbash sums up what he believes to have been the virtues of labor's contemporary political activity: it increases political participation throughout the nation, it spreads the benefits of our affluent society more broadly across the populace, and it reinforces pressures for a broad range of welfare and social security legislation.

In summary, it does not appear at any time in the foreseeable future that the American labor movement will attempt to form a labor party similar to those existing in many other industrialized democracies of the world. No prominent or responsible trade-union leader today espouses such a course. Without exception they realize that the structure of existing American politics, the fact that organized labor is still a minority in this country, and the fact that union members are not a class conscious group would make any such attempt futile. Moreover, there is no important pressure for a labor third party at any point in American society. This is primarily because both of the major political parties are reasonably responsive to the needs and aspirations of workers.

The future of labor in American politics appears to be one of continuation and development of its contemporary activities, rather than any radical change in its political approach and orientation. Labor unions are working to make the differences between the American parties more specific and to bring about some political realignments so that the two major parties stand for more distinctive points of view.

Labor certainly contributes to the increasing democratization of American society. It broadens the base of the electorate; it informs those to whom it speaks about the major public policy problems of the times, and it encourages workers to participate in politics. Each of these efforts tends to make the average citizen's participation in politics more meaningful and creative.

Organized Labor and the Democratic Party

Nicholas A. Masters

Pennsylvania State University

[THERE IS] A WIDELY HELD POPULAR BELIEF that labor represents a monolithic force on the American political scene, capable of placing a massive vote at the doorstep of the Democratic Party. Yet recent scholarly studies demonstrate that, despite increasing political involvements of union leaders, particularly in campaigns, there are a substantial number of union members who vote contrary to the public endorsements of their leadership; who note with disapproval, as detracting from the vital business of contract and grievance negotiation, any display of political activity by union leaders; or who remain politically apathetic, leadership exhortation to the contrary notwithstanding. Moreover, within the union movement, a substantial number of union leaders still

Excerpted by permission of the publisher from "The Organized Labor Bureaucracy as a Base of Support for the Democratic Party," *Law and Contemporary Problems*, Vol. XXVII, Spring 1962, Copyright © by Duke University, 1962.

attempt to stay out of partisan election campaigns, and refuse to allow their unions to become closely identified with any political party or its candidates.

The intention of this paper is to discuss, first, the generalization that union organizations and their members occupy varying positions on a continuum of political opinion and activity, and that as a result the AFL–CIO cannot *guarantee* a substantial bloc of votes for candidates in national campaigns. In the light of previous studies, this point does not merit detailed documentation and analysis. And second, the major focus of this discussion is on an analysis of organized labor, particularly the AFL–CIO nationally, as a base of support for Democratic candidates for presidential and congressional offices. Such analysis involves two questions: Why is labor sought as a base of support? What are the effects, positive and negative, of such support?

I

Diversity in Labor Support

While union leaders have over the years fought for the right to strike, to organize, to bargain with employers, and to engage in the collective promotion of their economic and social welfare by means of the ballot-box and lobbying, they seldom agree on candidate, parties, or issues. It is not a novel proposition to point out that "the American labor movement is a highly complex social phenomenon with myriads of dissimilar features at lower levels. These diversities are multiplied in the alliances and organizational arrangements improvised for political purposes within organized labor and between organized labor and other political groups."[1] For example, the bulk of the political activity carried on by the AFL–CIO in national campaigns is supported extensively by only a few unions, namely, the United Automobile Workers of America (UAW), the United Steelworkers of America (USW), the International Ladies Garment Workers Union (ILGWU), and the International Association of Machinists (IAM). And even within this group, there are some variations. The UAW in Michigan is openly partisan and for all intents and purposes is an integral part of the Democratic Party in that state. In New York State the ILGWU's political arm is the Liberal Party, which occasionally nominates its own candidates, but usually gives its support to the Democrats.[2] A more moderate approach is taken by the USW which, under President David MacDonald's leadership,

---

[1] Alexander Heard, *The Costs of Democracy*, 176 (1960).

[2] Seidler, "The Socialist Party and American Unionism," 5 *Midwest J. Pol. Sci.*, 207, 228 (1961).

has stopped short of *open* affiliation with the Democratic Party and extensive participation within the Party's internal framework.

Furthermore, a substantial part of the union movement has been conservatively oriented politically. Conservativism among unions might be defined in the following manner: (1) apathy toward or avoidance of national election activity; (2) an overwhelming concern with the political and economic problems of their own union, with little or no interest in the problems of other unions or other segments of society; (3) tight control from the top, with few avenues open for membership participation in policy decisions. Dominated by the late William Hutcheson, a Republican, the United Brotherhood of Carpenters and Joiners of America has a reputation for headquarters control and political conservatism and disinterest. Building and other skilled trade unions have manifestly turned their energies toward control of jobs rather than concern with political issues, and have avoided direct participation in election campaigns. This is not to suggest that conservative unions are politically apathetic and never press for legislation or participate in the determination of state and local governmental decisions. On the whole, however, this type of union deliberately and carefully avoids *partisan* commitments. In brief, organized labor is not unified politically and it is very unlikely that it will be in the foreseeable future. Strictly speaking, organized labor is not, in terms of its organization and leadership, a unified base of support for any candidate or party. . . .

II

Advantages of Labor Support

A. *Votes*

The closeness of the 1960 presidential election again brought home the point to politicians that any strategem that will affect even the slightest sprinkling of votes may be extremely critical to the final result. The same election also showed the tremendous influence of the large urban areas on electoral vote majorities. In view of the concentration of the most politically active and vigorous unions' membership—unions which support the Democratic Party—in the large urban areas within states having the largest electoral votes, AFL–CIO support has come to be regarded as essential for the effect it may have on perhaps only a small portion of the total union membership in these areas. That is, endorsement and active leadership support may persuade a few more unionists and members of their families to vote for endorsed candidates, or simply to vote. Although political scientists have not yet developed precise methods for measuring the effect of open support and related activity, Campbell *et al.* have hypothesized that when individual members of a group begin to get a clearer perception of the proximity of the group and the world of politics—and presumably aggressive political action programs are more likely to generate clearer perceptions—the susceptibility to group influence in political affairs increases.[3] True, politicians may not use these terms or they may not be able to articulate the point at all, but most of them are aware of the fact that the elaborate political activities of unions have had an impact on the voting decisions of *some* members. Consequently, candidates for the Presidency and for Congress in areas of labor concentration want identification with, and the support of, both unions in the area and the AFL–CIO nationally. Support is desired not because union political actionists control a large bloc of votes that they can swing one way or another—they have never had this kind of control—but rather because they may be able to affect the *size of the urban majorities* for the Democratic Party. This fact alone, despite the political variations within the labor movement, gives the AFL–CIO nationally a much greater voice in the Democratic Party and governmental affairs.

In politics, power relationships are determined and affected by the resources at the disposal of the participants. An important element of power is control over votes. The bureaucracy of organized labor realizes that this resource, this element of its power, is not an entirely flexible one, that it can be used only in a restricted manner. Labor's political strength lies in cities like Detroit, Chicago, Pittsburgh, New York, Los Angeles, and St. Louis, that produce the large majorities for the Democrats in presidential and statewide election contests. This means that the AFL–CIO must remain Democratic in order to maintain a strong and viable bargaining position in politics. It is extremely doubtful that the AFL–CIO could directly influence the size of the Republican minorities in these areas, and the idea that an independent third party can be formed in the event of dissatisfaction with the Democrats is ridiculous. . . . Labor's influence over votes presumably prevents incumbents from using their power indiscriminately against labor, or guarantees that incumbents will be favorably disposed toward labor's goals. This being the source of its political bargaining power, the AFL–CIO's alliance with the Democratic Party is firm, although not always openly espoused.

In addition to the influence labor leaders may have on the size of urban majorities, organized labor has gained representation at Demo-

---

[3] Angus Campbell, et al., *The American Voter* 311 (1960).

cratic national conventions. Approximately one-eighth of the delegates to the 1960 Democratic National Convention were unionists. It comes as no surprise that the majority of the union delegates were from the big industrial states, although there were a few from southern and western states. Organized labor, obviously, did not control the convention, but its delegates, coupled with the votes of delegates not directly involved in the labor movement but committed to its objectives, gave labor a strong voice in the choice of candidates, and an even stronger voice in the formulation of platform provisions. The following data illustrate the delegate strength of unions from some of the large industrial states:

> Michigan—102 delegates, 50 alternates; 34 union officials and 7 industrial workers.
>
> Minnesota—62 delegates; 10 union.
>
> California—162 delegates; 16 union.

On the Republican side, only ten delegates to the Party's national convention were unionists.

B. Money

Organized labor has been able to extend its influence outside the areas of labor concentration by offering candidates who are pro-labor a scarce and essential commodity—namely, money. Alexander Heard points out that: [4]

> . . . the two million dollars or so of free funds that 17 million union members gave in 1956 about equalled the reported voluntary contributions of $500 and over made by 742 officials of the nation's 225 largest business concerns.

(The two-million figure is equal to approximately only three-tenths of one percent of annual union dues.) Candidates for Congress in predominantly rural and nonindustrial areas, e.g., Montana and Idaho, where labor identification does not mean the kiss of death, but where local labor unions are not large enough to be affluent, seek labor endorsements "from the East" in order to obtain AFL–CIO money. In such instances, both labor and the candidate may have to play down labor support somewhat because the popular image of organized labor is not entirely favorable, and some of the members of a candidate's own party may resent "outside" influence. Of course, the source of money in campaigns is seldom kept quiet, at least for very long, and

---

[4] Alexander Heard, *The Costs of Democracy* 196 (1960).

opposing candidates have not hesitated to use the labor domination theme. The influx of labor money has resulted in situations today where conservative forces are using a traditionally liberal symbol. Conservatives, rather than liberals, since they are now able to finance their own political activities almost entirely out of local and state sources, are the ones who charge the opposition with "domination of the monied interests from the East."

How extensively national labor money is brought into the various states during a campaign can be noted from data on the 1956 presidential election. In that year, national labor money "went to back Democratic senatorial candidates in 22 of the 33 states from which Senators were elected, the remaining 11 consisting of seven Southern and two Northern one-party states plus Arizona and Kansas." In the same election "one or more Democratic candidates for the House of Representatives received national labor gifts in every state but six, all of the latter being one-party states, except New Mexico." . . .[5]

C. *Organization*

Party professionals seemingly complain more about the lack of party organization and money than anything else. The AFL–CIO has been able to provide for the Democratic Party one thing business interests have been unable to supply for the Republicans—namely, organization. The most fundamental point to emphasize is the sheer muscle union workers can provide in a campaign. It is easy to say organized labor provides workers, but it takes almost direct involvement to appreciate what this means. "Getting out the vote" involves . . . performing a multitude of unglamorous tasks which most middle-class suburbanite Democrats or ADA-type Liberals will not perform or are physically unable to perform. . . .

D. *The Liberal Sanction*

Endorsement and support from organized labor, or some segments thereof, frequently help a candidate to rally support from other self-designated liberal groups. Organizations, such as the Americans for Democratic Action, the National Association for the Advancement of Colored People, the American Civil Liberties Union, and their thousands of local chapters or units, usually will not back a candidate whose acceptability to organized labor is highly questionable. Moreover, the National Committee for an Effective Congress seldom supports a candidate with an antilabor background.

---

[5] *Id.* at 187.

The importance of the liberal sanction is illustrated by the pre-convention struggle among the Democrats prior to the 1960 election. The discussion that follows, however, rests primarily on newspaper accounts, which, although perhaps generally reliable, certainly do not provide a detailed account of exactly what happened. Preliminary discussions of the desirability of union neutrality in the 1960 presidential election ended with the realization that in the impending presidential contest, labor neutrality would increase the chances of a Republican President. In fact, it was soon realized by some union leaders that even though no formal action could be taken nationally before the Democratic nomination, organized labor had to get into the pre-convention fight to insure the nomination of a liberal candidate. Early in that year, Democrats Kennedy, Symington, and Humphrey were busy lining up labor endorsements not only because labor could affect votes both at the convention and in the election, but also because labor support helped to pave the avenues toward other liberal endorsements and acceptability. But failure to attract organized labor as a base of support significantly damaged Lyndon Johnson's bid for the Democratic presidential nomination.

For a number of reasons, Johnson was almost totally unacceptable to organized labor, and even after he received the vice-presidential nomination many labor leaders remained decidedly cool. Unacceptability to organized labor made it difficult for Johnson to gain support from other liberal groups, and without it he was virtually cut off from the large body of delegates representing the Northeastern industrialized areas. Party professionals in these areas, who perhaps may have been sympathetic toward Johnson, simply would not risk the alienation of organized labor. . . . Johnson was distrusted by labor primarily because he was trusted by Southern Democrats. It was felt, particularly by the UAW in Michigan, that Johnson, despite his New Deal background, had too many commitments to Southern legislators and the oil interests of his native state of Texas to use the power of the Presidency to protect and promote the interests of labor. There is little doubt that labor support might have gained Johnson the nomination. Support is a significant input factor in campaigns which functions so that the acts and statements of the endorsee will be accepted and understood by the public. Such support serves to prevent distrust or lack of confidence in the candidate by those sympathetic to or appreciative of a group's views, and who judge a candidate as to whether he can speak authoritatively in approval of programs advocated by a particular group. Johnson, despite his record, could not speak authoritatively in support of labor's goals before liberal groups committed to labor's programs.

It is not intended to imply, however, that organized labor support guarantees that other groups will be similarly inclined. A candidate for the presidential nomination with labor support simply has a better chance than others. . . .

E. *Propaganda Advantage*

A significant part of the success of any candidate is to gain and hold the attention of the attentive public, to make sure that informed people are aware of his candidacy and his position on the various issues in the campaign. The difficulty involved in becoming known is not commonly appreciated. Money is a crucial variable and labor supplies some of the funds necessary for purchasing TV time, radio programs or announcements, and newspaper advertisements. Articles about candidates and their backgrounds in labor publications—and there are hundreds of them—which reach and are read by intermediate level union leaders help to provide a flow of information to the rank and file membership. Invitations to candidates to speak before union meetings, furnishing them with captive audiences, also contribute to the significance of labor as a base of support for candidates for public office. Perhaps of greatest significance, however, is that a candidate can cut into the network of interrelationships among community elites through labor leaders. AFL–CIO leaders, through overlapping memberships, help to do this for presidential candidates. Labor leaders within particular internationals, or who are part of the state and local AFL–CIO bureaucracy, help candidates for other offices. Today labor leaders participate extensively in a variety of civic, fraternal, and political groups in their communities, and they are included in all types of academic, governmental, and business conferences where they interact with the leaders of other groups. . . . Labor leaders, acting in these arenas where their opinions are respected, can and do advocate candidates for office.

III

Limitations of Labor Support

A. *"Excessive" Liberalism*

In assessing labor as a base of support it is necessary to look into its limitations. The political education programs initiated and conducted by the various political arms of the labor movement have borne fruit, *but* the fruit is often unsophisticated and the efforts have frequently promoted a rigid, closed-minded adherence to pat liberal solutions for complex issues. Almost necessarily the programs have stressed slogans and been superficial; and the propaganda has insisted on what many regard as an uncompromising liberal, pro-labor commitment. This commitment has frequently made it difficult for Democratic candidates to maintain full labor support and at the same time adjust their positions to what they think or believe are existing political realities. Intermediate and lower-level union leaders have in a great many cases shown a reluctance to support, or have refused to support vigorously, candidates who do not buy in toto *the* "Labor" position on economic and social issues. In the eyes of some veteran observers, "the screaming liberal line" found in the political education programs has made it difficult for labor's top echelon, whenever they desire to take a more practical position, to sell their members on candidates who do not meet all the issues head-on. Moreover, the tough ideological line in some instances has even forced the leadership to narrow its perspective in order to keep faith with the local and intermediate level of the union bureaucracy. . . .

B. Decline of the Industrial Unions?

Labor leaders have begun to express grave concern about the future. For some time they have been talking about the threats of technological unemployment both to the union movement and the national economy. In a few states unions have proposed the creation of some kind of state commission to control the effects of automation. Today, technological unemployment is no longer merely a threat to unions; it is a reality with which they must cope. Membership has begun to drop off significantly in some unions, especially the UAW and USW. For the first time, union leaders are accepting the idea that they do not have a self-perpetuating future. Until very recently, labor leaders, somewhat like our early pioneers who thought there were endless forests, looked at all the unorganized workers and felt that they could always maintain their relative power in society through periodic expansion.

But now they can see that before very long their political and economic power will begin to decline unless something happens to alter the picture. . . .

What does this mean politically? In the first place, the big industrial unions have been hit the hardest by automation. And, as mentioned earlier, these are the unions that are the most active politically, that contribute most of the money and organization in national campaigns, and that have their membership most strategically located in terms of affecting the outcome of presidential elections. If the resources and membership of these unions begin to dwindle, the significance of labor as a base of support for the Democratic Party will dwindle. It is, of course, plausible that union leaders will turn more to pressure group politics and away from party and campaign politics nationally to delay uncontrolled change and to compensate for the economic power slipping from their grasps. Walter Reuther's increasing concern about the outcome of decisions affecting agriculture is, in part, explained by a desire to forge stronger alliances with other economic groups, in this case the Farmers Union, to offset labor's declining political power. But the road ahead for the AFL–CIO looks rough; it may have fewer votes to play with, less money, and a weaker organization. . . .

C. *The Popular Image*

It is not difficult to substantiate the point that organized labor still conveys a poor image. The publicity engendered largely by investigations conducted by Senator McClellan's Committee has hurt American trade unions. . . . Such adverse publicity has served to confirm in the minds of many the negative stereotype they have of trade unions in general and union leadership in particular.

The image labor conveys, of course, limits and affects its political role. As previously mentioned, in some areas labor endorsement carries the kiss of death, and even in Michigan, where organized labor is recognized and accepted as an integral part of the Democratic Party, elaborate efforts are made by Party professionals to make certain that the public does not think the Party is dominated and controlled by the UAW. More widespread participation by labor leaders in community affairs has helped to change the image, but many people in rural and nonindustrialized areas still view unions with suspicion and massive distrust and refuse to support candidates prominently identified with them.

Labor Should Get Out of Politics

Dick Bruner

MANY OF LABOR'S "FRIENDS" will win at the polls this fall—and some "enemies" may lose. The unions will claim—and get—a good deal of public credit for these victories. But AFL–CIO leaders and even the rank-and-file know that—with brilliant exceptions—their campaigning has been ineffective and their spirit dull.

As a former union staff man and a continuing supporter of organized labor, I think the AFL–CIO should pull out of party politics right

Reprinted by permission of the author from *Harper's Magazine*, August 1958.

now. Their candidates will do as well or better without them, will be just as grateful or ungrateful if they win, and will respect their influence more deeply the next time. Just possibly, labor could do worse than sit out the campaign in 1960 too.

To insiders in the labor movement, Senator Barry Goldwater's nightmares about the political power of American unions are just plain laughable. I doubt whether even the United States Chamber of Commerce took him seriously when he told them:

> If you continue to sit on your hands in the 1958 Congressional elections, the labor leaders can again get done what they want done . . . [and] in 1960 the President of the United States will be picked . . . by the labor leaders.

Not long ago I sat down as a union staff member at a dinner meeting with community leaders in Des Moines and heard them argue that Walter Reuther could get the Democratic Presidential nomination in 1960. So the Senator from Arizona is at least representative of some pretty widespread myth-making among the American people.

Yet I can assure you that nearly everywhere the political power of organized labor is nothing but a myth. Professional politicians and labor leaders pay lip service to it, but they bluntly deny it in action. William Levi Dawson, for example—a veteran machine politician on Chicago's South Side—put the situation in a nutshell when he asked a labor lobbyist who approached him for support of a particular bill:

"How many votes you got?"

The truthful answer would be: "Pretty few." . . .

Collapse of a Mission

The unions' waning political power reflects a basic loss of strength and prestige of organized labor among working people. A year ago in *Harper's,* I pointed out that labor's present inability to organize successfully can be explained by the revolutionary shifts in occupation which are replacing many blue-collar jobs with white, and so are changing both the status and the loyalty of the mass of workers.

This means a crisis for labor's hierarchy, and a loss of mission for many liberals who have pinned their hopes on a politically strong labor movement. For, at one time during the New Deal, organized labor seemed about to assume the role of a "social movement." Daniel Bell, writing in the February issue of the English magazine, *Encounter,* has described this earlier period as follows:

> The emerging CIO, faced by the attacks of the industrial combines, tended to take on an ideological coloration. The influx of the

intellectuals, particularly the Socialists and the Communists, heightened this radical-political quality. Support by the federal government gave labor an awareness of the necessity for political action. And John L. Lewis, a shrewd and dynamic labor leader, realized the possibility of welding together a new political bloc.

Bell goes on to say that from 1940 to 1955, labor lost this ideological flavor and concentrated instead on "market unionism." However, Bells sees in Walter Reuther a man whose energies and ideas may act as catalysts for "a new unionism as a social movement"—once the UAW chief takes over from the more conservative, market-oriented George Meany.

After four-and-a-half years on the staff of an AFL–CIO union, I am much less hopeful than Mr. Bell that trade unions will soon be able to shake off their lethargy and play any significant role in American politics. The union-voter registration figures are discouraging enough, but in addition, I see three other reasons why organized labor is short of political vitality:

1. It lacks ideas of its own. On many of the most fundamental political and social issues, it is hard to distinguish labor's position from that of the National Association of Manufacturers.

2. It is pathetically weak on political organizing ability.

3. It has adopted the "mass market" concept of many big organizations, and its leaders treat the rank and file with cynicism.

Recently, I asked the highest placed labor official I know what he thought the ideological future held for the American labor movement. He smiled wryly as he answered, "To continue the defense of the status quo."

Labor's Own Bureaucrats

A hard look at the AFL–CIO reveals little to attract the liberal citizen who is searching for alternatives to the mediocre leadership that our political parties have to offer. Once considered a haven for bright young intellectuals seeking a mass "base," the trade unions have evolved into a shelter for bureaucrats. As Harold Wilensky said in his book, *Intellectuals in Labor Unions*, the ideologically motivated youngster who joins a union's staff either adjusts to becoming a hack or ultimately seeks another creative outlet.

Currently, according to the *AFL–CIO News*, "labor has a vital interest" in taxes, jobless pay, minimum wage, schools, public works, social security, depressed areas, housing, welfare funds, federal pay, Taft-Hartley, foreign policy, and civil rights (in this order).

It is no discredit to a service organization to give priority to economic issues which bear most heavily on its own members. However, a "social movement" which lists foreign policy and civil rights at the bottom would seem to have a somewhat parochial view of society.

The innocent citizen who thinks that unions can be a rallying point for the common good, approaches them only to find a mare's nest of intrigues and conflicting vested interests. If he is a Negro in Chicago who wants to do away with the corrosive influence of the South Side political machine, he discovers that local labor leaders have long ago made their peace with the party bosses. If he is a member of a foreign policy group concerned about this country's apparent race toward oblivion, he will find that most labor leaders merely echo the uninspiring statements of George Meany.

Labor's contribution to whatever debate exists on civil rights, foreign policy, civil liberties, and taxes usually consists of mouthing cliches originated by some other group. Mountains of literature are printed and sent out to collect dust on tables in the backs of union halls. It deals with such "safe" issues as Dixon-Yates, offshore oil, or Hell's Canyon. Union pamphleteers, further, seem convinced that organized labor consists of a greedy army whose minds can be reached only through their pocketbooks. Even matters like race relations and civil liberties are approached from an economic point of view. White workers are urged to treat Negroes as brothers because "discrimination costs money." Their consciences and their public spirit are seldom appealed to.

State labor groups rarely develop and fight for broad legislative platforms which include planks of any substance on taxes, mental health, fair employment practices, education, or welfare. The council-manager plan, for instance, attracts strong interest among liberals in some communities—but it provokes enormous resistance from the craft unions which have developed a stake in the municipal inspection departments. Through control of these departments, construction unions are able to exert pressure on nonconforming contractor-employers. They seldom sacrifice this weapon willingly. In view of these myriad tie-ins of special interests, it is merely quixotic to expect any one man—even Walter Reuther—to cleanse the AFL–CIO of its provincialism and lift its horizons.

Smothered in Oratory

No other group of full-time functionaries in the American labor movement is as skilled in the art of political organizing as those who serve the Auto Workers. Their success is the exception which makes even more glaring the political collapse of labor in general.

While I was working in Des Moines in 1954 as the employee of another union, I watched Robert Johnston, a UAW International Representative at that time, initiate and administer a campaign plan that successfully captured for Democrats all but a very few of the offices in Iowa's most populous county. Johnston thought of it as an experiment, whose pattern could be used by labor groups throughout the country.

Essentially, the operation was this: Johnston and local Democratic leaders studied precinct returns of the past several years. It was a fairly simple, though laborious, job to compile a complete list of the names and addresses of every registered Democrat in these areas. Using the resources of CIO women's auxiliaries and Democratic women's clubs, Johnston worked with the party chairman to prepare a comprehensive card file. Then, in the frosty pre-dawn hour before the polls opened, CIO block workers convened at homes in the strategic precincts and were given envelopes containing the names and addresses of approximately 200 professed Democratic voters. The workers were told to get these voters to the polls. They did.

Johnston, who now serves as director of Region IV of his union, with headquarters in Chicago, spent the next few months traveling around Iowa trying to inspire other labor groups to show the same initiative. His audiences were always dutifully attentive. When the meetings were over, however, they promptly went back to business as usual. Except for Michigan, no other area in the United States has consistently organized people for election work as Johnston did in Des Moines.

I am convinced that one reason why most unions have not done so well is that their leaders have been hypnotized by their own oratory. I got this idea from spending a quarter of my time at conferences designed to draft plans for union political campaigns. This is how such a conference goes.

Before you sit down you pick up from your chair several pounds of pamphlets, graphs, charts, and tables of organization. Then come several blackboard lectures on the art of getting workers registered to vote, of organizing committees, of setting up block and precinct structures, and of soliciting dollars from members in the shops. Perhaps a movie or two is shown.

Once these preliminaries are disposed of, one of the conference coordinators says cheerfully, "Well, let's get started on the planning."

These words are the cue for a series of long-winded speeches from the floor. One grizzled veteran will spend most of a half-hour endorsing every suggestion that has been offered up to that point and conclude by excusing himself from any activity on the grounds that "it's a job for the younger men in the movement."

Often at least one person works up the courage to question the entire notion of union political activity. Another spends a great deal of time apologizing for the poor showing his constituents have made up to that time. Still another boasts of the achievements of his group and explains, in great detail, "how we did things when I was back in the shop."

By this time, the conference leader is wondering, desperately, how he can infuse enough direction into the group to get them to function together. For part of the problem, of course, is the actual hostility among the various unions represented. Craft versus industrial unionism is implicit in many of the speeches. So difference of procedure and protocol suddenly become magnified into major obstacles.

Somehow, miraculously it seems, a nucleus is formed, and pledges of support are made. The conference breaks up and the delegates adjourn to the bar, grumbling about the length of the sessions and the monotony of the speeches.

After that, nothing much happens. The international representatives and business agents—preoccupied with the routine problems of administering local unions—find it easy to postpone the unglamorous business of card-filing and tending to the countless grubby details which go into building an effective political organization. The union leader has become used to his labor-saving devices. The dues of most union members are collected through a payroll "check-off." Clerical functions are efficiently managed by office secretaries.

Of course, such methods are the earmarks of any modern organization. Yet they create barriers between the leaders and the members, and block those clear lines of communication which are absolutely necessary for effective action. And most staff workers can always plead lack of time.

Enter the "Specialist"

So an international union hires a "specialist" to work with its locals on a regional basis in the field of politics.

He is usually young. He probably did not come up through union ranks, but graduated from a state university where he was active in liberal student organizations. He may have been a newspaperman for a while. Hired primarily for his writing skill, he edits a newspaper or mimeographed newsletter as part of his job. He is idealistic about political issues. His desk is piled high with periodicals, books, and pamphlets, ranging from the *Congressional Record* to the latest report of the Anti-Defamation League. He may be an active member of a num-

ber of organizations such as the United World Federalists or the National Association for the Advancement of Colored People.

He is treated by his colleagues with mixed emotions, sometimes
with reverence ("he's terrific with words") and sometimes with a mix-
ture of contempt and good humor. But his fundamental trouble is lack of
power; or, put in trade union terminology, lack of a base. He is a general
without an army, an apex with no foundation. He is, in short, a nobody.

He can do an excellent job at the blackboard during a meeting
of department stewards or a local union committee on political education. He is a veritable encyclopedia of statistics and voting records
of Congressmen. He composes discussion guides that will stimulate a
committee's dullest member. But he can't knock heads together and
get the job done. Therefore, his effectiveness depends upon the enthusiasm he can generate.

I held just such a job. During an election campaign, my first
step would be to write or telephone a few union presidents and arrange
a schedule of meetings with their executive boards. Then, I would
collect enough literature to distribute to the board members, and
organize some notes.

Usually, I would be the first to arrive at a meeting and, while
the board members were filing into the room, I would introduce myself
and smile at the private jokes they exchanged about life in their industry. The presiding officer would open the meeting and call for a reading of the minutes. After a financial report, the chief steward would
take the floor for a summary of the major—and minor—difficulties he
was having with the local management. The board members would begin to nod sleepily during the discussion that followed and glance fur-
tively at their watches. Then, as a preliminary to adjournment, the
chairman would introduce me.

I would hastily adapt my notes to the changed time limit. When
I had finished, one of the group would make a motion to hold the matter over until the next meeting. I would climb back into my car for the
weary drive home.

"If you guys aren't after us for one thing, it's another," said one
local union president to me after I had finished plugging my program.
"You must think we got nothing to do after eight hours in the plant but
take care of your pet ideas."

The veteran local union leader wears an expression of intense
weariness. He is badgered from below and berated from above. His
members feel that he fears to stand up to the demands of the international union, while the international's staff accuses him of lacking
the courage to needle an apathetic membership. Caught in this vise,

when it comes to politics, he procrastinates—simply because politics never has the urgency of the everyday bread-and-butter problems his local faces.

Lacking the genuine inspiration that goes with a "social movement," union leaders find the mechanics of shaping a political machine dull work. Therefore, it simply doesn't get done.

A Little Baloney

Beyond the failures in ideas and in staff work that I have described, labor is even more devitalized in political action by the leaders' cynicism toward the members. If the leader regards the rank and file as his customers, then politics is just another commodity to sell them.

I first caught on to this attitude when I attended a seminar with other union representatives, sponsored by the American Labor Education Service at the University of Iowa. We were sitting around one evening discussing candidates for Congress. Trying to apply some of the lessons I had learned that day, I questioned the convictions of the leading candidate on international relations.

"I don't think he's square on these issues," I said.

"So what?" said a friend.

"Well, isn't that important?"

"Listen. Politics is like anything else in this country. You spread a little baloney around while you're campaigning, but the important thing is to get elected."

I don't mean that these staff members were selling their members a bill of goods about the labor movement. Nowhere in our society could you find people who more fervently believe that they have the key solutions to the nation's ills—i.e., a reduction in workers' taxes, more unemployment compensation, a higher minimum wage, etc. Like any other interest group—veterans organization, chamber of commerce, or trade association—the labor movement has decided to live with what its leaders think of as the realities of politics. Thus, they make only limited demands on the men and women they back for public office.

Occasionally, the officeholder dares to bite the hand that purports to feed him. Shortly after William Proxmire's startling election to fill the short-term Senate vacancy created by the death of Joseph McCarthy, labor newspapers around the country quickly recovered from their shock and gave credit for his victory to the Wisconsin labor movement. But the new Senator just as quickly turned it down. Speaking to delegates at a state CIO convention, he said:

"I would rather lose an election than yield my independence to the will of any group." To this heresy he added the positively treasonous comment that "merged labor may constitute a danger to American society."

Proxmire challenged the contention that union members make their own political decisions. This is a valid question. For despite the fact that the majority of union leaders are dedicated to the proposition that—in the larger sense—the mass of "people" should make political decisions, they hardly ever allow their members to accept or reject the political stands taken either by the AFL–CIO or by individual unions.

As any piece of AFL–CIO political literature will tell you, the basic policy decisions of the federation are made at the biennial conventions. In reality, however, the policy resolutions are ground out by the staff members of various AFL–CIO departments and constituent bodies. I would guess that less than one percent—if any—of the resolutions adopted by the conventions originate in local union meetings.

Moreover, such lack of rank-and-file expression is not limited to fundamental statements on major political issues. The Committee on Political Education (COPE) is supposed to have its facsimile at every level of the labor movement—city, county, Congressional district, state, etc.—yet even these bodies are made up largely of persons appointed to their offices. Endorsement of candidates is a ticklish business and is done in a semi-conspiratorial way by county and district committees.

In my experience union members are rarely encouraged to go into politics on their own. In 1954, in Iowa, CIO leaders made an attempt to encourage their members to join political parties and seek offices within them. There was some talk about trying to take over the direction of the Democratic State Central Committee. To that end, functionaries held classes for workers in several communities, instructing them in the laws which governed party caucuses and how union men should seek election as delegates to conventions. Some union members began to take part in grass-roots politics. However, when the plan was outlined to a man from the national office of the CIO Political Action Committee (this was before the merger of AFL–CIO) he immediately discouraged its further operation.

"We don't want the responsibility of running a party," he said.

Another example is a man I knew who worked in a meat-packing plant. He took a keen interest in politics, and he got elected delegate to the national Democratic convention in 1952. When he arrived in Chicago he expected to be part of a national labor pressure group. He sought out labor celebrities at the convention to ask when the first labor caucus would be held. None ever was. He was sorely disappointed to find out that union members acted no differently from other delegates and had no intentions of working as a national team.

The Worker as "Outsider"

When, occasionally, union members are provoked into political action, they may be frustrated by a decision made higher up the line. Recently, members of the United Packinghouse Workers of America in the corn-belt states were urged by their leaders to seek out farmers and organize joint committees for the purpose of endorsing mutually acceptable candidates. I was instructed to go to Sioux City, Iowa, to help organize such a committee. After many days' work we were able to hold a meeting of some 300 farmers and workers. Within a week, however, orders came down to abandon the committee since it might offend the officers of the National Farmers Organization. I knew, from the talk I heard among Sioux City packinghouse workers, that I would have a hard time developing their enthusiasm for future political projects.

Shut out from any decision-making in politics, the worker feels all the more insulated from real control of his union. Why doesn't he revolt? He is constantly being urged to do so by many persons, ranging from Senator Goldwater and David Lawrence to his own clergyman. But the worker is not inclined to revolt because he is too institutionalized. His opportunities to make decisions affecting his own destiny have been limited to those which he can make within his own home (and with the advances of child guidance and family counseling, this last frontier is rapidly closing). Unless he is a skilled worker, even his place of employment is the result of sheer accident: he was standing in the right line when a factory needed employees. He does not decide whether or not he will pay his taxes: they are withheld from his paycheck and extracted "painlessly" from him through excise and sales taxes. If his plant has a union-shop contract, he has got to join the union whether he wants to or not. And if he attends meetings, he becomes a ratifier or rejector, not an initiator. He has no more influence on his international union's major demands during contract negotiating time than he has on the design of next year's automobile models or on this country's foreign policy. Walter Reuther and John Foster Dulles are equally inaccessible to him.

Whatever dissent the American worker offers takes the form of apathy. In politics he fails to register or vote—thus defying the urgings of posters, slogans, speeches, and editorial sermons. He may also refuse to contribute money to his union's political fund. Since the Taft-Hartley Act forbids the use of union dues money for a federal office-seeker's campaign, COPE attempts to secure a single dollar from each of the estimated fifteen million AFL–CIO members. In 1956, a Presidential election year, its drive for contributions netted only $456,293.55 to be spent on candidates—less than one dollar for every thirty members. (Of course, COPE does not get all the political money collected by labor.)

Repair Job

The situation is not hopeless. But the cure demands something more profound than catchier slogans, more colorful posters, and bigger labor paper headlines. If union leaders persist in treating their members like consumers, they had better take a lesson from the revolt of the American car buyer: the customer is fed up with gimmicks. Therefore, any re-appraisal must deal with the fundamentals.

First of all, I believe that American labor should call a temporary halt to attempts to organize more workers. Union recruitment has reached the saturation level. Drives aimed at bringing more money into union treasuries only increase apathy and cynicism; while attempts to open new frontiers—such as the white-collar workers—merely frustrate energies which could be better spent reflecting on the present plight of unions, if nothing else. Such a moratorium might thrust American labor into a new period, during which it would attempt to raise the horizons of those within its ranks. And it would inhibit some of the rapacious "business-oriented" activities of unions by eliminating fratricidal "raiding."

Secondly, unions should withdraw for a while from the entangling alliances of partisan politics. This would mean: no endorsements of candidates; no collection of COPE dollars; and no compromises with politicians. Instead, it should redouble its efforts as a *pressure* group, in the manner of the American Civil Liberties Union, the American Friends Service Committee, the National Association for the Advancement of Colored People, and the League of Women Voters, whose influence is out of all proportion to the sizes of the membership. The AFL–CIO could be the biggest nonpartisan pressure group in our society. Its dissents would be bound to provoke refreshing debate. But no group can attempt to "deliver" a mass vote without curtailing the free voice of its members.

Finally, the direction that unions should take on any issue should be left wide open. Let many flowers bloom. The top brass should encourage debate among staff and rank-and-file. And I mean *real* debate. Many leaders and members of the AFL–CIO take violent—but private—exception to George Meany's views on foreign policy, for instance. Someone should take the initiative in challenging Meany's convictions (which now purport to represent all of labor) in debates before rank-and-file unionists across the country.

As a supplement to this first step toward genuine democracy, the AFL–CIO and all its constituent bodies should circulate *all* resolutions slated for conventions to *all* local unions. Staff members and officers and, of course, local unions should be urged to express any disagreement. At the very least, this method would give leaders a more accurate sounding of member sentiment. Besides—if the system were free of restraint and threat of reprisals—it would be certain to provoke controversy, a sense of rank-and-file participation in policy decisions, and, inevitably, a quickened interest in politics.

None of these recommendations can be embodied in federal or state legislation. I do not side with such enemies of labor as Goldwater and Senator Carl Curtis of Nebraska, and I reject their contention that labor is politically either so powerful or so sinister that it needs legal restraint. Unions should, of course, continue their practice of exposing the voting records of politicians and of urging their members to vote.

But I am convinced that if organized labor will adopt this counsel of abstention—*at this time*—and go in for an honest appraisal of its real function, it can become a new progressive force in our democracy. And its influence "next time" may be equal to the weight of its numbers and consistent with the interests of our society.

A Conversation with Walter Reuther

Henry Brandon
Sunday Times of London

BRANDON: What puzzles Europeans most about the American trade union movement is that it has not tried to create its own political party to advance labor's own interest. I mean, trade unionism here sees as its main function the bargaining for higher wages. How do you explain that?

REUTHER: To begin with you need to understand that the structure of American society is, I think, more in a state of flux than is the case of the European countries, and that political parties reflect that essential difference in the structure of our societies. A Labor

Excerpted by permission, from Henry Brandon, *As We Are*, New York: Doubleday and Co., 1961.

Party, as such, in America, could not possibly succeed because a political party to succeed has to have groups that go way beyond labor as a group; you've got to have farm groups, you've got to have small businessmen.

The American labor movement is essentially trying to work within the two-party structure, but to bring about a basic re-alignment so that the two parties really stand for distinct points of view. And I think that this process is happening very rapidly. More and more the Democratic Party is coming to reflect the kind of programs and policies that the American labor movement can support, while the Republican Party more and more becomes the party of big business.

BRANDON: But didn't a lot of labor people vote for the Republican Party in the last election?

REUTHER: Well, some . . . but I think in terms of percentages it was a small percentage. In the Detroit area, the surveys here indicate that about 21 percent of the vote was Republican but only for the Presidency. Because Eisenhower could give us greater assurance of world peace—that obviously had some impact upon working-class groups as well as upon people generally. But I think Detroit is a good example where roughly 80 percent voted for the Democratic candidates and 20 percent for the Republicans.

BRANDON: But if it is possible in England for a labor party to get enough support from a broad section of the public, why shouldn't that be possible here?

REUTHER: Well, I think America is quite different from England. In England you've got a much more rigid class structure—the middle class is less important in England than it is here—and the labor movement in America is developing a whole new middle class. Last year the average automobile worker got more than $5,000 a year income.

BRANDON: Isn't the reason that the labor movement here has not been able to create a broader political base that it has no real ideology apart from bargaining for higher wages?

REUTHER: I think that an ideology is developing. I agree that the original labor movement was basically pure and simple trade unionism—bargaining for wages and for hours and for working conditions. But the labor movement cannot carry out its historic mission if it continues to be no more than that. As the problems of our modern society become more complex and interwoven, their solution cannot be economic or political—the solution has got to be economic *and* political.

And we are developing in that direction. In 1945 and '46, for example, we had a strike with the General Motors Corporation and it lasted 113 days. The auto workers had raised a new demand for higher wages without higher prices. We said that the labor movement had to take into consideration the impact of its wage demands upon the price structure, because the price structure may determine the general economic climate and may have an impact upon employment opportunities. Well, in 1945 we were criticized by corporation executives, by people in government, and I think by 80 percent of the leadership of the American labor movement, who took the position that prices are no concern of labor. Yet today—only a few years later—I think that 90 percent of the leadership of the American labor movement now accepts the basic concept in respect to the relationship of wages, prices, and profits that we advanced in 1945.

Now the same thing is true about other things. The AFL has moved a long way toward accepting the beginning of an American trade union ideology. In 1932 the AFL convention for the first time went on record in favor of unemployment compensation. They had been against any government action that bore upon the economic position of the wage earner. They wanted only the unions to deal with such things as minimum wages or unemployment compensation. But in 1932 unemployment had become so overwhelming that they knew they couldn't cope with it by pure and simple trade unionism, and therefore they turned to government action. I cite this merely to indicate that gradually we are developing a trade union ideology which is not being borrowed from anywhere. It isn't based upon Marxism; it's not based upon any other preconceived, thought-through philosophy: it's a special American trade union philosophy that is coming out of the problems as they develop in a complex technology.

BRANDON: Why did you think in the early '40's that there was a need for a third party?

REUTHER: Well, at that time we hadn't made as much political progress inside the labor movement itself, and I was influenced in believing at that time that maybe our own party would be a more effective vehicle for getting broader participation than the labor movement itself. It was also true that the Democratic Party earlier was essentially a party in which the major industrial states were controlled by machine politics, and as a result the labor movement was having little influence upon the policies or the programs of those machine-controlled state organizations. We have made considerable progress now. The old machines are falling apart: new leadership is coming up, which more nearly reflects the kind of programs and policies that we think are adequate to meet these new economic and social problems. The combination of these things are the things that have influenced me.

BRANDON: Influenced you that the third party is not necessary—

REUTHER: That's right. I think you can get participation of labor in the structure of the parties on a basis where you can have some influence. The old machines are disintegrating and new forces and new faces are bringing about a basic change. For this reason we felt that instead of trying to create a third party—or labor party—that we ought to try to help accelerate the realignment that is taking place.

I argued with Wayne Morse on this 10 or 12 years ago. We had an educational conference in Cleveland where he said that he disagreed with my philosophy—that we ought to bring about a realignment and get the liberal forces in one party and the conservatives in another party. He argued that this contest ought to go on within each party. I pointed out that in that case no party will ever have the clear-cut policy and the leadership to translate and implement policy, because the power of the party will be diluted on basic questions and the parties will never develop sufficient internal discipline to be effective instruments for carrying out policy. The Democratic Party adopts a good policy, a good program at every convention—just as advanced as the Labour Party. But what happens is that you get the right words in the platform but when the party gets power, because it's "all things to all men," it lacks the internal discipline to translate party platform into specific legislation. . . .

BRANDON: How do you foresee the relationship between the labor movement and the Democratic Party, because it seems that up to now it was the Democratic Party that wagged the tail?

REUTHER: Well, I would be opposed to the labor movement trying to capture the Democratic Party. I think that at the point the labor movement captures the Democratic Party, you then destroy the broad base that is essential to make a political party an effective instrument to translate sound policy into governmental action. The essential problem for the labor movement is to learn to work with a party without trying to capture it.

BRANDON: But in Britain a man of your calibre and your oratorical gift would have a good chance to become Prime Minister. You haven't got that in this country—or do you think you have?

REUTHER: I suppose that the day will come when a labor leader could aspire to the top job of America. I personally do not aspire to that. I mean, I have no political ambitions whatsoever. I made a decision a long time ago that what little contribution I could make I would make inside the labor movement, trying to get American labor to mature philosophically and to change its basic character. The labor movement can only be effective if it becomes less an economic movement and more a social movement. . . .

BRANDON: You mentioned automation. . . . Now it seems to me there are two serious problems for the future of the trade union movement. One is the impact of automation and the other that white-collar workers are now outnumbering blue-collar workers.

REUTHER: Well, the problem of automation is actually the problem of learning to live with abundance, and the only way you can learn to live with abundance is to learn to manage it, and the only way you can manage it is to share it. There are really two basic questions. Number one: We've got to learn to distribute the abundance that we know how to make. Number two: Ultimately we've got to find a way so that people can be given a more rational means of choosing between gadgets and leisure.

How many cars should a family have? How many television sets? How many bathrooms do we need in an ordinary house? Ultimately when we have reached that plateau of economic living standards, where the law of diminishing returns sets in very rapidly, we've got to give people the educational background, the stimulations so that they would be interested in another kind of consumption. And that means the ability and the desire to spend a larger portion of their time, not making gadgets, but in the pursuit of constructive and creative leisure. We will be confronted very soon with this very real problem, that we may overfeed the outer man and starve the inner man.

The thing that bothers me is that the fellow working in the Cadillac Motor Company making the Cadillac motor car can be a part of making that Cadillac, and yet when he looks at it he gets no sense of creative achievement. In an earlier technology, a craftsman—no matter what he made—there was a little bit of him in what he made. There was a sense of creation. And when God made us in his own image, he also gave to each of us some creative capacity. That is being starved.

We've got to begin now to stimulate people in terms of interest, in terms of knowing how to find a way to achieve creative expression in our leisure hours.

BRANDON: But we may then have your—let's call them "tycoons of leisure"—go fishing and learning how to paint, how to garden— while the working class of the professionals, the scientists, teachers, doctors, civil servants—will be working long hours. I'm wondering whether this will not spark off a new kind of class war between the haves of leisure and the have-nots of leisure.

REUTHER: I think that we're going to have to shift more people into these categories. We obviously need more doctors; there's already a very acute shortage of medical personnel in America. There are thousands of young people with the potential capacity to make wonderful medical people but they don't have the economic resources to get access to medical education. So that our society as a part of this whole question of working out a proper balance between gadgets and between leisure has also to work out a proper balance in the area of human services—teachers, medicine, music, etc.

All of these things are a matter of deciding what kind of society we are really trying to make. Are we trying to build a society so that every kid of 18 has a sport car, every room in a house has a built-in television, and we have so much plumbing in the house that you need three plumbers on every block to keep it going? We are now in that place in human history where instead of the few on top having access to culture based upon the poverty of the great mass at the bottom, because there wasn't enough to go around, we can now give the great mass of people access to culture and learning and the opportunities to facilitate the growth of the inner man.

Now the trade union movement is important only as it facilitates these long-range objectives. Automation is important only as it provides the tools to create the economic base upon which the mass can have access to what only the few have had access to in the past. . . .

Unions and Politics

Jack Barbash

University of Wisconsin

COLLECTIVE BARGAINING POWER is the fulcrum for political power. Collective bargaining is still the overriding union function, having achieved a depth of penetration, scope, and systematization unprecedented in American industrial relations history and unrivaled by collective bargaining anywhere else in the world.

The labor movement's approach to politics partakes variously of the pressure group and of the political party. It is the pressure group strategy aimed at the preservation of collective bargaining and institutional power that engages union activities most insistently. But the reach of the pressures which a labor union needs to exert in order to preserve collective bargaining and institutional power has expanded until it fuses into broad economic policy.

Labor's political action assumes something of the shape of a political party because there is an inclusive labor program taking in the whole range of public policy. The program is more than decor, representing an authentic guide to the labor movement's policies in practice, subject to the discount that some unions take the program less seriously than others and that some stress one part of the program more than others.

The influences acting on the labor movement to commit its forces to a comprehensive political program have come first from its own assessment of the fitness of things—that an institution of power and position in the society must go beyond being "a narrow pressure group"; and then from the expectations that the labor movement, having matured or arrived, must "take its place as an equal among the trustees of the society and the political system." [1]

The labor movement lacks only its own national electoral instrumentalities to make it a full-dress political party. This gap is partly filled by the national Democratic party and the Democratic parties in many non-Southern states. Now, the national Democratic party is surely not a labor party, but the unions are the single most important force in it and, subject to the usual qualifications, that force is mainly exerted

Reprinted by permission of the publisher from *Challenge, The Magazine of Economic Affairs*, Vol. XII, December 1964.

[1] David B. Truman, "Labor's Responsibility in Public Affairs," *Labor's Public Responsibility*, National Institute of Labor Education, 1960, p. 109.

in the direction of program. In contrast to the pure model of European labor politics, the American labor movement does not strive for class political power within the Democratic party or, for that matter, outside of it. The source of labor movement strength in the Democratic party is the effort, money, facilities, and votes it will enlist in behalf of the party's candidates. There is a substantial involvement of local labor leaders in behalf of Republican candidates and prominent labor leaders identified as Republicans, but it is rare for the union to function as an institutional force in the Republican party. . . .

The labor movement's political action is decentralized, following in this respect the decentralized character of the total movement and the decentralized character of the political system in which the unions must function. The political and legislative line of the AFL–CIO as a federation has no binding force on affiliates who do, in fact, run counter to the federation's position at various times—and to each other's positions.

Union political action has had at least three concrete effects on the political process:

1. It has increased working class participation in voting.

2. It has provided a training ground in the organizational skills of politics, a point of access to influence in the political party, and a feeling of self-confidence by workers in aspiring to political power.

3. Unions have provided the base of political strength for the welfare state program in the Democratic party and have confronted the Republican party with the need to moderate its tendency toward doctrinaire conservatism if the party is to be a mass party rather than an ideological party.

In respect to political programs beyond bread and butter the union effect has been mainly by way of support and reenforcement. While the unions have been involved in the development of programs they have not been the initiating force in the creative stages of a program. Once a program is conceived in broad outline, however—and this is more true nationally and of course during Democratic administrations—the labor movement's technicians will be active participants in drafting, massing legislative support, and if the program is enacted, in maintaining a permanent vigil over its administration. If not enacted, then the labor movement will be the chief prod for another try. Minimum wages, "medicare," and social security are current cases in point.

For the left-oriented intellectual this limited reacting posture is a defect in the quality of labor's political performance; "reaching out for the stars" is more in keeping with labor as an historic *movement*.

For the economist this political power, whether reactive or creative, only extends the labor movement's inflationary thrust from collective bargaining to legislation.

There is a substantial distance between the political commitment of the union leadership and of the rank-and-file. For the rank-and-file member politics has the reenforcement of job rights as its main purpose. The widest perspective on political action is viewed by the federation leadership, and the angle of political vision narrows but also intensifies as the leadership moves closer to the actual work situation. This is probably in keeping with the political habits of the population at large.

The radical transformation that has taken place within a generation in the union concept and execution of political action has been obscured by what seems to be continued adherence to the Gompers "reward your friends, and punish your enemies" maxim. Nonpartisanship in the present period is supported by a going political concern composed of labor leaders who "belong" in the circles of political power and who matter in the nation's politics. This was not so under the older pre-1933 nonpartisanship and is a difference in degree that becomes a difference in kind. . . .

The secular trend for the labor movement in politics is upward. The decisive element in the trend is the expanding economic role of government to deal with military security, inflation, and unemployment, economic growth and social welfare. Price and wage restraints, full employment, poverty, and "automation" are the ways in which these issues become politically meaningful for workers and unions. At this moment it is the limitations of collective bargaining in dealing with the employment consequences of technological change that is and will continue to be a major spur to union political action. Inasmuch as "automation" ties in with every major economic problem, the labor political program will continue to be wide-ranging.

Labor's political role will be accelerated by ideology, but in this case not so much by the labor movement's own ideology as the ideology of the liberal intellectual community. However labor leaders may deprecate liberal criticism and expectations, union leadership at the higher levels of union government has historically been sensitive and responsive to the liberal climate of opinion. The pressure which union leadership has been reacting to on such issues as civil rights, foreign aid, and trade, has been the liberal's ideological pressure as much as, if not more than, the political pressures of the union constituency.

From the very origins of unionism, the middle-class intellectual as utopian, Marxian socialist, or contemporary liberal, has assigned the unions an historic mission which goes beyond the job interests of the union's constituents and makes it an instrumentality of progress in the larger social realm. Lenin was right, of course, when he said that "the working class, exclusively by its own effort, is able to develop only trade union consciousness."[2] In the United States the liberal has almost completely rejected formal socialism but this has not deterred him from urging (and getting) a larger political responsibility from the labor movement—but not so large as would be sufficient for the liberal's conception of the union role. The source of the intellectual appeal to the labor leadership is that at bottom they both, even the narrowest "business" unionist, share the same sentiment of the unions as a social movement.

The restraining influence on the leader in enlarging the union scope is his membership which holds him close to job interests. This insight and the special way he put it is Selig Perlman's enduring contribution to union theory. Since Perlman wrote, the dimensions of job interests have expanded from the craft unionism which was Perlman's prototype, to the industry interest of the mass-production/industrial-union unionist.

A "business in politics" movement has developed recently as a countervailing force to the union in politics. Businessmen had just about begun to understand that the union as a system of power in the plant need not be subversive to the enterprise when the implications of union political power reached them. As the businessmen view it, the union as a system of power in the political society is fraught with the greatest danger to the free enterprise system as well as a challenge to their own long-held positions. What distinguishes this "business in politics" movement is its self-consciousness, for, in point of fact, business has never been out of politics in the United States or anywhere else.

The self-consciousness of business politics raises up for the union the threat of external aggression that has always been a powerful drive to union political action. Nothing quite imparts the zing and the sense of outrage to labor politics as do injunctions, Taft-Hartley laws, right-to-work laws, and now possibly the "business in politics" movement—if it ever amounts to anything. The really massive political efforts by the unions have always been mounted *against* something.

The Negro worker in the civil rights upsurge is moving out of the working class substratum into an assertive role in the main line of

---

[2] Robert V. Daniels, "What Is To Be Done," *A Documentary History of Communism*, Vol. I, Vintage Russian Library, Random House, New York, 1962, p. 11.

the manual working class and its unions. The politicalization of Negro workers will give the labor movement's politics a strong civil rights thrust for a long period ahead.

What will finally sustain politics as a vital union function is the large extent to which the political interest has been institutionalized in the form of organizations, programs, and specialized personnel; and institutions do tend to develop momentum on their own.

All the portents, then, are for a broader political scope and for a more systematic political performance by the labor movement. But there are no signs that the expanding political vision will come to include a labor party because, to put it summarily:

1. There is little or no rank-and-file sentiment for it.

2. The union leaders are strongly committed to the established political arrangements and they believe that they haven't done too badly under them.

3. Labor leaders have no confidence that they can bring their constituents along with them into a labor party.

4. The leaders fear the class isolation which would follow and that, in any case, a labor party would insure the election of antiunion, reactionary forces.

5. Given the federal structure, the labor party could hardly expect to be more than a local institution.

6. American political parties are mass parties, not doctrinal parties, and they will ultimately take over the most viable parts of the labor party's program.

American unionism is emerging with a conception of its political role that is flexible, realistic and responsible: flexible because it is willing to experiment with both collective bargaining and legislative enactment and, as the situation demands, to have one complement the other; realistic because program has some relationship to capabilities; and responsible because the effective political goals go beyond parochial job interests and assert a serious union concern with the larger national and international community. Self-interest politics have not been bypassed but self-interest is moving away from catch-as-catch-can.

The wholesale effects of the labor movement in politics have been to strengthen democracy in two ways: (1) by diffusing political power but not polarizing it, and (2) by challenging our economic system to share its favors broadly. These effects may very well be the chief factors responsible for the viability of Western "capitalist democracy."

Index